Season of Ghosts

ALSO BY HOWARD BURMAN

Gentlemen at the Bat: A Fictional Oral History of the New York Knickerbockers and the Early Days of Base Ball (McFarland, 2010)

Season of Ghosts
The '86 Mets and the Red Sox

HOWARD BURMAN

McFarland & Company, Inc., Publishers
Jefferson, North Carolina, and London

All photographs herein courtesy of National Baseball Hall of Fame Library, Cooperstown, New York

LIBRARY OF CONGRESS CATALOGUING-IN-PUBLICATION DATA

Burman, Howard.
　　Season of ghosts : the '86 Mets and the Red Sox / Howard Burman.
　　　　p.　　cm.
　　Includes bibliographical references and index.

　　ISBN 978-0-7864-7042-6
　　softcover : acid free paper ∞

　　1. New York Mets (Baseball team) — History.　2. Boston Red Sox (Baseball team) — History.　3. Sports rivalries — United States — History.　4. Nineteen eighty-six, A.D. I. Title.
　　GV875.N45B87　2013
　　796.357'64097471— dc23　　　　　　　　　　　2012044026

BRITISH LIBRARY CATALOGUING DATA ARE AVAILABLE

© 2013 Howard Burman. All rights reserved

No part of this book may be reproduced or transmitted in any form or by any means, electronic or mechanical, including photocopying or recording, or by any information storage and retrieval system, without permission in writing from the publisher.

On the cover: The Mets' Mookie Wilson reacts after colliding with Red Sox first baseman Bill Buckner in the seventh game of the World Series at New York's Shea Stadium on October 27, 1986 (AP Photo/Susan Ragan)

Manufactured in the United States of America

McFarland & Company, Inc., Publishers
　Box 611, Jefferson, North Carolina 28640
　　www.mcfarlandpub.com

Contents

Preface 1

1. One of the Best Ever 3
2. Ueberroth in Control 6
3. The "C" Word 14
4. The "D" Word 18
5. Hopes and Dreams 22
6. Bullies in Pinstripes 25
7. Won't This Curse Ever End? 30
8. The Chicken Man 37
9. Rickey Knows Rickey 44
10. Where's the Can? 49
11. A Hitch in His Gait 52
12. Nearing the End 54
13. Everybody Loves Kirby 62
14. That Was Last Year 67
15. Abner Doubledata 69
16. A Talent the Likes of Which Are Seldom Seen 75
17. The Wild Boys 82
18. Doc Ain't Stupid 87
19. Welcome to the Alpha Male Club 98
20. Class 104
21. Signs of Trouble 108
22. Opening Day 111
23. Early Season Oddities 118
24. The Rocket 121
25. La La Land 125
26. You Gotta Believe 127
27. Darling of the Mets 136

28. Living in Another World 139
29. Clean Living 145
30. Drugs of Choice 153
31. Fight On 159
32. Renaissance Scholar in a Baseball Cap 162
33. Gambling on the Game 167
34. The Way They Used to Play 174
35. The Image of the Game 179
36. It Pumps Up Your Confidence 182
37. Lawyer on the Bench 186
38. Bunyanesque Feats 189
39. Here Comes the Judge 194
40. Baseball Exorcist 198
41. All About Money 203
42. The Big Silence 205
43. Mid-Season Form 209
44. Like Attila the Hun 211
45. Looking for Heroes 214
46. Wally's World 222
47. Family Values 224
48. As Mellow as Mr. Rogers 227
49. Misunderstood 230
50. Who's In: Who's Not 236
51. Signs of Confusion 239
52. The Tony Gwyn of Pitching 242
53. Challenges to America's Game 244
54. Making Waves Is Dangerous 249
55. The Fine Art of Cheating 254
56. Best and Worst 260
57. The Cowboy and the Goat 269
58. Just What Everyone Wanted 277
59. Disaster Wrapped in Catastrophe 285
60. Symbol of Failure 289

Bibliography 303
Index 307

Preface

A recent ESPN readers' poll ranked the 1986 Major League Baseball season one of the top three greatest ever, climaxing in one of the finest postseasons in baseball history, including an incredible Game 5 of the American League Championship Series and a dramatic Game 6 of the World Series. More than anything, though, the season was driven by a cast of amazing characters involved in an engaging narrative story.

Characters-in-conflict is the engine that drives baseball just as it drives narratives. It is why we stay with a story. We like watching controlled tension as long as it is in someone else, and if we care about the characters, it makes us want to know how the situation will turn out. Will the hero achieve his goal or will he be thwarted? Baseball, like all competitive sports, is driven by tension brought on by conflict—tension over an at-bat, tension over the outcome of a game, and tension over the placement of our favorite team in the standings. A baseball season unfolds like a good story.

Major League Baseball is also an ongoing ghost story. The players and plays of the past are part of the story of today, part of the context in which the game is played. Some of baseball's past is known to all true baseball fans; all of it is known to some. Because we know something of the game's rich history we are always comparing today with yesterday. When Pete Rose tops Ty Cobb in career hits it means something to us because we know who Ty Cobb was.

We know the players in the sense of having information about who they are, their athletic and personal backgrounds, their idiosyncrasies, their behavioral patterns, their ideas about the game and maybe about issues on a broader scale. Without this knowledge, the game loses much of its appeal.

So watching Charlie Hustle leg one out, or Mr. October hit a long one, or Doc bringing heat takes on a new level of significance because we know something about Rose, Jackson, and Gooden. We may or may not "like" them, but we know who they are and we know something about their struggles and accomplishments. Major League Baseball promotes its players with all their virtues, foibles, and faults, as well they should. Barry and Rickey sell tickets.

The more interesting a player seems, the more attention he will draw. It's why screenwriters create eccentric or unusual characters. The guy dancing on the tables in a sophisticated bar will have more appeal to the audience than the guy sipping his martini and reading a book in the corner. Dull characters are ... well, dull. They don't sell unless their dullness is so extreme that it becomes eccentric.

Jackson, Henderson, Hernandez, Boggs, Strawberry, Boyd, Joyner, Bonds, Gibson, Gossage, Puckett, Carlton, and the other characters of '86 are what drew so much attention to the game. Gooden staring down at Carter for a sign becomes interesting when we know that Boggs is the hitter and has gone hitless his last 9 at-bats. We sense his frustration because we know something about him.

Like many baseball seasons, '86 was rife with problems and rich in drama and, in its variety and scope, mirrored much that was a part of the evolving times—both the good and the bad. When Jacques Barzun, the French cultural historian, suggested that in order to understand the American heart and mind one need look no further than baseball, he might have had seasons like this in mind.

Baseball may mirror our society, but in some ways, our society mirrors baseball, too. Because it is followed by so many, its players often serve as popular models. Why not? Measured by any standards, they are wealthy, successful, good at what they do, and thus admired. It is but a short step from admiration to emulation and maybe just as short from emulation to justification.

We hold up the actions of the Cal Ripkens, Mookie Wilsons, and Dale Murphys of the game as models of admirable behavior in a way that reflects credit on us, and when the Steve Garveys, Dwight Goodens, and Kirby Pucketts let us down with behavior less than admirable we often lay blame, with the implication that we are, or should be, above such actions.

Certainly the '86 season had its examples of good and bad behavior.

Baseball survives because it continually tells new stories, compelling stories. Every season starts new ones and continues old ones because the game is at once linked with ghosts from the past and the promise of new stories to come. Some stories are so compelling that they survive the re-telling and endure for years. We call them classics. The '86 season was a classic. Here, then, is the story of that baseball season as it stretched both backwards and forwards—from the ghosts of seasons and players past to the reality of what followed.

1. One of the Best Ever

At the beginning of 1986, most of the baseball talk was about money; at the end it was about the great season, particularly the postseason — one of the best ever.

On an institutional level the game was facing critical issues — player contracts, collusion, drugs, free agency, charges of racism, cheating, gambling, the growing popularity of professional football, and the influence of cable TV and satellites.

As Tom Seaver said, "Like every family, ours has its problems."

In a sense, baseball reflects the nature of the times. A. Bartlett Giamatti, who was all too briefly commissioner, commented in late '86:

> Babe Ruth was a symbol of the Roaring Twenties. Through the Depression and World War II, the game waxed and waned with the nation. From the mid-60s to the mid-70s, baseball attendance plateaued as the nation went through a period of volatility that included Vietnam and the civil-rights struggle. Then in the late '70s, people wanted some stable form of leisure they could count on and turned to the game again. Since then attendance has taken off.

Still, baseball is resistant to change, or at least to rapid change. As a business it has been around since before the Civil War. As a game it goes back even earlier than that, to the earliest days of the colonies.

The first rule-makers, the Knickerbocker Base Ball Club of New York, played the game with underhanded pitching, no called balls and strikes, and one-bounce catches for outs. Despite repeated requests to alter these and other rules, it took many years for the changes to take effect. Baseball moves slowly.

To the slogan-happy writers, the '80s were often referred to as the "Greed decade." Corporation mega-mergers and leveraged buyouts produced highly visible celebrity billionaires like Donald Trump and Leona Helmsley.

The baby-boomers were growing up and becoming the greatest consumers of all time. They were the "Me generation," or as Tom Wolfe called them, the "Splurge generation," and they borrowed on a massive scale, handing the bill on to the unborn. The term "yuppie" entered the lexicon, referring to the rise of the new young urban middle class. They were commonly thought to be the most self-absorbed generation in American history.

They had disposable income for such things as going to baseball games, and the players in the game knew it and demanded more. As the owners were crying poor-mouth, salaries were skyrocketing. "The game is headed toward banditry," cried the principal owner of the Phillies.

Player demands were killing the game, claimed owners.

"We just want what's ours," responded the players.

"You telling us George Steinbrenner and Ted Turner are losing money?" asked the fans.

"I get sick of hearing about the poor owners," said Baltimore manager Earl Weaver. "Baseball owners today are happier than pigs in slop. They're making money hand over foot."

"It isn't really the stars that are expensive. It's the high cost of mediocrity," claimed Bill Veeck.

Aggressive player agents became important figures in the operation of Major League Baseball. They went to the owners armed with facts and figures showing how the game had prospered since free agency in 1976.

Some owners were holding the relative line on spending, but others kept pushing the price of desirable players higher and higher. The average salary had gone from $52,300 in 1977 to $363,000 in 1985.

Did an agent hold a gun to the head of the Giants' Bob Lurie when he paid Rennie Stennett $6 million? Rennie Stennett was not Pete Rose. Animosity broke out between the free-spending owners and those who wanted to hold the line.

Someone crunched the numbers and figured that teams were paying over $40 million to athletes under contract who were no longer in the game. "Players are sitting at home in rocking chairs and collecting wages," noted Tigers president Jim Campbell.

Then there were players like George Foster who was collecting $2 million annually from the Mets but batted only .263 in 1985. Nevertheless, the possibility of another strike was being widely discussed.

"If it weren't for baseball, many kids wouldn't know what a millionaire looked like," quipped comedienne Phyllis Diller.

"You don't stop an avalanche of 10 years in one month," said John Schuerholz, Kansas City Royals general manager. "But some moderation is beginning to take hold."

In a show of economic solidarity, baseball reduced its rosters by one man to 24, saving each team approximately $112,000. "They told me I was the 25th man," Mike Stenhouse said upon being released by the Montreal Expos, "but I talked to somebody else and he said he was the 25th man."

The financial issues in the game were out front for all to see, but the problem of drug use was being talked about in much quieter but no less urgent tones. It was a national issue not limited to baseball. Alcohol and drug education were front-burner topics, bringing about movements such as M.A.D.D., Nancy Reagan's "Just Say No" campaign, and D.A.R.E. By 1990 every state in the U.S. mandated the legal drinking age to be 21, the only country ever to do so. A crack cocaine epidemic occurred in urban areas of the U.S., such that violent crime and drug trafficking soared to record levels in most large American cities.

Many of the top stories of the '80s began in secret — the Iran-Contra affair and the savings and loan scandal are just two examples. But as the '80s wore on, secrets in America were becoming much harder to keep. The rise of cable news networks and the beginnings of widespread computer access made information much more difficult to keep hidden. So it was with the stories about drug use in baseball.

Major League Baseball was concerned, whether about the reality or the image is debatable. They were about to go on the offensive to rehabilitate their image by staking out the moral high ground against the players.

With all the off-field problems, what baseball needed more than anything else was a great season on the field, a memorable, problem-dulling season with great drama and larger-than-life heroes.

It was about to get it.

2. Ueberroth in Control

Most who knew him, and many who didn't, referred to Albert B. Chandler as "Ol' Hap." While governor of Kentucky, he signed 36 death warrants, two of which were for men who were hanged in the courthouse yard. So, looking for a job that might prove a little less stressful, he signed on as commissioner of baseball.

It wasn't quite what he expected. Ol' Hap later said:

> Baseball owners are the toughest set of ignoramuses anyone could ever come up against. They always have been. Refreshingly dumb fellows: greedy, shortsighted and stupid. They created this job in 1921 only because, after the 1919 Black Sox scandal, the American people needed a symbol of complete authority and absolute integrity. But I don't expect baseball ever really wanted a commissioner at all. When the clubs pushed me out in 1951, they had a vacancy and decided to keep it. So they named Ford Frick.

After that he was virtually ostracized by the baseball establishment and was never invited to World Series games or Hall of Fame induction ceremonies.

"They forgot about me and I forgot about them."

By 1984 Bowie Kuhn, in his 15th tumultuous year as commissioner, was under fire mostly due to issues of labor strife. His many detractors claimed he was self-righteous, pompous, inconsistent in his policies, and a puppet in the hands of the owners. "The village idiot," said Charles O. Finley, the maverick owner of the Athletics.

The game was in serious trouble (again). The Major League Umpires Union was threatening to strike the postseason. The Players Association was demanding a new labor agreement or they would strike the following season. Many fans were turning their attention to pro football, deriding baseball as slow and dull in comparison. Stories of rampant drug use by players were everywhere. Most importantly, Major League Baseball hadn't turned a profit for 11 straight years and now 21 of the 26 clubs claimed they were losing money.

The "Dump Bowie" movement won the day.

Get someone in who knows how to make a profit. Get a promoter. Get a salesman.

How about Maryland's governor, Harry Hughes? He's expressed interest. Maybe President Reagan's chief of staff, James Baker.

Peter Ueberroth. Didn't he just run the privately-financed Los Angeles Olympics and contrary to all predictions turn a huge profit? A two-hundred-and-fifty-million-dollar profit! And without the Soviets showing up! The man's brilliant.

He's shown he's a damn good negotiator. Look what he did with the Olympics. He knew TV would be the cash cow and engineered a huge payday from ABC. He talked corporations into unprecedented multi-million dollar sponsorships. He got Coca-Cola to ante up $12.6 million. Then when IBM balked at participating, Ueberroth told their chairman, Frank Cary, it was no matter because NEC was interested. IBM took the bait and signed on. When Eastman Kodak refused to pay $4 million for a sponsorship Ueberroth turned to Fuji Photo. And on and on.

Does he know anything about baseball? Does it matter?

"I played third, caught a little, pitched," Ueberroth says. "American Legion ball, sandlots, high school. I wasn't very good. But baseball is a sport I've cared about — it's not a made-up thing. I started out a Cubs fan, moved over to the [minor league] San Francisco Seals, then to the Dodgers."

Ueberroth is always in control. He hides it with his studied laid-back manner, but make no doubt about it. He is — has to be — in control. He is something of a paradox. He will walk along the fine edge between principles and goals. He can be at once self-deprecating and ego-driven, tender and tough. He is tall, blue-eyed, appealing — like a young John Kennedy.

He'll put a good face on baseball, and he's a fighter.

Ueberroth is not interested in any post–Olympic position that isn't a challenge. He likes challenges. Seeks them out. "I've always hunted for challenges," he says. He gave the Olympic workers scores of work-together-to-scale-the-impossible-mountains speeches. "That's the fun," he says.

But he has demands, too. The commissioner's fining authority was in most instances limited to $5,000 a club, and $500 a player. "That's no good," he says. "I have to be able to fine an owner a quarter of a million dollars. Somebody has to be in charge. In the past the position has been too reactive and responsive to ownership. The first responsibility of the commissioner is to the game and to the fans — it starts with them. Then to the managers, the players, the owners — no the players before the others."

He makes other demands, but he is so popular and so promising, the owners give in.

"I warned the baseball owners that they were electing a commissioner who may be the most criticized man in the country for months before he even arrives," says Kuhn.

Ueberroth gathers his employers/owners at the headquarters of Anheuser

Busch. He tells them bluntly that if he put a red button and a black button in front of each of them and they knew that by pushing the red button they'd win the World Series but lose $10 million or by pushing the black button they'd have a $4 million profit but finish in the middle of the pack, "you are so damned dumb, most of you would push the red button. Look in the mirror and go out and spend big if you want, don't go out there whining that someone made you do it. I know and you know what's wrong. You are smart businessmen. You all agree we have a problem. Go solve it."

He is often this blunt, but usually gets away with it because he is so damned charming.

Even as a kid he had an independent streak and a need for challenges. Some he found in playing sports. Some he found elsewhere. While he was still in high school he moved out of his parents' house and into an orphanage for children from broken homes. He was paid $125 a month to be the school's recreation director.

He paid his own way through San Jose State by working at various jobs—at a shoe store and a chicken farm. He tried out for the Olympics as a water polo player but didn't make it. He claims he spent a lot of time in college partying. "Outside of the classroom, my Delta Upsilon brothers basically helped set me straight about a lot of things. Fraternities get a bad rap sometimes. But you know, I didn't originally want to go to college. I didn't own a tie. My D.U. brothers taught me how to conduct myself in so many situations. And they remain as my friends."

Inside the inscrutable exterior is a man who is driven to succeed like few others. He might have been a great ballplayer had he the skills. Shortly after college he took a job as an airlines operation manager for Trans International Airlines, a small nonscheduled airline owned by Kirk Kerkorian, the man who later took over MGM. Stationed in Hawaii, Ueberroth threw himself into the position with such passion and commitment that he soon held out and got 3 percent of the airline's ownership. Shortly thereafter he opened up Transportation Consultants to serve as a reservation service for small airlines, hotels, and cruise ships. The company quickly became profitable and at 28 he became one of the youngest ever to join the Young Presidents Organization. Here was a young man to keep an eye on.

By 1978, the business now called First Travel had 1,500 employees in 200 offices worldwide and gross revenues in excess of $300 million. Then came the Olympics. When the Soviets announced their boycott just two weeks before the Games, financial disaster seemed imminent. It was likely the audience would fall off. After all, the drama of the Cold War American-Soviet showdown is what drew much of the interest in the Games. If the audience fell below a pre-established level, as much as $70 million would have to be returned to ABC. Ueberroth immediately dispatched his lieutenants to capitals all over the world to make sure other countries held the line. He went to Cuba himself to meet with Castro.

He had shown in quick order that he was shrewd, indefatigable, daring, and one hell of a negotiator. Some of his employees claimed that Ueberroth was cold and inhuman. More often he was described as a no-nonsense manager. Either way, he was getting results.

Ueberroth and his crew worked feverishly up to and through the games. Crisis after crisis was handled adroitly. The image of America was at stake. With all the cold war tensions we simply had to show the world that we could pull off the most successful Games ever. Ueberroth was in the spotlight and every move he made was open to criticism, but he kept his resolve and ever-steady hand on the controls and by the end of the Games he was a genuine American hero.

By any measure, the Games were more successful than anyone except Ueberroth might have imagined. Called to the platform during the closing ceremonies, he received an overwhelming ovation from the crowd of 93,000 — and it was seen by billions on television all over the world. He stood with princely bearing, smiling and teary-eyed.

To many people he was the man who had restored pride in being an American. "People weren't afraid to stand up and cheer for their country," he says, "and the rest of the world saw how caring America can be. There's a spirit of can-do, can-work, can-accomplish — you can do things without being on the Government dole. People want to know that something can work, that somebody can step up and turn a situation around."

President Reagan brought him to the White House and asked him to serve on a committee to energize the private sector to combat world hunger and urban blight. He was asked to take responsibility to restore the Statue of Liberty. A movement arose to urge him to run for president. He reminded many people of the old-fashioned American adventurer/entrepreneur/zealot who could convince the good folk to pull together for the common good. He seemed to genuinely care about patriotic issues.

Yes, the baseball owners had found a promoter who was loved, successful, patriotic, and charismatic — a true-blue American hero. And oh, yes, he knew how to turn a profit.

Not everyone is thrilled with Ueberroth's penchant to attract corporate sponsorship for the game, but the commissioner's office assures anyone who complains that they'll never see a day when there's a "Burger King World Series or any such honky-tonking of the grand old game." Corporate sponsorship, Ueberroth insists, is a form of revenue sharing that helps all teams. Now as to possible corporate sponsorship of individual teams or their stadiums ... well, that's another question altogether.

As part of the package to entice Ueberroth, the club owners agreed to expand the Commissioner's powers by amending the Major League Agreement such that the presidents of the American and National Leagues were required to answer to the Commissioner. Ueberroth would be the sole CEO of baseball. Ueberroth said this would only enhance, not diminish, the authority of the league presidents.

The commissioner's office holds an unusual position in that while it is charged with defending "the best interests of baseball," the commissioner is elected by the millionaire owners and as such is not directly answerable to the players, umpires, or fans.

Some club owners believe that Ueberroth's tenure as commissioner may be short. He's got political ambitions, they say. "I'm a businessman, I'm a leader, and I'm a problem solver. I'm not a politician," insists Ueberroth. "I'm not good on television, and I can't give answers in sound bites."

September 2003
Television commercial:
Dominant images: Ueberroth is shown in various settings — at the 1984 Olympics, meeting with advisers, business leaders and workers, and shaking hands with former Los Angeles Mayor Tom Bradley.
Script (announcer's voice): Peter Ueberroth took the LA Olympics from a deficit to a $200 million surplus and helped lead California out of its last recession. Leadership in crisis is what Peter Ueberroth does best. Bringing together the finest talent regardless of political party. Ueberroth will make the tough decisions needed to balance the budget. Peter is a proven problem-solver who can help save jobs and create more jobs. Peter Ueberroth, governor.
Ueberroth (on camera): "Let's make California work again."

Baseball had endured strikes in 1972 and 1981 that had tested the loyalty of baseball fans. Now a similar situation is pending. Drug violations have sent four players to prison. It looks as if million-dollar salaries may become commonplace. "I have studied the financial position of baseball and it is not viable," says Ueberroth. "It loses an awful lot of money."

He probably would not have taken the position had the situation been otherwise. After all, to be a hero, you have to overcome great odds.

"He's walking into a hornet's nest," the White Sox president says.

Ueberroth wants to hear more of the same. He wants the challenge to be unmistakable.

First things first. The thorny issue with the umpires. Time for the negotiator to negotiate.

He quickly sizes up the situation and concludes he could use the umpire negotiations to put pressure on the players. What if he negotiates a deal favorable to the umpires? Wouldn't that send a message to the players that he wasn't simply a rubber stamp man for the owners? So in his best imitation of Henry Clay, the great compromiser, a man in whom labor could put its trust, he brokers a deal generous to the umpires. Now, surely the players can see he is a fair man. At the same time, he convinces the owners they are getting a good deal. The settlement for the three-year contract is $1.4 million, less than the price for one top player. It is instant credibility for the new commissioner at a bargain price.

Ueberroth is off to a good start, but he knows, as do the owners, that the escalating salary level of the players is a problem. A big problem.

At the general managers' meeting in Florida, Ueberroth tells them: "It's not smart to sign long-term contracts. They force clubs to want to make similar signings. Don't be dumb. We have a five-year agreement with labor."

The owners, eager to support their new savior, quickly fall in line. Contracts for hitters will run for no more than three years; for pitchers, no more than two. Most clubs give up on the idea of free agents altogether.

The Players Association chief, Don Fehr, can scarcely pick up his phone without hearing from a furious agent using the dreaded "C" word—"Collusion." In early February 1986, the union files a grievance which comes to be known as "Collusion I."

The greedy owners are working together to limit salaries, says Fehr.

Collusion? What collusion? responds Ueberroth. "They aren't capable of colluding. They couldn't agree on what to have for breakfast."

The issue of collusion in baseball goes back at least as far as 1918. After that season, the club owners entered into a "gentlemen's agreement" by releasing all their players and agreeing not to sign players from any other team. The aim was simply to artificially force down salaries.

After the Dodgers won the 1965 World Series, their two star pitchers, Don Drysdale and Sandy Koufax, agreed to hold joint negotiations with the club and thereby put additional pressure on the general manager, Buzzie Bavasi. For the season they had gone 49–20 and were grossly underpaid. In those days, there was no free agency, no organized arbitration, and holdouts were about as common as spring training aches and pains. Lots of players held out. Mickey Mantle, for example. It was said that one year he refused to sign a contract with the Yankees until George Weiss, the general manager, supposedly came up with photographs of the Mick cavorting with a woman who bore no resemblance to Mrs. Mantle. Perhaps the press would be interested. Mickey signed.

Since this was before free agency, it meant that the Dodgers' dynamic duo would play at the terms the Dodgers set or they would not play Major League baseball at all. Since they were in Southern California, perhaps they could act in movies.

Drysdale and Koufax held out for more than a month of spring training before agreeing on the two largest contracts in baseball history — Koufax for $125,000 and Drysdale for $110,000.

"Let's put it this way," Koufax said when the acrimonious negotiations were over, "Don and I are both happy." It wasn't about money, he insisted as so many do, but about self-respect.

That's player collusion! scream the owners. My God, what if this ploy catches on?

So in 1968, new union chief Marvin Miller negotiated a Collective Bargaining Agreement with the owners stating that "Players shall not act in concert with other Players and Clubs shall not act in concert with other Clubs."

That's the way it is, Mr. Ueberroth.

Except we're losing money, counters the new commissioner, and if we continue to do that, we'll soon all be out of business.

We don't believe that, says the union. The game generates more than $500 million in revenues annually, drawing 45 million Americans to big-league games.

In 1976 Andy Messersmith paved the way for the downfall of Major League Baseball's reserve clause and began the current era of free agency. Deciding to negotiate his own contract in 1974, Messersmith asked the Dodgers for a no-trade clause. When the Dodgers refused, the pitcher declared he should be a free agent and able to sign with any club of his choosing.

Many fans turned against him.

Look, he made $115,000 last season and he'll probably get around $150,000 for the upcoming season. Where the hell does he get off complaining about his station in life?

Other fans sided with him against the big, bad owners.

What gives the rich guys in the gray suits the rights to run their teams like feudal estates?

One thing was indisputable, though. The laws of the land favored baseball over all other professional sports. They all get certain tax breaks, but baseball alone has an exemption from federal anti-trust laws. It can legally structure certain player-owner relationships in unique ways. Football, basketball, hockey have no such arrangement.

Unlike Curt Flood who went to court to challenge the reserve clause, Messersmith was only dealing with the renewal aspect of the reserve clause and he was asking for arbitration, not a court decision. According to Major League Baseball, a player's contract was for one year plus an option year. So if a player does not sign a contract, the club can unilaterally renew the contract for one year plus an option year, and they can do this theoretically forever.

Messersmith played the 1975 season without a contract and because of that, in December, an arbitrator, Peter Seitz, ruled Messersmith a free agent. The next day the owners fired Seitz. The entire structure of baseball had changed.

Looking back on the decision of a decade ago, Messersmith says, "It was less of an economic issue at the time than a fight for the right to have control over your own destiny, It was a matter of being tired of going in to negotiate a contract and hearing the owners say, 'OK, here's what you're getting. Tough luck.'"

Ten years on and the issue is still a concern. "Ten winters ago, after the Messersmith Decision was handed down, that was the most important off-season in baseball history," says agent Tom Reich. "This one may be the second most important."

Going into this season, the owners hold ranks and stay away from any bidding war involving Kirk Gibson, the only big-name free agent on the market, and they are saying they will do so again.

"We went through a decade of wild inflation," says one agent. "Now we're entering a new era. The ride is over, and the owners are dead serious. We just have to accept that contracts are going to be shorter and tied to performance. Eddie Murray probably got the last five-year contract. I don't know what's taken them so long to become businessmen."

It appears that 1986 will be pivotal in determining whether the days of rapidly escalating salaries for ball players is over. Encouraged by Ueberroth, the owners vow to get costs under control by limiting spending on players.

3. The "C" Word

Kirk Gibson played baseball and football at Michigan State and was named an All-American flanker in 1978. He was drafted by both the Tigers in baseball and the Cardinals in football. Both sports were drooling for his services.

"Why play baseball? It's truly the best of all possible worlds," claimed a promotional pamphlet put out by Major League Baseball in an attempt to lure blue-chip athletes away from football and basketball.

"If I had to compare him with anybody, he's like Mickey Mantle," says the Braves' Paul Snyder of Gibson. "You don't see that combination of speed and power very often."

Still, most people thought he'd play football.

"One of our scouts talked to him and he said he liked baseball but he loves football and that's the difference," said Snyder.

But Gibson did sign with the Tigers for a $200,000 bonus saying that the possibilities for injuries are greater in football and he liked the idea of playing close to home. The agreement allowed him to complete his senior year in college and play football before engaging in a full-time baseball career, at which point the Tigers immediately took out a personal disability insurance policy.

By 1984, Gibson was a pivotal player for the Tigers. He was voted the American League Championship Series Most Valuable Player and led them into the World Series. In Game 5 he came to bat against Goose Gossage, one of the game's best relievers. Gibson had already homered earlier in the game and with first base open an intentional walk seemed to be in order. Sparky Anderson, Detroit's manager, called out to Gibson, "He don't want to walk you," and made the sign for him to hit away. Gibson did, sending a Gossage fast ball into the right field upper deck for a three-run homer. Series over.

The next year he had his best season, collecting 29 home runs, 97 RBIs, 30 stolen bases, and a .287 batting average. He wasn't yet 30.

By this time, free agency was a fact of life and after the season Gibson opted for it. Certainly he would be in great demand. He went home after the Series and waited for the phone to ring off the hook — as surely it would. He knew he would shortly become a very wealthy young athlete and he imagined what pleasures these riches would bring. He read time and again in the papers that he and Donnie Moore would be the most sought after of all the free agent players.

Donnie Moore, an engaging youngster who grew up in Lubbock, Texas, was drafted by the Red Sox but chose instead to go to Ranger College, which he promptly led to the national junior college baseball championship. While there he married his childhood sweetheart with whom he had already fathered a daughter. Family difficulties followed, but he mostly kept them to himself as he began his baseball career.

After three seasons in the minors, he finally landed with the Cubs. Then it was on to the Cardinals, Brewers, and Braves. It looked as if he was destined to become a journeyman pitcher, good enough to sustain a career on the margins of stardom. When left unprotected in the 1985 free agent draft, he was picked up by the Angels to shore up their leaky bullpen.

All of a sudden, he became a star. For the '85 Angels he racked up a club-record 31 saves, eight wins, and a Koufax/Gibson–like 1.92 ERA. He was selected to the All-Star Game over future Hall of Fame teammates Rod Carew and Reggie Jackson.

"I never thought I'd make the All-Star team," he said. "I never gave it any thought."

Then he went out and pitched two scoreless innings. At season's end he received Cy Young Award consideration. Nintendo even put him in their R.B.I. Baseball video game.

He was famous, well-liked by his teammates, one of the best stoppers in the game, and a free agent. Millions of dollars awaited him. He was so confident he announced he intended to negotiate an All-Star Game bonus into his next contract.

Through all of this, Donnie Moore was fighting his demons, but saying little about them. Still, the always perspicacious Reggie Jackson saw things in Moore that warranted concern. "A man is only as good as how he weathers bad times," Jackson tells reporters with Moore in mind. "And you're going to have them in this league."

Even the observant Jackson didn't realize how prophetic he was.

So as the winter meetings for the season of 1986 were about to begin Moore, like Gibson, waits for the offers from other clubs that he will then sift through to choose the most appealing one. Clubs will vie with each other for the privilege of signing these two dominant players.

Wait they do. So do the other free agents like the knuckleballing Niekro brothers and Tommy John. But offers just aren't coming in. The agents press hard, make calls to general managers in both leagues.

"I don't think so," come the replies.

"We're not really going to go that way."

"Doesn't fit into our plans."

"Not someone we're going to pursue."

Only Carlton Fisk gets a nibble. The free-spending George Steinbrenner of the Yankees makes an opening offer for Fisk, but soon, after a cautionary phone call from White Sox chairman Jerry Reinsdorf, he withdraws it. The Yankees have had a change of plans. They'll be happy to platoon three or four different catchers. Sorry, Carlton.

Everyone knows what's happening. The fix is on. At Ueberroth's urging the owners are holding the line. If any of them plans on offering a contract of more than three years, Ueberroth tells them, "I want you to come and tell me eyeball-to-eyeball that you're going to do it."

Doug Baldwin, Gibson's agent, working the phones is frustrated. "I think their actions speak louder than any of the announcements the clubs have made about why they're not pursuing free agents," he says.

The words "collusion," "conspiracy," and "contracts" are on every agent's lips. When confronted with the "C" words, Ueberroth says, "You'd have to ask the owners. I don't think there's any kind of conspiracy or collusion at all. I haven't seen any signs of it."

Many an agent thinks he is either a liar or blind. The evidence is everywhere.

In defense, the owners produce scores of reasons why no one is pursuing long-term contracts for free agents.

After players sign long-term contracts, they spend more time on injured reserve, and we have the statistics to prove it.

After signing long-term contracts, players don't perform as well, and we have the statistics to prove it.

Baldwin says numerous clubs had interest in Gibson — the Cubs, Royals, Braves, White Sox, Angeles, Dodgers, Padres. Gibson was particularly interested in the Royals, but the GM for the Royals says, "Free agency only costs us time and energy, and we've never, ever benefited from it."

If not the Royals, then perhaps the Braves. Ted Turner has been known to open his checkbook for someone who can help his club, and certainly Gibby can do that. Baldwin talks directly with Braves manager Bobby Cox, who is very encouraging. Maybe a deal can be worked out. Baldwin comes away from the meeting sure that Cox will get Turner to ante up for the slugger. Then Ueberroth flies to Atlanta and meets with Turner. The next day Cox says the club has decided to exercise "fiscal responsibility."

"Ted and I had a quick bite to eat," says the commissioner. "There's no connection between my discussion with Ted and their not going after him."

For their part, the Angels say they are interested in re-signing Moore. Well and good, but where's the bidding war Moore and his agent expected?

Moore is left with only the Angels' offer; Gibson with only the Tigers'.

Gibson is the premier player on the market and the Tigers' offer of $3.6 million for three years would make him the highest paid Tiger.

Nevertheless, Gibson, never wont to mince words, says if he were to sign a three-year deal and then have to shake the hands of the club's president, "I think I would vomit." Gibson often talks the way he plays—with swagger, aggression, maybe even anger. "Over the years the Tigers have told me to be patient and my time would come and I feel I have been patient. Now my time has come and they've turned their backs on me."

Bill Campbell, the Tigers' president, insists Gibson shouldn't take it personally. Gibson does. Campbell says it's not about collusion. Gibson doesn't believe him. If they don't sign him to a five-year, $8 million contract, he says, "I will not be a Tiger." If not a Tiger then what? A Lion? Go back to football? At 28 that's not likely. With the deadline for signing looming, Baldwin plays *Beat the Clock* with the Tigers and, on the day Willie McCovey is elected to the Hall of Fame, agrees to a three-year, $3.9 million deal for his client. Gibson has no comment. He's honeymooning in New Zealand.

March 1987

Tigers president Jim Campbell throws up his hands when told Gibson will attempt to co-pilot his Cessna to a world altitude record for planes in its class.

"Nothing about anything surprises me anymore," Campbell says, probably remembering that both Thurman Munson, the Yankees' All-Star catcher, and Ken Hubbs, the Cubs' second baseman, were killed in recent years while flying small planes.

"If I could break a record in the 100-yard dash, I'd do it," Gibson said. "Why do you go on a roller coaster ride? It's just a thrill. No one has ever done it."

Gibson takes the Cessna to 25,200 feet which is more than 5,000 feet higher than the previous record.

Moore also signs. His $3 million, three-year contract is considerably less than he had expected, but he says he really always wanted to be an Angel after all.

The "C" words will not go away. Neither will the "D" word.

4. The "D" Word

Two days before his heart stopped beating, Len Bias, the University of Maryland basketball star, was at Madison Square Garden in New York. Hundreds of kids pressed against police barricades to get a look at the player who would be the second player picked in the NBA draft. He would be playing for the legendary Boston Celtics.

Before they bury him, hundreds show up at Maryland's Cole Field House to say goodbye. How could this have happened, ask his family and friends? They all swear he was clean. But cocaine killed Len Bias. The consensus is that he may have gone out to celebrate and used it once and once may have been enough.

The day after his death the police report finding a plastic bag with between $800 and $1000 worth of cocaine in the athlete's newly leased sports car.

Eight days later the Cleveland Browns' Don Rogers dies the day before he is to get married. Again, cocaine.

Drugs in sports are getting a lot of attention. The NBA bans the Nets' point guard, Sugar Ray Richardson, after he tests positive for cocaine use for the third time, and dozens of other NBA players are said to be using. The NFL suspends running back Chuck Muncie after he fails to show up at mandatory therapy sessions following his drug-treatment program.

In an effort to give their athletes a competitive edge in the Cold War days of the '50s, the Russians supplied some of their best male and female athletes with the male hormone testosterone and they went on to dominate many international sports.

Not to be outdone by the dastardly Russians, an American doctor developed a form of anabolic steroid, a drug that was a variation of testosterone. It was given to some of our weightlifters with the idea that it would build muscle while minimizing masculinizing side effects. The weightlifters who tried the 5 mg pills thought they noticed an increase in muscle mass. So, if that's the case, went the logic, two pills should add even more, and if two, why not three? The race was on.

Steroids are all about gaining an "edge," and often that's all it takes to throw or hit something farther or faster or lift something heavier. With all the money to be made playing sports, a little edge may be the difference between a career as a plumber and a Hall of Fame plaque.

It wasn't just athletes, though, who were looking for that edge. According to reports, law enforcement officers were starting to use steroids to make themselves more imposing to criminals. A Florida police chief was quoted as saying officers should be careful when taking steroids because "there's a great potential for an officer abusing steroids to physically mistreat people." In fact, the Nazis in World War II sometimes administered anabolic steroids in order to make their troops more aggressive.

The idea that really big muscles were appealing got a huge boost when the Arnold Schwarzenegger movie *Pumping Iron* transformed barbells and massive biceps into status symbols, and local gyms and health clubs were more than happy to point young men in the direction of steroids. It was good for business.

The "coked-up '80s," they're starting to call it. Since 1983 when Steve Howe was suspended for a year and four Kansas City Royals players, including the once-heralded Vida Blue, were sent to prison for cocaine use, drugs have been a front-burner issue in baseball.

Ueberroth has to do something. He has to show the public that baseball will clean its own house. He has to do something very public. "We have to get rid of drugs, not people," he says loudly and often, wanting to be seen as a savior, not a nuisance. Some see him as an inveterate publicity hound, but everyone agrees that drugs in sports is a problem that must be addressed.

The commissioner invites 24 players to come and visit him for a little chat. He wants to talk to each about his admitted or alleged involvement with drugs. Nineteen of the 24 either testified at the 1985 Pittsburgh cocaine trial of Curtis Strong or were mentioned in testimony during the trial. Strong, the former Phillies clubhouse cook, had been accused of distributing drugs to players, and seven admitted that they had purchased drugs from him.

Chuck Tanner, the Pittsburgh manager, was one of the central witnesses. He claimed to be unaware of any use of cocaine on his team. Dale Berra, who had played shortstop for the Pirates, testified that the manager once instructed him not to talk to Strong before a game. "Don't talk to that gentleman," Berra quoted Tanner as saying referring to Strong. Tanner not only denied the incident, but denied even knowing who Strong was. Berra and outfielder Dave Parker, then with the Reds, testified that at least five Pirates used cocaine while they were with Pittsburgh.

"Chuck Tanner cautioned us about Curtis Strong, that a drug probe was going on," Parker said. "Gary Matthews was telling players to watch out for Curtis Strong ... that he was 'hot,' to stay away from him."

Parker said that Willie Stargell and Bill Madlock freely dished out amphetamines, known as "greenies," to any player in need, the need being fatigue, stress, or injuries.

"Amphetamines improved my performance about five percent," wrote pitcher Jim Bouton. "Unfortunately, in my particular case that wasn't enough."

John Milner, a former player, also testified. "Did I use them with the Pirates? Yes, I got them in the clubhouse from Stargell, from Madlock." He said that at times pills would be left in his locker before games. "I don't know who dispensed them. They'd always be in my locker. Not every game. Usually games in the second half of the season when the players are worn out and a little tired. Everybody doesn't take them. I don't know how they got there. I just know I'd take 'em."

Milner turned out to be a rather dramatic witness, drawing gasps from spectators when he said that Willie kept a "nasty, potent" stimulant called "red juice" in his locker with the Mets.

Asked who "Willie" was, Milner replied: "Mays, Willie Mays. The great one. Yeah. I tasted it once during his last year and it was really nasty. I guess the pharmacist made it for him. I don't know what kind of speed it was but it kept your eyes open."

It's bad enough to have the Milners of the game implicated, but Willie Mays?

"I consider cocaine the devil on this earth," the Mets' Keith Hernandez testified. He calls coke "a demon in me" and claims he used massive amounts starting in 1980 when he separated from his wife and then developed an "insatiable desire for more." He terms the baseball/cocaine connection a real "love affair."

Ueberroth is unsure whether he will, or even if he can, take action against players who admitted use or gave testimony in the Strong trial. Everyone who testified said they ended their drug use before the trial. Besides, they reminded Ueberroth, they testified under a grant of immunity from prosecution.

"Major League Baseball is not on trial here," said the prosecuting attorney, "Curtis Strong is." Strong's attorney countered by saying that players were "nothing but junkies." They're "hero-criminals" who "are still selling drugs to baseball players around the league." His client was merely a scapegoat for the rich and powerful players who were immune from doing jail time.

Strong was sentenced to 12 years in federal prison. Still, there is pressure from the public for baseball to take action. Sorrow, regret, anger seem to be the prevailing responses.

It's terribly disappointing to have someone as a role model and have them turn out to be tainted.

It's a damn shame that these guys can't depend on their talent to see them through.

Making that kind of money they ought to set a better example.

What's the matter, a million bucks a year ain't enough to get the cheatin' slime buckets through a season?

Toronto outfielder Lloyd Moseby, wanting to help in the war on drugs, puts out a record called *Just Stick to It*. "It warns kids to stay away from drugs, stay in school, that scene," Moseby says. "I wouldn't have done it if not for the lyrics, the message. I'm no singer; no way am I doing love songs or anything."

It may do more to warn kids to stay away from singing.

If for no other reason, Ueberroth, ever the skilled public relations man, has to act for the image value. He orders a conditional one-year suspension of seven admitted users with the caveat that they would still be allowed to play if they donate 10 percent of their yearly salaries to drug-prevention programs, commit to 100 hours of drug-related projects over each of the next two years, and submit to random drug testing for the remainder of their playing careers.

Will this help stem the tide of diminishing public esteem for the national pastime? Maybe it isn't the national pastime anymore anyway.

What about mandatory on-the-spot drug testing of all players? Absolutely, says Ueberroth. No, says Fehr: "Chemical abuse is a medical problem and should be treated like one, presupposing the doctor-client relationship and its confidentiality." Ueberroth is left to limit his tough mandatory drug testing policy to umpires and minor league players.

Nevertheless, not everyone is convinced Ueberroth is doing all he could or should.

Peter-the-Would-Be-Great's crackdown on nose candy is too little, too late.

Some writers love to knock supposed heroes like Peter the Olympic savior. There's something about him that always smacks of insincerity, they opine. Could it be his apparent fascination with seeming to be more important than the straight-arrow stars of the game? What is he afraid of, that they might be more deserving of the public's oohs and aahs than he? Maybe he's appealing to the voters. What voters, you ask? Isn't it obvious he's setting the stage to run for public office? President Ueberroth has a nice ring, don't you think? Look, he had plenty of time after the Pittsburgh mess to come up with a substantive response but look what we got. The game's "image" was more important than the reality. He's too damn busy conceiving a bigger, better publicity bombshell, too busy counting imaginary votes.

The commissioner knows, the owners know, the players know, and the fans hope, that the only way this will recede, if not disappear altogether, is for spring training to begin. Once the balls begin flying through the Florida and Arizona sunshine, attention will turn to hope. Isn't that what spring training is always about — hope?

5. Hopes and Dreams

The game's fans are by nature optimists. No matter how poorly their team is performing this year, there is always the hope of better things to come — if not today, then tomorrow, and if not tomorrow, then soon. According to that great American philosopher John Wayne, "Tomorrow is the most important thing in life."

If baseball fans have a biological predisposition to be hopeful, then it is spring training that feeds the soul with the rampant imagination of tomorrow's victories.

"Hope smiles on the threshold of the year to come, whispering that it will be happier," wrote Alfred Lord Tennyson.

The last time Boston won the World Series, the Great War (the first one) was raging in Europe, Manfred von Richthofen — the German ace known as the "Red Baron" — had just been shot down, the Spanish flu was on its way to killing 25 million people, Ted Williams was a newborn, Knute Rockne was getting ready to take over Notre Dame football, and Woodrow Wilson was president.

On Wednesday, September 11, 1918, the Boston Red Sox, behind their ace right-hander Carl Mays, shut down the Cubs on three hits. The 15,238 fans who left Fenway Park that afternoon were flush with the glow of victory and the promise for the future. And why not? Their Sox had just won their fourth World Championship in the last seven years and their fifth overall. Could anyone stop them? Not likely.

The Chicago White Sox thought otherwise. The following season the Red Sox finished sixth, 20½ games behind Chicago.

Sixty-seven years later they still haven't won another championship. The last time the Red Sox had even won a postseason game was 1978. In 1983 they finished sixth in the seven-team AL East, their worst record since 1966. After the season, their superstar, Carl Yastrzemski, ended his 23-year career. The following season they finished 18 games behind the Tigers, and then in '85, 18½ games behind the Blue Jays.

5. Hopes and Dreams

Now with the season opener just around the corner, the Red Sox are crossing their collective fingers that Roger Clemens' surgically-repaired shoulder is going to hold up. In his last tune-up appearance he goes seven innings, striking out nine while giving up only three singles to the Tigers and one of those a bunt.

"I'm very satisfied where I am right now," he says. John McNamara, heading into his second year as manager, is hopeful but not sure, so they are pursuing Tom Seaver from the White Sox. Seaver has said he wants to play closer to his Connecticut home. The on-again/off-again talks are a source of frustration to both pitching staffs.

Clemens and his shoulder are a concern; pitcher Oil Can Boyd and his attitude are a concern; Al Nipper and Bruce Hurst, both of whom had losing records last year, are concerns; bullpen ace Bob Stanley's surgically-repaired finger is a concern.

They are going to score runs aplenty, no doubt about that. With the alliterative trio of Baylor, Buckner, and Boggs, they are capable of bludgeoning teams. Now if only their pitching holds out...

Detroit with Gibson back in the fold will be formidable. In New York, new 42-year-old manager Lou Piniella inherits a team that led the Major Leagues in runs scored last year, and they still have MVP Don Mattingly, as well as Dave Winfield, and Rickey Henderson. The Jays won 99 games last year without a 20-game winner, a 30-home-run or 100-RBI hitter, or a 20-save reliever. What they do have is maybe the best outfield in baseball with Jesse Barfield, Lloyd Moseby, and George Bell. With Eddie Murray and Cal Ripken, Jr., the Orioles can hit and if they can shore up their pitching staff they could contend.

Once known as baseball's Skid Row, the AL Worst, the Mild Mild West, a congeries of mediocrity wrapped in failure, the AL West is now formidable. Before the season is over, it will showcase a boatload of young talent—Jose Canseco, Pete Incaviglia, Wally Joyner, Kirby Puckett, and Mark McGwire among others.

Harrah's betting book says the money is on the Kansas City Royals to repeat as division champs. Why not? They're loaded with pitching and they've got George Brett, the hitting machine.

"Repeating is very difficult," says their manager, Dick Howser, despite winning six of the last 10 titles. With a pitching staff led by Cy Young Award winner Bret Saberhagen and Dan Quisenberry, they're not going to get blown out of a lot of games. They've got some speed and a little punch with "Bye-Bye Balboni."

Some will argue veterans Reggie Jackson, Bobby Grich, Doug DeCinces, and Don Sutton give the Angels a lot of experience and leadership. Others say it gives them an achy-kneed, aging lineup. Maybe the promising young Wally Joyner can help.

White Sox manager Tony LaRussa plans on playing his catcher in left field to "lengthen his career and make his bat available for 150 games." The catcher, Carlton Fisk, is not thrilled. The shallowness of their pitching staff is not being helped by 41-year-old Tom Seaver's pleas to be traded back east. The Athletics are counting on the homer-happy Dave Kingman. They also have hopes for Jose Canseco who, after hitting 41 home runs in the minors last year, added five for them as a late-season call up. And prepping in the minors is Mark McGwire.

The Twins have big boppers in Kent Hrbek and Tom Brunansky and a solid starting four led by Bert Blyleven. They're hoping that Billy Beane can nail down the left field spot.

The Seattle Mariners have been collecting good young talent for a number of years and have now brought in 37-year-old catcher Steve Yeager to mentor their pitching staff. Rangers manager Bobby Valentine says, "The 1986 season could be the start of something very exciting." True, their best pitcher, Charlie Hough, broke his finger shaking hands and will be lost to start the season, but Pete Incaviglia, the hard-hitting outfielder who homered 48 times in 75 games last year for Oklahoma State, could be a savior.

The Royals and Red Sox may be favored, but where there is imagination there is always hope. Miracles do happen.

For many fans, though, as long as the miracles don't happen to the Yankees, they'll be happy.

6. Bullies in Pinstripes

There is rooting for and there is rooting against, and fans can become as impassioned about the "against" as they are about the "for."

"Hating the New York Yankees is as American as apple pie, unwed mothers and cheating on your income tax," says columnist Mike Royko.

An old joke: A Mets fan, a Braves fan, a Yankees fan, and a Red Sox fan are climbing a mountain. Each is arguing about how loyal they are to their team and what they would do for that team. Upon reaching the top, the Mets fan shouts, "This is for the Mets!!!" and throws himself off the top of the mountain. Next the Braves fan yells, "I love Atlanta... This is for you, Braves!!" and he, too, jumps off. Then the Red Sox fan reaches the top and screams, "This is for EVERYONE!!" and pushes the Yankees fan off the mountain.

To many, the Yankees represent the rich bully they love to hate. "The Yankees... are a family," wrote *Sports Illustrated* contributor Ron Fimrite. "A family like the Macbeths, the Borgias, and the Bordens of Fall River, Mass."

If they were located someplace else, it would probably be different, but the Big Apple magnifies everything. "I could never play in New York," says Baltimore pitcher Mike Flanagan. "The first time I ever came into a game there, I got in the bullpen car and they told me to lock the doors."

As one-time presidential candidate Thomas E. Dewey said, "If you're not in New York, you're camping out." It's often claimed that when you leave New York, you "ain't goin' nowhere." To most New Yorkers, their city is not only the cultural center of America, it is also the business, political, and administrative center.

"This is the town that never sleeps," wrote quintessential New Yorker Woody Allen. "That's why we don't live in Duluth. That plus I don't know where Duluth is."

To much of the rest of the country, rooting for a New York team is like rooting for the house in a blackjack game or pulling for IBM. Oh, of course, the people who root for the Yankees are the people who would take the lions over Daniel. To hate New York and the perceived arrogance of its inhabitants is an art form easily mastered.

"Damn Yankees" is more than just the title of a Broadway musical.

George Steinbrenner, the billionaire owner of the Yankees, graduated from a military academy and served as a graduate assistant to Woody Hayes. Perhaps it's not a total coincidence that he is such a control freak. "The Boss" doesn't take his title lightly.

He meddles, claim players, coaches, and managers alike. He interferes with baseball operations; he tampers with things with which he has little or no experience.

"It's a good thing Babe Ruth isn't here," says third baseman Graig Nettles. "If he was, George would have him bat seventh and tell him he's overweight."

When he took over the Yankees in 1973, he said owning the Yankees was like owning the Mona Lisa and he vowed he would be a hands-off owner and leave the day-to-day operations to others more qualified. After all, his business was shipbuilding, not baseball. The vow apparently expired on his first day at Yankee Stadium. As he explained to the *New York Daily News*: "I walked in and saw flowers on every desk. Freshly cut flowers. I said, 'What the hell is this? Is it Flowers Day? Is it Secretary's Day?' Somebody said, 'Isn't that wonderful? Mr. Burke does this every day for us.' [Former Yankee president] Mike Burke is a guy who I admired tremendously. He was a real heartthrob type of guy. Everybody liked him. I loved him, but for what I wanted, he didn't fit with me. When I saw the flowers, that was the trigger. I got involved."

And he stayed involved, changing the managers and general managers on his team more often than most people change the oil in their cars. He fired Billy Martin five separate times.

One of the great Yankee traditions is the retiring of the uniform numbers of its greatest players and the placing of plaques in center field to honor them. Naturally Ruth, Gehrig, DiMaggio, and Mantle are among them. Steinbrenner added Billy Martin, whose lifetime batting average was .257, who won the same number of world championships as Joe Altobelli (one). The Yankees press release announcing the enshrinement referred to "the plague in centerfield."

"All I know is, I pass people on the street these days," says Martin, "and they don't know whether to say hello or good-bye."

Steinbrenner became known as the most manipulative, controlling, domineering owner in professional sports, a cold schoolyard toughie. Many owners dislike him because he has paid so much for players that he has driven player salaries far too high; many players dislike him because he is outspoken and publicly critical of them; fans of other teams dislike him because the Yankees win too often; managers and coaches dislike him because he meddles in baseball matters; and team executives dislike him because of the unreasonable pressure he puts on them.

As devout Red Sox fan Ben Affleck says, "George Steinbrenner is the center of evil in the universe."

In "Homer at the Bat," a *Simpsons* parody of a real-life event, Mr. Burns fires Don Mattingly for refusing to shave his sideburns. Mattingly walks off the field proclaiming, "I still like him [Burns] better than Steinbrenner."

Shortly after taking over the Yankees, Steinbrenner was indicted on 14 criminal counts for making illegal contributions to Richard Nixon's re-election campaign and for obstruction of justice. He was originally suspended from baseball for two years by Commissioner Bowie Kuhn, but later the suspension was reduced to nine months, and then in one of the final acts of his presidency, Ronald Reagan pardoned him.

In one of the "off-again" moments in their on-again/off-again relationship, Billy Martin said of Steinbrenner and his high-priced outfielder Reggie Jackson, "The two of them deserve each other. One's a born liar and the other's convicted."

That comment brought the end of Martin's first tenure as Yankee manager, but The Boss liked winning more than revenge so he was re-hired before the year was out.

July 1990
Commissioner Fay Vincent bans Steinbrenner from baseball for life for the "Howie Spira" affair that had been sparked by a Steinbrenner/Dave Winfield feud.

Steinbrenner signed Winfield to a $15 million contract, but when Winfield failed to lead the team to the successes Steinbrenner expected for his investment, he called Winfield "Mr. May," a sarcastic reference to the more productive "Mr. October," Reggie Jackson. Winfield bristled at the comparison but let it pass. However, when Steinbrenner refused to pay Winfield's foundation the $300,000 guaranteed in his contract, a series of lawsuits followed.

Steinbrenner did what he could to discredit Winfield and his foundation, claiming at one point that an audit revealed that the foundation spent $6 for every dollar it donated to worthy causes.

Spira, a 21-year-old go-fer for Winfield and small-time gambler, asked Winfield for a $15,000 loan to pay off gambling debts. When Winfield refused, he approached Steinbrenner and offered to dig up "dirt" on Winfield for a reasonable fee. Steinbrenner thought $40,000 a reasonable business fee to disgrace Winfield.

When the deal came to light, Steinbrenner claimed he paid off Spira because his family was being harassed by the little man.

When asked if he was really $40,000 afraid of Spira, Steinbrenner said, "You're damn right I was! And after that, there was a death threat at my hotel... Now, everybody says, 'Yeah, but look at Howard Spira. He's a little guy.' But Sirhan Sirhan was a little guy. Lee Harvey Oswald was a little guy... I was scared stiff... I told him to take the $40,000 and go away."

The Commisioner didn't buy the scared story and thus the banishment.

When fans at Yankee Stadium heard the news on their radios, they gave a standing ovation in response.

Winfield would later go into the Hall of Fame as a San Diego Padre and Steinbrenner would be reinstated.

After 16 games of the 1985 season, the Yankee managerial musical chairs game was on again. Steinbrenner fired manager Yogi Berra and replaced him with Billy Martin. It was the second time he fired Berra and the fourth time he hired Martin.

Martin's relationship with The Boss was, at best, always on the edge of collapsing.

Alfred Manuel Martin, Jr., whose mother called him "bello," or "beautiful" in Italian, collected about as many nicknames as he did Steinbrenner pink slips—"Billy," "Billy the Kid," "The Brat," "The Little General," and "Whiskey Slick."

He grew up on the gang-infested streets of Oakland, California, and — as the legend goes — developed his fighting style there.

As a player he got into celebrated fist fights with Jim Brewer, Jimmy Piersall, Clint Courtney (twice), Matt Batts, and Tommy Lasorda. He also got into a highly publicized fight in the Copacabana nightclub. During his managerial career he took on a fan, a sports writer, a cabbie who professed he preferred soccer to baseball, two traveling secretaries, two bar patrons, two bouncers in a topless bar, and then as his crowning boxing achievement, a marshmallow salesman. He even made beer commercials glorifying himself as the toughest bar fighter of them all.

"I don't throw the first punch. I throw the second four," says Martin.

He seemed to court crises like Hugh Hefner courted women.

Around two o'clock one morning, he got into a fight with Ed Whitson that began in the hotel bar and then moved throughout the hotel. During a losing streak he had dropped Whitson from the lineup referring to him as "Whatchamacallit." It seems that Whatchamacallit got the better of his battling manager, because Billy ended up with a broken arm.

Goodbye, Billy ... again. The message is delivered not by Steinbrenner, but the team's general manager.

Christmas Day 1989.
Martin is drinking heavily with his friend William Reedy in upstate New York. The two are heading home in a pickup truck on icy roads, when it skids 200 feet off a winding rural road and careens another 100 feet down a gully. Martin is killed when his neck is fractured. Considerable speculation arises as to whether it was Martin or Reedy who was driving.

Someone suggests they should put up plaques in all the bars where Billy had fights and they would become great collectors' items. Psychologists have a field day suggesting various causes for his apparent death wish and need to make headlines for all the wrong reasons.

Also grist for the speculation mill was the question of why Steinbrenner chose the fiery Lou Piniella as Martin's replacement for the '86 season. Maybe it's Steinbrenner with the death wish. *Sport* magazine refers to the curious situation as "The Case of the Pinstripped Volcano."

"I'm 43, and I'm still married to a four-year-old," says Piniella's wife, Anita, after one of her husband's foot-stamping, dirt-kicking, hat-throwing demonstrations.

Piniella swears he's mellowed, swears he's given up punching water coolers and dugout walls. The implication is that he's not a bully like Martin, but a passionate man who has matured since his playing days as a Yankee. He understands the Bronx Zoo atmosphere here. "I know managing the Yankees is a tough job, but, my God, it wasn't easy playing here, either."

He also claims he has a non-interference pledge from Steinbrenner.

Sure, Lou.

7. Won't This Curse Ever End?

The Boston Americans were one of the eight teams that formed the new American League in 1901. The league was the brainchild of Ban Johnson, who wanted a league to compete with the established National League of Professional Baseball Clubs that had been operating more or less successfully since 1876 when it supplanted the floundering National Association of Professional Baseball Players. Johnson's plan was for the new league to be a "clean" league free from the gambling and shady business deals that characterized the National League. To compete successfully with the older league, Johnson made sure there were teams in two of the National League's biggest cities—Philadelphia and Boston. He had wanted to include New York, but the New York Giants of the National League had enough political muscle to keep them out.

The Americans, led by the rubber-armed Denton True Young, otherwise known as "Cy," were successful right from the start. In their first four seasons of play they came in first twice, second once, and third once.

In 1903 a "peace conference" was held between the leaders of the two leagues and, as a result, the Giants begrudgingly withdrew their opposition to an American League franchise in New York. So Johnson convinced the Baltimore Orioles to move to uptown New York and they changed their name to the New York Highlanders in deference to the location of their playing field and to the Gordon Highlanders, the venerable British fighting unit. Not coincidentally, their owner was Joseph Gordon.

That year the Americans played in the first official World Series, then a nine-game affair pitting the winners of the two leagues. The Americans defeated the highly favored Pirates, five games to three.

The next year, on the last day of the season, the Americans beat the Highlanders to take the AL championship, but the Giants refused to meet them in a World Series because they were still pouting about the Highlanders invading their city. Nevertheless, a great rivalry had begun, a rivalry that has persisted and maintained its intensity to this day.

The Highlanders eventually moved from their high lands down to the Polo Grounds, and gradually the name "Highlanders" faded away to be replaced by "Yankees" as a synonym for Americans. The name stuck and by 1913 it was official.

Meanwhile the Americans, with Tris Speaker—popularly known as "Spoke," or "The Grey Eagle"—leading the club on the field, changed their name to the Red Stockings. Newspapers found that a trifle long so they started shortening "Stockings" to the more headline-friendly "Sox." (The "Red Stocking" name actually migrated to Boston from Cincinnati where it was used by the first all-professional baseball team in 1869 in reference to their white knickers and red stockings.)

In 1914, the Red Sox called up a young pitcher from their top farm club, a kid named Ruth.

When he was seven George Herman Ruth, Jr., was dumped in St. Mary's Industrial School for Boys, a reformatory and orphanage. The wild youngster, whose parents seldom visited him during his 12 years there, was considered by the Catholic brothers who ran the institution as "incorrigible." One man, though, Brother Matthias, became a surrogate father figure to George. He offered guidance and help with the kid's batting stance.

George proved to be a good athlete and quickly became the regular catcher on St. Mary's baseball team. When he was 15 he began pitching, and pitching well enough to catch the eye of Jack Dunn, one of the best scouts in baseball. Dunn signed the strapping youth to a contract with a Red Sox–affiliated minor league team. The other players on the team referred to the kid as "Jack's newest babe." George Ruth had become "The Babe," or "The Bambino."

It didn't take the Red Sox long to see what they had, and after only five months in the minors, they called up the 19-year-old pitcher. Within two years he was the ace of their staff.

The Sox made the World Series in 1916 and sent Ruth to the mound in Game 4 against the National League's Brooklyn Robins. He gave up a run in the first inning, and then settled down to pitch 13 scoreless innings. His 14-inning masterpiece remains the longest complete game in World Series history.

He also pitched the Sox to victory in the 1918 Series. Now, 68 years later, they are still looking for their next World Series title. Despite having had some of the greatest players ever to put on a baseball uniform, players like Bobby Doerr, Joe Cronin, Carlton Fisk, Carl Yastrzemski, and Ted Williams, they always came up short.

What happened? As all Red Sox fans know, their fate is the result of the "Curse of the Bambino."

After the Sox dropped to sixth place in 1919, the team's new owner, Harry Frazee, sold his star to the New York Yankees for $100,000 and a $350,000 loan. It seems Mr. Frazee had showbiz fever and wanted the money to invest in Broadway productions, but he was broke. Or so goes the story.

Frazee produced *No, No, Nanette*, a Broadway musical about a man who makes millions in the bible publishing business and then wants to teach his ward, Nanette, how to be a respectable young lady. The play makes money for its producer but presumably nary a Red Sox fan goes to see it. The very mention of the name "Frazee" raises the hackles of true Red Sox aficionados to this day.

Prior to the sale of Ruth, the Red Sox had won five World Series, the Yankees none. After the sale, the Yankees played in 39 World Series, winning 26 of them, while the Sox played in four, losing each in seven games.

Over the years, fans obsessed with the Curse tried about everything they could think of to break it. Exorcists and witch doctors were hired, a Sox cap was carried to the top of Mt. Everest, Yankee caps were burned, a Boston street sign for Reverse Curve, was repainted to read "Reverse the Curse," "Reverse the Curse Ice Cream" was churned, and more prayers were offered up than any priest could count.

One frustrated fan even scoured the bottom of a Massachusetts pond with sophisticated scanning equipment in a failed bid to find a piano Ruth had supposedly dumped there. Somehow, the fan believed, finding the piano would have reversed the curse.

The facts of the Ruth sale, however, are rather at odds with the widely accepted image of the broke Frazee and *No, No, Nanette*.

Frazee wasn't close to being broke. The club had made money the year before, and he had a show running on Broadway that was bringing him $3,000 a week. Rather, he was fed up with Ruth, who although performing well on the field, was a troublemaker in the clubhouse, was agitating for a new manager, asking for a new contract, and demanding special treatment. Frazee had enough and he started asking other owners if they were interested in the pitcher who was also demonstrating skills as a power hitter. The White Sox offered their star outfielder Joe Jackson and $60,000 for Ruth, but the illiterate Jackson presented his own problems, so when the Yankees trumped that with $100,000, Frazee took the deal. The Yankees were looking for box-office help in their battle with the National League Giants.

It was "bye-bye, Babe, hello, losing" for the Sox.

Throughout most of the '20s and '30s they put up poor records. Then in 1939, they purchased the contract of Ted Williams from the San Diego Padres of the Pacific Coast League. Williams showed his batting brilliance right from the start, hitting .327 as a rookie and then going on to play 19 seasons for the Sox, amassing a lifetime .344 average. He was the last player to hit .400 for a full season.

"If there was ever a man born to be a hitter it was me," he said modestly. And he was probably right. He could hit for average and he could hit for power.

In case there's any doubt, he added, "A man has to have goals—for a day, for a lifetime—and that was mine, to have people say, 'There goes Ted Williams, the greatest hitter who ever lived.'" After he retired that's exactly how he insisted he be introduced.

"He could hit better with a broken arm than we could with two good arms," said Jerry Coleman.

Some writers started calling the team the "Ted Sox," but not all of them loved him. He could be a prickly character and he got into scores of feuds with writers, or as he called them, "The Knights of the Keyboard." His relationship with the fans could also be rocky and more than once he was known to spit in the direction of the stands.

Eddie Collins said of him, "If he'd just tip the cap once, he could be elected Mayor of Boston in five minutes."

But that was not Williams. He even refused to tip his hat to the fans when he hit a farewell home run in his last at-bat in 1960. He was argumentative, brash, often offensive.

"Gods," John Updike later famously remarked, "do not answer letters."

Wherever he was, whatever he was doing, his magnetic personality could not be ignored. For better or worse, he was always at the center of attention and gradually the legend grew.

They say his eyesight was so good he could actually read the words on the ball before he hit it.

They say he could hold a bat in his hand and correctly tell you its exact weight to the ounce.

They say had he not spent all that time in the military, he would have been the greatest home run hitter ever.

Although missing nearly five full seasons due to military service and two major injuries, he still hit 521 home runs, won six batting titles, two Triple Crowns, two Most Valuable Player Awards, and was an eighteen-time All-Star selection.

About the only thing he didn't win was a World Series title.

The Curse affects even the great ones.

July 1999

Fenway Park, Boston. The All-Star Game turns into a tribute to Ted Williams.

With Kevin Costner narrating, Williams, now 80 and feeble, is driven out onto the field in a golf cart and immediately surrounded by the greatest names from baseball's past and present. Hank Aaron, Willie Mays, and Pete Rose are there. So are Tony Gwynn, Mark McGwire, Jose Canseco, and Cal Ripken, Jr.

The event planned as a salute to the all-century team, quickly turns into a one-man love fest for the great hitter who was once so disliked. Thirty-four thousand people stand as the cart drives him around the park.

Now, for the first time, he takes off his cap and waves it to the crowd. Fans are crying; other players are crying; Williams is crying.

The players crowd around his cart. "When you see Ted Williams, and tears are running from his eyes, it's a very emotional time," McGwire says.

"When I got up there, tears were coming out of Ted's eyes," says Colorado's Larry Walker, who digs up a piece of the right field turf as a memento. "The greatest player in the world is surrounded by more great players. I know Ted was extremely touched by it."

Williams drinks it all in. "I can only describe it as great," he says. "Hell, I haven't had a base hit in 30 years, and I'm a better hitter now than I've ever been in my life."

Three years later Williams dies and his son has the body frozen so that someday, when the technology permits, the body will be thawed out and "the greatest hitter who ever lived," will live to hit again.

With Williams leading the way, the Sox made it to the 1946 World Series, but lost to the Cardinals in part because they employed the "Williams shift," moving the shortstop to the right side of the infield, thus daring Williams to try to hit to left. He didn't take the bait and had a poor Series. Some people think he let pride get in his way.

He was a stubborn sonovabitch, that Williams.

He just didn't want the Cards to think they could dictate to him.

By the time Williams returned from the Korean War where he was a fighter pilot, the Sox had lost most of the top players from the '40s. They were so bad their lineup was sometimes called "Ted Williams and the Seven Dwarfs."

The team's fortunes weren't helped by the owner's refusal to sign black players. Tom Yawkey, then the club's owner, passed on signing two black players who had been praised by his scouts and brought in for private workouts. One can only think what the team might have been had Yawkey listened to his scouts and signed Jackie Robinson and Willie Mays to play alongside Williams. As it was, they were the last Major League team to play a black player — Pumpsie Green in 1959.

At the age of 38, Williams hit .388. He retired two years later.

Carl Yastrzemski took over as the next great hope for the Sox faithful. There was tremendous pressure on him from the first day he took the field in 1961. He was, after all, expected to replace Williams.

"I remember I was scared as a rookie, hitting .220 for the first three months of my baseball season and doubting my ability," he says.

He was a good hitter and a better fielder than Williams and went on to a long and successful career.

"I loved the game. I loved the competition," Yaz says. "But I never had any fun. I never enjoyed it."

7. Won't This Curse Ever End?

He did, however, work hard at it.

"Yaz did it all the time," says outfielder Joe Lahoud. "We'd be on the road and he'd call, 'C'mon, we're going to the ballpark.' I'd say, 'Christ, it's only one o'clock. The game's at seven.' He lived, breathed, ate, and slept baseball. If he went 0-for-4, he couldn't live with it. He could live with himself if he went 1-for-3. He was happy if he went 2-for-4. That's the way the man suffered."

Yaz didn't bring the personality of Williams to the club, but he was generally liked and respected by his teammates.

"He's a dull, boring potato farmer from Long Island who just happened to be a great ballplayer," says his teammate, Bill Lee. "But he was the worst dresser in organized baseball. He made Inspector Clouseau look like a candidate for Mr. Blackwell's list of best-dressed men. He had the same London Fog raincoat during his entire career. We'd throw it in trashcans all around the league, and somehow it mysteriously made its way back."

Taking their cue from the big number in the Broadway play *Man of La Mancha*, the press took to calling 1967 the year of "The Impossible Dream." Behind Yaz's Triple Crown season, considered by some as one of the greatest single offensive seasons in history, the Sox made it to the World Series, only to lose to Bob Gibson and the Cards. That was the year, too, that their young slugger, Tony Conigliaro, was hit in the face by a fastball from Jack Hamilton. Tony C, as he was usually called, had put up home run numbers that no one his age had ever done before.

Tony C was a local kid, part choir boy, part hellraiser. On at least one occasion in New York, he spent the night on the town and then on the team bus threw up on himself and everyone near him.

The Vietnam War was building up steam at the time and the military was drafting young men. To avoid losing players, most teams were able to get them into the Army Reserves. According to Bill Lee, however, the Red Sox were "having trouble with the military at that time, because one of our players allegedly told an officer to shit in his hat and the officer told him, 'I'm going to have you and the rest of these ballplayers walking point in Quang Tri.' That really hurt the club's relationship with the Army. Somebody told me later that player had been Tony Conigliaro. That made sense — old spur-of-the-moment Tony."

After his beaning, he sat out a year with headaches and blurred vision. When he came back, he was never the same and was soon out of the game altogether.

The team didn't win the pennant again until 1975. By that time, Yaz was surrounded by a talented and colorful cast including "The Gold Dust Twins," Jim Rice and Fred Lynn; "Dewey" Evans; "Pudge" Fisk; Luis "El Tiante" Tiant; and Bill "The Spaceman" Lee.

In the World Series they faced Pete Rose and Cincinnati's "Big Red

Machine." Trailing three games to two, they played the sixth in Boston's Fenway Park. In one of the greatest games in World Series history, Pudge hit a twelfth-inning high fly ball deep down the left field line. As he made his way down the line to first he frantically waved his arms as if trying to push the ball fair. It must have worked. The Boston crowd went wild and pictures of the arm-waving catcher have become a permanent part of the game's iconography.

Early in Game 7, leading 3–0, they called on the Spaceman. He threw a pitch he called a "pace ball." Tony Perez called it a home run, hitting it over the Green Monster left field wall and across the street.

Pudge later said of that Series, "We won that thing three games to four."

Bill Lee may not have been the best pitcher Boston ever had, but he was probably their best quote machine.

"Baseball's a very simple game," he once told a reporter. "All you have to do is sit on your butt, spit tobacco, and nod at the stupid things your manager says."

When asked about drug testing he said, "I believed in drug testing a long time ago. All through the sixties I tested everything."

Any rules you live by, Bill?

"The only rule I got is if you slide, get up."

What about the Yankees? Any thoughts about them?

"You take a team with twenty-five assholes and I'll show you a pennant. I'll show you the New York Yankees."

What, if anything do you think about when you're on the mound?

"I think about the cosmic snowball theory. A few million years from now the sun will burn out and lose its gravitational pull. The earth will turn into a giant snowball and be hurled through space. When that happens it won't matter if I get this guy out."

If you could change the game, what would you do?

"I would change policy, bring back natural grass and nickel beer. Baseball is the belly-button of our society. Straighten out baseball, and you straighten out the rest of the world."

At one point in 1978, the Yankees were 14½ games behind the Sox, but then in September after a four-game sweep they called "The Boston Massacre," they ended up in a dead heat with the Sox. Boston lost the one-game playoff on a Bucky Dent home run. Bucky who?

Won't this Curse ever end?

For the next seven years they failed to make the postseason. In 1983 they finished in sixth.

But now in '86, with Clemens leading the way on the mound and Boggs at the plate, hope is running high again. It's cautious hope because they've been here before only to be disappointed.

8. The Chicken Man

Wade Boggs is the only Major League player known to have been beaten up by *The Simpsons*' Barney Gumble. It happened after an argument over who was the best prime minister in England's history. Barney claimed it was Lord Palmerston; Boggs, William Pitt the Elder. Boggs had been to a junior college so he should know these things.

The incident occurred as part of the episode "Homer at the Bat." It seems that Mr. Burns bet Homer that his baseball team could beat Homer's. To win the bet he brings in a few ringers, including Boggs, Roger Clemens, Ken Griffey Jr., Ozzie Smith, Jose Canseco, Don Mattingly, and Darryl Strawberry.

However, before the game is played, Boggs gets into his fight, Griffey Jr. overdoses on a nerve tonic, Smith disappears into the "Springfield mystery spot," Mattingly is kicked off the team because he sports sideburns, Canseco misses the game while rescuing a woman from a fire, and other misadventures cause all the ringers except Darryl Strawberry to miss the game.

The players all recorded their parts while they were in Los Angeles playing the Dodgers or Angels. All of the players enjoyed the experience except Jose Canseco, who proved to be uncooperative from the start. He insisted his part be rewritten to suit his liking — making him appear more heroic. The writers groused but grudgingly agreed. He complained that the animation looked nothing like him. When the script had him waking up in bed with Edna Krabappel, Canseco's wife objected.

No, it was no fun working with Canseco. Later when asked by the *San Jose Mercury News* for an interview about the part, he hung up the phone and refused the paper's subsequent calls.

Boggs, though, loved doing the show and the notoriety that followed. He claimed it made him more famous than he already was.

Boggs was nothing if not idiosyncratic. Appearing on *The Simpsons* was almost normal compared to some of his antics. His superstitions for example.

Lots of players in the long history of baseball adhered to odd rituals in the name of preserving their sanity. Routines are comforting; they imply a sense of order. From the Curse of the Bambino to the rally cap, from freezing out a pitcher in the midst of throwing a no-hitter, to ignoring the razor after a first postseason win. Rich Donnelly, a long-time coach, says of players:

> They're like trained animals. They come out here and everything has to be the same, they don't like anything that knocks them off their routine. Just look at the dugout and you'll see every guy sitting in the same spot every night. It's amazing, everybody in the same spot. And don't you dare take someone's seat. If a guy comes up from the minors and sits here, they'll say, "Hey, Jim sits here, find another seat." You watch the pitcher warm up and he'll do the same thing every time. And when you go on the road it's the same way. You've got a routine and you adhere to it and you don't want anybody knocking you off it.

Babe Ruth, however, said the only superstition he had was to make sure he touched all the bases when he hit a home run.

Still, among the great superstitionists in the game, Wade Boggs is in his own world.

He eats chicken before every game. If he missed his chicken he probably wouldn't play that day. The chicken has to be baked or broiled, never fried. Lemon chicken is best. He wakes up at the same time every day and takes exactly 150 ground balls in fielding practice. When finished, he steps—in order—on the third-, second-, and first-base bags. He then steps on the base line taking two steps in the coach's box, then trots to the dugout in four steps. At exactly 5:17 he takes batting practice. At 7:17 he runs sprints. Although he is not Jewish, he draws the Hebrew word for "life" in the dirt before every at-bat.

Quirky Boggs doesn't do anything to dispel the stories of his superstitions, true or not. He doesn't mind the attention. Boggs the flake, Boggs the iconoclast are labels that fit nicely on him. In fact, some of his teammates think he goes too far out of his way to encourage the idiosyncratic image.

According to oft-encouraged stories, Wade "the Chicken Man" Boggs can down more Miller Lites than anyone in the history of ... well, anyone ever. Has to be Miller Lite. Chicken and Miller Lite.

Kornheiser and Wilbon cemented the legend of Boggs on their ESPN show, alleging Boggs downed 64 beers on a cross-country flight. Jim Rome upped the number to 72.

Jeff Nelson, who was his teammate for a time, says, "Oh, I'd say, on a typical road trip, east coast to west coast, say a road game to Seattle ... Wade would drink anywhere between 50 and 60 beers."

Nelson, you must be drinking yourself. That's impossible.

"No, I know ... I know how crazy that sounds, and I wouldn't believe it myself unless I saw him do it ... numerous times."

He'd have to spend the entire flight in the bathroom.

"Seriously. Wade was the kind of guy who was always the first one at the clubhouse. So he'd get to the clubhouse, and he'd bring a six pack with him. He'd be there drinking a beer when someone showed up, and as we were all packing our stuff up out of our lockers and getting our bags ready for the trip, Wade would sit there and drink that whole six pack.

"Now, at the time, we were flying out of New Jersey, so it was somewhat of a drive from Yankee stadium to the airport in New Jersey. Wade would drink another couple of beers on the bus to the airport. At the time, we were flying this older airplane, it couldn't make it across the country without refueling, and it wasn't the fastest airplane in the sky. So we would stop in North Dakota or something. Wade would drink about a half rack between New Jersey and North Dakota, and it would take about a half-hour to an hour to refuel once we got there, so he'd have a few more beers while we were grounded in North Dakota.

"Once we got back up in the air, Wade would drink another 10, 11, 12 beers on the way out to the west coast. The whole flight from coast to coast usually took us well over 7 hours. We'd touch down at Sea-Tac, hop on the bus headed to the Kingdome, and Wade would have another beer or two on the bus. Then, all of us would get to the Kingdome and unpack our bags and sit around and BS with each other, and Wade would have a beer in his hand the entire time.

"He was always one of the last people to leave the club house, too. So I'd say that all in all, he drank over 50 beers on the trip, and this wasn't just an isolated incident, he did that almost every time."

Paul Sorrento, another former teammate, when asked to confirm the number of brews Boggs-the-Miller-Lite-king can consume on one cross-country flight, says, "Oh, geez, I don't know. Like 70."

When asked to either confirm or deny the story, Boggs says with a wry grin, that it wasn't 70.

The legend grows with the telling. Spot the Boggs in a bar becomes a popular game. One college student and part-time bartender says:

> After Wade's 4th bottle in less than an hour, I realized that the group wasn't going anywhere anytime soon and there were only two Lites left in the fridge. When I delivered the next to last bottle, I told Wade that we were going to run out and rattled off the list of other beers we carried. Wade wasn't having any of it and asked me to send someone out for more — which I did. We only had two hours to closing time and while the rest of group ordered three more rounds, Wade downed 11 more Miller Lites — 17 total in less than three hours. And it was only 11 pm when we closed ... so I am sure the night continued somewhere else. The next day, Boggs got two hits.

The stories are everywhere. He'd go with his wife to a '50s themed bar after Saturday games at Fenway and bang down 60 to 70 Millers before closing. Great guy, though. He'd sign autographs and roll off a couple of hundred dollar bills as tips.

How the hell can he function the next day and go 4-for-4? Shouldn't he be in a hospital somewhere getting a blood transfusion?

Must be genetic, like a weird gene that sucks up the alcohol or something.

It's amazing that the catchers didn't keel over with the fumes reeking from his pores.

Mostly he is mellow when drinking heavily, but occasionally he can become bellicose. One story making the rounds is that on one flight he told a flight attendant that he would "kick her fat lip in," if she didn't bring him another beer before the plane landed.

Boggs does little, if anything at all, to dispel the rapidly escalating stories. It was inevitable that he would make an appearance on *Cheers*, the popular television show set in a Boston bar. He played Wade Boggs sitting in a bar drinking beer.

Yes, drug use in the clubhouse is getting a lot of attention these days, but no one's talking much about the beer guzzling.

"It's so easy after you're hot and sweaty to just go in and pour a cold one," says Jim Sundberg, the Rangers catcher. "Of course, that can just continue to grow and grow and grow. Guys stay in the clubhouse and end up having a talk session afterwards and they stay an hour, two hours and end up putting down a lot of beer before they're through. Nobody addresses alcohol abuse. Drugs have been the big thing. Alcohol has kind of taken a second place."

But Wade-the-Drinking-Machine stories aren't the only ones making the rounds. Wade-the-Sex-Machine stories are running a close second. There are episodes about VD, and abortions, and strippers.

He has at least two addictions teammates claim — beer and love. Boggs doesn't deny either. He has a lovely wife, Debbie, and a lovely mistress, Margo. It's pretty common knowledge in the clubhouse.

Boggs was born in Omaha, Nebraska, but almost died when going into violent convulsions when he was 18 months old. Petrified that their third child might die in his sleep, his parents kept him in their bed for three years.

"It was very threatening," he says. "A couple of times I had to be rushed to the hospital and packed in ice, and on a couple of instances I swallowed my tongue. I turned blue a couple of times, and those kinds of things."

He dated Debbie through his high school years and they were married after he was drafted by the Red Sox and playing in the minors. Shortly after, he noticed he played better on days when he ate chicken. It's part of what he calls his "cocoon"—the protective shell that deflects all the distractions and allows him to concentrate on his hitting, something he does better than almost anybody else. By following all those routines, all those repeated actions, he's free to focus all his attention on what he has to do on the field.

As the son of a career military man, Boggs learned about regimentation early. "It was strictly by the book," he remembers. "It was a very strict household, but it makes for a better life growing up. I was up by 7, off to school, and had to check in when I got home from school. Dinner was at 6:30, and if you were late, you went hungry."

Margo Adams is a buxom former Miss Anaheim runner-up and frequent road trip companion of Boggs. It's no secret. She claims to have made 64 trips with him, staying with him in fine hotels and sharing expensive meals. She took vacations with him and he showed his appreciation by showering her with expensive gifts like a gold Rolex and diamond earrings.

Margo, who some of the other players call "the bimbo," recalls how she met Boggs. "He told me that he had been married seven years and was bored. I was enamored with him; I thought he was so adorable."

In true bimbo fashion she says she doesn't know what the word "bimbo" means.

The Sox players know Debbie, who goes to many home games, but they don't say anything to her about Margo even as some see big trouble ahead. Teammates don't do things like that. Some think she probably knows.

His teammates tolerate his eccentricities because he is a very good player and many believe they have a standing invitation to this year's World Series.

For all his weirdness, the Chicken Man has fashioned a .351 average in his four seasons with the club.

But Boggs is a prickly character at best and has already gotten into a few hissy matches with teammates.

He's selfish, some players say privately, and some fans publicly. He cares more about his numbers than about the team. He'd rather go 4-for-4 and lose than go 0-for-4 and win. It's a comment he hears a lot and it rankles him. To a reporter he says:

> You know, I'm trying to figure out why they call me a selfish ballplayer. Everybody wants to be the best player that they can be in this game, and how do you classify somebody as selfish? Don't you care about writing good articles? Doesn't a doctor care about making people well, and doesn't he get upset if someone dies on him? A carpenter knows measurements. I know numbers, but it's my livelihood. I mean, I'm not selfish. I don't feel that I'm selfish. I feel that somebody just came up with that and said, "Okay, let's say Wade Boggs is selfish." I'm not selfish. If the job has to be done, I do it. There's one thing that means more to me than any batting title, any 200-hit season in the world, and that's wearing a World Series ring and having that parade down Main Street.

Ask him about the 0-for-4 and 4-for-4 claim and he says, "I'd go 0–4 and win if the main goal was getting to the World Series. A few years back — and I've learned to curb this — if we won as a team and I went 0–4 and didn't contribute, I'd be frustrated. But that's not a classification of a selfish ballplayer. I mean, I'm going to take these frustrations, and we're going to win again tomorrow, and I'm going to contribute. That's not being selfish."

Debbie, like the good wife she is, comes to his defense. "We've been married 13 years, and I've never seen him be selfish. You can ask anybody on any level. Never on a personal level. In ball playing, I go to every game, and I don't see it. I'm like him — the first time that I read he was selfish, I couldn't understand why."

Another quality that irks some of his teammates is his habit of referring to himself in the third person.

"I'm trying to figure out why people knock me for doing that," he says. "See, I'm not into the 'I, I, me, me.' I don't toot my own horn. That's why I sit there and say, 'Well, as far as Wade Boggs is concerned.' I'm talking about a guy, okay? I mean, I'm talking about my best friend. I don't know if you can call it intellectual or what you can call it, as far as talking in the third person, but it's something that I've always done."

Just ask Rickey Henderson, the undisputed king of third-person references.

Boggs also claims the first time he went invisible was when he was 12. He claims it occurred during his second go around in the fifth grade. While his older and bigger twin brothers were playing football, he was off playing jacks. One of the football players took a break from knocking into the opponents and decided to take on the jacks players instead. As Boggs tells it:

> I closed my eyes and I wished and I wished and I wished as hard as I knew how. The next thing you know, baby Jesus came down and lo he said: "Thou art a special child, Wade Boggs. In the future you will inspire millions of children and become a Major League Hall of Famer. With the power vested in me, I hereby grant you the superpower of invisibility and all of the perks that go with it."

Later he will claim he willed himself invisible when threatened with a knife outside a bar in Gainesville, Florida.

He likes these stories.

So he's not the most popular player among teammates who think him a whiny, wacky, self-obsessed, wife-cheating ingrate. But he can hit and he has one heck of a good eye.

One day while the Red Sox are taking batting practice in Tiger Stadium, several players contend that home plate is incorrectly aligned. Boggs dropped to the ground to get a gopher's-eye view and then announced that it is turned two inches to the right. Despite the protest of the sharp-eyed Boggs, the groundskeeper refused to have it moved. It's an optical illusion he claimed.

A few weeks later Boggs insisted the pitching rubber at Royals Stadium was closer to home plate than it should be. After all, the batting champion can tell about these things. He knows the distance is off by 3 feet 6 inches — exactly, and that gives the Royals pitchers an advantage. The cheating Royals are getting away with it because few, if any, other batters have his eye. So before a game with the Kansas City Slickers, he found a tape measure and measured for himself. Sixty feet, 6 inches to the inch — exactly the correct distance.

It must have been the beer that threw him off.

His eccentricities are tolerated in a game that has more than its share of eccentric characters. One — Will "The Thrill" Clark — freely admits he's afraid of aliens. He also is known to shoot a bow and arrow in empty stadiums after games. Whether these two facts are connected is not clear.

Compared to Clark, Boggs looks almost normal and he's certainly not the only eccentric character on the club.

9. Rickey Knows Rickey

Rickey Henderson may be seen as the personification of the Yankees image. He's good; he knows he's good; he tells you he's good; and in many quarters he's disliked.

But Rickey can really run.

"I did a lot of study and I found that it's impossible to throw Rickey Henderson out," says veteran manager/coach/scout Charlie Metro.

"I started using stopwatches and everything. I found it was impossible to throw some other guys out also. They can go from first to second in 2.9 seconds; and no pitcher-catcher combination in baseball could throw from here to there to tag second in 2.9 seconds, it was always 3, 3.1, 3.2. So actually, the runner that can make the continuous, regular move like Rickey's can't be thrown out and he's proven it."

At the age of 28, Rickey has 620 stolen bases. On their 28th birthdays, Ty Cobb had 485 and Lou Brock 220.

Julius Caesar of Gallic Wars fame, Elmo of *Sesame Street* fame, and Rickey Henderson of Baseball Hall of Fame are all well-known illeists. Some argue that Jesus Christ of "The Son of Man" fame was also an illeist.

Illeists are fond of referring to themselves in the third person, as in "Don't worry, Rickey, you're still the best."

Once when his career took a dip, he called San Diego GM Kevin Towers and left the following message: "This is Rickey calling on behalf of Rickey. Rickey wants to play baseball."

Rickey knows Rickey.

"Listen, people are always saying, 'Rickey says Rickey,'" says Rickey. "But it's been blown way out of proportion. People might catch me, when they know I'm ticked off, saying, 'Rickey, what the heck are you doing, Rickey?' They say, 'Darn, Rickey, what are you saying Rickey for? Why don't you just say, "I"?' But I never did. I always said, 'Rickey,' and it became something for people to joke about."

He often refers to himself as the game's greatest base stealer. He is that, at least statistically — 1,406 to be exact, or 50 percent more stolen bases than the next man on the list, Lou Brock. Of all the career statistical records in all professional sports, this remains one of the most significant in terms of proportional margins.

"He's like a little kid in a train station," says former pitcher Doc Medich. "You turn your back on him and he's gone."

Rickey can steal a base.

Run, Rickey, run.

Because of his high on-base percentage, stealing ability, and power, many consider him the greatest lead-off hitter ever to play the game. In addition to his stolen base record, he ranks among the top in career records for games played, at-bats, hits, runs scored, walks, and lead-off home runs.

Oakland pitcher Curt Young, after giving up a long home run to Henderson, says, "He really jumped on it. He hit it a lot farther than it went."

Bill James, baseball's statistical wizard, claims, "Without exaggerating one inch, you could find fifty Hall of Famers who, all taken together, don't own as many records, and as many important records, as Rickey Henderson."

Rickey agrees.

May 2004

Rickey Henderson is riding on a bus to a game with his new team, the Newark Bears of the independent Atlantic League. He is making $3,000 a month.

Rickey says Rickey can play and still steal bases and can continue to do so until he's 50. Someone reminds him that Willie Mays played until he fell down running in the outfield. Rickey smiles. Rickey don't fall down running.

Rickey is one of the rare ones, he says.

"I didn't get no job, so I'm back here," he says. "Gotta do it again. Gonna do it again. God gave me this body, this gift, these skills to play this sport. Until He says, 'Enough,' this is what I'm supposed to be doing."

May 2005

Rickey Henderson is sitting in the dugout at Tony Gwynn Stadium on the campus of San Diego State University. He is an outfielder on the San Diego Surf Dawgs of the Golden Baseball League.

In an hour he'll be playing in a game against a team from the Marine Corps base at Camp Pendleton.

C'mon, Rickey, you made your big league debut in 1979. Why the hell you still hanging around?

"I ain't hurt," Rickey says. "You ask the guys who quit the game, they're hurt. Listen, I'm not aching. Tony Gwynn once told me he was aching so much, he said, 'Rickey, man, I want this jersey to be tore off me. My body's killing me.'"

The Dawgs equipment manager asks Rickey what size waist he needs in his uniform pants. Rickey tells him still "34."

His manager, former catcher Terry Kennedy, calls Rickey a freak of nature like Cal Ripken, guys born with something nobody else has. Yes, of course, signing Rickey was a publicity stunt, Kennedy admits. But you know what? He still picks up balls during batting practice and hits fungoes during infield practice.
On bus rides, his teammates let Rickey sit up front.

Rickey Nelson Henley was born in 1958 in the back seat of a 1957 Oldsmobile. He was named after Ozzie and Harriet's singing son Ricky. To this day Rickey with an "e" claims he has no idea where the extra letter came from, but he does occasionally knock out his own rendition of "Hello, Mary Lou."

After his father, John Henley, was killed in a truck accident, Rickey's mother married Paul Henderson, so Henley became his middle name, replacing Nelson, and Henderson his last name.

The family moved to Oakland where Rickey became an All-American running back in football and was highly recruited by colleges. But Rickey preferred baseball. He was drafted by Oakland in the fourth round and went to the minors where he once stole seven bases in one game. That was enough for the Athletics. They called him up in 1979 and then, in 1980, Billy Martin took over as manager. His "Billy Ball" style of play was perfect for Rickey, and he started running wild.

In 1982, he shattered the Major League record for steals in a season, then held by Lou Brock. By the All-Star break he already had an astounding 84 steals, which no player other than Rickey has managed for an entire season since. He ended the year with 130. The closest to him was Tim Raines with 78.

It was truly a remarkable feat acknowledged by everyone in the game, including the never-shy-about-self-promotion Rickey. Upon breaking Brock's record, Rickey gave a speech:

> It took a long time, huh? (Pauses for cheers.) First of all, I would like to thank God for giving me the opportunity. I want to thank the Haas family, the Oakland organization, the city of Oakland, and all you beautiful fans for supporting me. (Pauses for cheers.) Most of all, I'd like to thank my mom, my friends, and loved ones for their support. I want to give my appreciation to Tom Trebelhorn and the late Billy Martin. Billy Martin was a great manager. He was a great friend to me. I love you, Billy. I wish you were here. (Pauses for cheers.) Lou Brock was the symbol of great base stealing. But today, I'm the greatest of all time. Thank you.

Rickey was roundly criticized for the speech.

That arrogant S.O.B. He thinks he's the greatest, eh? Bullshit. Couldn't hold a candle to Maury or Lou.

Stole bases just to steal bases. Didn't matter what the score was. Didn't matter what the game situation was. What mattered was Rickey adding one to his steal column.

Selfish bastard. Cared about Rickey and only Rickey. "As soon as I said it, it ruined everything," he says. "Everybody thought it was the worst thing you could ever say. Those words haunt me to this day and will continue to haunt me. They overshadow what I've accomplished in this game. If you talk about baseball, you can't eliminate me, because I'm all over baseball... It's the truth. Telling the truth isn't being cocky. What do you want me to say, that I didn't put up the numbers? That my teams didn't win a lot of games? People don't want me to say anything about what I've done. Then why don't you say it? Because if I don't say it and you don't say it, nobody says it."

The New York Sun sportswriter Tim Marchman wrote about Henderson:

> He stole all those bases and scored all those runs and played all those years not because of his body, but because of his brain. Rickey could tell from the faintest, most undetectable twitch of a pitcher's muscles whether he was going home or throwing over to first. He understood that conditioning isn't about strength, but about flexibility. And more than anyone else in the history of the game, he understood that baseball is entirely a game of discipline — the discipline to work endless 1-1 counts your way, the discipline to understand that your job is to get on base, and the discipline to understand that the season is more important than the game, and a career more important than the season. Maybe he'd get a bit more credit for all this if he were some boring drip like Cal Ripken Jr., blathering on endlessly about humility and apple pie and tradition and whatever else, but we're all better off with things the way they are.... Everyone had their fun when he broke Lou Brock's stolen base record and proclaimed, "I am the greatest," but he was, of course, just saying what was plainly true.

Yes, he's a hot dog. He readily admits that with the proviso that it must be understood that the term can only be applied to players who are good, who have style. Who ever heard of a lousy player being called a "hot dog"?

In 1985 he was traded to the Yankees for five players and then proceeded to score more runs in one season than anyone had since Ted Williams in 1950.

Despite his productivity for Steinbrenner's Yanks, the season was anything but a love fest. His cavalier attitude and apparent disregard for his teammates and the team were a source of continual exasperation. He led the league in runs scored, stolen bases, and unmitigated arrogance, including, but not limited to, telling the media that Steinbrenner owes him an apology for publicly lambasting him for basking in the California sun while the rest of his teammates were getting ready to begin the season.

When he showed up after missing the first ten games while he was resting an injury, the first thing he said was, "Don't need no press, man." Steinbrenner, who was paying him $8.6 million, thought otherwise.

When informed he would talk to the press or else, he began his campaign to endear himself to the New York fans by telling them that he neither knew nor cared about the accomplishments of Mickey Mantle or Joe DiMaggio. History, as one writer claimed, is irrelevant when you live, as Rickey does, in a vacuum.

It's Rickey time, Rickey says.

In 1985, the players staged a two-day strike. The Yankees player rep Dave Winfield informed the team they should not leave town because he expected the labor issues to be solved in a day or two. In the world according to Rickey, however, Rickey lives by a different set of rules, so he flew to California. Sure enough, the strike was quickly settled. When told Rickey couldn't make it back in time for the doubleheader the team was to play against the Indians to re-start the season, Steinbrenner blew up. While his team was taking two from the Tribe behind Don Mattingly's two home runs, he announced he was fining Rickey $24,000.

Upon hearing about the fine, Rickey says if it's true he'll be "real ticked off and they don't want me ticked off right now." He claims the reason he didn't get back from California in time is that the plane from San Francisco to New York was full.

The only plane, Rickey?

But Rickey has his staunch defenders, too. The narcissist Reggie Jackson comparing the narcissist Rickey Henderson to the narcissist Jose Canseco says, "There's a difference between a Jose and a Rickey Henderson. Rickey gets embarrassed if he doesn't do well. Rickey's a little ... um ... different, but he strives to excel every day. He listens because he really cares. He hates not doing well because he gets embarrassed, and he cares whether he wins or not because he's embarrassed to lose. But some other players don't get embarrassed."

As the columnist Alan Greenberg once noted, "Rickey Henderson is 26. Born on Christmas Day. Yes, a child will lead them. A spoiled child. One who understands, instinctively, that when you can put together a season like he has, there will always be room for Rickey time."

Now if only Rickey time is in sync with Yankee time, they'll have a chance. Only the Red Sox appear as if they might give the "evil empire" of the Yankees a run for their money.

10. Where's the Can?

Where's the Can? Who the hell knows? Half the time the Can don't even know. Oil Can time ain't the same as anybody else's time. Talk about different drummers.

Two things you immediately know about Dennis "Oil Can" Boyd are that he's as skinny as a bird and about as flighty.

At the beginning of spring training he's 6'1" and maybe 130 pounds. Maybe. Anyway, it's all rumor because nobody's seen him.

"Lost 10 to 12 pounds," says Lou Gorman, the exasperated Sox GM.

Boyd's been sent to the University of Massachusetts Medical Center in Worcester. The team physician, Dr. Pappas, tells the press he's there for "routine tests to evaluate liver function and see if there's any evidence of infection."

Last year the Can became Boston's first 15-game winner since 1979, but nothing was ever routine with him. He was either a free spirit or a nut case, take your pick. Either a colorful character or a severely troubled one. He was passionate, though, loved baseball — when he showed up.

So, how sick is the Can?

After a few days of tests Doc Pappas announces that all the results are negative.

The Can says he has hepatitis — viral, non-contagious hepatitis.

His agent, Dennis Coleman, tells one reporter there's "nothing at all wrong with him, period" and tells another reporter he has "some type of virus."

Gorman says, "Nothing, zero, nothing, there's nothing wrong with him at all. I have no idea why he lost weight. But if he had any kind of hepatitis, he wouldn't be coming back here to camp."

Boyd, the son of a black league player, comes from Mississippi claiming that the "Oil Can" moniker stems from the local name for a beer can. He had made his debut with the Sox as a September call-up in 1982 and then, after a few ups and downs between Boston and farm-club Pawtucket, he more or less became a regular in 1985.

This spring when he finally shows up at Winter Haven for his first start of spring training he is nearly two hours late.

Maybe they don't have clocks down there.
Maybe he can't tell time.
Maybe he doesn't want to tell time.
Hepatitis can do that to you.

John McNamara immediately calls him into his office, slams the door none too gently. McNamara has scheduled the spring training activities down to the minute. He was a peripatetic Major League catcher for years and has been a baseball manager since 1959. He knows how to run spring training. Done it many times. Players are to be in uniform and ready to work by 9:45. That's 15 minutes before 10:00, Mr. Boyd.

Already in his brief Major League career the Can has a history of lateness. Last season he completely disappeared for more than a day. McNamara says he won't put up with that kind of behavior again. At the very least, he's got to make a show for the other players.

The Can says he called and told the club he'd be a little late because his wife was sick. Mac had it timed precisely. The Can showed up at 11:34. Exactly one hundred and eight minutes late. That's not a few minutes. That's a lot of minutes. That's almost two hours.

The Can apologizes and says he's turning a new page.

The crane-like Oil Can Boyd about to deliver a pitch in the '86 World Series. He ended the Series with a 7.71 ERA in seven innings and no wins.

10. Where's the Can?

After the meeting that lasted exactly 17 minutes, Mac tells the press that the Can said he'd be a few minutes late and that he was very disappointed that it was much more than a few minutes. Mac says this time there won't be a fine. "It's rectified," he says. "It's resolved and he knows where I'm coming from."

After throwing a few innings Boyd announces:

> I was pleased with my outing. I got into the groove and would have liked to go one more inning, but they said three was enough. My relationship with the manager is fine. This is my job, this is my life and I'll be dammed if I don't take it seriously. This man understands me. He could see through it if I was lying, so I was straight with him. I know him. With him, it's cuss me out or pat me on the back. He never falls in between. It's always one or the other.

Talk around the Sox camp is that Mac and his pitching coach, Bill Fischer, still want the club to go after Tom Seaver. They were with Tom Terrific in Cincinnati from 1979 through 1982 and think he would be good insurance. Publicly they are saying that Boyd is getting stronger after his mysterious virus and that Clemens is coming around from his shoulder blowout.

The truth is, though, that anyone watching spring training can see that Clemens is pitching scared and Boyd isn't going to be ready for the opener. He is, in his own words, all mixed up.

11. A Hitch in His Gait

Billy Buckner isn't mixed up, but he is messed up. When he leads your club in stolen bases you know you have a slow team. How slow? Well, for one, he's 36. On top of that, he's got a bum ankle. Still, last year he led the sodden-footed Red Sox with 18 stolen bases.

Oh, once upon a time Buckner could run. When he came up as an outfielder with the Dodgers in the early '70s he could do it all — hit for average and power, field superbly, and he had good speed. Then in 1975 he severely sprained his ankle and the speed was gone, never to return.

Now he plays first base where he doesn't have to do much running. The ankle is still not right but he does his best to ignore it. What choice does he have? It's either that or quit, and he's making too much money to do that. Besides, he still likes playing.

"It hurts even when I walk," he confesses. "I found out that I have a bone spur that has to be removed. But that won't happen until after the season and next year I'll come back and run better than ever."

Wishful thinking. For christsake, next year he'll be 37. You don't get faster at 37, period.

McNamara knows his team can't run. They'll have to score runs some other way because they sure as hell ain't going to steal their way to the pennant.

"Sure, we'd love to have more speed on this team," Billy Buck says, "but we've got some great hitters, so you can't have everything."

Sure you can, but they don't.

This year the Red Sox will steal all of 41 bases for the season — 100 fewer than the Indians.

Mac likes Billy Buck. He's one of the hardest workers in camp. Even after he adds a hamstring pull, he still doesn't stop working. He takes extra batting practice. He takes more infield practice than anyone else. You can see the little hitch in his gait, but that doesn't stop him. He's pushing 3,000 hits for his career and he didn't get them by loafing.

"If I stay healthy and play four more years," he says, "I think I can make 3,000."

Stay healthy? Is he delusional? He hasn't been healthy for years. Still, there's that work ethic and that's worth something. That's worth a lot.

"I try to lead by example," he says. "I know I have a job to do, but at the same time baseball is supposed to be a fun game."

Buckner has always been a contact hitter, striking out only 370 times in 7,795 career at-bats. That's why two years earlier the Sox gave up Dennis Eckersley for him. He can still spray line drives to any field, has that fan-favorite swashbuckling style, doesn't hesitate trying to stretch a single into a double if the opportunity arises, and never jogs to first base.

Mac watches Billy Buck limp into the batting cage. He's counting on him to be healthy enough to put in a full season. No, he's praying for him to be healthy. Those are two very different things.

"Some players ask for a king-size bed or a water bed when they check into a hotel," says Buckner. "All I ask for is a room near the ice machine."

Line drives fly out of the cage to every field.

Atta way, Billy Buck.

Fans may be drawn to the game's flakes, but they always love the dedicated, hard-working professional like Buckner. Now if he could only run.

12. Nearing the End

While at home watching TV, Rod Carew sees plenty of examples of older athletes still competing at a high level — Pete Rose; Reggie Jackson; Kareem Abdul-Jabbar who is 38 and balding; Jack Nicklaus at 46 wins the Masters; Bill "Willie in My Younger Days" Shoemaker, 54 and still winning Kentucky Derbys. And the president of the United States. Isn't Reagan the oldest president ever?

Carew wants to play another year, maybe more. He's 40. That may be old for a ballplayer but it's not like no one ever played well at that age. Ty Cobb hit .357 at 40. Last year Carew hit .280 — not exactly Cobb-like, but not bad either. All he did was lead the Angels regulars in hitting. Doesn't he usually? He's already won seven batting titles, owns a gaudy .328 lifetime average, was AL Rookie of the Year, has won the MVP award, and was named to the All-Star team for 18 straight years.

Surely there's a place for him on the Angels, or if not the Angels, some other team. Rod Carew can, as Wee Willie Keeler used to say, "hit 'em where they ain't." His bat control is as good as anyone's.

"I get a kick out of watching a team defense me," Carew says. "A player moves two steps in one direction and I hit it two steps the other way. It goes right by his glove and I laugh."

Ken Holtzman, a pitcher who faced him many times, says, "He has an uncanny ability to move the ball around as if the bat were some kind of magic wand."

Add to that, he's a terrific base stealer. Billy Martin says he taught him how to steal home, but that's all he ever taught him because nobody ever tells him how to hit. That he does naturally.

Pitchers respect him probably about as much as anyone in the game.

"He's the only guy I know who can go four for three," says Alan Bannister.

"Greaseball, greaseball, greaseball, that's all I throw him, and he still hits them," says Gaylord Perry. "He's the only player in baseball who consistently hits my grease. He sees the ball so well I guess he can pick out the dry side."

12. Nearing the End

He's always worked for what he's got. Everybody knows that. He changes his batting stance more often than Madonna changes costumes because he's always looking for that little edge.

Carew's black Panamanian mother was forced to ride in the back of the train as it passed through the town of Gatun in the Panama Canal Zone while the whites sat up front. When she went into labor the call went out for a doctor. Fortunately Dr. Cline appeared. The appreciative mother asked his name. "Rodney Cline," he said, and so the baby got his name — Rodney Cline Carew.

Years later, after becoming one of the greatest hitters in the game, he would remember his days in Panama. "There is a special sensation in getting good wood on the ball and driving a double down the left-field line as the crowd in the ballpark rises to its feet and cheers. But, I also remember how much fun I had as a skinny barefoot kid hitting a tennis ball with a broomstick on a quiet, dusty street in Panama."

While he was a teenager, they moved to New York, where he attended high school and then, after graduating, signed a contract with the Minnesota Twins.

He made his Major League debut in 1967 when he got a hit on Opening Day, and then went on to add another 3,052 during regular-season games.

By his own admission, when he came up he was something of a loner, prone to temperamental outbursts and sullen spells. He was not popular with many of his teammates and often quarreled with his managers. "I was always moody with managers ... threatening to jump the club," he writes in his autobiography.

While with the Twins he once went off on a tear against the owner, Calvin Griffith, and the team. "Griffith is horse spit. They are penny pinchers. They take everything they can get and give nothing in return."

Over time, though, he mellowed and became a solid, if soft-spoken clubhouse presence who tried to keep his private life just that. That's not easy when you're as public a figure as Carew.

When in 1970 he married the former Marilynn Levy he received death threats for converting to Judaism. To some he was the Sammy Davis of baseball, a famous Jewish convert of color, and belonged with Sandy Koufax and Hank Greenberg among the great Jewish ballplayers. Adam Sandler even included him in his long list of famous Jews in "The Hanukkah Song." The fact is, though, like Ron Cey, Al Leiter, and other Gentile players who married Jewish women, he never converted.

Now the Angels want to go with Wally Joyner at first base and have not offered Carew a contract for the '86 season. So he sits by the phone in the southern California hills and waits for the phone to ring. It doesn't. This is what they mean by collusion he thinks. "I don't understand it," he says. "No one has even taken the opportunity to call and say, 'Can we work something out?'"

Definitely collusion. He's financially secure but he's played his way to a good salary level and he's not going to sign for peanuts. Still he's in shape and the way he plays the game, he could be ready to hit Major League pitching in a matter of days.

"I hate to go out this way," he says. "If I'd known last year that it was going to be this way, I probably would have retired. If I didn't think I could play, if I thought I didn't still have it, I wouldn't want to play. I know I can still hit."

Reggie Jackson will be 40 in a few weeks.
Time to mellow out. Time to play the role of the mature veteran leader.
No one really believes that. Reggie plays by his own rules.
"I've got miles to go before I sleep," he says hoping someone will ask him to identify the source.

Reggie is running hard to first base on routine ground balls—every time. Who does he think he is, Pete Rose?

"How many home runs I end up hitting in my career is just a number," he says. "I've hit a ton of home runs in my career. I can't hit any any differently than the ones I've already hit. I can't hit any any further or hit any any harder. What I want is to still be a factor. I don't want to be one of those guys who just hangs around."

Reginald Jackson's parents divorced when he was six and he was raised by his father, a former player in the Negro Leagues. He attended Arizona State on a football scholarship but while there he also played a little baseball. He was drafted by the Athletics in 1966 and sent to the A's Class A team in Modesto, California. The next season he was moved up to Class AA Birmingham, Alabama, where as the team's only African American player he got his first taste of racism. The man who helped him through the tough times was manager John McNamara, now leading the Red Sox. When the A's called him up the next summer, he quickly blossomed into one of the best power hitters in the game.

After running ahead of Roger Maris' home run record pace for part of 1969, he asked owner Charles O. Finley for a raise in the off-season. In typical fashion, Finley told Jackson what he could do with that idea and said to his young power hitter that despite his 47 homers he would send him to the minors before he'd agree to the raise. The commissioner had to step in to resolve the dispute, but the next season Jackson hit only 23 home runs and ended with a batting average of .237.

Some people thought he was either pouting or trying to get even with Finley. Nevertheless, he went on to have some very big seasons.

There are some who ended their careers by hitting more home runs than he did, but nobody struck out more often. He swung for the fences. Singles and doubles were accidents.

12. Nearing the End

He was also less than sterling in the field. As Billy Martin once said sarcastically, "It's not that Reggie is a bad outfielder. He just has trouble judging the ball and picking it up."

Jackson lives for show-off home runs, and no home runs show better than those hit in the World Series. Three times he won the World Series Most Valuable Player Awards, hence the nickname "Mr. October." Of his ten World Series home runs, three came in 1977 when he connected off three different pitchers, each on the first pitch he saw.

Reggie Jackson courts/needs the limelight like a rose needs the sunlight. Controversy? Bring it on — just so long as people are talking about him. Had there been reality shows when he was playing, he undoubtedly would have had his own *Reggie Show*. Jackson has many fans, none greater than Jackson. More than once he has used the phrase "the magnitude of me" and referred to himself as "the straw that stirs the drink."

Al Michaels, the ABC baseball announcer, who knows a little about Jackson's need to be the center of attention, says, "Reggie wouldn't get in the batter's box until he knew we were back from a commercial."

Catfish Hunter once said of Reggie, "He'd give you the shirt off his back. Of course, he'd call a press conference to announce it."

Dave Anderson, the veteran *New York Times* writer, thinks Jackson is the second most quotable athlete of all times, following only Muhammad Ali.

"The only reason I don't like playing in the World Series is that I can't watch myself play," he says as if he knows exactly how to phrase his words for media consumption.

"Part of the reason they pay me is that ... I'm the hunted. I'm the hunted on the team of the hunted."

Say what you really mean, Reggie.

"You never met anyone like me. I'm not just a ballplayer. I'm a multifaceted person, a myriad of personalities. I'm a businessman who happens to be an athlete."

Jackson loves the press coverage and the press loves him. But there are limits. "There are certain things I don't want made public," Jackson says. "I don't want strangers in my home, or around my children, or in my personal love life. If you see the lifestyle I have, to some people it would be offensive."

Offensive?

"Because of the monetary things that I have, the way I live, that's what I mean. It winds up being me flaunting it. Why see me get on a private jet? Who would want to see that? Who wants to see me buy a bracelet for my girlfriend for $20,000? It would make someone sick."

Jackson claimed he had an I.Q. of 160, to which outfielder Mickey Rivers replied, "Out of what, a thousand?"

Before he had moved on to New York, Jackson and several other A's moaned loudly about being trapped in Oakland. When asked by a reporter if he might like to play in New York, he responded, "Man, if I played in New York, they'd name a candy bar after me." Then along came the Great Free Agent Revolution, and, voilà, he was in New York with a candy bar named after him.

"We're calling it 'Reggie, Reggie, Reggie,'" announced the president of Standard Brands Confectionary at a posh Manhattan restaurant press conference. Along with the candy bar, he laid out a plan that included a monetary contributions for each of Jackson's home runs and reserved block of 140 seats at Yankee Stadium called Reggie's Regiment. These would go to youngsters accompanied by members of the New York Police Department's Community Relations Program.

"The most important thing in this world is what you give back to the community," said Jackson. "You know, when I go to the ballpark every day, I drive through Harlem. One day I pulled over and parked by a playground up at Madison Avenue and 115th Street. The kids were playing basketball — that's what they do up there — with rundown sneakers, no nets on the hoops. The next homer I hit, I'm going to get them $500 worth of nets."

Reggie, Reggie, Reggie would make confectionery history, the sweets president said.

You're forgetting the Baby Ruth bar named after the Bambino.

Nope. Contrary to popular belief that bar was named after Grover Cleveland's daughter.

Is it true the Reggie bar will be shaped like a hot dog?

Right now that's a tightly held trade secret.

Is it true the Butterfingers candy bar was named after Dick Stuart?

Oakland pitcher Catfish Hunter says of the Reggie Bar, "When you unwrap one, it tells you how good it is."

The Reggie Bar doesn't sell well outside of New York and is eventually discontinued, going the way of Beech-Nut Spearmint and Wintergreen Gum Pine Brothers Cough Drops. Wrappers, however, are still on display at the Candy Wrapper Hall of Fame next to the Pete Rose Energy Bar — "Nature's Answer to Candy."

April 2006

"I'm more amazed than anything when a kid 8 or 9 years old knows who Reggie Jackson is," he says. "So I've done something right."

With all the talk about better batting through chemistry, Jackson remains free from aspersions. Noting that he has recently been passed on the all-time home run list by Bonds, McGwire, and others he says coyly, "In the last, what, how many months, I have gone from six to ten. Something went on sale."

12. Nearing the End

He is almost as famous for his feuds as he is for his home runs—those with Billy Martin, Thurman Munson, and Goose Gossage among the most notorious.

Steinbrenner was happy to add him to the Yankees' Bronx Zoo in 1977; Martin wasn't. Jackson had been quoted as saying he "hated Martin," not a remark presaging a cordial relationship. It was probably only a matter of time before Jackson's huge ego and Martin's quick temper collided. In a game with the Red Sox, the $3-million-outfielder and the pugnacious manager got into it. The dynamite keg that so many people knew would eventually explode, did when Jackson lit the fuse by taking his time going after a Jim Rice double.

Martin thought his narcissistic star was loafing, and loafing on a Martin team brings an immediate, and usually volatile, response. Without waiting for even one more play, he waved Jackson into the dugout and sent Paul Blair in to replace him. Jackson then went into a protracted petulant stroll back to the dugout. When he finally got near the dugout steps, Martin screamed at Jackson and then, with Yogi Berra and Elston Howard moving between them, tried to climb over them to get at Jackson. Berra grabbed Martin and Howard grabbed Jackson. Jackson shrugged and headed down the runway toward the locker room at which point Martin threw off his restrainers and tried to chase Jackson but was blocked by other players.

Scuffles between players and managers, while not common, are not unknown either. What made this fracas unusual, though, is that it was being watched by the thoroughly amused Red Sox, a national TV audience who saw the entire episode, and 34,603, delighted fans, many of whom began cheering wildly.

Never underestimate the entertainment quotient of a Jackson-Martin exchange.

And if the TV cameras hadn't been there?

Later the firebrand manager said, "When a player shows up the team, I show up the player. I don't run my team for television. I'm not going to wait until next week to say something just because it's on TV. This is between Reggie and me."

Jackson must have had 40 pounds on the eighteen-years-older manager, but the betting money was on Battling Billy.

"Words were said that I didn't like... We won without him, didn't we? All he has to do is what I ask every player to do—hustle. I play this game one way—win, play hard, and give your 100 percent best. Players make errors, strike out, that's part of the game. I accept it. But if they don't hustle. I don't accept that."

Jackson had no comment.

January 2000

Jackson pleads no contest in Carmel, California, to disturbing the peace during a fight with a former business partner and is sentenced to three years' probation and ordered to perform 40 hours of community service.

Jackson has been charged with misdemeanor battery after Jeffrey Haney, who co-owned a gym with Jackson, accused Jackson of grabbing him by the throat and throwing him against a wall. Jackson denies the nature of the encounter and sues Haney, accusing him of embezzlement.

Earlier in the season, Martin had benched Jackson because he wasn't hitting. In his first game back he hit a home run against the Red Sox and then went directly to the far end of the bench, refusing to shake Martin's hand, or any of his teammates either.

"It's not good here," Jackson said.

Steinbrenner didn't seem too concerned. "I buy advertising in the New York papers," he said, "and I know how expensive that is. One way to look at the Jackson newspaper stories is that they're free space."

Jackson told a magazine reporter that other Yankee players seemed insecure and petty. After that comment surfaced, and a fresh uniform was brought to him, someone had taped an obscenity to the hanger. "You know," Reggie said, "whatever I said to the fellow from the magazine was off-record."

Sure, Reggie, magazine reporters never print what athletes tell them — like the story in *Sport* magazine, the one that quoted Jackson as saying, "This team, it all flows from me. I'm the straw that stirs the drink. Maybe I should say me and Munson, but he can only stir it bad."

Jackson denied he said anything negative about Munson and used the accused's favorite defense — that his quotes were taken out of context.

He may be a show off, he may be argumentative, yet he is anything but a fool. He is bright, articulate, thoughtful, and outspoken.

"It's a shame, an absolute shame," Jackson tells reporters during batting practice before meeting the Twins. "You got players who can't even play and there are colored boys who need work."

On the Twins, only Kirby Puckett is an American-born black player. Their only other black is a Dominican, Alex Sanchez.

Twins vice president of player personnel, Andy MacPhail, says he can understand what Jackson says, but the team doesn't eliminate players because of race. In fact, he insists, anyone looking through their farm system roster can see that. The Twins roster is dominated by white players at the moment, he claims, because the team has traditionally relied on power rather than defense and speed.

Jackson tells the Minneapolis reporters, "The real story is why aren't there colored boys on this team. Why don't you write it? I shouldn't have to say it. You should write it. But you make me say it and sound like a pop-off and a racist. There aren't prejudiced people here. It's a beautiful place. There are more interracial marriages here than anyplace in the country."

Minnesota manager Ray Miller reacts angrily. "If you ask me, there is no prejudice in baseball. If a guy is hitting .350 in the minors and he is black, you don't think I'd have him sent up? You'd have to be crazy not to."

Despite their denials, three days after Jackson's tirade about racism they add black players Roy Lee Jackson, Al Woods, and Ron Washington.

Baseball has long been popular with black players, long before Jackie Robinson broke the recognized color barrier in Major League Baseball, long before Larry Doby became the first black player in the American League, and long before Dan Bankhead became the first black pitcher to play in a Major League game. Like so many other young men, blacks first came into contact with baseball during the Civil War, when thousands of soldiers learned the game as a way to fill the time in military encampments. When the war ended they took the game home with them and thus spread it across the country.

A few years later, black teams like the Philadelphia Excelsiors and the Philadelphia Pythians began playing regular schedules against each other. When Octavius Catto's Pythians applied for admission to the first organized league, the National Association of Base Ball Players, they were denied.

"We all agreed that to admit colored clubs would inevitably have led to a division of feelings," said the committee chair responsible for new admissions, "whereas by excluding them, no injury could result to anyone. It was in the best interests of both our clubs and the colored clubs to keep the groups separate."

By the 1880s there were more than 200 independent black clubs playing more or less regularly and a few blacks playing on otherwise all-white clubs, some as blacks and some who could "pass" for white or American Indian. Moses Fleetwood Walker is generally credited with being the first black Major League player when he went 0-for-3 with Toledo of the American Association.

In 1920 the Negro National League was formed and developed many great players.

In his 1966 Hall of Fame induction speech, Ted Williams said, "I hope someday Satchel Paige and Josh Gibson will be voted into the Hall of Fame as symbols of the great Negro players who are not here only because they weren't given the chance."

Baseball took note and soon the Hall established a committee to review the great black players from the past. Paige and Gibson were the first to be admitted.

"Baseball is very big with my people," says comedian Dick Gregory. "It figures. It's the only way we can get to shake a bat at a white man without starting a riot."

Reggie is right at least about one thing. He is the straw that stirs the drink.

13. Everybody Loves Kirby

Kirby Puckett chooses to remain in the gray area of the black/white issue. "If I was a veteran, I might say something, but I'm not, and the Twins have always treated me well."

He could star in his own Twin Cities sitcom —*Everybody Loves Kirby*. Why not? He walks, he talks, he smiles, he hits home runs. Because of his gregarious personality and his puckish charm he is probably as popular as anyone on the team, a true fan favorite.

Little Kirby, the man with the big heart.

Loves the game, absolutely loves it.

Plays with that big smile like he really enjoys playing the game ... really, really, enjoys it.

He has that zest for the game, for life, that you can't teach people. Either they've got it or they don't. Kirby's got it.

"Can you all just do me one favor?" he says. "Don't take life for granted, because tomorrow isn't promised to any one of us."

Along with Mr. T, Puckett is a product of Chicago's Robert Taylor Homes project, a drab collection of 28 16-story high-rise buildings decorated by scores of arson-fire scars, stretching for two miles alongside the Dan Ryan Expressway. It was not a happy place.

Designed to house 11,000, its population swelled to 27,000, 99.9 percent of whom were African American. At any given time, 95 percent of the residents were unemployed and claimed public assistance as their only source of income. The U.S. census once claimed it contained six of the poorest census areas in the country.

Littered streets, broken glass, and drug paraphernalia were everywhere where one might have liked to see trees and grass. According to the Chicago Housing Authority, it wasn't unusual to find $45,000 in drug deals taking place daily. On some weekends, hundreds of gunshots could be heard echoing off concrete walls. It was much easier to find a turf war than a baseball game as drug dealers continually fought for control of the towers.

In 1983, an infant was abducted from a hallway after her grandmother left her alone for a few minutes to make a phone call. Police say some 50 people were in the hallway at the time of the abduction, but no one came forward with information that would lead to an arrest. The child has not been seen or heard from since.

How could Puckett possibly have come away from this with his perpetually sunny disposition?

"My mom was determined that the baby of the family would stay out of trouble," he writes in his autobiography. "I was sheltered. I didn't hang out. I didn't even go to many movies. At night I was home. It's as simple as that. Baseball and school, that was it, that was my whole life. School let out at three-fifteen, I was home by three-twenty-five, three-thirty at the latest. I'd race in and change, grab something to eat, and be ready to go. But Mom would always ask about homework and I'd have to do my math or whatever before she let me go play ball."

He'd play any way he could — with rolled up socks, with balled-up aluminum foil, with ten-cent rubber balls. During the summers "I'd be playing somewhere by eight o'clock every morning and wouldn't come home until sunset," he says. "Even then, I wouldn't come home until I heard my mother's voice calling from the fourteenth floor, Kiiiiiiirby! ... KIRBY!"

By the time the streetlights came on, he was allowed out on the balcony but never down on the ground. From the balcony of the family's cramped apartment, he could see the lights of Comiskey Park. That baseball would be his way out was never a sure thing. Oh, he loved to play and he was good at it, but was he good enough? He was short and squat — not exactly the physique of an Aaron or a Mays, or for that matter, of anyone else then playing in the Major Leagues.

"You look at him," Twins manager Ray Miller says, "and you think he's a little fat kid. You touch him and he's like concrete." Jim Murray describes him as "a cantaloupe with legs."

The man with the Dickensesque name is also called "cute," "adorable," "teddy bearish," and a "real-life smurf."

To some extent, an if-Kirby-why-not-me reaction accounts for his popularity.

If a stubby fat kid can play at that level, maybe there's hope for me.

So, you don't have to look like a Greek god to play the game well.

Then there was that infectious smile that never seemed to desert him. "You never see me down. I'm always a person that says, 'If things aren't going my way now, hey, they'll change.'"

In high school he was a solid, albeit not a spectacular player. While working at a Ford plant and as a census taker, he continually improved his game. For a short time he went to Bradley University and then Triton College, a two-year community college hardly known for preparing athletes for professional careers.

"Playing in the rain, in cold and on fields that aren't in the best shape ... no matter what the conditions were, you never heard a word of complaint from Kirby," notes his Triton coach. "He just wanted to play."

The Twins took note of the little embonpoint outfielder who ran faster than he should have for his size, threw harder than it looked like he could, and hit for more power than his stubby frame suggested. They drafted him in 1982 and sent him to their rookie-level team, the Elizabethton Twins in the Appalachian League. Two years later they called him up to replace center fielder Jim Eisenreich, who was suffering from Tourette syndrome, a physical disorder of the brain that caused him to exhibit brief, repetitive, purposeless, and involuntary motion and vocal tics.

Although he had not yet been diagnosed with the syndrome, Eisenreich had been taking terrible abuse from some fans. When he was playing the outfield in Fenway Park, fans chanted "shake, shake, shake." He had heard these and similar remarks from classmates while growing up, but this was public humiliation. A camera caught him fighting back tears and then struggling to get into the dugout and away from Boston's insensitive fans.

When he was six he developed tics and jerks and couldn't stop blinking his eyes. He was regularly teased and ridiculed by others including his junior high coach and so spent a lot of time alone in his home. Before the syndrome was diagnosed, he was simply thought to be crazy.

He excelled at baseball, but even when he came up with the Twins, he had to take nights off due to the uncontrolled tics. Newspapers portrayed him as cracking under the pressure of playing in the Major Leagues. In 1984, unable to cope with the taunts, he walked away from the game he loved. Although, after a proper diagnosis and treatment, he later returned to the game to play for four other teams. His defection from the Twins opened the door for Puckett.

Puckett was an immediate success on and off the field. In his rookie year he hit .296, led all American League center fielders in assists and, despite his squat physique, demonstrated he was one of the best defensive outfielders in the league. American League managers voted Puckett and Boston's Dwight Evans as the outfielders with the best arms. With his quick wrists, he also showed the promise of developing into a true power hitter similar to another short power hitter, the Toy Cannon, Jimmy Wynn.

"He has as much power as anybody on the team," says the Twins resident power hitter, first baseman Kent Hrbek. "He can hit the ball as far as I can."

The Minnesota fans quickly adopted him as a favorite. When in 1985 John Fogerty recorded his song "Centerfield," the fans associated it with their new fireplug of a star player. Thereafter he was frequently referred to as "touch 'em all Kirby."

He is particularly good with the press, always upbeat, and usually good for a positive quote.

"I was told I would never make it because I'm too short," he says with his signature big smile. "Well, I'm still too short... It doesn't matter what your height is, it's what's in your heart."

He's always a good story: Chubby kid from the slums makes good. Everyman in center field.

There's a story, too, about his tattoo at a time before many players had them. The tattoo says simply "Kirby" written in a tasteful script with the cross of the "Y" forming a sword-like emblem.

What's the story, Kirby? How come the tattoo?

According to him, shortly after being drafted by the Twins, he reported early to the instructional league in Clearwater, Florida, and having nothing better to do, he roamed the streets and wandered into a tattoo parlor. That's all there was to the story.

He is reminiscent of the equally ebullient Roy Campanella and his famous line: "To be good you've gotta have a lot of little boy in you. When you see Willie Mays and Ted Williams jumping and hopping around the bases after hitting a home run, and the kissing and hugging that goes on at home plate, you realize they have to be little boys."

Kirby Puckett certainly is that.

Some years later, Don Deford wrote of him, "He was given the Branch Rickey Award and the Roberto Clemente Man of the Year Award—both for service to the community—and inducted into the World Sports Humanitarian Hall of Fame. Bob Costas, the Cupid of baseball, named his firstborn after, of all the players on all the teams of all time, Kirby Puckett. Kirby Coins were minted. For the children: Kirby Bears. When a local magazine listed 'The 100 Best Things about the Twin Cities,' Puckett was the top-rated citizen, ranked fifth overall, just ahead of the Mississippi River and Betty Crocker."

He is popular, he is good, and he is loyal, saying he wants to stay with the Twins for his entire career. Minneapolis needs a star. By Major League Baseball standards it is a small city—smaller than Fresno, or Omaha, or Long Beach. Kirby Puckett looks to be a star with a very bright future.

March 1996

Puckett wakes one morning with a black dot in his field of vision and is diagnosed with an early form of glaucoma.

Said Puckett: "I've got the best doctor there is. All I can do is pray. I can still see my beautiful kids and wife. Even if I can't play anymore, all I can do is be thankful. As soon as my vision comes back, I'll be playing that day,"

July 1996

The Minneapolis Star Tribune *runs a story on Puckett, writing: "Can there be a Minnesotan, or a baseball fan anywhere, who is not affected by the shattering news that Kirby Puckett will play no more? Damage from the glaucoma that struck him from the Twins lineup at the end of spring training apparently has not cleared up. So he has announced his retirement. Over time, this has increasingly come to seem the likely outcome of his damaged eyesight, but that makes the reality of it no easier to take — possibly not for him, certainly not for his fans.*

In an era when sports stars too often behave like overpaid spoiled brats, Puckett has been that rare commodity: a player awestruck by his own success, ebullient, open, friendly and — yes — well-paid and well-worth every penny of it. With Major League baseball seemingly intent on doing everything possible to antagonize its fans, Puckett has been a happy reminder of the joy and satisfaction that the game can provide."

September 2002

Puckett goes on trial for false imprisonment and criminal sexual assault after allegedly pulling a woman into the men's room.

Since retiring, he has gained a great deal of weight — some reports have him at over 300 pounds.

March 2006

Puckett suffers a massive stroke. Surgery is performed to relieve pressure on the brain. The surgery fails and Puckett dies at 45.

April 2008

Don Deford writes in Sports Illustrated: "Anyway, the mistress of many years says that when Puckett couldn't play baseball anymore, 'he started to become full of himself and very abusive.' He began to perform lewd acts in public, such as going to a fancy shopping center, parking there, then opening his car door and stepping out and peeing in plain view of other people (Twins fans presumably included)."

There is no question about it, Kirby Puckett is easily the best player on a team that may find wins tough to come by this year. So the Twins will continue to promote him as a classy player and the face of the organization and hope for the best. It's going to be a long season.

14. That Was Last Year

The Dodgers' Tommy Lasorda would be optimistic in a POW camp. In spring training his ebullience is only dampened when no one asks him for a quote. He's been known to offer them up even when not asked.

"The difference between the impossible and the possible lies in a man's determination."

"The only way I'd worry about the weather is if it snows on our side of the field and not theirs."

"Guys ask me, don't I get burned out? How can you get burned out doing something you love? I ask you, have you ever got tired of kissing a pretty girl?"

"I love doubleheaders. That way I get to keep my uniform on longer."

"I bleed Dodger blue and when I die, I'm going to the big Dodger in the sky."

Tommy says the Dodgers will be in the World Series.

Romanticism runs wild in spring training. So what if his Phillies came in 26 games behind the Cards last year? That was last year. Last years are last years. There is always hope, but hope requires belief.

So what if the Phillies of late have been considered talented underachievers? They've got Mike Schmidt so they've got an offense. All right, pitching and catching might be problems, but they've got some kids. You never know.

The Cards, who did win it all last year, are one of the best defensive teams in the history of baseball, says manager Whitey Herzog. Just look at Ozzie Smith. They're fast, too. The Cubs are old but Ron Cey and Gary Matthews can produce. The Expos have two of the game's best in Andre Dawson and Tim Raines. The Pirates don't have much but they do have rookie slugger Barry Bonds who may provide some punch. The Braves can always count on a solid performance from Dale Murphy and could mount a serious challenge if they can bring some stability to the pitching staff. The Padres need production from an aging Steve Garvey but they do have strong pitching headed by Goose Gossage. The Astros can count on the potent arms of Nolan Ryan and Mike Scott. As long as Roger Craig can convince his pitchers to throw his signature split-finger pitch, the Giants will be competitive. Pete Rose is counting on a revitalized Dave ("They ought to pay me just to walk around here") Parker to lead his Reds to the NL West title and many prognosticators believe he will, Pete Rose among them. "I don't want to go out on a limb," he says, "but I'll be very disappointed if we don't win the west." They are seen as the most improved team in the division. Most of the betting money is on them.

The Mets look like the team to beat in the NL East. They've got the pitching led by the phenom Dwight Gooden; they've got hitting with Darryl Strawberry and Keith Hernandez; they've got the down-and-dirty scrappers Wally Backman and Lenny Dykstra; and they've got leadership with Gary Carter. Had it not been for the injuries last year, they might well have won it all. Davey Johnson, their manager, says they will win this year. He said it last year, too.

15. Abner Doubledata

Davey Johnson had a 13-year Major League career and then added a couple of seasons in Japan. Undoubtedly, his high point came in 1973 when he broke Rogers Hornsby's single-season record for home runs by a second baseman. He also makes the trivia lists in being the only man ever to hit behind Henry Aaron and the great Japanese hitter, Sadaharu Oh.

Sometimes his confidence comes across as arrogance. He can be downright stubborn and, to some in the Mets dugout, he comes across as a man who thinks he knows more than anybody else — and he probably does. He has a degree in mathematics from Trinity University in Texas and could, if asked, either demonstrate proof of the Laplace transform of a function's derivative or how to calculate your batting average if you got 10 hits in 100 at-bats. He could answer this question: If you're flying in his Cessna and the magnetic heading is 330 degrees and the relative bearing is 270 degrees, what is the magnetic bearing to the station? The answer: Remember the formula: MH + RB = Mbto. So, 330 + 270 = 600. Well, there is no 600 degrees, so we subtract 360 from it and get 240 degrees, which is the magnetic bearing to the station!

Want to buy a small scuba compressor, something in the 110v, 80cc/20min range, under 200 lbs? Johnson can make a recommendation since, in addition to being a licensed pilot, he's also a licensed scuba instructor. Want to buy some Florida property but aren't sure of the zoning restrictions? Ask Johnson. He's got a license for that, too. Despite the fact that he is frequently feuding with his employers about his salary, he made his first million in real estate and owns numerous properties.

In his spare time he's attended Johns Hopkins University and plays golf with a three handicap.

Some in baseball opine that he spreads his interests too thin and that winning is not high enough on his priority list. Johnson vehemently disagrees. He cares greatly about winning he insists, and his frequent inability to sleep nights is ample enough proof.

If asked, he'll remind you that when he took over as the Mets manager in October 1983, the club was in absolute shambles. Not only had they just finished the season dead last, more than 20 games out, but they weren't in any conceivable way an interesting team to watch, not like back in the days of Casey Stengel. They had barely drawn a million fans in New York and, in his opinion, had been losing for so many years they simply took it for granted.

Yeah, we lost today. What's new? Take a shower and go home.

Johnson came in expressing confidence from the start. Hadn't he won as a player with the Orioles and in Japan? Hadn't he won all three years he managed in the minors?

Tom Chandler, who coached Johnson when he played at Texas A&M, never considered him managerial material. "He always had leadership abilities, but I didn't even know if he could play in the big leagues," Chandler says.

When Johnson threatened to quit the A&M team, Chandler jumped all over him. "I told him if he was going to quit now, he'd be a quitter all his life. I was pretty vocal about it. The next night, I went to the ballpark and there he was, smiling ear-to-ear. He wanted to stay."

Johnson says what he remembers most about the school experience is that "it was all-male then, so I put a lot of miles on my old '49 Ford driving around Texas looking for girls. I mean, a lot of girls. On cools nights, I'd stick my head out the window, trying to stay awake driving back."

He is not always the most affable guy around. As Orioles coach Elrod Hendricks says, "There was never an Oriole player who was more intense. And he played a little bit dirty, too."

There's a little Philip Marlowe in Johnson. Once, when Leo Durocher was riding Johnson during batting practice, Davey came right back with "Leo, you're washed up. You won't even be in baseball next year." During the game, Leo responded by having his pitcher drill Davey. Johnson's shoulder was bruised enough that he believed it cost him a legitimate shot at the home run championship, which he lost by one. Says Johnson, "I figure, let 'em do whatever they want. I'll do what I want."

"My first memory of Davey is in Elmira in AA," says Baltimore General Manager Pat Gillick. "He really got gonged good. It was bad. I never saw a guy who wanted to get back in the fire that fast. It really spoke to the competitor in him."

"I missed two curveballs to fall in a hole," Johnson recalls. "I thought he'd throw another one and I remember telling myself, 'Don't budge, Davey, and you'll just kill it.'"

But Johnson didn't see the fastball until it was a foot from his nose. "I saw it here," he says, holding his hand in front of his face.

> I knew I was going to eat it. Broke my nose and a couple of teeth. The ball went all the way back over the pitcher's head. Somebody on the bench yelled, "Run." They thought it must have hit my bat from the sound and where the ball went.

> Unfortunately, I never passed out. At the hospital, the nurse looked at me — my nose spread all over my face — and said, "Where did it hit you?"

The next day, after morning surgery, Johnson was back in the dugout, his nose full of stuffing and his body full of codeine. "I'm ready to play," he told Weaver, who put him in against a junkballer named Grilli. Johnson remembers the situation very well:

> He threw me three big slow curves and I swung at 'em after they were already in the catcher's glove. I didn't know that the pain pills had slowed down my reflexes. All I remember that night was crying. I thought that was my career. "Now I can't even hit a slow curve with the bases loaded." I'd be the guy they pointed out who'd lost his nerve after getting hit in the head."For a year and a half, I could be walking down the street and see a ball coming at my face. I'd throw up my hands and dive out of the way.

"What the hell you doin' Davey?" his teammates would ask. "I had to dodge that thing. Didn't you see it?" he'd say.

Despite all his resolute ways, Johnson bristles at criticism real or imagined. Any suggestion that he is wrong will usually bring some form of rebuttal. Davey Johnson, the tough-guy manager, is easily hurt by criticism.

He's got so damn many outside interests how can you expect him to concentrate on baseball?

He runs a loose ship. He needs to be tougher with some players who are getting away with hell.

He gets so stressed out that sometimes he ends up drinking too much.

Don't count the Cardinals' Whitey Herzog among the Johnson fans. After reading parts of Johnson's book *Bats*, he says sarcastically, "I thought Harry Caray invented baseball, but after reading Davey's book, I think Davey did." When asked if this year's Mets team is among the all-time greats, he just shakes his head and walks away.

When the Mets TV broadcaster Tim McCarver criticizes Johnson for putting Ray Knight into a game because he's more worried about hurting Knight's feelings than in winning the game, Johnson explodes, "For McCarver to say I'm not concerned about winning a game, them's fighting words. And I will let Timmy know it when I see him. But it just goes to show you that in this town, even your best friends will say things that may undermine what you have going."

He complains about the second guessing that all managers face.

He complains about the heat from the press.

He frequently clashes with Mets general manager Frank Cashen. Once Cashen went to Johnson and told him he didn't want Jesse Orosco used that day. Johnson was furious and told Cashen that if the GM wanted to manage the club, he'd quit.

When Yankees manager Billy Martin was quoted in the press saying,

"Davey Johnson is a nice guy, but what has he ever won?" Johnson went on a tear about the Yankee penchant for ripping other players in the press.

What Davey Johnson does is win baseball games. When they gave him his first chance to manage in the Major Leagues, he led the team to a second place in the NL East in his first two seasons.

Now the expectations are higher. Anything less will be considered a failure and Johnson knows the pressure is on. Cashen understands that Johnson is a knowledgeable baseball man but he also finds him stubborn and manipulative. He will bend rules if it is in his interests to do so and will upend the apple cart to get what he wants.

To Cashen, he is ego-driven, self-centered, and maybe self-destructive.

Johnson sees himself as highly competitive, driven to win at all costs and unsure that Cashen understands this. Cashen meddles in team issues that are the sole province of the manager.

To Cashen, Johnson is over-committed. He still owns a real estate company, a restaurant, and a fishing camp. He's also having family problems. They are paying him a lot of money to manage the team and that should be his sole focus.

Johnson sees himself as a man with more interests than just baseball, but when he is managing, he gives the game his full attention.

To Cashen, Johnson constantly complains that he is not being paid enough and he often does so in the press. Johnson sees himself as more valuable to the club because they are winning and winning brings people to the ball park.

Cashen tells Johnson, "I don't want you saying things where you and I are in disagreement. We can disagree in private, but not in public."

The friction between the fractious manager and the front office will not go away. During his managerial career, Johnson will post winning records everywhere he goes— New York, Cincinnati, Baltimore, Los Angeles— but he will be fired from each club nevertheless.

"A lot of the problem with the Mets concerned the public airing of his contract difficulties," Joe McIlvaine, a Mets executive says, "and in Baltimore, it seemed like the public airing of his contract situation got him in trouble. It happened in New York, constantly, and it could have been handled easily behind closed doors."

"You knew the personalities were not going to work," says one Major League executive. "Davey knows how to manage a game as well as anyone, but he's not a disciplinarian. He's going to get his time in on the golf course. You just can't evaluate him the way you evaluate somebody in the business world."

He may insist on playing by his own rules, but he's no fool. He may run a slack clubhouse but not one without reason. He remembers how Gene Mauch was dubbed "the boy genius" but he never won a pennant.

While he was still playing, his teammates sometimes called Johnson "Dum-dum" as a backhanded tribute to his intellect. He was always analyzing, always trying to find an edge that might lead to success.

After he retired as a player, one of Johnson's many activities was as a computer salesman for Litton Industries. This was in the '60s, long before most people saw practical applications for the behemoth card-chewing machines. Johnson, though, believes strongly in the symbiotic relationship between probability and baseball. He sees a computer as a tool that can do for the manager the same thing it can for the businessman. It can't make decisions but it sure can make any needed information instantly available. In his office is a computer displaying such information as batting averages and RBIs of certain batters against certain pitchers. Every day he checks it for data on pitch-selection patterns of the day's opposing pitchers and numerous other game variables. Someone suggests that on the other side of town Yankees manager Yogi Berra uses a computer to play Star Wars.

Abner Doubledata is accused of relying too heavily on a machine and some players resent it. "I'll tell you what," says one of his players, "when a damn computer can steal signs and ride pitchers, let me know, until then it's all bullshit, but don't tell the skip I said that."

With his mathematics background, Johnson calls himself "the perfect mix for baseball and computers." Once when he was playing for Earl Weaver in Baltimore, Johnson waved a computer printout in front of the manager claiming it showed he should be batting cleanup. Weaver looked at him like he was crazy. He had Boog Powell and Frank Robinson in the lineup and he's supposed to bat his little second baseman cleanup? Weaver just smiled and wrote in Johnson's name near the bottom of the order. Tool or no tool, instincts are a helluva lot better than a machine.

August 2008

Johnson, no longer wanted by any Major League team, has turned to international baseball. After leading the Holland team for a time, he is now in charge of the American team at the Beijing Olympics.

He leaves no doubt about where he stands on the wacky new format the games are using. If the game is deadlocked after ten innings, each team begins its half of the 11th with men on first and second and nobody out. The managers can select any part of the order they like to do this.

This is not exactly what the Knickerbockers had in mind but then again neither was baseball in China.

"I'm a baseball dinosaur. A baseball purist. I don't like the idea of putting guys on base and then trying to defend them," says Johnson.

Two runs down in a critical game against the Cubans, Johnson puts the ninth and leadoff men on base in the bottom of the 11th. His first batter of the inning is hit in the head while attempting to bunt. "He threw it at his head. No game of baseball is worth that, as far as I'm concerned," *says Johnson.*

"That is a lack of respect on the part of the U.S. manager to say that," *says the Cuban manager.*

The player is sent to the hospital, and the U.S. loses the game.

While some players see Johnson as an arrogant, I'm-a-whole-lot-better-than-any-of-you-guys, heartless manager, Johnson sees it quite differently. He says he carefully balances what is best for the team with what is best for each player. When he has to discipline players as he did last year with Doug Sisk, he banks on the other players understanding that what he did was best for the club. Winning is everything for a manager. Lose and you're gone. That doesn't take a computer to figure out.

In an effort to seem to be a buddy to all the players, he subscribes to the "y-is-a-friendly-letter" school. Everyone gets the happy letter added to his name. Ron Darling is "Ronny," Mex Hernandez is "Mexy," and Ron Gardenhire is "Gardy." One big happy family.

The way he sees it, some managers have to show they're the boss by fining, shouting, or demeaning players. He says if he make the right decisions and is consistent with the players they will respect him.

Tell that to Darryl Strawberry.

16. A Talent the Likes of Which Are Seldom Seen

Almost from the moment Davey Johnson joined the Mets, there has been friction between slugging outfielder Darryl Strawberry and his manager. Subtle, tacit at first, it has slowly continued to build. Johnson says he can tell when a player's grinding, giving it his all. He can also tell when a player's slacking off, going through the motions. Strawberry can do both and Johnson is conflicted over how to handle his slacking days. The two don't talk a lot. Johnson says, "To communicate you don't necessarily have to have a conversation. A player goes by you, and as he's getting ready to go out onto the field, you can hit him on the arm or tap him on the ass, or say, 'Have a good one.' Often that's enough."

For the "sake of the team," though, Johnson frequently fines Strawberry for a variety of offenses, but insists that Darryl knows how he feels about him. In spring training he tells him, "Darryl, you're my security blanket. If you play well, I'll be around. If you don't, I'll be gone."

Darryl puts his bat on his shoulder. "Dave," he says, "I'm ready. I'm going to tear them up this year. I'm sleeping, eating, drinking nothing but baseball. You ain't going to worry about me, not once, not one time."

Johnson can only hope. "I'm counting on you," he says.

"Don't worry about it. You're not going to get my money this year."

"Darryl, the boys at the orphanage sure appreciated your money that I gave them last year."

The manager and the star player smile broadly at each other. Will it last? wonders Johnson. Still, Darryl seems more mature this year. He almost has to. He was so young when he came up and he was saddled with the most dangerous of all baseball labels—the dreaded "P" word—potential.

He was such a naturally talented athlete that the assumption was that everything should come easily to him.

Darryl struggle? Why would he do that? He's a talent the likes of which few have ever seen.

"Someday he's going to hit the ball farther than anyone has ever hit a ball," Davey Johnson says.

In New York they compare him to Joe D and the Mick, elsewhere to Ted Williams.

When the Mets brought him up in 1983, writers said he'd likely win the Triple Crown, something that hadn't been done in the National League since Joe Medwick did it in 1937. When he didn't, they said he wasn't living up to his potential. His game began to suffer and he started to pout. He wasn't smiling anymore and he was making all sorts of mistakes in the field — missing cutoffs, throwing to the wrong base. And to make matters worse, he looked as if he were dogging it, not giving it all he had. So the fines followed.

At first, Johnson tried to buck him up. "Listen, you're in a little slump, and you feel you're letting yourself down, the team down, me down. Forget it. Shake it off. You aren't letting anyone down."

For a while that worked, but then the old pouting came back. It was a tricky situation for Johnson, and the computer wasn't going to be any help. Criticize Darryl and he sulks even more. Leave him alone and it looks like the manager doesn't give a damn.

Take Darryl's second season escapades as an example. Once in San Diego he arrived at the ballpark an hour late, saw that Johnson had pulled his name from the starting lineup card and proceeded to throw a childish tantrum. Just days before, he had proclaimed that he wanted to be seen as the leader of the club. Leaders do not sulk and pout or question authority. These are the unwritten rules of the game. Johnson called him into his office and tried to explain the facts of baseball life to his young star. It wasn't the first time a manager had to do this. In Darryl's rookie season, big Frank Howard, then the manager, gave him a stern lecture after Darryl sauntered to first base on a hit he might easily have turned into a double. Howard told him he was getting a reputation as a player who didn't always give 100 percent.

"It's too bad you can't be happy with a bunch of guys you think are your friends," Strawberry says, not letting the issue die. "All I do for this team and I get criticized."

So the press starts doing just that. He is called "selfish," "childish," "unable to understand when he has made a mistake." One paper writes that he acts like a five-year-old and when he's wrong it's always somebody else's fault. They write about the tunnel vision of his selfish world.

When Johnson says, "As he gets older, he'll have higher valleys and shorter slumps," it's hard to tell whether it's a prediction or a prayer.

Strawberry, if anything, is even more sensitive to criticism than Johnson. "I don't know why Davey is always trying to bury me," he says. "I don't like it, the way he buries me all the time. He relates to some players, his favorites. But he comes down on me and two or three others."

16. A Talent the Likes of Which Are Seldom Seen

The last baseball prospect in New York who came with this much hype was Willie Mays. Like Strawberry he was rushed up from the minors ahead of schedule. The Giants needed help and Mays was crushing AAA ball. After his first three games at the Polo Grounds he was 0-for-12 and literally on the verge of tears. "Mr. Leo," he said to Durocher, his manager, "I don't think I'm ready for this. Send me back."

Durocher grabbed him hard by the arm. "Son, you're my center fielder whether you hit or not," he said.

Mays remembered those words years later when he watched Strawberry for the first time. "That was the key," he said. "That gave me confidence." After seeing Strawberry strike out six of his first eight times at bat, Mays observed, "He has a good swing. He'll get hitting. He looks like he has great potential. He doesn't show it by his voice, but he's probably nervous."

Darryl Strawberry played for the Crenshaw High Cougars in Southern California. He was the best player on one of the best high school baseball teams ever. He was slender like Ted Williams, graceful like Joe DiMaggio, and powerful like Mickey Mantle.

There were no "if" questions about him, only "when" questions, and those didn't last long. Diehard Mets fans tracked his progress from high school to the majors in three quick years.

From day one in the majors he felt the pressure. And why not? So much had been written about how he would be the savior of a franchise.

"He can go as far in baseball as any man living," Frank Howard said.

"If Darryl works at it, he could be the greatest player ever," catcher John Stearns said.

Say those things to Pete Rose and he would probably have loved you for expressing them, even if you were understating the case somewhat, but Darryl didn't want to hear more comments like that. It was like everyone was adding a little weight around his ankles slowing him down. Add enough and he'll stop altogether.

Some athletes when under pressure bear down and work harder to live up to expectations. Some athletes thrive only when under pressure. It is the catalyst that drives them. But not Darryl. Some like Willie Mays, Reggie Jackson, and Rickey Henderson learn to handle it. Some like Darryl Strawberry don't.

There were times during practices when Darryl was the first one to call it a day. This did not go unnoticed. Still, in his first three years with the team, he put up respectable offensive numbers and, on occasions, performed superbly in the field. At other times he seemed to lack concentration.

Off the field concerns were slowly mounting up. He seemed to be partying a lot and drinking more than he probably should. It was not unusual for him to down three or four drinks before dinner and then wash down his food with a couple of beers. It was Darryl's way of escaping the pressures and he certainly wasn't the first player in the game to use alcohol for that.

You think Strawberry drinks a lot, heck, you should have seen Babe Ruth. The Mick. Now he could drink. And Boggs, well he's in another league altogether.

Gradually but surely Strawberry began to isolate himself from the fans. He smiled less, sulked more. Darryl Strawberry was not having much fun, not like back at Crenshaw.

A national study shows that 75 percent of American fans stated that sports heroes are good models for our youth, and 60 percent said they are our best models. Dr. Bruce Ogilvie, a sports psychologist, says:

> Is it any wonder that when sports heroes of the stature of Dwight Gooden and Darryl Strawberry and other members of a championship team become involved in antisocial behavior that the fans feel cheated? Only months ago these players were cheered wildly as they reached the top of their profession. Now it is easy to understand the shattering effect of such behavior as the fans' idols slip, fall or are pushed off their pedestals.

Hopes for a calmer, more mature, more focused player arose in 1985 when, at 22, Strawberry announced he was marrying Lisa Andrews, a beautiful young girl he had met the year before. It was an ominous sign, though, when he finally showed up at his wedding an hour late. Probably not surprisingly, the marriage was a disaster from the start. Within two years, Lisa would file assault charges alleging Darryl broke her nose. That the marriage actually lasted as long as it did was remarkable given their continual rounds of fights, separations, and semi-reconciliations.

During the course of his trouble-ridden career, all manner of explanations are put forward for his behavior.

Deep down he had no self-confidence.

His father walked out on the family.

Ronnie, his older-brother role model, was habitually in trouble with the law.

He did not have an extended family for support.

He grew up a product of inner-city Los Angeles and we all know what that leads to.

Too much was expected of him too soon.

He should have been a basketball player. He always liked that game better anyway.

Although he didn't always perform like one, he was so often referred to as a superstar that he adopted all the accouterments that the label suggested, including drugs and alcohol.

"Baseball is the easy part," he has said. "Living is the hard part."

"He's just Darryl," his mother says, "just like the rest of the children I have raised, and maybe sometimes all the status makes a person try to be what

16. A Talent the Likes of Which Are Seldom Seen

Darryl Strawberry takes his long home run cut in the 8th inning of the seventh game of the '86 Series against Al Nipper. It is his only round tripper of the Series.

other people think they are. To me, if you do that you are living outside yourself. In that sense, that might have been the case with Darryl."

He was getting a reputation, too, of a player who wouldn't play hurt, and this never goes down well with those who do. One night in the clubhouse after Strawberry had scratched himself from the lineup, Lee Mazzilli, a reserve outfielder/first baseman, exploded.

"Swollen glands," said Strawberry.

Swollen glands! A broken leg and you take yourself out of the lineup. Swollen glands, you play.

"They don't believe I'm sick," Strawberry said, referring to his teammates. "I feel terrible. Why wouldn't I want to play? I'm having a good year and I'm putting up good numbers. You can't believe I'd skip playing against the Cardinals if I could."

"He said he couldn't play, so he didn't play" is all Johnson said — in public. But Johnson was angry. He had already fined the sulky kid $1,500 for showing up late for a workout and walking out of another practice.

After Mazzilli's outburst Strawberry avoided crossing paths with him in the locker room. He sat near the trainer's room in the back of the clubhouse while Mazzilli showered and dressed.

What was particularly galling to teammates was that Strawberry had spent the morning in a sound studio working on a rap record. Presumably swollen glands don't prohibit rapping but they do batting.

"There are some times you just have to play," third baseman Howard Johnson said. "I would have to have something broken before I wouldn't play."

Strawberry described his critics as "back-stabbers" and threatened to punch second baseman Wally Backman. "I'll bust that little redneck in the face," Strawberry told reporters.

"If that's the case," Backman replied, "do you think I'm going to back down?"

"Patience with Darryl has run out with a lot of guys," Hernandez said later. "You never know what side of the bed he's going to wake up on."

Maybe it isn't swollen glands that Darryl's got but rather the "southpaw disease," a not-so-mysterious ailment that attacks some left-handed batters when they have to face left-handed pitchers. The two games he missed against the Cards were both pitched by lefties.

"Nobody in the world that I know of gets sick 25 times a year. There's only so much you can take," reiterates Backman.

January 1987
Strawberry's wife accuses him of breaking her nose and files for divorce.

April 1989
Strawberry is sued; it is claimed that he is the father of another woman's son. Tests confirm the allegation.

February 1990
Shortly after being arrested for hitting and threatening his wife, he checks into rehab for alcohol addiction.

September 1993
He is arrested for hitting his pregnant girlfriend.

April 1994
Now with the Dodgers, he fails to show up for an exhibition game just as the season is about to begin. The team announces he has a drug addiction problem and puts him on the disabled list.

December 1994
He is indicted for failing to report more than $300,000 of income from autograph and memorabilia shows.

February 1995
He is suspended by Major League Baseball after testing positive for cocaine and is released by the Giants.

December 1995
   He is charged with failing to make child support payments.

August 1998
   He is sued by his attorney for unpaid legal fees.

October 1998
   He is diagnosed with colon cancer and undergoes surgery and chemotherapy.

April 1999
   He is arrested for soliciting sex from a police woman posing as a prostitute and for possession of cocaine. He is again suspended by Major League Baseball.

January 2000
   He tests positive for cocaine and again is suspended.

July 2000
   He has surgery to remove a tumor and a kidney after learning his cancer has spread.

September 2000
   He is arrested at gunpoint as he tries to drive away after blacking out and rear-ending another car.

October 2000
   He is arrested after leaving a drug treatment center to use drugs with a friend.

November 2000
   He tells a judge that he has lost his will to live and has stopped chemotherapy.

April 2001
   He is arrested again for disappearing from house arrest at a drug treatment center.

August 2001
   For the third time in 10 years, Strawberry has entered a treatment center to deal with his addiction to drugs and has been suspended from baseball for failing his drug test.

March 2002
   He is back in jail for violating drug treatment center rules.

September 2005
   He is charged with filing a false police report claiming his car had been stolen.

December 2005
   His second wife files for divorce.

17. The Wild Boys

You don't call a synchronized swimmer "Nails." It suggests someone strong, tough. Lenny Dykstra is Nails, a scrappy player with a perpetually dirty uniform and a seldom-say-die attitude. He appears to be something of a paradox. On the field, a bundle of nervous energy; away from the field, a bundle of restraint.

When Lenny Dykstra wonders aloud why Strawberry gets sick so often, Johnson brokers a meeting and the two agree publicly that the feud is over. Backman says, "I am a redneck," but the friction between the two lingers. "I've always been known to speak my feelings, say whatever I want to say. I'm not going to let anybody force me into saying something or not say something. If people don't like it, that's up to them."

Between and near the chalk lines he dives for balls, runs into railings, slides head-first into first base. He is the personification of the aggressive ballplayer playing right on the edge of being out of control. Yet off the field he is a neat freak, an obsessively organized man whose life is synchronized perfectly. His personal motto might be "everything in its place and a place for everything." Every night before going to bed, he neatly lays out his clothes for the next day so that when he wakes up there will be none of that sloppy indecision. He is precise in a way that fans never see nor would they ever guess.

To the fans he is simply Nails, the hard-nosed player, an image that is only reinforced when he sheds his shirt to pose for a Nails beefcake poster.

A woman wearing a wedding gown and veil walked through the Shea Stadium stands in the middle of a game carrying a sign that read "MARRY ME, LENNY." Lenny Dykstra, who already is married, refused to comment.

With his curly blond hair sticking out from beneath his batting helmet, and his boyish blue-eyed fresh face, he hardly looks like the Mets center fielder, but watch him hustle and you can't help thinking about a young Pete Rose. He seldom walks any time he can run and he seldom runs slowly if he can run fast.

To other teams he is a pesky player, a real pain in the ass. The way he tries to distract pitchers by inching ever farther from the base, the way he dives across the railing in quest of a foul ball.

"This is the way I've always played ever since I was in the Little Leagues. I don't know any other way," he says.

Billy Beane, a one-time minor league teammate of Dykstra, commented that Dykstra is perfectly designed emotionally to play baseball, if for no other reason than he had no concept of failure.

His first manager in the minors, Danny Monzant, says: "My first impression of him was here as a feisty little son of a gun with an overabundance of energy and confidence who had ants in his pants and didn't know how to sit down. Everybody else was just in gear but he was in overdrive." He tells a story of how Dykstra's left foot slid under a wire outfield fence while chasing a line drive:

> His foot is stuck and he's holding up the ball to show the umpire it should be a ground-rule double. But it's not a ground-rule double and the ball is still in play. Our whole team stands up in the dugout and yells at him, "Throw the ball, Lenny!" He refuses. In his mind it's a ground-rule double so the hitter winds up with an inside-the-parker. But Lenny doesn't make too many mistakes on the field. He's a catalyst, a live wire, the kind of guy who makes things happen.

Last year, doing his best imitation of Pete Reiser, he ran into the center field wall and knocked himself silly. Reiser won the batting crown in his first full season with the Dodgers and then put so many dents and cracks in his body that his career ground to a premature halt.

"You gotta look out for them walls," Ed Lynch warned him on the Mets bench.

"I thought I could catch the ball," Dykstra said, as if that explained everything.

Davey Johnson worries about that, too, but he also understands that if he tries to change the way Nails plays, he won't be Nails and that means he won't be as valuable to the club. Although he often talks about hitting home runs, his game is singles, stolen bases, and covering as much ground in center field as his never-stop feet can take him.

Last year he actually did hit one home run out of Shea. Johnson, who has been on him to forget about swinging for the fences for fear it will foul up his natural line-drive swing, says he forgives him just as long as it doesn't go to his head.

"The last time I did it was in Strat-O-Matic," Dykstra said. "It's a baseball game where you roll dice. It was against my brother. I was always Rod Carew. I still play it."

The Mets had signed him out of Southern California as a 13th round draft pick in 1981. He quickly put up big numbers in the minors, and last year in May the Mets brought him up when their starting center fielder, Mookie Wilson, went down with an injury. His high-octane play clearly energized the team.

The Mets' outfield seems set. Dykstra and maybe Wilson in center. Strawberry has a lock on right, so that leaves left field up for grabs. The aging George Foster, the highest paid player on the team, will probably start the season there despite the fact that among all players, only Joggin' George Hendrick is booed by home fans more often than Foster.

February 2008
Lindsay Jones, onetime business partner and close friend of Dykstra, is suing the former ballplayer to regain an interest in their lucrative car wash business. Jones claims that on Dykstra's advice, he gambled an average of $2,000 on specified Phillies games in 1993.

His sworn statement alleges these wagers were a payment to him "on the basis that Lenny would cover all losses, and I would use the winnings to live on."

Also included in the suit is a sworn statement from Jeff Scott, convicted drug dealer and bodybuilder, alleging that Dykstra paid him $20,000 plus "special perks" to "bulk up" the three-time all-star.

In a subsequent interview, Scott says he injected Dykstra with steroids "more times than I can count."

Dykstra absolutely denies all the allegations, claiming it is a fabricated story from a disgruntled partner.

Probably the only player on the team who can match Dykstra for scrappy play is Wally Backman. Together they come to be known as the "Wild Boys." The two seemed to be starring in a *Who Wants to Get His Uniform the Dirtiest?* reality show. Why go into a base standing up if you can win points with a good bellywhopper? Make a running catch or a diving catch? Silly question.

Then there was the out-jockey-the-opposition competition. These are the types of players you love if they're on your team but hate when you have to play them. They are a combustible duo but an important part of the club's character as aggressive hellions.

Backman had been up and down a couple of times between the Mets and Tidewater, their Triple A affiliate, but when Johnson took over, he made Backman one of his priorities. Johnson likes his scrappy play and his ability to get on base as a slap-hitting switch-hitter even if he didn't hit left-handers very well and didn't cover a lot of ground at second base. What he lacks in defense, he makes up in other ways.

Despite his on-field bravura, Backman worries about being sent back down so he spends his entire first season living in a mobile home with his wife and daughter at a New Jersey campsite. It's a fickle game; you never know what may come your way. Best to play hard every day.

"All I expect is to see my teammates play hard," Backman says. "When you're getting paid as much money as we are, you should be giving over 100

The scrappy Wally Backman digs one out of the dirt in the '86 World Series. He batted .333 in the Series, walked three times and stole a base.

percent. If you're not, you're not only hurting yourself, you're hurting the team. And when you're hurting the team, somebody shouldn't be afraid to tell you, 'Hey, you gotta get out there and bust your butt.'"

November 2004
The Diamondbacks hire Backman as manager. He has been a successful minor league manager for seven years. He had hoped to manage the White Sox while managing in their system, but reports said he had been not-so-secretly rooting against the Sox in the hopes that the current manager, Jerry Manuel, would be fired and the position given to him. When the club heard about this, they let him go and he was picked up by the Diamondbacks.

Shortly after he is named as manager of the Diamondbacks, they learn Backman had been convicted of DUI a few years earlier, pleaded guilty to harassing a female friend of his family, had been accused of spousal abuse by his ex-wife, and had filed for personal bankruptcy.

The Diamondbacks, admitting they had erred in not conducting a financial or criminal background check on their new manager, fire him four days after he is hired.

Like most of the team, Backman thinks this might be the year for the Mets to take the last step to winning their division. "It'd drive us nuts if we came real close and came up empty again," and like most of the team, he realizes a lot will depend on the not-always-dependable Doc Gooden.

18. Doc Ain't Stupid

The he's-the-best-prospect-I've-ever-seen stories are legion.

Howie Haak, the man who scouted Roberto Clemente, Frank Robinson, and scores of others who went on to solid Major League careers, says that the best player he ever saw was Alfredo Edmead, a Dominican outfielder.

> He was 17 years old and so good that he skipped the rookie leagues and started in the Carolina League. He was hitting .314 with 7 triples, 18 doubles, and 61 stolen bases when he collided with friend and second baseman Pablo Cruz in Salem, Virginia. Cruz's knee crushed his [Edmead's] skull and he was killed. Doctors later learned that his skull was so thin that, had he been beaned, even if he was wearing a helmet, he'd have been killed. But he had the best skills I ever saw.

George Digby, who has been a Red Sox scout since 1944, says in high school Dwight Gooden was the best pitching prospect he ever saw, and he's seen many of the greats.

There is already talk about his Hall of Fame prospects. Dwight Gooden is a superstar no matter how that word is used, abused, or revered.

Now in spring training beginning his third Major League season, he is showing off his 98 mph fastball and sweeping curve they call "Lord Charles," a conscious upgrade from the more common name for a curve, "Uncle Charlie." Since the common scorekeeper's abbreviation for a strikeout is the letter "K" he is dubbed "Dr. K," which is then shortened to a simple "Doc."

Doc played only one season in the minors before Davey Johnson had heard enough and called him up — and that was from the Class-A Carolina League. He won 17 games in his first year, 1984. He went to the All-Star Game as the youngest pitcher ever and struck out all three stars he faced. He led the league in strikeouts, set records for consecutive strikeouts, and was voted Rookie of the Year. In 1985 he turned in one of the most dominant pitching performances in baseball history. He led the league in wins, strikeouts, ERA, complete games, and innings pitched.

Then he became the youngest-ever recipient of the Cy Young Award and was named the Associated Press Male Athlete of the Year, beating out Walter Payton, Pete Rose, and Kareem Abdul-Jabbar for the honor. He also won the

Black Athlete of the Year award, beating out Abdul-Jabbar and track star Valerie Brisco-Hooks by amassing the greatest number of votes ever accumulated for that award.

Umpire John Kibler says of Gooden's rookie season, "If he was throwing the ball any better, we'd have to start a new league for him."

That fall, Doc turned 21.

New York can't get enough of him. A giant mural of Doc in mid-delivery adorns Pennsylvania Station, another is painted on the side of a Midtown building. He was on the cover of *Time*. They called him baseball's hottest pitcher. Forget Tom Seaver, the Doc is here. The greatest pitcher since Sandy Koufax. He's already been on the cover of *Sports Illustrated* three times. Harry Reasoner came to St. Petersburg to do a story on him for *60 Minutes*.

He's the hottest property in sports marketing — not Gretzky, Bird, Dickerson, or Palmer. The kid on the Mets tops them all. He is simply the most recognized athlete in America.

Sponsors can't get enough of him. Pepsi has engaged him to sell cola and Kellogg to push Corn Flakes. He endorses sunglasses and bats for Toys R Us and with his father he plugs AT&T on television.

The way Cashen puts it, "The two players in baseball who have instant recognition are Dwight Gooden and Pete Rose. They are household names. You mention them and everybody instantly knows who you mean."

When Sandy Koufax says, "I'd trade anyone's past for Gooden's future," people listen.

"If I could pick somebody to be," says Mickey Mantle, "that's who I'd be. He knows there is a wonderful ride ahead."

The kid has it all. He is young, famous, graceful, talented, charismatic, and wealthy.

In February he had signed a contract for $1.32 million. His agent had wanted a multi-year contract, but the Mets don't give that to players with little experience in the Major Leagues. The Mets knew that this phenomenal young talent was going to cost them plenty in the years to come. Gooden vowed to get a long-term contract next year and said that the first thing he'd do with his big haul was "turn some over to my mom and pop."

He already owns a Mercedes, a Corvette, and three condominiums. He bought a house for his parents.

Dwight Gooden enterprises is raking in the money with no end in sight. Oh, sure, an athlete's time in the spotlight is limited, but he's 21. Need more cash? Endorse another product. Spalding shoes wants him for a long-term deal.

His agent, James Neader, says, "Sure he could make $3 million this year. He can make as much off the field as on it. We get calls about Dwight every hour or so. Charity appearances, autographs, insurance, commercials, everything. I like to let him know everything out there, so I keep him posted on the requests, tell him what I think and let him decide which ones to handle."

"Money is good to have," Doc says. "It gives you security. You can do a lot of things for your family. But money hasn't changed my whole way of life. I don't go out and buy a dozen suits. I don't even carry much money around with me."

The Mets are lucky to have such a phenom. Baseball is lucky to have such a young star. He is good for the game. He is the future.

When he arrives for spring training he is surrounded by the press unlike anyone else. He's already won 41 games. Project that ahead for say 20 years and he'll end up with 440 wins. And why not? He would still only be 39 and lots of pitchers have played at that age. He'd pass Spahn, Mathewson, Alexander, and Johnson. Only Cy Young would rank ahead of him and he was of another time.

Such is the talk among those who follow these things. This brilliant young player — emphasis on the "young" — is all about the future. It's why fans follow the game — to imagine what could be. They follow the game because the hope for what is to come is always bright.

This is before the cocaine addiction. It is before the financial and marriage failures. Before the sexual assault charges. Before the violence and battery of a police officer. Before the arrests. Before the suicide attempt. Before the once promising career shatters into pieces.

As fans arrive at Al Lang Stadium in St. Petersburg, they are greeted by a life-sized cutout of a beaming Doc Gooden. For $5 you can have your picture taken with the cutout. Someday you can show your grandkids a picture of you and a cardboard Hall of Fame legend. Five dollars seems a bargain.

Doc's father and twelve other members of his family have made the trip across the bay from Tampa to watch their famous relative go three scoreless innings against the St. Louis Cardinals in his first spring outing. They wouldn't have expected anything less.

"He's just the same shy kid he always was," says Dan Gooden, his father. "It amazes me the way he handles it."

The photographers crowd around the 58-year-old arthritis-ridden man. Anything Gooden-related makes a good story.

"I think this year he feels like he belongs."

Well, that's not much, but at least it's a quote they can use. They've got to have something. This time of the year any news about the phenom will be welcome back in New York.

"He just likes to hang around the neighborhood, same way he always did. He was down here three days after the season. He doesn't like New York."

The reporters scribble in their notepads "Doesn't like N.Y." Now, that's a tidbit worth something.

When Doc finally emerges from the clubhouse smiling, the reporters converge on him. The smile seems more genuine, more relaxed than last year.

"I was nervous in spring training 1984 and 1985, but not this year. This year all my family and friends make it easier. In other years I would have been worried about throwing certain pitches in certain situations. Not this year. Now I just go out and work on things and have a little fun."

"Doc, what are your expectations for this season?"

Gooden smiles the smile of a confident young man.

"A pennant would be nice," his father interjects. "I'll just be tickled if he has another year like the last one."

This seems like undue modesty to many of those wielding pens, pads, and microphones. Players only get better after 21. Joy comes from imagining what will be.

The Cardinals are the team that knocked the Mets from contention in the final weeks of last year's season, so his good performance on this day as they beat the Cards, 8–1, is nice — even if it is only spring training.

No doubt about it, as advertised, Doc is much more relaxed and confident. The Mets fans back home will be pleased.

Neither Doc nor his parents are worried about it, but some think he's being exploited.

Exploited? That's what being a sports star means. Play me, pay me, exploit me, and pay me some more.

General manager Frank Cashen is concerned. Yes, the popularity is good for the club, and yes, he sells tickets — lots and lots of them. Still, the kid can't be pulled in so many directions that he forgets his way to the pitcher's mound.

"Our orders are to protect him, not exploit him," he says. "I give those orders twice a week. All the money they're trying to heap on him could be a curse. It could rob him of his youth. He hasn't yet had the opportunity to enjoy being Dwight Gooden. On the mound, you can see him but not touch him, and that's about the only place in the world where he's safe."

Gooden acts young, talks young, giggles like a kid.

When talking about Gooden as he so often does, Cashen uses words like "protect," "protection," "guard," and "assist." The Mets seem to understand that they're going to have to proctor their huge investment.

Cashen doesn't say it, but he wants to avoid making the same mistake the club did when Darryl Strawberry arrived so highly hyped. Valuable properties have to be protected and they didn't do that with Darryl. He, too, had his face on posters and magazines. He, too, was popular and in demand but he's become difficult to deal with and, at times, a disruptive presence in the clubhouse. Cashen vows to steer Doc in a different direction. If being a general manager these days means babysitting young millionaires, so be it — just so long as they continue to produce on the field and put butts in seats. Cashen has seven kids. He knows a little about babysitting.

Johnson is particularly defensive when it comes to Gooden. One of the first things Johnson did when he took over as manager of the Mets in 1984 was to argue to keep the 19-year-old Gooden on the roster. Cashen was wary about rushing the phenom as he felt they had done a year earlier with Strawberry. Strawberry was coming off a good year at Tidewater and the Mets manager at the time, genial George Bamberger, talked Cashen into keeping him against the GM's better judgment. When the young outfielder struggled to live up to expectations, Cashen believed he should have stuck to his guns. Even years later he believed Strawberry would have developed into a better player with another year of minor league seasoning. He certainly didn't want to make the same mistake with Gooden, but Johnson pressed his case and Cashen let his first-year manager have the kid. Ever since, Gooden has been "Johnson's project" and the manager would go out of his way so as not to be proven wrong.

Gooden's physical tools were obvious, but what particularly intrigued Johnson was the young man's killer instinct. Get two strikes on a batter and he gets even tougher and toughness appealed to Johnson, who always saw himself as that type of player. Gooden, a terrific athlete, was poised, too, Johnson

Dwight Gooden checking a base runner in the first game of the '86 World Series. He will give up only one run but the Mets will lose to the Red Sox 1–0.

observed, as level-headed as any kid his age he'd seen. That and the fact that the Mets had the worst record in the majors the previous year convinced him they needed Gooden a lot more than Tidewater did.

Make no doubt about it, Cashen is the architect of this team. He had played a little ball at Loyola College in Maryland, tried journalism and law school for a while after graduation, and then ended up as advertising director for Hoffberger's National Brewing Company. When that company bought the Baltimore Orioles, he found himself executive vice president of the team. Later when he was part of a cabal trying to oust Baseball Commissioner Bowie Kuhn, he went back to the brewery as senior vice president of marketing and sales.

When Nelson Doubleday, Jr., and Fred Wilpon bought the struggling Mets franchise in 1980, they asked around baseball circles for suggestions as to a strong general manager. When Cashen's name kept coming up, they interviewed the advertising man. Cashen promised to promote the team aggressively. This was, after all, New York and New York was, after all, storied Yankee territory. His idea was to advertise the team on television, emphasizing the old glory days of the team in the '70s with the slogan "The magic is back." Doubleday and Wilpon liked the idea. Cashen promised the new owners a franchise turnaround in four or five years. They liked that even more and offered him $500,000 for a five-year contract. He took it and immediately went to work.

One of his first moves was to draft Strawberry. He promoted Hubie Brooks and Mookie Wilson from the minors and traded for cheeky slugger Dave Kingman, whom he then dumped. Then he brought in the former MVP George Foster, Ron Darling, and Howard Johnson. In one of the most lopsided trades in club history he traded for another former MVP and batting champion, Keith Hernandez, and finally future Hall of Fame catcher Gary Carter. The pieces were almost in place. All he needed was a top-of-the-rotation pitcher.

In 1982 he drafted Dwight Gooden. In 1985 they barely missed the playoffs.

Now if he can just juggle the pieces, handle the diverse personalities, the playoffs seem within grasp.

Cashen knows he needs a strong season from Gooden. Oh, they have Rick Aguilera, Ron Darling, Sid Fernandez, and Bob Ojeda, but no one is thinking about the wording on their Hall of Fame plaques.

In the clubhouse, Cashen sees Gooden acting like the kid he is until the hordes of TV people and reporters descend on him and then all the fun is put away and he tries to act like a grizzled veteran, but it never fits well on him.

Gary Carter glows in the attention he gets. Looks for it, craves it. He almost invites reporters to hang around his locker. Not Dwight. He'd rather hang out with other kids and maybe shoot a few hoops or listen to the radio.

He likes eating his mother's cooking. He likes to go back to Hillsborough High to play in the annual alumni-varsity baseball game. Of course, they don't let him pitch. What would be the fun in watching everyone strike out? No, he plays right field and loves to bat against his nephew Gary Sheffield, who some scouts think might make it to the majors someday — if he can control his temper. He was a star in the Little League World Series of 1980, but even then he had an "attitude" about him.

When a reporter asks Dwight about the last alumni-varsity game, he giggles a little and says, "I went one-for-three. Hit a double off Gary; it was great." He said: 'I'll get you next time.'"

During one spring training game, Doc says a few words to reporters but isn't available afterwards to meet the press.

The next day, Leigh Montville writes in *The Boston Globe*: "What was the big deal? Has the pedestal become so high for these guys that they will sit at the top and dispense a crumb here, a crumb there, and then be carried away by flunkies and attendants on an elevated chair, someone cooling their fevered brow with a large fan?"

Jay Horowitz, the Mets public relations director, takes the blame saying when Daryl Strawberry came along he was supposed to be the savior of the franchise, but the club made so many mistakes by saying yes to all the requests for his time, that they really wore him down.

"When Dwight arrived. I talked with people like Steve Brener of the Los Angeles Dodgers about the way they handled Fernando Valenzuela," Horowitz says. "There are a couple of basic rules: Do nothing on the day he pitches, nothing at all. And don't go into his home. Look, in the spring of 1985, after his rookie season, I could sense he was tired. He didn't smile a lot."

Yes, Gooden is a superb athlete, yes, he along with Strawberry is the future of the franchise, and yes, he is still a kid and a kid with a lot of money and a lot of pressure. What kid doesn't get into some mischief?

"I hear things and read things and, of course, I worry," says Dwight's mother, Ella. "A mother worries about her children all the time. People ask us about Dwight, we tell them, then they don't print it anyway. They only print what they want to print."

And they do.

First comes a report that before spring training even began Dwight was on crutches. His agent says there's nothing to the story. Gooden is just fine.

When he is told Gooden was spotted on crutches near his home in Tampa, he says, "He isn't on crutches now."

Then a story comes out in a New York paper claiming that the ankle was injured when Gooden stepped on a sprinkler.

"He's fine now, he's fine," says Neader. "He'll be working out in a few days again. It was just a little twist."

Not everyone believes the sprinkler story, but then stories about famous people are often viewed with skepticism if not cynicism.

The Mets have the ankle examined by their team physician who declares the ankle will be 100 percent in time for the season. Gooden says he injured the ankle when he tripped over a drainpipe while shagging fly balls hit by his young nephew.

Gooden's former high school basketball coach says he hurt the ankle while playing in a pickup basketball game. Another report says he hurt it while pitching.

Skepticism is rife.

When Gooden misses a spring training workout, he says he and a friend had been in a minor car accident. Later a story comes out saying he wasn't even in the car. Davey Johnson has a closed-door meeting with his pitching ace and then announces Gooden is not injured but he has been fined.

The New York papers refer to the "mysterious auto accident," and wonder about the behavior of their young star.

Then Gooden, his sister, and his fiancée are involved in a shouting match at an airport rental car counter. Gooden reportedly cursed the rental agent. The police are called and his sister is charged with harassment for tossing whiskey in the agent's face. Gooden claims it was only soda.

For days the story is all over the tabloids. Forget about the bombing of Libya. "Doc in Tussle" is more intriguing.

"Dwight is Dwight," his father says. "He can handle himself. He's old enough to know what he should do. He's a good kid."

It's not easy being a superstar in New York. Just ask Mickey Mantle or Roger Maris. The glare of the spotlight is brighter than maybe anyplace else. This is not Kansas City, Doc. This is the biggest apple on the tree.

"I can't do anything right anymore," says a laughing Gooden, who adds he's thinking of bringing all his furniture and moving into the Mets clubhouse so that he doesn't have to deal with the rest of the world.

Billy Reed, his coach back in Tampa, says, "I told Dwight that he was going to the majors, the fast times. I told him New York was the fastest of them all. The people who put you on a pedestal overnight want to tear you down just as fast."

Rumors are the lifeblood of the tabloids. "I was abducted by two-headed aliens" is of more interest to the subway riders than "Reagan to address Congress." Even a rumor without a leg to stand on figures out some other way to get around, and Gooden rumors are getting around just fine.

The Mets brass tolerate, even encourage, some rumors about their players. The right type, of course, just creates more interest in the team and more interest means more tickets sold. But some rumors...

One making the rounds is that Gooden is doing, or has done, drugs. He denies it, of course.

"A month before Dwight went north, I told him what I'd heard," Reed says. "I said, 'Watch yourself.' He said, 'Hey, Coach, you know I'm not doing it.'"

The old coach believes him because he wants to believe him and because he has no concrete reason not to. Still, rumors always leave a little doubt, and doubt no matter how slight is still doubt.

A cop back in Dwight's old neighborhood says there's nothing to the rumors. "Down here word travels fast. If Dwight Gooden were up to anything, believe me, we'd know about it. Believe me."

Many do.

"Doc ain't doing drugs. I know he ain't," says a young fan from Bayside, New York. "Why would he? I mean he's too good and too rich to need anything like that. He wouldn't risk all that. That would be just plain stupid and Doc ain't stupid."

November 1994

Now 29, Gooden, struggling with a 3–4 record and a 6.31 ERA, tests positive for cocaine ... again. He is suspended for the entire 1995 season. His wife finds him in his bedroom with a loaded gun to his head.

His once-promising career is a shambles. According to Sports Illustrated, *he has become "Thor without the thunder." Injuries, alcohol, and cocaine abuse have taken their considerable toll. So too, has the heavy, early-career workload. Before he was 21, he had thrown more than 10,700 pitches. More than half of his career wins will have occurred before he is 25.*

Once a phenom, he is now struggling to hang on to his fast-fading career.

Some papers send reporters down to Tampa to go quote fishing to see what they can come up with about Gooden's past.

"Dwight is a young man I have noticed and observed for a number of years," says a local Sunday school teacher. "He has a lot of friends in the neighborhood and he speaks to everybody. He has not allowed stardom to go to his head. I've seen him try to give notice to everyone, rich, poor, famous, not-so-famous. This is the mark of a positive man."

Some locals suggest that whenever he's in town, Gooden always takes the time to say hello to the good folks of Tampa and to sign autographs. As a result, lots of people claim they "know" Dwight, that they're friends. So when they're asked what Dwight's like, they make up things to demonstrate their connection. Things like knowledge of drug use. Hence the rumors.

"I'm not saying he has never done anything wrong," says Bob Gilder, president of the local NAACP. "But I know of nothing in his life that makes him less than a perfect model for the youth of this city."

Before the year is out, Gooden will be involved in an ugly incident in

Tampa. With a group of friends he spends the evening enjoying himself at a neighborhood Chili's restaurant. When the group becomes a little boisterous they are asked to quiet down. Chris Sullivan, a Chili's manager, later says the group wasn't intoxicated. They were just having fun and got a little loud, that's all.

On the way home, Gooden is stopped for a possible traffic violation and a scuffle with police follows. He is arrested on charges of battery on a police officer, resisting arrest with violence, disorderly conduct, and traffic infractions. So is his 18-year-old nephew, Gary Sheffield, who had recently been drafted by the Milwaukee Brewers.

Battery of a police officer and violently resisting arrest are third-degree felonies carrying maximum penalties of five years in prison and $5,000 fines. The disorderly conduct charge, a second-degree misdemeanor, carries a maximum penalty of 60 days in jail.

The police report says Gooden was driving his silver Mercedes, and Sheffield, a red Corvette. An officer sees the two vehicles weaving toward each other in heavy traffic. When he stops them, Gooden gets out of his car using profane language and refuses to surrender his driver's license.

According to Earl Williams, a Tampa police officer, Gooden took off his gold necklace, stuffed it in his pocket and told officers, "You're not going to take me anywhere."

"One guy pulled a gun and shoved the barrel into my neck," says Gooden.

He is taken to a hospital emergency room where he is given a blood-alcohol test.

"I wasn't drunk," Gooden says.

The hospital says he was.

After he's released, Gooden goes on the offensive. "The cops hit me first. They were laying for me ... it happens a lot with me and the group I hang around with and the cops down there. They put shackles on me for no reason and beat me."

Any Gooden news is grist for the tabloids. They immediately send reporters scurrying to find witnesses who line up for a chance to make the papers in connection with the celebrity.

One says his children were crying when they saw what the police were doing to Gooden.

One says Gooden was being held down by three officers when a female officer rushed across the highway and hit him in the face with a flashlight.

One says he saw a policeman knee him in the back.

One says he saw Gooden hogtied.

He wasn't hogtied say the police. He was handcuffed and his feet were restrained by rope to keep him from kicking. He had already kicked one officer in the head. "That's what we train the officers to do."

Cashen puts the team's spin doctors to work.

Dwight's a good kid. Really he is.

This is just one of those things kids sometimes get into. None of this is his fault but he'll learn to avoid situations like this in the future. And, too, there is veteran leadership on the team.

19. Welcome to the Alpha Male Club

He may be in his fifteenth Major League season, but it's a tough spring for the moody Keith Hernandez. He's going to play first base and bat third for what may prove to be the most talented team in baseball, but he's having a hard time concentrating.

The drug allegations and Ueberroth's response are still very fresh in his mind. The Mets' fans, though, give him a warm welcome when he reports to camp. It's not that they forgive or don't believe the drug charges, but they know they have a chance to go all the way this year, if (and it's a big if) Hernandez doesn't let the distractions get the better of him and affect his play on the field. More than once he's been called "the house pro."

Few of those who were involved in the recent drug mess are having much to say publicly. Hernandez, however, is. He isn't above admitting he is angry about his punishment — the loss of 10 percent of his 1986 salary, the hours of community service, and the random drug tests that would follow him for the remainder of his career.

Yes, he is furious with Czar Peter.

No, he isn't doing coke anymore. Been clean for years. Even the Commissioner acknowledged that.

Yes, he may file a grievance.

No, he's not going to walk away from a $1.35 million contract over a $135,000 fine.

Yes, he confessed publicly, he paid his dues, and now is unjustly being pilloried.

Justice William O. Douglas once wrote: "Once privacy is invaded, privacy is gone. Once a man is forced to submit to one type (of invasion), he can be forced to submit to another."

And what about alcohol abuse? Is that different from cocaine abuse? Does the game suffer more from the image of a coked-up player than from a boozed-up player? What about the lush, Bob Welch? He admitted to being soused half the time. Who knows, maybe even on the mound. What did Ueberroth do? Told him to stop drinking.

Hernandez has certain obligations as the Mets player representative to stand firm against Ueberroth's strong-arm, despotic, dictatorial ploys to enforce mandatory drug testing. If necessary, he will play the martyr's role.

Backman, among others has concerns, though, that despite what everybody is saying, the Hernandez issue is a distraction.

"I'm not saying it was wrong for Ueberroth to do something," Backman says. "Drugs definitely shouldn't be in any sport. I feel for Keith and those other guys. It's bad for the players, bad for the fans, bad for everybody. Nobody's a winner."

Certainly not the Mets, but some of the problem stems from the way Hernandez has chosen to handle the problem. After the first day of spring batting practice, he goes to the clubhouse and sits alone reading his mail. Hate mail or fan mail? He doesn't say. He is proceeding cautiously, quietly. Later he comes out and joins the others for running and exercises. Fans line the fence watching.

"Pay the fine!" a fan shouts.

But how will the fans greet him when he appears in the other teams' stadiums? The question lingers.

Most of the fans want the issue simply to fade away. Take your medicine, Keith. Shut up about it, and lead us to the Promised Land. A flawed hero, maybe, but a hero nevertheless. Besides, you're lucky you didn't get a jail sentence like Vida Blue and the others.

This not the first time he has been angry at baseball. Not by a long shot.

While playing as a junior for Capuchino High School in San Bruno, California, baseball scouts followed him like hounds tracking a fox. A natural, they said. He sprays line drives to every field, and those soft hands at first base ... a can't-miss prospect. There wasn't a Major League team that didn't know about him.

He would very likely be the first pick in the 1971 player draft. The scouts all nodded knowingly whenever someone brought it up. In one day he would go from high school athlete to a wealthy professional.

Then something very strange happened. He deserted the team as a senior. Something about problems in school. Maybe a childish reaction to something or someone, but the scouts didn't like what it suggested. Would he be a problem? Down the draft list he fell.

It wasn't until the 42nd round that the Cardinals finally called his name. Seven hundred and seventy-five players were chosen ahead of him. The Cards' first two picks were Ed Kurpiel and Gary Christophel. He was angry and resentful of the way he was treated.

Everyone knew how good he was and he was determined to prove it. He moved quickly through the Cards' system and in 1974 they called him up. By then he was being hailed as the next Stan "the Man" Musial, a comparison resented by some fans. Musial was a god to the Cardinal faithful and few believed they would ever see his likes again. He was seen as not only a great player, but a great man. So who is this guy they're calling Musial II? The pressure was intense.

The skeptics believed they were right, when after his first two seasons he couldn't get his batting average out of the .250s. What did Musial I do in his first two seasons? Only .350.

In 1979, however, Hernandez raised his average to a league-leading .344 and won the MVP award.

In the 1982 World Series against Milwaukee, he went 0 for his first 15 at-bats, but in the seventh game when he singled with the bases loaded, he became a true Cardinal hero. Nobody played a better defensive first base. Surely he would be a fixture there for years to come. Some long-time followers of the game even opined that he was the greatest fielding first baseman ever.

He moves around first base with the grace of a panther — lithe, agile, and smooth. Who has ever seen better? Mattingly over on the Yankees is good, but he's no Hernandez. Gil Hodges was slick but not too many around now remember him. The old-timers claim that Hal Chase, the Black Prince of Baseball, was the best but no one around now ever saw him play, not even on film. No, put Hernandez in the fielding Hall of Fame alongside the likes of Fox, Mazeroski, Smith, Speaker, Ashburn, Mays, and Clemente.

Then, seemingly out of the blue, Whitey Herzog, the Cards manager, traded him to the Mets for Neil Allen and Rick Ownbey. Allen, the Mets pitcher who had fashioned a less-than-sterling career record of 25–40, and Ownbey, who had won all of two games in the Major Leagues and who would go on to win only one more? And for one of the best players in the game? It didn't make any sense

In addition to the MVP award, Hernandez was a two-time all-star, had won four Gold Gloves, a Silver Slugger Award and owned a .298 career batting average. For Neil Allen and Rick Ownbey? Something was terribly wrong.

The Cards' boo birds, now firmly in Hernandez's corner, had a field day.

The stupidest trade the Cardinals ever made.

We was robbed.

Joe McDonald, the GM, tried to justify what looked as if it were a one-way deal. "It's hard to trade a player of Keith's stature, but we've demonstrated in advance that we have traded many popular players like Ken Reitz and Garry Templeton and Ted Simmons. We're not afraid to do what is best for this club."

The fans were having none of it. Allen was a stiff and Ownbey was useless. Besides, stories said Allen had a drinking problem.

Hernandez told the Mets they would have to pay a heavy price when he became a free agent the next year. He hinted at $2 million.

He was angry. Then he got even angrier.

On the day Willie Wilson and Jerry Martin, two former members of the Royals who had been serving sentences at a federal prison in Texas, were released, Kenneth Moffett, former head of the players union, speaking at a sports symposium in Washington, insinuated Hernandez had been traded because of drugs. He claimed that Herzog had told his players the year before that the FBI had photographs to prove that three players on the team were using cocaine. "Shortly after that," he said, "Lonnie Smith asked to be admitted to a rehabilitation center, then Hernandez was traded to the Mets, and Doug Bair was waived, cut, traded, whatever, and went to Detroit. Draw your own conclusions."

Despite the stories, allegations, apologies, and suspicions, Met fans loved the new first baseman with his magic glove and matinee idol good looks. And why not? All he did in his first two full seasons with them was hit over .300 each year and finish no lower than eighth in the National League MVP voting. During that time Rick Ownbey had won one game and the Cards had already dumped Neil Allen.

Now, as the '86 season is to begin, Hernandez is widely considered the soul of the team — a solid performer offensively and defensively.

Hernandez also has a terrific sense of when and how to calm down an excitable pitcher. A couple of years ago, when he first came over to the Mets, they had a very young pitching staff headed up by 23-year-old Ron Darling, and 19-year-old Dwight Gooden, with 23-year-old Mike Fitzgerald doing the catching. In the field, the shortstop, Jose Oquendo was 20, the second baseman, Wally Backman, was 24, and out in the outfield, Darryl Strawberry was 22.

Cashen pulled Hernandez aside and said, "We want you to handle the press and take the burden off the other players."

So the elder statesman (he was 30) took on the role of mentor, freely distributing the wisdom of his advanced years. He often went to the mound and took upon himself the traditional role of talking with pitchers about pitch selections and generally settling them down.

Later this year in a critical game he will saunter to the mound with Jessie Orosco fast running out of gas and say to Gary Carter, the catcher, "You call one fastball, and we're fighting."

He appears fearless, too, in bunt situations as he comes creeping in so close to the batter that a hard hit ball coming his way will about take his head off. Hernandez's response is that he had his glove to protect his face, his cup to protect his balls, and the baseball could have the rest of him. Like many batters, at the plate he goes through a set routine. He starts by mashing down his dirty helmet with his right hand, and then cleans it off on his pants. Then he windmills his bat and settles into his fidgety stance, pumping his bat a little and shifting his weight until he finds the right alignment.

His father sometimes would call and tell him that if he couldn't see the "Z" on his uniform then Keith wasn't keeping his shoulder in enough. That couldn't have happened too much, because Hernandez was always a solid hitter and a particularly good one in critical RBI situations.

With his teammates, however, he isn't always everyone's favorite. He can be, in the words of one observer, "testy." He is opinionated, strong-willed, and arrogant, wont to hand out advice — some wanted, some not — particularly to Gooden and Strawberry. His influence on them does not go unnoticed and it is a concern.

Gooden/Strawberry/Hernandez may not be the best mix. Exactly what type of advice is Hernandez dishing out? Adopting the older brother role can have its benefits, but it also carries dangers. Davey Johnson sees this but there is not much he can do save for a fatherly conversation with his two young superstars. Who they listen to off the field is up to them. He just hopes they're mature enough to handle any off-field advice from Hernandez with due caution.

Hernandez advises Strawberry on how to break out of a batting slump: Go out and get totally smashed. Strawberry remembers the time Hernandez told him he'd found a dry martini to be the perfect drink because you only need five or six in a night.

Keith's best friend in the clubhouse may be a mirror. At 6 feet, 195 pounds, he is the epitome of what has come to be called the alpha-male. They are ambitious, self-confident, competitive, opinionated, and often difficult to work with and unpleasant to be around.

Animals such as chimpanzees exhibit such behavior as bowing to the alpha male of the group, allowing him to walk first in a procession, or moving away when the alpha challenges. Among humans they often dominate in any group of men and their influence usually carries the day. When it comes to sex with women they take priority.

Welcome to the alpha male club, Mr. Hernandez.

His carefully-groomed hair, full mustache, and athletic body lend an air of unmistakable sex appeal. The days of the paunchy Babe Ruths as baseball sex objects has given way to the sleeker look of the Hernandezs and Cansecos.

Hernandez, who had been involved in a messy divorce the year before, is a sexual animal. But then, many ballplayers, especially on the road, are notorious tomcats and are proud of it. Just ask Mickey Mantle. A certain excitement goes with being a celebrity in a strange town. Still, a ballplayer's notoriety often works as much against him as it does for him. True, it is easier for them to meet women, get into clubs, and receive free drinks, but they can also be devastated by the same type of publicity that makes a rock star legendary. Rock stars represent rebellion; baseball players, true-blue American virtues—a father-son thing.

Hernandez is mentioned frequently in connection with various "affairs," although nothing like outfielder Luis Polonia who was convicted of having sex with a 15-year-old girl.

April 2006

Hernandez, now a broadcaster, complains on air that a female massage therapist is in the San Diego dugout. "I won't say that women belong in the kitchen, but they don't belong in the dugout," he says.

New York Post columnist Phil Mushnick *responds to the controversy: "He's arrogant, vain, condescending, impolitic, opinionated, judgmental, profane, sarcastic, obnoxious and scornful. And because of it, rather than in spite of it, he's among the best pure baseball analysts we've ever heard or ever hoped to hear."*

Someplace along the line somebody hung the nickname "Mex," on Hernandez even though his heritage is Scottish and Spanish with nary a drop of Mexican blood. He has taken a liking to the name as in "Mex, Prince of the Dark Hours."

While he was involved in a particularly acrimonious divorce, he continued to date young ladies. What a catch he was—young, handsome, and rich. The papers linked him with numerous celebrities, most notably Carly Simon. When asked to verify the story, he breaks into a big smile and says, "She's a nice lady."

When she sings "You're so vain, you probably think this song is about you," people nod towards Hernandez.

When Wade Boggs' one-time mistress says, "Wade would jokingly say Keith was a homosexual," most people put the remark down to a last resort comment of a bitter woman.

"It's too ridiculous to even comment on, not even worthy of an answer," says Mex. "I don't know what went on there, whether she said it or not. It's quite apparent that the woman has sunk to the lowest depths."

There are certainly issues all spring swirling around Hernandez, Gooden, and Strawberry. Johnson has his hands full with his talented but contentious club. Thank goodness he has other players on whom he can count to provide stability.

20. Class

Mookie Wilson is, in the words of many a sportswriter, a "classy player." On a Mets team with so many abrasive personalities, he is anything but. He is seemingly always a gentleman, always cheerful, and often underappreciated by the club.

Sometimes his fielding in the outfield is an adventure. He might make a brilliant catch on one ball and then a bonehead error on the next, but he is fast, he hustles, and he is uncommonly loyal to the team and his teammates. He is the team's best base runner, sporting a truly Robinesque style that made a first to third dash one of the most exciting things to witness in baseball.

His gusto and determination make him a fan favorite. When "the Mookster," does something special, the chorus of "MOOOOOOOOOKIE" echoes across Shea.

Some years later when David Letterman put together a list of "Mets Excuses" after one of their dismal seasons, the number one excuse was "No one named Mookie."

Whenever the Mets need someone to represent the club for some civic or charity event, Wilson usually is the first to volunteer.

Need someone to talk the Boys Club? Go ask the Mookster.

He does so much public speaking he should run for office.

Some players do all that stuff for their image, Mookie does it because he actually believes in giving back to the community.

Really?

Really.

He neither smokes nor drinks, but unlike some abstainers, he doesn't make a big deal about it. This automatically eliminates him from some activities of his teammates, but he doesn't seem to mind. He's got other things to do with his time.

"Mookie's Roses," for example. It's a club for young girls that meets once a week at a local community center, where Mookie and his wife invite speakers to talk on such topics as teenage pregnancy.

Mookie Wilson at bat with Ray Knight leading off second in the 10th inning of the sixth game of the World Series. Spike Owen is at short. Wilson will hit a ground ball that rolls through the legs of Bill Buckner for one of the most famous errors in World Series history.

When an ugly racial incident broke out on the University of Massachusetts campus, Mookie and the Red Sox' Marty Barrett went over there to counsel students about race relations.

He spends so much time in the community that he has a much better handle on baseball fans than most players:

> I find that people have no idea about what professional athletes are like. They treat them like statistics. And then people come up to me and have the nerve to criticize ballplayers they don't even know. They completely ignore the fact that they're people. "He makes $500,000? Why should he have the same problems we do?" That attitude upsets me more than anything else. That's part of why I go into the community — to let people know that ballplayers are people, too. But I'll tell you something. In the 10 years I've been speaking in churches and banquets, not once has a fan asked me about my involvement in the community. They want to know what really goes on in the clubhouse, not about my charity work.

There isn't a hint of bitterness when he says this, just disappointment.

He is often called a great "role model" for kids, but he shrinks from the suggestion.

"The future of your kids depends on me? Then you're in trouble," Wilson says. "Your kid sees me play baseball once a week and I'm supposed to be a role model? You sit there with your five Jack Daniels and make me a hero for your kid?"

But Mookie, you've got to understand as a ballplayer you have certain responsibilities.

"Believe me, I realize there's some responsibility. It comes with the territory. But I don't want the responsibility of raising your kid. I don't want eight million Mookies walking around the world. I don't get it."

To a lot of young kids, you guys are gods.

"Why are we gods? How come we have to live above reproach? How come when politicians make mistakes people say, 'Oh, that's politics,' and when show biz people do the same thing, it's the same thing, but when athletes make mistakes, it's BOOM!"

It's just the way it is. It's how things in our world work.

"I don't like it. I don't understand it. We're human, but apparently we're not allowed to make errors."

1999

Wilson, now a coach with the Mets, gets his license to drive tractor-trailer trucks and begins hauling freight in the offseason. He says it's a profession he'll continue after he leaves professional baseball.

The Mets need Wilson's lucidity and focus on a club not loaded with either. They need him, too, to get on base before the big bats come up, but then in a routine spring training run-down drill, a ball thrown by Rafael Santana hits him square in the face, shattering his sunglasses and leaving cuts that need 17 stitches above his right eye and four on the side of his nose. Blood collects in the anterior chamber of the eye in what doctors are calling a "hyphema." They project he will be out for two months.

This is not the way they need to start the season. There is already enough gallows humor in the clubhouse as it is. In 1985 they finished second for the second straight year.

"And next year the Pirates probably'll win 105 games and we'll come in second to them," Ron Darling says facetiously. "We laughed about it then, but sometimes you wonder what it will take."

Coming close sets up expectations, and expectation means more pressure, and more pressure on young players like Gooden and Strawberry is probably not good.

"Coming in second then made us look to first place last year. That was natural," Ron Darling says. "And then, when we didn't win it all last year, it made it a little more urgent for us this year. Second place is getting a little old. People are patting you on the back. But at the same time they're saying, 'Of course you're going to win it all next year. Right?' And I say, 'Right,' because that's what I expect, too."

Maybe coming in third would even be better. "I don't know that I'd want to finish out of it after being so close for two years," Backman says. "It'd drive us nuts if we came real close and came up empty again."

No one says it out loud but there is clearly a "we'd-better-do-it-this-year-or-else," where the "or else" probably includes wholesale personnel changes, including but not limited to players, manager, and coaches.

It's a "must win" situation despite the protestations. "That's putting too much pressure on ourselves." says Hernandez. "What happens then if we come in second again? What do we do, disband?"

"It's not desperation. I don't want to be that negative about it," Johnson says. "I'd rather say this is the year we expect to win."

By the end of spring training, Johnson feels he has the team, with the exception of Wilson, about as ready as he can get them. Lenny Dykstra will have to fill in for Mookie until he's ready to go. "I've been telling people all spring I'm tired of catching the bouquets at weddings. I don't want to be the best man again this year."

Maybe you won't have to be, Davey.

21. Signs of Trouble

Amidst the hopes of spring, there are signs of trouble.

The Chicago White Sox are anything but one big happy family.

Carlton Fisk has his eyes on a Hall of Fame plaque as one of the game's best catchers but they've got him in left field and he isn't happy. "This is like bringing Seaver over here, 27 games from his 300th win, and saying, 'Tom, we want you to be a middle reliever, and it'll only take you 15 years to get your 300th,'" he says.

Tom Seaver isn't happy. "After 300, I'm seriously wondering if it's worth another season of being in Chicago," he says.

Tony LaRussa isn't happy that General Manager Ken Harrelson keeps trying to trade Seaver to the Yankees or Red Sox. He isn't happy either that Harrelson has put in a direct phone line to broadcaster Don Drysdale's booth.

Harrelson isn't happy with LaRussa period and is intrigued by Dick Williams' availability.

It could be a long season in Chicago. Neither the Chisox nor the Cubs look as if they're going to contend.

In Baltimore Cal Ripken is complaining that he keeps hearing the club wants to move him to third base, which would halt his string of 5,457 consecutive innings at short. "It gets tiresome just talking about it," he says. "In a game where stats are so important, they seem to be overlooked in my case. Nobody thinks you're a shortstop unless you're flashy. People don't understand that all the plays are routine when you play where you're supposed to play."

Despite a lineup loaded with top hitters, few things are going right for the Red Sox this spring. Jim Rice is lumbering around on gimpy knees, Wes Gardner, the relief pitcher they picked up during the winter from the Mets, has a bum shoulder and may not even pitch this season, and Sammy Stewart allows 19 base runners in his first 5½ innings and then hurts his leg.

If these aren't enough problems, the team is making so many stupid mistakes that McNamara's hair is turning white and his stomach sour. Runners are regularly being picked off, cutoff men are waiting in vain for throws that never arrive, balls are dropping between fielders as if they were grenades, and hitters are grounding into double plays as if they were being paid by the out.

Even Ted Williams, who makes a trip to the Red Sox training complex in Winter Haven, leaves shaking his head. This does not look like a team ready to contend.

McNamara is widely known to be the quintessential Mr. Nice Guy. Maybe too nice. He had been a peripatetic minor league catcher and manager before getting his first Major League managing shot with the As. He has also had managerial stints with the Padres, Reds, and Angels. The Red Sox brought him aboard last year after the Angels let him go following a season in which they went 81 and 81.

He's gotta toughen up, say his many critics.

With that lineup they should be scoring a zillion runs. Last year alone, the first two hitters in the lineup reached base 621 times in front of sluggers like Rice, Armas, and Buckner and still they finished 18½ games out.

You've got to look at the manager. Something's wrong someplace.

McNamara decides to let everyone know he's a changed man, a new tough boss. He vows the old country club atmosphere will no longer be tolerated:

> I want everyone to know who the manager is and what he expects. They're going to understand that you don't get superstar status until you earn it. You don't just throw your glove out there, you have to go out and do the job. I want 100 percent out of 80 percent if that is all a player can give. Even 100 percent out of 40 percent. If a wife is ill or the kids are sick, I expect the player to block it out of his mind and give his best. I want everyone to do his job to the best of his ability. That would include taking out the garbage. If you take out the garbage, do it right.

McNamara, the new whip-cracker, begins holding closed-door meetings to make his point. First up is the wacky kid, Steve Lyons, whose obvious talents are being overshadowed by his lapses in concentration. He has been known to play tic-tac-toe and hangman with his spikes in the infield dirt.

After a heated exchange between Oil Can Boyd and Bob Stanley over Boyd's agent, McNamara angrily summons both into his office.

"I talked a little about attitudes and the approach to the game," McNamara says. "I asked if anybody had anything to say. I told them to air it all out. I told them my door was always open, that if they want to talk we'll talk and if they want to fight we'll fight. Nobody said a word."

Then on the day of Boston's final exhibition game, the Can is nowhere to be found. He isn't scheduled to pitch in the game with the Tigers, but he is scheduled to sit in the dugout. When he finally makes his appearance more than an hour late, he says he was packing, his dog ran out of the house, and he couldn't find the dog. He is fined $2,150 by the club. They suggest he get psychiatric counseling. He refuses.

Out in Arizona, without any meetings, the tough-talking Padres manager is making lots of players happy—by quitting. Dick Williams is widely recognized as one of the game's premier strategists, and as one of the game's most disliked managers. He knows baseball, when to bunt, when to run. He knows how to win. What he doesn't know is how to keep his players content.

"I got along with the guy good," says Jack McKeon, the Padres vice president of baseball operations. "He didn't bother me, and I didn't bother him. But his attitude toward players was terrible. We knew what we were getting into. He was the right guy for us at the right time. We needed somebody just to get tough, intimidate them and get them to play. He did. But after the players get to know him and live with him long enough, he wears out his welcome."

Williams carries a big chip on his shoulder, say some of the players. He's angry all the time, angry at the money some players make without producing like they should. He's an arrogant, angry, aloof man.

Steve Garvey, hardly a complainer, says,

> It was just an uneasy atmosphere. There were certain relationships that were irreparable. I mean, they couldn't be corrected and would have had an effect on the ball club. It would have been a heavy weight to bear for the team. I think it's better for all this way. Dick would have had as much pressure on him [as the players]. If anything had gone wrong—a losing streak, a problem with a player—all the attention would have been on Dick. It's not fair when that happens.

Williams is replaced by Steve Boros, Williams' emotional opposite. Boros is low key, sensitive, contemplative.

"I think most managers fall into two categories," Boros says. "Some of them keep a certain distance between themselves and the players. I'm with Tommy Lasorda and some of the others who like to stay close, communicate with them. I'm a relaxed type of guy. I just manage that way. It's my style."

Williams had taken the Padres to the World Series just two years earlier, but now the club will turn to a kinder, gentler hand in hopes of returning.

The Mets end spring training in disarray when Rafael Santana badly bruises his left thumb, Gooden is fined for misleading Davey Johnson about his automobile accident, and the team drops four straight games.

"We've stunk it up the last three or four days," Johnson says in a burst of pique after the final game. "The dog days of spring."

Ready or not, it's time for the season to begin.

22. Opening Day

According to a diary left by a soldier, George Washington played an early version of baseball with his men at Valley Forge. John Adams and Andrew Jackson were known to have played bat and ball games, and Abraham Lincoln was apparently a real devotee. One story that made the rounds of the Civil War camps was that the President and his son Tad used to watch Union soldiers play games behind the White House. The story claimed that the President himself played the game back in Springfield, Illinois, and that when informed that the Committee of the Chicago Convention was waiting for him, Lincoln responded: "Tell the gentlemen that I am glad to know of their coming; but they'll have to wait a few minutes till I make another base hit."

President Ulysses S. Grant invited the first all-professional baseball team, the Cincinnati Red Stockings, for a visit to the White House in 1869.

President Taft apparently had less to occupy his presidential time than other presidents as he is known to have attended at least 14 games while in office. He is also the first president to throw out the season-opening pitch, which he did to Walter Johnson in 1910.

President Grover Cleveland, on the other hand, felt quite differently. "What do you imagine the American people would think of me if I wasted my time going to the ball game?" he said.

Pitcher Grover Cleveland Alexander, aka "Old Pete," struggled with almost everything in his life except pitching. Among his other less-than-admirable traits, he was an alcoholic who was known to take the mound under the influence. At least that's the way he was portrayed by Ronald Reagan in the 1952 film *The Winning Team*. In the biopic, poor health and alcoholism force Alexander out of the game and to the brink of complete despair, but through Doris Day's steadfast devotion as his long-suffering wife, (surprise!) Alex the Great battles his way back and gains redemption.

Former player Peanuts Lowery, who was cast in the film as a player, remembers one scene in particular: "I was the player that plunked Reagan with a ball between the eyes as he was heading for second. We used a cotton ball and when I hit him I shouted, 'Look out!' But the director said, 'Cut.' He figured I would get an extra $350 for having a speaking role so we reshot the scene, and after I hit Reagan, I had to look sad and keep my face down as Reagan was sprawled on the ground."

Now President, Reagan takes advantage of the presidential helicopter to make the short trip from the White House to Baltimore's Memorial Stadium. He participates in the pre-game festivities and makes himself at home in the Orioles dugout while the crowd chants, "Ron-nie, Ron-nie." Before the game begins, he strolls out to the infield to join 11-year-old cystic fibrosis victim Brian Gray for the first ball ceremony. Gray throws a perfect strike to Orioles catcher Rick Dempsey. Then it's the president's turn. His ball sails wildly over Dempsey's head, narrowly missing the media.

Nah, the pres wasn't sending a message, was he?

When he returns to the Orioles dugout, he sits next to Ueberroth. Some pundits wonder if the Commissioner is getting tips from the President that he might file away if (when?) Ueberroth decides to change offices again.

Reagan polishes off a hot dog and then leaves after two innings with the Orioles trailing, 3–0. He tells the Oriole players maybe his leaving will bring them luck.

It doesn't.

The season is officially opened and Reagan goes back to the Oval Office where such issues as the Iran-Contra affair will be waiting.

Reagan's political instincts apparently come naturally to him. At one point he says, "I really do love baseball"; another time, "I never cared for baseball."

Either way, he has had a long connection with the game. In the '30s he called baseball games for radio station WHO in Des Moines, Iowa, where "Dutch" (a childhood nickname because of his "Dutch boy" haircut) gained national media exposure recreating Chicago Cubs baseball games. He delivered play-by-play accounts of the games from the radio's studio by reading the telegraph accounts of the games in progress and then inventing the details.

Calling one 1934 game between the Cubs and the Cardinals, he was handed a note in the ninth inning: "The wire has gone dead." Not a man to be thwarted, or to let reality get in his way, he went on to improvise for six minutes during which hitters on both teams suddenly developed a superhuman ability to foul off pitches. As Reagan recalled:

> There were several other stations broadcasting that game and I knew I'd lose my audience if I told them we'd lost our telegraph connections so I took a chance. I had Billy Jurgens hit another foul. Then I had him foul one that only missed being a home run by a foot. I had him foul one back in the stands and took up some time describing the two lads that got in a fight over the ball. I kept on having him foul balls until I was setting a record for a ballplayer hitting successive foul balls and I was getting more than a little scared. Just then my operator started typing. When he passed me the paper I started to giggle — it said: "Jurgens popped out on the first ball pitched."

Tip O'Neill, the longtime liberal Democratic congressman and Speaker of the House, was named "Tip" after James Edward "Tip" O'Neill, a Major Leaguer in the late 19th century. He remembers once when Reagan was sitting by his desk in the Oval Office. "He's sitting over there and says, 'Hey! Grover Cleveland. I played him in the movies.' I said, 'No, you played the baseball player.' From that moment on I knew the nation was in tough shape."

George Bush is often ballyhooed as a "former owner of the Texas Rangers." The fact is, he borrowed $500,000 to buy a very small piece of the club. Tom Hicks remained the CEO and owner. For his investment, Bush reportedly earned a $200,000 annual salary and the public exposure he needed to convince the Texas voters that he had the administrative experience to run for governor. His contribution to the team consisted solely of lobbying for a new stadium for the steroid-riddled club.

April 2008
President Bush is scheduled to throw out the Opening Day first pitch at the Nationals' new stadium. Normally this would go to the club's catcher, but on this day, Bush throws it to Manny Acta, the Nats' manager. It seems associating with the catcher, Paul LoDuca, an apparent life-long juicer, would have been considered detrimental to the president's already plummeting approval rating.

When asked about the steroids issue, the president issued the following statement: "I'm at the ballgame, people. Leave me be."

On Opening Day players find a letter from Ueberroth in their mail boxes. In it are details of his plans for drug testing. According to the commissioner, the players are to be tested up to four times a year for cocaine, marijuana, heroin, and morphine. There will be no test for amphetamines and no penalty for first-time positive test results.

The Players Association is irked that the letter bypassed them and went directly to the players, but at least for now they will whine but refrain from action.

The Red Sox open at venerable Tigers Stadium on a typical chilly Michigan spring afternoon with more than 51,000 fans expecting big things from their Sparky Anderson-led team. With Jack Morris pitching for the Tigers, Dwight Evans, who has promised to swing at more first pitches, drives the first one of the season into the stands. The Sox go on to hit three more, but they can't overcome Kirk Gibson's 4-for-4 day including two long home runs and lose, 6–5. After each of his blasts, Gibson tips his hat to the crowd.

"I put a lot of pressure on myself to justify all I went through over the winter," he says, referring to his bitter contract negotiations with the Tigers. "The last day I can compare this with is the last game of the 1984 World Series."

This doesn't happen very often." In the final game of the '84 Series Gibson also hit two homers and drove in five runs to pace Detroit as they beat the Padres.

The White Sox lose two of the three games in the opening series with Detroit and then move on to Chicago where Roger Clemens gets his first start for Boston and his first win. He scatters 6 hits over $8^{2}/_{3}$ innings handing the Chisox, who are off to their worst start since 1974, their fourth straight loss.

The Red Sox finally get home to celebrate Fenway Park's 75th birthday and the club's 86th American League home opener. It does not go well for Oil Can as the Royals jump all over him and reliever Bob Stanley when they send 12 men to the plate in the league's biggest inning of the season on their way to an 8–2 victory. The packed crowd of 34,764, many of whom had read about Oil Can's shenanigans in spring training, boo him lustily.

Doubts about the pitching are deepened.

After the bullpen blows another save, reliever Bob Stanley is still sitting in the dugout two hours after the game. "I want to make sure no one has a chance to shoot me," he says.

Why can't they get Seaver? Tom Terrific may be 41, but he's no flake and at least he shows up when he's supposed to.

In Milwaukee, Seaver, still pitching for the White Sox, notches his 306th win then calls it "nothing fancy. "I wasn't real pleased with my control," he says. "I would like to be a great artist. I would quit pitching if I could paint like Monet or Rousseau. But I can't. What I can do is pitch, and I can do that very well."

Milwaukee manager George Bamberger agrees. "He still throws good. He knows what he's doing all the time."

Tom Seaver, who virtually single handedly changed the New York Mets from lovable losers into formidable foes, joined the Marine Corps when he was 18 and continued to serve in the reserves until 1970, three years into his Major League career.

The Dodgers drafted him while he was pitching for the University of Southern California, but when he asked for $70,000, the Dodgers passed. The Mets were eventually awarded his rights in a lottery draw. Seaver spent one season with the Jacksonville Suns before the Mets called him up in 1967. He was an immediate sensation, throwing 18 complete games, winning 16 with a 2.76 E.R.A. He was named National League Rookie of the Year and an All-Star. Two years later he led the "Miracle Mets" to the World Series championship by winning 25 games and his first Cy Young Award.

Reggie Jackson once quipped, "Blind people come to the park just to hear him pitch."

"My idea of managing," says Sparky Anderson, "is giving the ball to Tom Seaver and sitting down and watching him work."

Seaver's mechanics are as good as anyone's. He drops his knee almost to the dirt and drives forward powered by his muscular legs. He says it's the legs more than the arm that is responsible for his success. Unlike Boyd, he works hard at his craft and seems always to be prepared. Maybe that's why teammates call him "Boy Scout."

Late in April, the Red Sox are still talking about trying to land Seaver when they beat the Tigers behind Clemens' third win. It's a costly loss for the Tigers who, in addition to losing the game, lose Kirk Gibson to a severe ligament sprain. He was hitting .369. The trainers think he'll be out for 4 to 6 weeks. In the second inning, he cajoled a walk out of Clemens and was about to attempt to steal second when Clemens tried to pick him off first.

"I was leaning the other way a little bit," Gibson says. "I was just scuffling back a little. The bag seemed soft to me. It seemed I slipped when I stepped on it. I knew as soon as it happened I was hurt."

It's a serious blow to the team favored to take the title, but Sparky Anderson tries to downplay it. "This could be a blessing. People are going to have to pick up the load. Everybody is talking about Gibby, but now they have to step in front of a mirror and say, 'What about me?' We're a mediocre club if we can't win without one big man."

Yes, they are.

On Opening Day in the AL West, Bobby Grich and Reggie Jackson hit first-inning home runs to stake the Angels to a 3–0 lead. Jackson's homer puts him within three of seventh place on the all-time list, but the Angels lose the game when Seattle's Jim Presley hits a two-out grand slam in the bottom of the tenth.

The 80-year-old coach with the snow white hair and sparkling eyes sitting on the Angels bench just nods. Jimmy Reese has seen this before — this and a lot more. He has been involved in the game since he was a young boy who sneaked into minor league games in the old Pacific Coast League. Now 68 years later he can look back on a career as a player, manager, coach, scout, and, at one time, Babe Ruth's roommate. He's told that story scores of times and he'll continue to tell it as long as there is anyone to listen. After all, there are lots of guys who can tell stories of players, manager, and coaches, but how many can start sentences with "Oh yeah, the Babe and me, we used to..."

"I was going to have dinner at their house one night, and I sat in the car waiting for him for more than an hour while he signed autographs outside the stadium," Reese says. "He signed them all. His wife was mad when we were late for dinner, but it was OK when I told her what he'd been doing. The Babe never refused a kid an autograph and never took a penny for doing it neither."

Reese says that a lot of people don't realize how influential his buddy the Babe was. "He made the huge sum of $80,000, and that allowed other players to say to the owners, 'Let's see, if Babe's worth $80,000, I'm worth $20,000.' It changed everything," Reese says. "And after the Black Sox Scandal, a lot of people stayed away from baseball. But they came back to see the Babe. When he just walked onto the field, you could feel the electricity in the crowd."

Reese's favorite subject, though — and he'll talk for hours about it if given the chance — is how the game has changed.

The fields were a lot rougher back then. No bad hops on the carpets.

There were no fancy toys like radar guns or video tape machines.

The diets are better today, though, so the players are in better shape.

Can you imagine what the Babe would do on a diet of supplements other than scotch? No, wait, maybe not as good. Stengel was known to argue "I have found that the ones who drink milkshakes don't win many games."

Nevertheless, the players play longer today because of being in better shape, and for the most part, they're better educated. "I think John McGraw would have trouble with the players today," Reese says. "That old type of roughness, where the manager was king, just wouldn't work."

Dan Quisenberry once said of the Braves' Ted Simmons, "He didn't sound like a baseball player. He said things like 'Nevertheless,' and 'If, in fact.'"

Any way you look at it, says former pitcher Jim Bouton, baseball players are smarter than football players. "How often do you see a baseball team penalized for too many men on the field?" he asks.

The reality is, though, that baseball changes very slowly — and that's the plan. It's the tradition of the game that goes back to the 1840s that is a large part of its appeal. It's the fathers-playing-catch-with-their-sons idea. Too much change, or too fast change, and the connections stretch and break. It is a conservative game at heart. Former club owner Bill Veeck says, "Baseball is the most unchanging thing in our society — an island of stability in an unstable world, an island of sanity in an insane world."

Orioles owner Edward Bennet Williams says of his fellow owners: "They move very, very, reluctantly. I think it was a long time before any of them had inside plumbing."

"I believe in the Rip Van Winkle theory," says Bowie Kuhn, "that a man from 1910 must be able to wake up after being asleep for seventy years, walk into a ballpark, and understand baseball perfectly."

In fact, one could look back on a Knickerbocker game of the late 1840s and have no difficulty at all in understanding the game the hirsute men were playing. A few things would look odd — underhanded pitching, no called balls and strikes, no fielder's gloves, outs made by catching the ball on one bounce, the catcher standing well behind the batter, and uniforms that looked more like firemen's. But the field would look similar and so would the position of the players, although the basemen played a little closer to their bases than they do today and there may or may not have been a shortstop. The rules played were not significantly different and the object was, as always, to score more runs or "aces" than your opponent. In the very earliest days, they played to 21 aces, but later they put in the 9-inning rule.

Who invented the game? Nobody. Certainly not Abner Doubleday or Alexander Cartwright. The game simply evolved from a myriad of earlier stick-and-ball games and probably trumped other similar games here like cricket, because cricket was British and at a time when anti–British sentiments still flourished.

So baseball was adopted by the Americans as theirs, and woe be to anyone who tried to alter its essential characteristics. Such radical changes as the designated hitter rule still strike the purists as sacrilege.

"The designated hitter rule is like letting someone else take Wilt Chamberlain's free throws," argues Rick Wise.

"Putting lights in Wrigley Field is like putting aluminum siding on the Sistine Chapel," says Roger Simon.

"Every player should be accorded the privilege of at least one season with the Chicago Cubs. That's baseball as it should be played — in God's own sunshine. And that's really living," says former shortstop and manager Alvin Dark.

Despite its problems and its reluctance to change, this deeply rooted game remains popular. Early attendance figures this season are at an all-time high. Then again, maybe it's because it doesn't change rapidly that it remains so popular.

23. Early Season Oddities

The season is off to a start with about as many surprises as a Gene Autry western. By the end of April, the Mets are already showcasing their dominance; the Angels and Astros are in front in their divisions; and the Red Sox are within 2½ games of the Yankees.

It is, however, already showing signs of the oddities that seem to imbue every year with the personalities and quirks that keep fans engaged in the long summer of games, many of which have no bearing on the eventual outcome of the season.

Like all the other Indians, Jamie Easterly wears a uniform with his name on the back. The fact that he was playing in the misspelled shirt goes unnoticed by him for five days.

Mickey Mahler is quoted in *USA Today* as saying that were he commissioner of baseball for a day, he'd send every player with three straight years in the majors "back to Triple A for one month, just to let them see what it's like so they won't forget how good they have it now." As poetic justice would have it, the next day the Rangers ship Mahler to Triple A.

After the Angels' Jim Slaton goes six straight starts without a win, his 260-pound brother, Frank, announces he's going on a hunger strike until Jim wins another game. A few days later Jim is removed from the rotation. Presumably Frank is wasting away someplace.

How long can you go without eating? Someone tells him the longest hunger strike on record is something like 75 days but he can expect to die well before that. When, at the end of June, Jim is released by the Angels, Frank is either very hungry or has decided the deal is off.

While the Angels are playing the Twins at the Metrodome, heavy rains and winds rip the roof open, dumping rain on the field and causing the lights to swing wildly. It is, as Yogi Berra once said, déjà vu all over again, as fans remember "the sky is falling" episode, when snow caused the roof to collapse.

"I wanted to get out of there," says Joyner. "I've never seen anything like it."

Given the number of home runs being hit this season, pitchers are searching for excuses. Twins pitcher John Butcher, who by mid-June is 0–3 with a 6.30 ERA, thinks he knows the reason for his struggles — the ball, which is being made in Haiti, has been juiced up because Haitian women aren't raising their kids to be pitchers.

"They want their sons to grow up to be hitters," he claims, "so they're wrapping the ball real tight. What we [pitchers] need is for more Haitian women to want their sons to grow up to be pitchers."

Teammate Gary Gaetti concurs that the balls are being wrapped tighter. However, he opines that the reason is more political than it is sociological and stems from the deposing of the Duvalier family of dictators. "Since the overthrow of the government," he says, "the women are happier. They're doing a better job."

Like everyone else in their division, the Phillies are rapidly losing contact with the Mets. Nevertheless they decide that alienating the beat writers can't make things worse so they ban them from traveling with the team on their charter flights. It seems that on a flight home from the West Coast the plane was so overloaded that the players were asked to leave their golf clubs behind. So that this terrible fate wouldn't befall them again, the writers would henceforth be left behind in their stead. Upon careful analysis, *Philadelphia Daily News* writer Bill Conlin estimates that this will allow the Phillies to accommodate 13 sets of golf clubs.

The Dodgers announce they will build the Dodger Baseball Field at the Tianjin Institute of Physical Culture in the People's Republic of China. Dodger president Peter O'Malley and Institute president Jia-Oi Chen participate in the opening ceremonies.

"All of us in the Dodger organization believe that this contribution to international amateur baseball will encourage the athletes in China to participate in the great game of baseball and, hopefully, hasten the growth of the sport throughout the country," O'Malley says. "The future of baseball in the People's Republic of China is very bright."

In March 2008, the Dodgers and Red Sox play the first Major League exhibition game in China. The stands are full of Chinese, Japanese, and South Korean baseball enthusiasts, as well as Beijing Little League and high school teams in full uniforms.

The American ambassador throws out the first ball to wild cheers. The first ball hit is a high pop foul and the cheer is even louder.

In the top of the ninth inning, the Dodgers' Taiwanese shortstop, Chin-Lung Hu, comes to the plate.

An American reporter asks a fan, "Are you cheering for the Dodgers because this Taiwanese guy is on their team?"

"I was," the fan says, "but he seems to commit double murder more often than he gets on base."

The translation of "double play" needs a little work yet.

With the first pick in the amateur baseball draft, the Pirates take power-hitting third baseman Jeff King, out of the University of Arkansas. Broadcaster Ralph Kiner, known for his malapropisms, said of King, "Half of Jeff King's extra-base hits last year went for extra-bases."

The Mets would love to have drafted Gooden's nephew Gary Sheffield, but he goes to the Brewers with the sixth pick. He is highly regarded as a pitcher-shortstop at Gooden's alma mater in Tampa. His fastball has been clocked at close to 90 mph, but it is more likely that he will be used as a third baseman. In last year's alumni game he got a hit off of Uncle Dwight. The Mets end up selecting Lee May, a player with the same name as the big first baseman who played for four teams from 1965 to1982 and ended up hitting 354 home runs. The Mets' Lee May hits none as he never makes it to the Major Leagues.

The Mets haven't cornered the market on fighting. In St. Louis, with the Cardinals leading, 10–2, Vince Coleman steals both second and third. When the Giants' reliever retaliates by hitting Coleman with a pitch, the obligatory fight breaks out, injuring several players.

The Cardinals' Whitey Herzog defends the steals by saying that if Giants manager Roger Craig "will send a promissory note guaranteeing they won't score any more, then we won't run. I hope Roger Craig loses 20 games in a row. He thinks he invented the game."

Craig responds, "If Vince Coleman wants to steal 100 bases and get 50 in situations like that, the hell with him. I'd rather see a real professional like Ozzie Smith who steals bases when it means something. He doesn't pull that bull for personal glory."

24. The Rocket

There are those in the game who think the 23-year-old pitcher Roger Clemens is already on track for Hall of Fame induction someday. He's big, he throws hard, he's intimidating the way he throws inside so much, and maybe he's an angry pitcher.

"Everybody kind of perceives me as being angry. It's not anger, it's motivation," he insists.

His intensity is what gets the attention of so many players. Derek Jeter says he's "in another world when he's pitching. He's there but he's not there."

But there are those who begin to notice the diva-ish behavior that will come to characterize him later in his career. Within the year he will grant an interview to a Boston TV station, in which he complains about the Red Sox, the cramped amenities at Fenway Park, and about having to carry his own luggage through an airport. Other players whined to each other about the same things, but they didn't embarrass the team that paid them by saying it on television.

Clemens will also be accused of racially insensitive comments. When asked why so many Japanese and Korean fans were at the World Baseball Classic, he said, "All the dry cleaners were closed."

The biggest complaints about him, however, will come from those who think that once he becomes a star, he will continually ask for special considerations, setting him apart — above — his teammates. Roger cares about Roger's stats and the hell with anything else, goes the complaint.

He's a great pitcher who wants to make damn sure everyone knows it.

He craves wins like an addict craves crack — wins in his column.

Team wins? Who cares about those?

At various times in his long career he will ask for — and get — such privileges as not having to travel with his team on road trips, and the "family plan" that allows him to leave the team to visit his family when he is not scheduled to pitch. Some players resent this but say little because Roger wins big games for them.

That man doesn't have a loyal bone in his big body scream those fans when he leaves their team to sign for more money elsewhere, something he will do frequently.

"A good for nothing mercenary, a money-grubbing scumbag who saddled his children with obnoxious, fake names that represent his achievement," says a fan.

"The modern day Judas," says another.

Then, too, despite his glowing statistics and stellar record, there are those who think Clemens fails to perform his best under pressure.

Clemens' parents separated when he was still an infant. He went to high school in Texas where he played baseball, football, and basketball. Drafted by the Mets, he elected instead to enroll in college. He pitched two seasons at the University of Texas, where he was an All-American and helped them to win the 1983 College World Series. On that same Texas team was Calvin Schiraldi, his current pitching teammate on the Sox. Schiraldi had also been drafted by the Mets, but after two seasons with them he was traded to the Red Sox in a multiplayer deal that sent Bob Ojeda to the Mets. All three pitchers will play important roles in this postseason.

At one point during the 1983 season while at Texas, Schiraldi headed their rotation, with Clemens dropping down to the third spot, but in the final game of the College World Series Clemens tossed a seven-hitter against Alabama to improve to 13–5 on the season.

"Some people said this wasn't a close ball club but we were close," said Clemens. "We wanted to win this one bad. The media has been on us all year and I tell you we came through when we had to." Clemens' reputation as a big-game pitcher had begun.

The first round of the '83 amateur draft was particularly pitcher heavy. Tim Belcher was the first overall pick, followed by pitchers Stan Hilton, Jackie Davidson, Darrel Akerfelds, Ray Hayward, Joel Davis, Rich Stoll, Wayne Dotson, Brian Holman, Erik Sonberg, and then Roger Clemens.

The Red Sox said he had a body that reminded them of Robin Roberts and Tom Seaver and sent him to Pawtucket of the International League. He didn't stay there long, however.

A dispute was ongoing between two groups fighting for ownership of the Red Sox. The judge hearing the dispute told the principles that while he was deciding the issue, they should "get some pitching."

So after only a couple of months in the minors, the Sox brought Clemens to spring training in 1984 where he made his debut by pitching three scoreless innings in an exhibition game against the Los Angeles Dodgers and their rookie prospect, Orel Hershiser.

"This is the best, most poised young pitcher I've seen since Tom Seaver: great rising fastball, pretty good curve, and he don't get scattery," said Detroit's Sparky Anderson.

Nevertheless, the Sox sent the 21-year-old back to Pawtucket to start the season. After seven appearances there, he was brought back up to begin what would become a long and productive Major League career.

In 1985, the Sox led by Buckner, Boggs and Rice came in fifth in the AL East. With Oil Can Boyd, Bruce Hurst, Al Nipper, and Bobby Ojeda getting most of the innings, Clemens was used sparingly. His ERA was the best among the starters, however, and the Sox think '86 will be his coming out year.

They call him "The Rocket." He works hard, too. McNamara likes that. He's a big kid, but he's not lazy when it comes to working out.

February 2008.

Roger Clemens, looking tense in a nice suit and tie, sits behind a microphone facing a congressional committee. "Let me be clear," he says. "I have never taken steroids or HGH."

Former Yankees trainer Brian McNamee says he did.

Former teammate Andy Pettitte says he did.

Most fans think he did.

Four professors from the University of Pennsylvania have recently completed a study of pitching statistics and have concluded that Clemens' late-career success was statistically highly unusual. Most pitchers, they claim, peak with their best numbers around the age of thirty and decline significantly in their mid-thirties — precisely the point in his career that Clemens has been accused of using performance-enhancing drugs. As he neared his 30th birthday his numbers declined, then spiked in his late 30s and early 40s.

Roger tells the Congressmen about his generosity, about his charitable works, about his good deeds.

Many think the Rocket, a serial retiree, is losing his PR battle as well as his ticket into Cooperstown.

The seven-time Cy Young Award winner, whose biography website says he is considered one of the greatest Major League pitchers of all time, is facing the toughest switch-hitters of his career. As Brian Wice writes in The Houston Chronicle:

> From my seat in Room 2154, an ornate chamber in the Sam Rayburn Office Building, I saw Roger Clemens painfully stumble through an almost five-hour hearing last week before the House Committee on Oversight. Clemens' helplessness called to mind the words of another Texan some 40 years ago. When asked about the morass that Vietnam had become, Lyndon Johnson remarked, "I feel like a hitchhiker in a Texas hailstorm; I can't run, I can't hide, and I can't make it stop." In about 60 days — less than one-third of a baseball season — Clemens has gone from icon to punch line; from Cy Young to sayonara.

As if that weren't enough, country singer Mindy McCready tells the press that she was a 15-year-old aspiring singer when she met Clemens in a bar. By that time, Clemens was married with children and an established star. She says they were romantically linked for years and that Clemens supported her financially.

Clemens' attorney admitted that a relationship existed, but described McCready as a "close family friend."

Clemens had shoulder surgery to repair torn cartilage last August. "All that injury is behind me. I'm tired of hearing about that. I'm going to come back from anything," he says and then goes out and sets the single-game strikeout record previously shared by Nolan Ryan, Tom Seaver, and Steve Carlton, by striking out 20 Mariners.

Clemens doesn't know he's on the verge of setting the all-time record, until the top of the ninth inning when fellow Red Sox pitcher Al Nipper tells him. Clemens says that after that the entire inning was all adrenaline.

Ueberroth doesn't think that's an illegal drug, does he?

The plaudits come rolling in.

"I have to say that was the most awesome piece of pitching I've ever seen," McNamara says. "I saw Catfish Hunter pitch a perfect game. I've seen Mike Witt pitch a perfect game. But this rates right at the top."

"The only one I've ever seen throw like that is Dwight Gooden," says Steve Yeager.

"I think we all should be happy we were here because I don't think we'll ever see that again," says Seattle's manager, Chuck Cottier. "I know I'll never see it again for as long as I live."

"Where's the asterisk?" cry the cynics. It was against the Mariners for christsake. Mother Theresa could strike out 15 and Helen Keller probably a dozen. The Mariners! They've already struck out 186 times this season and it's still April. That averages out to more than nine a game and they have a team batting average just slightly above .200. They have not had back-to-back hits in an inning over a 74-inning stretch.

Still, regardless of the competition, incredibly, he threw 97 of his 138 pitches for strikes and did not walk a batter.

The Sox and their fans are thrilled with the first true phenom they've had since Jim Lonborg's career came to a crashing halt in a skiing accident. After his record-setting performance against the Mariners, Clemens gets a call from Cooperstown requesting his glove, cap, uniform, and spikes. He immediately calls his family. "I'm in the Hall of Fame!" he tells them and promises he'll take them all there soon to look at his former equipment.

25. La La Land

In late May, the Dodgers come calling on the Mets with their ace, Fernando Valenzuela. Fernandomania may have quieted some since he made his debut in 1980, but his abilities haven't. He will win 21 games this year, but not this one. In the second inning George Foster hits a home run and the Mets go on to sweep the three-game series.

After the game Fernando's torso looks as if he's about to be mummified, wrapped as it is in elastic bandages pressing ice to his elbow and shoulder.

"I have to be careful of, of..."

In Spanish he asks Lasorda for the right word.

"Inflammation," Tommy says. Lasorda had spent a few years pitching for the Cristobal Motta's in the Canal Zone Baseball League, so he knows some Spanish. "All last year we tried to teach him English, and the only word he learned was 'million,'" says Tommy.

After Valenzuela pitches back-to-back shutouts, Lasorda says, "I want to thank the country of Mexico from the bottom of my heart for giving us Fernando. It's a great country and if they ever need me to fight for them, I'll be glad to go down there."

Lasorda, whose Major League pitching career consisted of $58⅓$ innings, insists he knows a lot about pitching strategy.

In 1984, Padres manager Dick Williams accused Lasorda of instructing Dodger pitchers to throw at his batters.

"I think that is very, very bad, for that man to make an accusation like that. That is terrible," said Lasorda, who added:

> I have never, ever since I've managed, ever told a pitcher to throw at anybody, nor will I ever. And if I ever did, I certainly wouldn't make them throw at a fucking .130 hitter like Lefebvre ... or fucking Bevacqua who couldn't hit water if he fell out of a fucking boat. And I guaran-fucking-tee you this, that when I pitched and I was gonna pitch against a fucking team that had guys on it like Bevacqua, I'd send a fucking limousine to get the cocksucker to make sure he was in the motherfucking lineup because I'd kick that cocksucker's ass any fucking day of the week. He's a fucking motherfucking bigmouth, I'll tell you that.

Lasorda can talk up a blue streak in at least two languages, and since he also played for several seasons in Canada, where he became the winningest pitcher in the history of the Montreal Royals, he could probably throw in a little French, too, if the occasion called for it.

With his arm in an ice holster, Valenzuela reminds Lasorda of Sandy Koufax and the elaborate post-game ice routine he went through after every game trying to stem the tide of his advancing arthritis. Valenzuela isn't nearly as brittle, but he does have to be careful. If the Dodgers have any chance at all this year, they will need him.

About his pitching staff, Dodger catcher Mike Scioscia says, "We have Mexicans, Hawaiians, Germans, and a couple of guys who have no idea where they come from or where they're going."

The Dodgers have already lost Pedro Guerrero. Guerrero, whom Bill James, the baseball stats guru, called "the best hitter God has made in a long time," may have been able to hit a ball but he couldn't slide as well as most Little Leaguers. In spring training he ripped apart a tendon trying and is now maybe lost for the season.

Guerrero, who comes from San Pedro de Macoris in the Dominican Republic, struggles with his English, but then as one fan suggested, "He's illiterate in two languages."

Don Rickles once asked him, "How long are you gonna make you wife clean hotel rooms?" Guerrero didn't seem to get the insult.

A few years later, his attorney, defending him on drug conspiracy charges, called Guerrero a "simpleton, an 11-year-old mind in a grown man's suit," who was easily manipulated because his IQ was in the low 70s. Guerrero was acquitted. After the trial, his attorney said, "Pedro told me I'm the greatest lawyer in the world, and I told him he's the greatest Dodger." When asked if 'dodger' should be capitalized, the attorney said, "I'll leave that up to you."

It doesn't take a genius to hit a baseball. Just ask Joe Jackson, even Pete Rose.

Regardless, last year Guerrero was easily the Dodgers' best weapon. He hit .320 with 33 home runs. This year they'll have to rely on Mike Scioscia, Greg Brock, and Steve Sax — quite a drop off.

So now it's Fernando and a few prayers. Just days before the Mets series, Valenzuela two-hit the Expos and then the Phillies. On three days rest.

"The last time there were two games pitched like that was Johnny Vander Meer when he pitched back-to-back, no-hit, no-run games against Brooklyn!" Lasorda said. "Fernando! Every time he goes out there, you see the tremendous ability he has! The tremendous poise he displays! The tremendous heart he has."

The loss to the Mets is but a small bump on the road to Valenzuela's superb season.

26. You Gotta Believe

For many Mets fans, games against the Dodgers are special. Beating them means more than just beating another team. In fact, many Mets fans were once Dodger fans, but when in 1957 that cigar-smoking, double-chinned, money-grabbing son-of-a-bitch Walter O'Malley unceremoniously carted the Dodgers off to La La Land, taking the Giants with them, they were left with but three choices: root for the Yankees, move to California, or wait and hope.

The Yankees? You kidding me? Those pin-striped, starch-collared, arrogant stiffs ain't getting my support. I'd rather root for the Soviet Union. No, the Yankees are definitely out.

And we ain't goin' to California, period. Don't you know New York is the center of the universe? Anyway, they got quakes out there and isn't the whole loony state supposed to fall into the Pacific Ocean or something?

We'll wait. Look, New York can't be without a National League franchise for long. It's New York, for christsake, not Skunk Hollow.

By pulling out, the unsentimental Walter Francis O'Malley ushered in the era of baseball as big business. That was almost thirty years ago but the consequences are still being felt.

No sooner had the Dodgers and Giants left for greener economic pastures than numerous proposals were floated for expansion, presumably to include a new team for New York. But owners balked.

The league revenues will be spread too thinly.

We don't want to lose players in whom we've invested considerable time and money to an expansion draft.

There just isn't enough baseball talent anywhere to stock new teams. The quality of play will be down everywhere and the fans won't support that. We'll all end up losing money.

Most New Yorkers couldn't understand how the universe could continue to remain in balance without a National League baseball club in their fair city. Washington may have been the center of political life in the U.S but New York was the center of just about everything else — art, commerce, culture, and delicatessens.

New Yorkers weren't going to put up with being shut out of the National League for long. Two years after being jilted, feisty attorney William Shea announced the formation of the Continental League, a third major baseball league. The new venture was to be run by men not associated with either the National or American Leagues and was intended to tap into new markets. Shea took on the herculean task because he said he was an Irishman who got mad.

He went to Major League officials for cooperation and they told him, in effect, to get lost. "They made a mistake when they said that to Bill Shea," said Wheelock Whitney, Jr., one of the potential new owners.

Shea likes to be portrayed as a spunky Irishman. "They kicked me in the teeth," he said. "I don't let anybody do that."

Until he was tapped by New York Mayor Robert Wagner to head up the city's efforts to acquire a new franchise, the six-foot, 200-pound New York native had lost interest in baseball. He didn't, however, lose interest in doing what others said couldn't be done. He basked in the attention when he did it anyway. "Bill Shea triumphs over impossible odds," is a lead story he is always eager to read.

He initially tried to talk any one of several existing franchises into moving to New York. "The New York Reds" had a nice ring to it he thought even if Joseph McCarthy would have screamed, but he was turned down by the Cincinnati owners. He was rebuffed, too, by the Pirates and Phillies. So, he was left with the new league idea. He wasn't particularly eager to take on Major League Baseball, but there didn't seem to be any other way to get the job done.

Publicly he said he was anticipating the full cooperation of organized baseball, but he knew the reality would likely be quite different. The pugnacious promoter went to work on potential owners in several cities and announced they would start with franchises in Houston, Minneapolis–St. Paul, Denver, Toronto, and of course, New York. Then he announced he would meet with American and National League officials to work out details of player distribution, territorial rights, pension plan inclusion, television policies and participation in the World Series.

Shea may be a dreamer (some say schemer) but he is not naive. He knew very well that organized baseball was scared stiff of at least two things: the courts and the Congress. A fight with their new organization could drag baseball into both. He told everyone willing to listen that he didn't want a war but wasn't afraid of one and argued that organized baseball had to accept them because he was offering them the "greatest deal in their history."

"It can't cost them a thing," he said. "It creates vast new areas of interest and income with no risk on their part. On what grounds would they object to a deal like that?"

His plans included the new league playing a 154-game schedule in 1961 with at least eight clubs, and then adding franchises to be selected from Buffalo,

Montreal, Atlanta, New Orleans, Portland, San Diego, Indianapolis, Dallas–Fort Worth, Seattle, and San Juan, Puerto Rico.

To add credibility to their efforts, the organizers brought in Branch Rickey, the former Dodger president, and named him league president. Rickey's name brought immediate credibility to the new enterprise.

Jack Kent Cooke, slated to be an owner, said their aim was to develop the new league quickly enough to enter into a round-robin World Series within a few years. "And the day will come," he said, "when the Continental League will win the World Series and we will really be made there."

Shea, not wanting to appear too aggressive to the Major Leagues, added, "Of course, the Continental League's champion might not win it for a while but can you picture anybody saying it's not a league when it does?"

Well, Ford Frick, the Commissioner for one, and then all the other owners.

So officials of the new league were forced to go to ask Congress for help. Surely congressmen would go to bat for their districts wouldn't they? Baseball, hot dogs, apple pie, and all those good American things bring in votes, don't they? Senator Estes Kefauver, who was then campaigning for re-election in Tennessee, introduced a bill calling for an unrestricted player draft in Major League Baseball to give the new league a boost. It would also have spelled out limited exemptions from the antitrust laws for professional baseball, football, basketball, and hockey. It would have made players owned by the Major Leagues subject to unrestricted draft once a year except for 40 on each club's roster. It would also apply to players with four years of service in the minors.

When the Senate handily defeated the fighting Irishman, Bill Shea called it a severe blow but swore they weren't finished.

The top brass in Major League Baseball wanted no part of a competitive league, so they were thrilled with the bill's defeat. But just to be sure that the idea wouldn't keep rising from the ashes like a Phoenix, they agreed to expand by adding two teams in each of the existing leagues. And so ended the saga of the putative Continental League.

New franchises were added in Washington to replace the team that had relocated to Minneapolis–St. Paul, and in Houston. Then to give the American League a presence on the West Coast, they added the Los Angeles Angels. The fourth franchise would go to a National League team in New York.

The Continental League's New York franchise had as its principal owners, Charles Shipman Payson and his wife, Joan Whitney Payson. M. Donald Grant was chairman of the board. As soon as they were offered an expansion slot by Major League Baseball they jumped at it.

New York baseball fans (those who weren't Yankee fans anyway) were ecstatic.

Good riddance to the turncoat Dodgers and Giants; welcome to the...

What should we call the new team? Certainly nothing that harkened to the deserters. Suggestions come pouring in, and for a time many New Yorkers became obsessed with the possibilities. The new club announced it received over 750 suggestions, "but none seem quite to fit."

Exactly what does it have to fit? Apparently they wanted a name that reflects New York.

For a time the front runner seemed to be the "Empires," since that's what New York calls itself. Then came the "Skyliners," presumably because it suggests what New York has, followed closely by the "Islanders," which suggests what New York is.

Since the team will probably be pushovers for a few years to come, someone suggested that as a name. Other names presumably reflecting the city were proposed: "Addicts," and "Muggers."

A young fan wrote to the club suggesting the "Impires," since they're so famous for the Impire State Building.

Another fan wrote, "I don't care what you call 'em. Just get the show on the road. I'm 86 years old and haven't got too much time."

The club even contacted the Hanover Farms who screen names for nearly 200 harness racing yearlings each year and they sent an SOS to Alfred Gwynne Vanderbilt who was famous for coming up with interesting names for his race horses.

Mrs. Payson prefered "Meadowlarks," since Flushing Meadows was the site of their proposed new ball park, and presumably because "Flushings" doesn't seem to convey the right image.

The club finally cut the list to these possibilities: "Avengers" (as in "avenging" the loss of the Dodgers and Giants), "Bees," "Jets," "Mets," "Rebels," "Continentals," "Skyliners," and "Skyscrapers."

Then ignoring the more poetic or romantic names, they settled on "Mets," as it reflected their corporate name — the New York Metropolitan Baseball Club, Inc. So much for creativity. The name was short and thus would fit nicely in newspaper headlines. It was also a name used by an early New York team playing in the American Association in the 1880s. Then, so as to appeal to the former Dodgers and Giants fans, they chose as their team colors, orange from the Giants and blue from the Dodgers.

In October 1961, the new Mets took part in the expansion draft. Rather than stocking up on young players with upside potential, they relied more on faded stars with Dodger, Giant, or Yankee connections. Nostalgia was to be the order of the day.

Understanding that it would be some time before they were a highly competitive club, they opted instead to be a highly amusing club. George Weiss, the president, signed 71-year-old legendary Casey Stengel to be the first manager, saying, "Casey is the ideal man to handle the type of team we will inherit."

"Most people are dead at my age. You could look it up," Stengel said.

For the new club, a clown was a better choice than a sage, and a clown with New York connections is even better. He was chosen as much for his publicity value as his baseball knowledge. He was a walking quote generator in a city with a lot of newspaper readers. "Good pitching will always stop good hitting and vice versa," he said. With the players the team had collected, they're going to need his quotes.

"You couldn't play on my Amazin' Mets without having held some kind of record," he said, "like one fella held the world's international all-time record for a pitcher getting hit on the ankles."

The fans didn't expect a great team, but few realized the depths to which a ball club could descend. Their first season was simply one of the worst in the long history of the game. Only the 1899 Cleveland Spiders lost more games in a single season than the 1962 Mets.

After a player disrupted the furniture in the clubhouse, Casey said, "If everybody on this team commenced breaking up the furniture every time we did bad, there'd be no place for us to sit."

Keep them coming Casey. We need the diversion.

"Been in this game one-hundred years, but I see new ways to lose 'em I never knew existed before."

Their ineptitude caused them to be the "loveable losers," and despite their record (or maybe because of it) the fans embraced them like no other expansion team ever. In true Chaplinesque fashion they were a terrible baseball team, but, oh, so loveable in their ineptitude. The adorable bumbling fools. Who couldn't identify with that? They were charming and empathetic, and in lieu of winning, they played up their maladroitness.

And the Old Professor, Stengel, kept adding fuel to the fire of love.

"Amazing strength, amazing power," he said of outfielder Ron Swoboda. "He can grind the dust out of the bat. He will be great, super, even wonderful. Now, if he can only learn to catch a fly ball."

"I got a kid, Greg Goosen, he's nineteen years old and in ten years he's got a chance to be twenty-nine."

How could you not like the Mets? Fans all over the country adopted the "Amazin' Mets."

Toots Shor, the New York restaurateur who frequently hosted the players, said, "I have a son and I make him watch the Mets. I want him to know life. It's a history lesson. He'll understand the Depression when they teach it to him in school."

With such ineptitude came fame for many who played for them. Players like "Marvelous Marv" Throneberry and "Dr. Strangeglove" (Dick Stuart) became celebrities because of what they couldn't do. Stuart, who tied or led the league in errors for each of his first seven seasons, once got a huge ovation from the fans when he cleanly fielded a flying hot dog wrapper. "Errors are a part of my image," he said. "I just want to walk down the street and hear them say, 'Jesus, there goes Dick Stuart.'"

He failed to mention that for most fans it was his only image. He acknowledged that he was the world's worst fielder, but defended it by insisting that nobody gets paid for fielding, only hitting.

According to another oft-told story, at a birthday party for Stengel everyone got a piece of the birthday cake, except Throneberry. When he complained, Stengel said to him, "We was gonna give you a piece but we was afraid you'd drop it."

In one of the team's first games, Marvelous Marv legged out a triple. While bent over on third base trying to recover from his unaccustomed long trip around the infield, Ernie Banks, the Cubs first baseman, called for the ball and appealed to the umpire that Marv had missed first base. When the appeal was upheld, Stengel raced out from the dugout to argue. The umpire shook his head and said, "Forget it, Casey. He didn't touch second either."

Jimmy Breslin, the columnist, once quipped, "Having Marv Throneberry play for your team is like having Willie Sutton play for your bank."

Once in their first season, Rod Kanehl, pinch hitting, said, "Don't ask me how the base-runners got there. I was asleep in the dugout."

Their catcher, Choo Choo Coleman, has to rate as one of the worst players ever to don a Mets uniform, which includes a long list of marginal players. One year he managed to amass more errors than RBIs which is no mean feat. One might be tempted to assume then, that he was playing because of his defensive prowess. The fact is, he couldn't catch or throw well either.

Casey was wont to forget the names of some players—probably a self-defense mechanism. Once he went to the umpire to tell him he was changing pitchers. When asked who he was bringing in, Stengel refused, saying, "Wait till he comes on the mound and then I'll tell you." By the time the pitcher arrived, Stengel was back in the dugout, probably trying to figure out the answer himself.

In July during their first season they held an "Old-Timers Day," but since there weren't any Mets old-timers, they imported some of the old Dodger and Giant stars from the past. The game featured Ralph Branca again pitching to Bobby Thomson, the man who hit the "home run heard around the world" giving the 1951 pennant to the Giants. It remains one of the most memorable hits in the history of the game. This time, however, Branca fared better and got Thomson to fly out.

Karl Ehrhardt was one of the Mets loyalists. Originally a devout Dodger fan, like so many others of that stripe he eventually switched allegiances to the Mets where he became a fixture at home games. Known as the "Sign Man," he became famous for holding up nicely printed signs reflecting either the appropriate joy or the disappointment of the moment.

Watch a play then look towards the Sign Man for a reaction from one of the 1,200 signs he had at the ready.

"There are no words."

"Just great!"

"Before I went to the ballpark, I would try to crystal-ball what might happen that particular day," he said years later. "I would read all the newspapers to learn who was hot and who was in a slump, stuff like that, and create my signs accordingly."

Some were player specific. After Jose Cardinal struck out: "Jose Can You See."

"Know Why the Mets Are Such Good Losers? Practice Makes Perfect." It was fun to have fun at the expense of the bumblers.

Without the hope of victory, fans can get behind the loveable losers, but when expectations rise and are not met, well, that's quite another thing altogether. Throughout the '60s the Mets continued their losing ways and the appeal of the bumbling losers began to wear thin on their faithful. It was time to start winning. This was, after all, New York.

By the late '60s things were beginning to change. They were fortunate enough to win the rights to top pitching prospect Tom Seaver and in 1967 he became Rookie of the Year. Then they added Bud Harrelson, Cleon Jones, Jerry Koosman, and several other strong players.

Losing was no longer fun. Expectations rose. The lovable losers had become competitive and in 1969 swept the Hank Aaron-led Braves in the first National League Championship Series. They were given little chance in the World Series against the Orioles and the Robinson boys— Brooks and Frank— Jim Palmer, and Davey Johnson. When they won the Series it was regarded as one of the greatest turnarounds in baseball history—a true triumph of the underdog.

The Mets were the best baseball story in years. They had gone from inept to heroic. They were an inspiration to the downtrodden everywhere. "Tom Terrific" was involved in a commercial proclaiming, "If the Mets can win the World Series, America can get out of Vietnam."

In the early '70s the team had its ups and downs. The "downs" included trading Amos Otis for Joey Foy, and Nolan Ryan for Jim Fregosi, and the sudden heart attack and death of their manager, Gil Hodges, soon after he had led them to their Series victory. The "ups" included coming from far back in 1973 behind Tug McGraw's "You Gotta Believe" to win 21 of their last 29 games, and then their shocking everybody by beating Cincinnati's unbeatable "Big Red Machine" in the NLCS championship. They pushed the A's to seven games in the Series before finally losing in the final contest.

To help bolster the sagging attendance, in May 1972 they gave to the Giants Charlie Williams, a pitcher who would win 23 games in his entire eight-year Major League career, and $50,000 for the aging Willie Mays. The "Say Hey Kid" was no longer a kid. He was 41 with rapidly diminishing skills. Still, it was in New York that he began his brilliant career. The Giants fans may have still hated the team for leaving, but it wasn't Willie's doing. He was revered as one of the greatest players (some would argue the greatest) ever. The Mets needed him not so much to play center field as to sell tickets. If they couldn't win their division, they could at least put up a good sideshow: "Come see the future Hall of Famer before it's too late."

Yogi Berra was then the manager and he said they'd play Willie some in center field to rest Tommy Agee and some at first base. The greatest center fielder ever was going to play some first base. It had come to that.

New York put out the welcome mat in fine style. With cameras rolling at City Hall, the always-campaigning Mayor John Lindsay welcomed him "home." "At my age," Willie said, "it makes you feel so good, so wonderful. I wish I could express my feelings. I only wish I knew how."

No player wants to be seen as an embarrassment — not the marginal players and certainly not the superstars — but by the end of the next season that's what Mays had become. Forget the .211 batting average, it was obvious that his once wonderful reflexes were no longer there. He had put in 22 years in the Major Leagues and now he was stumbling around like he belonged on the original Mets. In one game, he was sent in as a pinch-runner in the top of the ninth inning and the Mets leading, 6–3. When John Milner singled, Willie took off for second, but somehow his legs became twisted and he sprawled helplessly on the ground as he was making the turn around second. Once he would have easily made third, but now all he could do was half-crawl, half-fall back to the bag.

In the clubhouse later he said, "I guess I was trying to do two things at the same time — watch the ball and touch the bag. You see what happens."

Then in the bottom of the ninth, Deron Johnson hit a fly ball to deep center. It was the type of fly ball Willie had seen thousands of times. The crowd watched, waiting for Willie to glide effortlessly to the ball and then as his cap flew off, almost nonchalantly watch the ball settle softly into his waist-high glove. For any baseball fan it was truly a glorious thing to see, a balletic and athletic move that only Willie could do. This time, though, he slipped, pitched headlong on the turf, and tried to reach out with his bare hand and grab it, but he couldn't quite reach it.

It was a painful thing for any fan to see.

It's a shame really. He ain't Willie no more.

I can't watch.

Referring to replays, Willie said. "I didn't see it. But I didn't think it was that bad. Was it really that bad?"

Yeah, Willie, it was.

It was time to retire. Everyone could see that. Even Willie. So with his aching legs and rusting skills, he said he didn't want to let the kids down, announced his retirement, and waited for the Hall of Fame to call.

When in 1975 Joan Payson died and M. Donald Grant took over, the club entered another dismal period. Grant, ever tight-fisted, got into disputes with Seaver and slugger Dave Kingman, and soon traded both in what the tabloids were calling "The Midnight Massacre." The team's stadium had been named after Bill Shea but now with attendance falling and local interest in the team declining, they were calling it "Grant's Tomb." M. Donald had mismanaged just about everything that could be mismanaged on a professional baseball team. In a city which shared its fandom with the Yankees, the Mets were coming in a distant second.

It wasn't until the team was sold to the Doubleday publishing company and Frank Cashen was hired as general manager that the Mets fortunes began to rise again. Expectations were high. After coming close in 1985, they figure to be tough to beat in '86.

They got the pieces, now they damn well better win. Time for "you gotta believe" again.

27. Darling of the Mets

Ron Darling makes his best pitch to a group of about 150 junior high school students in New York. "Anyone who is on drugs is going to get caught," he says. "It doesn't matter who you are, what position you're in, whether you're a student 12 years old or a multimillion-dollar baseball player. There's only two places you can end up if you're on drugs— one's in jail and one's dead."

If any of the Mets players seem out of place in the clubhouse, it's Ron Darling. History has shown us there are Yale graduates lacking great intellects, but he isn't one of them. He is bright and his teammates know it. He actually reads books— even those without pictures— a trait he shares with Hernandez. And he knows things— things like which letters go in all those little boxes in *The New York Times* crossword puzzles that he works regularly, which wines to order with rack of lamb, and why Phan Boi Chau and Phan Chu Trinh led Vietnam's nationalist political movement. He is fluent in both French and Chinese.

His dual degree in French and Southeast Asian history is not posted on the outside of his locker but it might as well be. His erudition is hard to miss, if not ignore. It would seem logical that he and Johnson would be bosom buddies, that they could talk a common language without having to translate it for the other players, but the fact is the two often butt heads. Darling drives Johnson nuts the way he goes about pitching. Johnson thinks Darling overthinks everything, tries to be too fine with his pitches, tries too hard to outsmart the batters when all he has to do is trust his stuff and throw more strikes.

"But he was just so goddamned intellectual, he thought he could figure everything out himself," says the manager with the degree from Trinity University of the pitcher with the Ivy League degree.

So led by Johnson's acknowledged frustrations, the word on Darling around the league is that he doesn't trust his good stuff.

In the parlance of the game: Just throw the goddamned ball over the goddamned plate and let the goddamned hitter try to hit it.

In 1985 he won 16 games but led the league in walks, which according to Johnson came about largely because he was too damn stubborn to listen to the wise manager. This also accounts for why he has become a five-inning pitcher.

"I'm tired of that son-of-a-bitch having 110 pitches by the fourth inning," Johnson says. He tells his catchers to camp out in the middle of the plate on every one of Darling's pitches and never let him to pitch to the corners. "If he doesn't like it, blame me," he says. Darling does, and the two eggheads spend the season largely avoiding each other and communicating mostly through the press.

"This game is played with confidence because this game is played with your head. Most people have the physical ability to play the game. To excel in it, I think it's in your head," Darling says.

After raising their record to 16–4 in a May sweep of the Reds, Johnson says of Darling's pitching in the final game that they won, 7–2, behind two Strawberry home runs: "He was behind every hitter. It wasn't a pretty outing. He wasn't missing close; he was way out of the strike zone. It was a very ugly game. Very trying on the manager."

In mid–June, despite the fact that the Mets have won all of Darling's eight starts, the Darling-Johnson relationship continues to be frosty. Says Darling, "I seem to take the brunt of criticism on this staff." After Darling picked up his fourth straight win in a three-hit, two-run stint, Johnson called Darling's performance "terrible," adding, "He has flashes of brilliance, but he doesn't pitch as well as his ability warrants."

Darling counters by saying Johnson doesn't know how to communicate with his pitchers. "All I know about Davey Johnson," says Darling, "is what I see on the field and read on the back of his bubblegum card. I never sat and had a serious discussion with him about pitching. I never sat and had a serious discussion with him about anything."

This would appear to be just fine with Johnson.

"Every team is an extension of the manager," Darling adds. "Every team is what the manager wants it to be."

"I don't care if they like me or not," Johnson says. "I want them to like me. But it's not crucial."

Born in Honolulu, Hawaii, to a Hawaiian-Chinese mother and French-Canadian father, Darling is strikingly good-looking, always well-dressed, and so has become a real fan favorite, particularly with the young girls. Even after he marries supermodel Toni O'Reilly, with whom he has two children, he remains a poster boy for the handsome, preppy, clean-cut ballplayer, although he is seen squiring around scores of beauties and celebrities like Madonna.

While at Yale, he was considered the greatest player ever at that school. In his sophomore year be batted .386 as an infielder and racked up an 11–2 record on the mound with an impressive 1.31 ERA. "His season was probably the greatest a Yale player has ever had as far as both pitching and hitting go," his coach Joe Benato said at the time.

In what has sometimes been referred to as the best game in college baseball history, he hooked up with Frank Viola of St. John's University. Darling had a no-hitter going through 11 innings and then lost in the 12th, 1–0, on a double steal.

The Rangers made him the ninth player chosen in the 1981 draft that included Tony Gwynn going as the 58th player. He was acquired by the Mets along with Walt Terrell before the 1982 season and then made his Major League debut with the last-place Mets as a late call-up in 1983.

2006

After retiring from baseball following the 1995 season, Darling has been active in several banking ventures and in television as a color commentator. Along with Keith Hernandez and broadcaster Gary Cohen, he forms the garykeithandron charity.

"In order to even think about helping others," proclaims their organization, *"one must build a solid foundation within themselves. In order to do so with an open hand and heart, one must become a good neighbor. When you yourself decide to become a good neighbor, a community is born. Community, like charity, begins at home. It takes a community to effectively weather the storms of life. From that point on, anything is possible. This is our community and we can make anything possible."*

All of the net profits from their activities go to charity.

Darling remains a respected, level-headed presence on a team where level-headedness seems to be at a premium. He knows how to keep his ego in check even if he has to endure frequent run-ins with his manager.

28. Living in Another World

Because for years they had been led to believe they have a pass to behave almost any way they choose, many professional sports heroes then act in ways that have fundamental and detrimental consequences. Often top athletes are applauded and catered to beginning when they are young. The kid in Little League who is big and strong enough to hit a ball a long way quite naturally sees himself as better than the other kids, and where it comes to that quality, he is. He sees adults applauding him, telling him how wonderful his talent is, and treating him differently from the others. He feeds off the constant attention he receives. He loves to be loved. In time he comes to believe the special treatment is his due.

Some come to consider themselves as living outside the rules the other kids have to follow, and because they see it demonstrated time and again, they believe they will not be held accountable for any wrongful conduct.

Jim Bouton, the former pitcher, opines that "many players are in a dream world and out of touch with reality from the fourth grade on. As soon as they hit the first home run, they start living in another world."

These are the same players who are often unprepared for life after they can no longer play the game. When the spotlight goes off, they don't know how to behave because they've never been made to do so. They never grow up simply because they've never had to.

As Bouton has observed, "Athletes are not special people, they are people with special skills." In our society, throwing a ball fast or hitting it far are special skills we admire. In other societies the ability to hunt or to carve a spear tip might be considered far more admirable and so the best at doing those things are the ones lionized. Hitting a little round ball with a round stick might not be considered valuable at all.

The kid who excels in the science classroom is seldom given the same respect.

When we identify with our sports heroes, they can exert powerful influences on our lives. We celebrate their accomplishments just as we grieve for their inevitable decline.

Denny McLain, who went from being a 31-game winner to being a convicted felon, has described what it's like being put on a pedestal:

> I learned long ago that when you have a highly sought talent, you can write your own ticket. I was a damned good pitcher and I knew it. Unless I became intolerable, teams weren't going to discipline me much for breaking a few rules.... I blame sports writers in part for giving me the big head. Ever since I was a teenager, newspapers have run stories about how great a pitcher I was. That was nice, but the problem was that I started to believe what they said. And the more they wrote, the more I believed it. My ego grew to a proportion that was out of whack with reality.

If the Pirates are going to make their presence felt in the NL race, they may have to rely on the young Barry Bonds, who some scouts think is the most promising talent in their system. Certainly he comes from good stock since his father, Bobby, patrolled the outfield for the Giants with the likes of Orlando Cepeda and Willie Mays.

Pirates manager Jim Leyland is being bombarded by requests from some of his coaches to keep the kid on the roster. "He will hit more homers over his career than his father did," predicts Pittsburgh pitching coach Ron Schueler. He's got good speed, too. His father stole a ton of bases and his aunt, Rosie Bonds, once held the U.S. women's record in the 80-meter hurdles and competed in the 1964 Olympics.

Leyland knows they would have one heck of a player if Barry came anywhere close to his father's record of being only the second man to hit 300 home runs and steal 300 bases, but he feels his skinny outfielder would be better off developing his game with the Hawaii Islanders in the Pacific Coast League. Nevertheless, he is comparing Bonds with Kirk Gibson, whom he managed in the minors. "Bonds is crude, just like Gibson was," Leyland says. "They are both made out of the same mold. When they fall into a slump, they will figure a way to get out of it."

When he was in high school in San Mateo, California, he was known as Bobby Bonds' son. More than one scout thinks that before he's done, his father may be better known as Barry Bonds' father.

"I was a little bothered at first, being known as someone's son," he says. "I just love to play sports and I just happened to choose the same sport my father did. I didn't choose to play baseball because of the money or my dad, but because I loved the sport. I don't feel any more pressure than if I were the son of a successful plumber or a successful doctor."

As an indication of what they think of their prospect, instead of giving him a normal rookie number like 69 they assign him the number "7"— Mickey Mantle's number.

"James Bond was agent 007, so we thought Barry Bonds should be our No. 7," joked Greg Johnson, the team's publicist. Before the year is out he will

A svelte Barry Bonds beginning his Major League career with the '86 Pirates. He is one of 157 players to make their debuts that year in a class that included Will Clark, Barry Larkin, Greg Maddux, Jamie Moyer, Benito Santiago, Edgar Martinez, Ellis Burks, and Billy Beane.

change to No. 24. He'd rather have Willie Mays' number. Besides his birthday is July 24.

His distant cousin, Reggie Jackson, offers suggestions about how to deal with the pressure. Barry, though, seems confident, maybe even a little brash. Still, near the end of spring training, the Pirates, not wanting to rush him before he's ready to face the confidence-killing Dwight Goodens of the league, send him back to the minors for a little more seasoning. Near the end of May, with the Pirates already 12 games behind the Mets, they recall the slender but powerful and fast Bonds and install him in center field.

By all accounts, he is a good kid. The days when his ego swells to Ted Williams-like proportions and he becomes as unapproachable as Joe DiMaggio are still in front of him. For now he'll mind his business and play ball.

When asked how he felt about facing Dwight Gooden for the first time, Bonds says, "Don't forget, Dwight Gooden has to face me, too."

Nobody ever accused him of lacking confidence.

When he fails to back up second base on a steal and throws to the wrong base, he responds by saying, "There's still a lot of things I've got to learn about myself. It's not so much about the pitching or that anyone is better than you or that you're better than anybody else, it's learning about yourself, what you can do, what you can't do. That's what makes people like Keith Hernandez and George Foster and all the great players."

"He's worth the price of admission," Leyland says. "That's not to say our other players aren't. I mean he's a little extra."

Playing in his sixth game for the Pirates, Bonds hits his first home run. Later he will say, "I was born to hit a baseball."

At Serra High School, Bonds was swizzle-stick thin 6' 1", 175-pound, star jock in a school of jocks. On the baseball team, he was a gap-hitter if ever there was one. And he could run. A mediocre student at best, he spent little time on academics. To maintain his academic eligibility, he enrolled in the easiest classes he could, and even at that he was known to look over the shoulders of the better students. A former teacher remembers Barry taking tests with the answers pre-written on his hand. If the teachers knew, how did he get away with it? Simple. He was recognized as the school's best jock.

All right, he's got a few little answers on his palm. Look, we've got the championship game coming up this weekend. You want him sitting in detention or standing at the plate?

It's not that he wasn't bright enough to pass the tests on his own, but Barry had other priorities.

He was used to being treated differently because he could do things most people couldn't. A classmate, Scott Kockos, remembers, "If you were running late you got yelled at. But not Barry. I remember the looks on the faces of teachers when Barry did something wrong. They knew there was no point in going to the dean, because nothing was going to happen. He could get away with anything."

Barry Lamarr Bonds learned many important things at Serra that would stay with him throughout his playing days and beyond.

2005

The video game MVP Baseball 2005 is released using the names and likenesses of many Major League players. One character is a generic athlete called Jon Dowd. He represents Bonds who is the first player in the 30-year history of the Major League Baseball Players Association not to sign their licensing agreement. He believes independent marketing deals will make him more money. As a result his name and likeness cannot be used in any merchandise licensed by the Association.

May 2006

Jeff Pearlman's book Love Me, Hate Me: Barry Bonds and the Making of an Anti-Hero *characterizes Bonds as "an insufferable braggart with an incendiary ego who consistently alienated teammates."*

November 2007

A federal grand jury has charged Bonds with perjury and obstruction of justice over an inquiry into steroids use.

The federal indictment states: "During the criminal investigation, evidence was obtained including positive tests for the presence of anabolic steroids and other performance enhancing substances for Bonds and other athletes."

Bonds faces four counts of perjury and one of obstructing justice, which together carry a maximum penalty of 30 years in jail.

A statement released by the Bush White House says, "The President is very disappointed to hear this."

April 2011

A federal court jury finds Bonds guilty of obstruction of justice for giving an evasive answer under oath. Rather than say "yes" or "no" to whether he received drugs that required a syringe, Bonds gave a rambling response to a grand jury, stating: "I became a celebrity child with a famous father."

He is sentenced to 30 days house arrest.

Bonds will finish the 1986 season as the top rookie in home runs, walks, and stolen bases, but will end up 6th in the National League Rookie of the Year voting behind Todd Worrell, Robby Thompson, Kevin Mitchell, Will Clark, and Charlie Kerfeld.

Kerfeld's Fleer Baseball card lists the 6' 6", 250-pound reliever as being 5' 11" and 175 pounds.

Those damn relievers are always trying to deceive batters.

"I haven't weighed 175 since I was in seventh grade," says Kerfeld.

Bonds is 175 pounds, and at 6' 1" he is skinny. He will, however, fill out considerably as his career progresses.

Working out will do that for you.

29. Clean Living

Although he is 33, they still refer to him as "the Kid." Gary Carter loves the name. To him it suggests the youthful joy and enthusiasm with which he plays the game. He likes it when people think of him that way — a happy kid. For a while they called him "Teeth" because of his big smile, but that never stuck.

The "Kid" name was put on him when, during his first spring training camp in 1973, he found himself in a card game with some of the older players. "Hey, kid," said Mike Torrez, "why don't you run down and get us some ice cream?" The rookie did the veteran's bidding as rookies are wont to do and he was the Kid thereafter.

He plays with energy and passion. He plays hard and he is smart — baseball savvy anyway.

Carter likes to be liked and he works hard at it. He brings an upbeat personality to the clubhouse and is mostly respected for it.

In December 1984, Frank Cashen sent Hubie Brooks, a versatile and popular Met, along with three other players of little distinction to Montreal for the all-star catcher. Cashen knew his youth-laden team could use the leadership and steadying hand of the league's best catcher. At the very least, he would command the respect of the kiddy corps of pitchers the Mets were counting on. Dwight Gooden was 20; Ron Darling, 24; Sid Fernandez, 22; Roger McDowell, 24. Yes, the vet they called the Kid would definitely be a big asset.

The three-sport star from Southern California signed a letter of intent to play football for UCLA, but when the Expos drafted him and made him a nice financial offer, he left football behind and became a full-time catcher. In 1975, his first full season with the Expos, he made the All-Star team and was named *The Sporting News* Rookie of the Year. He was the only Expo player ever to take the time to learn French, which only helped boost his popularity.

In 1984, he led the league in RBIs and had his best season ever. Cashen was ecstatic with the trade. He found a fine defensive catcher, a good run-producer, and a solid citizen. The New York fans would fall in love with the ebullient, always-positive player. Who wouldn't love the Kid?

Well, some of his Expo teammates for openers. As soon as he was traded they said that he only played for himself and conveyed a phony image to the public.

Davy Johnson quickly jumped to his defense. "I think a lot of things that were said about Gary in Montreal were manufactured," he says. "Besides, you can't tell me that all the great players in the history of the game didn't play for themselves to some degree. Look at someone like Ty Cobb. Who played more for himself? And he was only one of the greatest players in the game. I tell our players they should go out and play as well as they can for themselves and let me worry about the team."

Carter readily admits that not all his teammates appreciated him and his gung-ho attitude. "When I came to the Mets," he wrote in his autobiography, "some of the guys told me straight out that they hadn't liked me. Bill Robinson, the first-base and hitting coach, broke it down in basic English: 'I thought you were an asshole.'"

Carter says he knows, too, why he is disliked more than the other Mets. "I know I have an image like Steve Garvey, except that I'm not going into politics. But I've got everything I could want in life — health, a great family, I'm on a winning team, and I make a good salary. I'm not a carouser who goes out and gets in trouble in bars like some guys I know. I've got that all-clean image. But I'm not going to change the way I play or the way I am."

Johnson thinks Carter is loathed by other players for the same reason opponents hated Frank Robinson. "Frank beat your brains out, like Gary does. Frank wouldn't try to hurt you, but he gave you no quarter."

The difference, though, is that Robinson was disliked because of his apparent meanness and Carter for his excessive effervescence.

What Johnson doesn't say is that he was of the same ilk. In his playing days he was known as "the second baseman you can't take out." To this day there is a nasty patch from a poorly done skin graft on the right side of his neck where doctors tried to repair a spike wound.

Carter may be one of the best catchers in the game but he's also one of the most disliked.

When *Sports Illustrated* conducted a poll of players asking them who they would select as the most valuable player in the league, one anonymous Giant responded, "I wouldn't vote for Gary Carter for MVP if he had 162 game-winning hits." Carter responded, "I don't try to insult anybody, but I can't help the way I play baseball. The raised fist, the smile, are sheer happiness."

Some players resent what they consider his I-holier-than-thou attitude.

In the early '70s Watson "Waddy" Spoelstra, a reformed hard-drinking *Detroit News* sportswriter, noted how hard it was for ballplayers to attend church services, since fans were often passing their bulletins down the pews for autographs and otherwise making it difficult for the devout to worship undisturbed. So he went to Commissioner Bowie Kuhn with the suggestion that baseball do something for the observant players, of which he said there were many, including the "Milkshake Twins," Tony Kubek and his Yankee teammate Bobby Richardson, known for their clean-living lifestyles sans alcohol and drugs. Together they were instrumental in forming Baseball Chapel Inc., an organization that supports the creation of chapels for the players. It also presents a Danny Thompson Award each year to the ballplayer who "best exemplifies the Christian lifestyle." Gary Carter was one of the recipients.

After winning the World Series, he will broadly smile before the cameras and proclaim, "My only dream was to give glory and praise to Jesus Christ."

He certainly wasn't the only active faith-proclaiming ballplayer. George Foster's bat is inscribed with scripture to "remind him who runs the game," and many others are outspoken in their faith — Frank Tanana, Tommy John, Orel Hershiser, Paul Molitor, Andre Dawson, Rick Sutcliffe, Harold Reynolds, and Eric Show among them.

Many of them eagerly appear on TV's *700 Club*, *The Jim and Tammy Show*, and with evangelists like Pat Robertson. They speak about how they now worship Christ where they once worshipped baseball.

If they can use their names to promote Gatorade and coffee makers, why not Christ?

Some players are skeptical of those who give thanks to God for, say, a particularly important hit. Are these really acts of God? And who exactly does he favor?

And how exactly can a pitcher who throws high and tight fastballs call himself a Christian?

Dugout theologian Sparky Anderson, a regular Baseball Chapel attendee, says, "No, I do not believe God cares about baseball. If He did, you would never have a loser. I am suspicious of guys who think that by attending chapel it is going to help them with their baseball."

Not everyone in baseball is happy with Baseball Chapel. Dick Balderson, the Mariners GM, blames Christian ballplayers for being weak athletes. "I thought we had a complacent bunch of people who were unwilling to accept their own failure," he said when chapel meetings delayed a couple of batting practices. A Christian radio station then blasted him, and some players said they were offended for being singled out for their faith.

Eric Show, the Padres' pitcher, says, "If a Christian pitcher wins 20, his faith is never mentioned. But if he loses 20 the reason given is that he loses because he is a weak, non-competing believer in Jesus."

The Royals' Rudy Law, Detroit's Chet Lemon and Lou Whitaker, and the White Sox's Jerry Hairston are all members of Jehovah's Witnesses, and all are refusing to come out of the dugout and stand for the traditional playing of the

National Anthem. "For the National Anthem, you worship the flag," Law explains. "I don't want to live like that."

Carter's teammate Ron Darling says that although he is "not a big fan of organized religion ... I don't knock these guys. I say if it works for them, it is wonderful. Baseball is a very lonely and trying experience, and going to Baseball Chapel on Sunday can be one of the best ways to handle that."

Without doubt, because he wears his faith on his sleeve, Carter gains respect from some and skepticism from others.

Oh, you mean Mr. Goody-Two-Shoes? He makes Steve Garvey look like Lex Lothor.

"I love my wife and children, I love God, and I love playing baseball," he often proclaims. "Like any ballplayer, I love to hear the cheers."

Most of the non-religious teammates simply ignore this aspect of the Kid. He catches a good game and he's good with the pitchers. When he's done with that, he can go off and do and think anything he wants.

Dale Murphy's image is also milk-drinking clean. He doesn't chew, spit, curse, tell dirty jokes, smoke funny cigarettes, take drugs stronger than aspirin, or drink alcohol. He is (take your pick) a choir boy, Eagle Scout, paragon of virtue, straight-shooter, or tower of strength. He will only endorse wholesome products such as milk and ice cream, won't appear for interviews until he is fully dressed, will pick up a teammate's dinner check as long as alcohol isn't on the tab, won't allow women to put their arms on his shoulders during photos, or even talk to anyone in the locker room if a woman is present.

"Guys walk around naked in there," he says.

Although some feminist groups see it otherwise, Chuck Tanner says, "God puts someone down here like Murphy only every 50 years. I'm not talking about baseball, either. I'm talking about him as a person. In my opinion, there's no finer fellow on earth."

"Just look at him over there," says Angels pitcher Terry Forster. "Doesn't drink, doesn't smoke, doesn't take greenies, nicest guy you'd ever want to meet, hits the hell out of the ball, hustles like crazy, plays a great center field and isn't trying to get anything from anybody ... doesn't he just make you sick?"

In a scene reminiscent of *The Pride of the Yankees*, Murphy once actually went into the stands to visit a six-year-old girl who had lost both hands and a leg in an accident when she stepped on a downed power line. After he presented her a T-shirt and cap, the girl's nurse innocently asked Murphy to hit a home run for her. "I didn't know what to say, so I just sort of mumbled, 'Well, O.K.,'" says Murphy. He then went out and hit not one, but two home runs.

He works with Athletes Who Care, the Make-a-Wish Foundation, and several other charities who call on him with the regularity of bill collectors.

"Dale may be the only guy I know who could call 24 guys in one locker room a good friend," says the Dodgers' Don Sutton.

Murph is easy-going, seldom argues with the umpires, and seldom gets angry. Once when, uncharacteristically, he smashed the water cooler in frustration, teammates stood open-mouthed in amazement.

Joe Torre says of Murphy, "If you're a coach, you want him as a player. If you're a father, you want him as a son. If you're a woman, you want him as a husband. If you're a kid, you want him as a father. What else can you say about the guy?"

Well, for one thing, he's an excellent baseball player.

"I can't imagine Joe DiMaggio was a better all-around player than Dale Murphy," says Nolan Ryan.

"The best player I've seen since Willie Mays," says Cubs pitching coach Billy Connors.

Mr. Perfect, as Chuck Tanner calls him, is not always appreciated by everyone. He doesn't hang out with the guys trading stories over a few beers. Anyone who sets himself up as a paragon of virtue is bound to be a target for those who don't.

"When Dale Murphy speaks, everyone in sports should listen," says sportscaster Jim Nantz. Some, however, would rather not.

If I want to listen to a sermon I'll go to church.

Yeah, I know he's a saint, but how the hell could a saint have dropped that fly ball?

There are always those who welcome the fall of the high and mighty.

The Braves are "America's Team"—at least according to their flagship station, TBS, but around the country they're about as popular as TB.

On a poor Braves team Murphy remains their only true star on and off the field. The Braves, needing to curry favor in the wake of their record, promote his wholesome image as if he were Frank Merriwell incarnate.

The fictional Merriwell's classmates once observed, "He never drinks. That's how he keeps himself in such fine condition all the time. He will not smoke, either, and he takes his exercise regularly. He is really a remarkable freshie."

The Braves selected Murphy in the first round of the 1974 draft as a catcher, but his throwing was atrocious, sometimes hitting his own pitcher while attempting to throw out runners at second base. The Braves moved him to first where he then led the league in errors. It looked for a while like he would have a very short career, but Bobby Cox decided to try him in the outfield. The results were ... Gold Glove good.

"He's scary," says former Reds manager Russ Nixon. "Do they have something above MVP?"

In eight seasons with the Braves, Merriwell/Murphy has compiled team career batting figures exceeded only by Hank Aaron. In 1983, he became only the fourth National League player to win consecutive MVP awards. Last year he hit 37 home runs, his fifth season with more than 30. Coming into this year he is the only NL player to have driven in 100 runs a season for four consecutive years since Steve Garvey in 1977–1980.

In center field, he shows all the instincts of the great ballhawks. About the only thing the four-time Gold Glove winner has dropped recently was a quiche in the church parking lot, says Bishop Gerald Bahr, the Mormon leader who presides over the church attended by the Murphys.

While a minor leaguer in the Braves system he met Barry "Preacher" Bonnell. They were both working their way up to the majors and became good friends. Bonnell, a devout Mormon, introduced him to his religion and then baptized his teammate the day after the 1975 season ended.

Then came the conflicting emotions. Play baseball or go on a Mormon mission?

"It was an emotional time," he says, "because I knew I wanted to play baseball, but more than that, I wanted to do what the Lord required."

He agonized over making a decision. He talked to his non–Mormon parents and they said they would support whatever he decided. He talked to General Authority Elder Dunn.

"We talked about my desire to do what the Lord wanted, and I said I would drop baseball then and there if it was the thing I should do," Murphy says. "I had been praying diligently about the matter but as yet hadn't been able to find the answer."

While Murphy was wrestling with his conscience, Braves owner Ted Turner was wrestling with his lineup. He had heard that his No. 1 draft choice, to whom they had given a significant signing bonus and trained for three years in their minor leagues, was thinking of giving up the game and going oversees to try to convince others to do as he did and convert to Mormonism.

Despite, or maybe because he grew up with an abusive father, Turner was very religious as a boy, at one point even intending to become a missionary. Then in his teens, he saw his younger sister Mary Jane come down with a form of lupus. She was in such intense agony that Turner prayed an hour every day for her recovery.

"She used to run around in pain, begging God to let her die," he recalled. "My family broke apart. I thought, 'How could God let my sister suffer so much?'"

When his sister died he began to turn away from religion completely. Now, publicly, he either describes himself as an atheist or an agnostic.

Turner, having little knowledge of Mormonism but a lot of knowledge of making money, wanted to protect his investment in this kid he thought could lead his team to the promised land, if not the holy land. He even facetiously said that if Murphy left to go on a mission he would kill himself and his family, but that if Murphy stayed and played for the Braves, he and his family would all become Mormons.

Murphy decided his mission "would be served for the time being there, playing baseball for the Atlanta Braves." Turner kept to his atheism/agnosticism.

On days when the Braves start their games at 5:40, their radio affiliate WTIK cuts away from 7:00 to 7:30 to carry "Back to the Bible." Someone suggests it's Murphy's doing, since it sure as hell isn't Turner's.

After his first season in Atlanta, Murphy spent some time at Brigham Young University where he met his wife, Nancy. They have four sons. Travis, their second oldest, suffers from Rubinstein-Taybi syndrome. Individuals with Rubinstein-Taybi syndrome typically have low IQs, are non-verbal, but understand signs.

Travis requires special attention and Murphy's baseball time away from his family is difficult for him. He's had to make hard choices he says but admits that fame is a Siren whose charms are hard to ignore. "The problem is that it's so much fun." he says. "It's more than fun. It's addictive. Playing baseball is not real life. It's a fantasy world ... a dream come true." Still, the pull of his family's need is strong and some wonder how long his baseball career will last.

"I'm trying to teach my kids principles that will keep them safe and happy in life. And I'm hoping they'll choose those principles when they grow up over the ones the world teaches. It's a big preparation. We're in a scary place," he says.

January 2007

Dale Murphy, now a grandfather and concerned about drug usage among young athletes, starts a grass-roots national organization called "I Won't Cheat," with the aim of teaching these grade school, high school, and college athletes the dangers and unfairness of taking performance-enhancing drugs.

About the use of drugs when he was playing he says:

> *I mean, it was obvious it was going on. We didn't address the issue as strongly as we should have. Everybody who covered it, everybody who watched it, everybody who was playing, everybody who was in the front office. Baseball, as an industry, we just buried our heads in the sand. So now what we've created is not only unhealthy players, but the temptation so real for college, minor leaguers, and high school kids. If you see dollar signs and people getting away with it, you're going to be tempted to do it. The more I read, and the more I understand of the challenge that high school kids are having, the more upset I get at the lack of what we did.*

Taking drugs to improve your performance, he lectures to youngsters, is simply cheating yourself, your sport, and the fans. He tells them the way to go is to develop relationships of trust and respect.

> *So that when a kid is faced with this decision, people he has respect for tell him there's a right way and a wrong way to do things. And this is the wrong way. Maybe this*

> will lead to some positive peer-pressure of little clubs in each high school — "I Won't Cheat" clubs. Our vision, maybe it's too Pollyannaish, is to bring up a new generation of guys who are going to say, "I see that guy in Triple-A that's doing this, and I'm in single-A, but I'm not doing it." Maybe what we can create is more positive peer pressure — you're going to feel ostracized if you go down that route. I don't think kids want to go that way. What we're seeing above them, that's the problem, I think.

And about Barry Bonds' breaking Aaron's home run record? "To me, Barry Bonds' career will always be, 'Yeah, but,'" Murphy says.

And then come the cynics suggesting that the "I Won't Cheat" program is similar to the "Just Say No" and "A Safe and Sober Prom Night" campaigns.

Since 1991 more than 300,000 students have signed a pledge not to drink or do drugs on prom night. Look, say the cynics, the kids who behaved well on prom night were going to do it whether they signed a piece of paper or not. Who really believes the kids who planned to drink or do drugs on that holiest of nights looked their teacher in the eyes when presented with the pledge paper and said, "Nope, sorry. I can't sign that because I'm gonna shoot up on prom night." Only a Goody-Two-Shoes would think that. They sign.

Same thing is going to happen with "I Won't Cheat." Those kids who end up cheating won't give a moment's thought to a piece of paper they signed when they were 12 — or so sayeth the many cynics.

Yeah, but as Murphy says, at least they're trying to do something about the problem, which is more than can be said for Major League Baseball.

> *August 2007*
> *Murphy calls Sports Radio AM 1280 to offer a statement about Barry Bonds:*
>
> This is a great teaching moment for a parent. You can explain to your kids why you're not watching and why it doesn't interest you.... Even in a court of a law you can have a preponderance of circumstantial evidence to convict somebody. Now, maybe I'm wrong, but when you get enough stuff on a guy, you can make a decision and it's just really a no-brainer. The guy would have been one of the great ones, anyway. But now, he sucked the fun and the life right out of it. I mean, there is enough evidence to me to say without a doubt he used performance-enhancing drugs. He hit 73 home runs when he was 37. I mean, Hank would have hit 855 if he had this same advantage. Barry's a great player, there's no question about it, but he put an asterisk by his name on his own. He's deserved all the negative publicity that he's getting. I mean, people are calling up and complaining that he's being treated unfairly. You know, life just usually isn't like that. You don't usually get treated unfairly. You usually get what you deserve. This is what Barry deserves. He's a hard guy to like. He's a hard teammate to have and, you know, he's set a terrible example for our kids. That's what you say to your kids. This is what happens when you take steroids. Your dad doesn't want to watch this because this is drug abuse, basically, as we all know. I am not really trying to jump on the last caller, but he's a Giants fan. Giants fans love it and they are blinded for some reason. But most people put an asterisk by it.

30. Drugs of Choice

Steve Howe continues to be a thorn in the side of Commissioner Ueberroth. He wants to play professional baseball again with the independent San Jose team and cannot do so without the commissioner's permission. Ueberroth has to make his hard-line position on drugs clear, yet there are union issues to consider and he knows if he comes down too hard it will discourage others from acknowledging their problems for fear of excessive penalties.

Howe was drafted in the first round by the Dodgers in 1979 out of the University of Michigan and quickly came up to the team in 1980, winning National League Rookie of the Year. He was a highly effective, hard-throwing left-handed relief pitcher. He was also the team's biggest problem child.

Don Newcombe, the director of community relations for the Dodgers, a former pitcher who had battled problems with alcohol, was quoted as saying that there's "a very serious problem" on the Dodgers. The Dodgers' team physician, Dr. Robert Woods, denied it. "If there were any heavy users, they couldn't function as well as they do. Their reflexes would be impaired, and they aren't."

Outfielder Rick Monday said the Dodgers were "livid" when Newcombe made his allegations. "We demanded he come down and explain to us what he meant," Monday said.

There was no doubt among some that Steve Howe and Kenny Landreaux were at the heart of the issue. Then, after displaying erratic behavior throughout the '82 season, Howe entered the Meadows drug rehabilitation center, the same facility that had earlier treated Bob Welch for alcohol dependency. He described the final month of the season as "the pits." He said he used cocaine "at Dodger Stadium, before games, in between, anytime." He claimed he spent $10,000 on his drug habit. "Now I'm a grateful alcoholic," he said after checking into rehabilitation.

He spent five weeks at the center, which was also treating Landreaux.

Since little is sacred around baseball clubhouses, jokes were making the rounds that the Dodgers led the league in get-well cards and that they might as well move one of their minor league franchises to the Meadows.

Howe pitched well in the early months of 1983, not allowing a single earned run. Then he re-entered the drug and alcohol treatment center. "To see it happen to him again makes us all feel bad. We feel bad the young man had to go back," said Lasorda.

This time when he was released he was fined $557,000 by Major League Baseball, the largest fine ever levied on a player.

At a press conference, Howe said, "I feel very good, probably the best I've felt in a long time. I'm confident, it's a good program, and I've got good people helping me. The single most important thing to me now is sobriety day-to-day. I am sober today and I look forward to being sober tomorrow."

Within a month of his return to playing, he arrived late for a game and was suspended for two games by the Dodgers.

When he returned he again pitched well, but then in September he missed the team's charter flight to Atlanta and refused to take a test to determine if his conduct resulted from the use of prohibited substances. He was suspended indefinitely by the team. Despite the fact that Howe again checked into the rehabilitation center, his lawyer insisted he was not using drugs.

In December he was suspended for one year. The Dodgers said they agreed with the decision but would stand behind their reliever. "We will do everything possible to hasten the day when Steve can join his teammates," said Dodger owner, Peter O'Malley.

His attorney, Roy Bell, didn't agree. "I don't think you should punish someone who has a disease," he said. Nor did his agent, Tony Attanasio. "There is no question Steve Howe requires assistance; he needs psychological and medical help. What he doesn't need is the whip and chain and being put in a stock."

"We are going to be trying some new approaches with Steve for what is a very difficult problem," said his doctor "This is not a hopeless situation."

Commissioner Kuhn decided to suspend him for the entire 1984 season. He returned for the 1985 season and made it to late June before problems arose again. The Dodgers fined him $300 for arriving late for a game. Howe said he was tardy because his wife accidentally left with his car keys and his wallet with his credit cards so he had no way to get to the park on time. Eventually he found enough cash to take an $80 cab ride to the game, arriving in the seventh inning, which as everybody knows is about the time he might be needed anyway.

"It could happen to anybody," said Lasorda. "It's not a bad sign at all. Those things happen."

A week later, Howe, who for some inexplicable reason was chairman of a Boy Scout dinner event, failed to show up for the dinner attended by many of his teammates. The next day he also failed to show up at Dodger Stadium for a game against the Braves. No one, including his wife, seems to have known where he was. The Dodgers, having lost patience, first put him on the restricted list and then, two days later, released him.

In an apparent effort to explain the situation, the Dodgers senior player, Bill Russell, said, "He's got a problem."

The Twins, desperate for relief help, signed Howe but then released him a month later after he missed three games.

Baseball has long reveled in its "character drunks." Old-timers love to tell the story of the great Grover Cleveland Alexander staggering out of the bullpen in the 1926 World Series with a world class hangover and then through blurry eyes staring down at Tony Lazzeri. He may or may not have noticed that the bases were loaded. He proceeded to strike out Lazzeri and then navigate through the haze back to the dugout. The story is never told without a chuckle and a smidgen of admiration. Good old Grover, what a guy!

And Paul Waner, didn't he used to claim he'd sometimes see two balls coming from the pitcher and had to decide which one to hit? Good old Waner, what a guy!

Of course, there is the great Bambino himself, that great real-life cartoon character with the big belly that everyone knew came from beer and bootleg whiskey. Well, maybe the kids were told it came from eating too many hot dogs, but the adults knew. Good old Babe, what a guy!

The myriad stories of the drinking bouts of Billy Martin and Mickey Mantle were legendary and, until their drinking led to the deaths of both, funny. The Mick and Billy the Kid, what great guys!

Unlike Howe, baseball never suspended these "characters" for their drug of choice, never fined them, and never disciplined them in any way. Rather they cherished them for their eccentricities, even promoted them as being good for the great old game. Fans like characters and characters sell tickets. The lore of baseball, the romance of the game prominently include the great drunks.

"What we have are good gray ballplayers, playing a good gray game and reading the good gray *Wall Street Journal*," wrote maverick owner Bill Veeck:

> They have been brainwashed, dry-cleaned and dehydrated! Wake up the echoes at the Hall of Fame and you will find that baseball's immortals were a rowdy and raucous group of men who would climb down off their plaques and go rampaging through Cooperstown, taking spoils. Deplore it if you will, but Grover Cleveland Alexander drunk was a better pitcher than Grover Cleveland Alexander sober.

Now that the drug of choice for some players comes in powder form, baseball no longer wants to ignore it because booze is funny, cocaine is not, and people don't buy tickets to watch coked-out players. Times have changed. Because Howe came forward and admitted his problem, asked for help, and publicly humiliated himself, baseball has punished him. Wade Boggs can brag about his drinking, but Steve Howe cannot brag about his cocaine habit.

As columnist Jim Murray wrote, "Steve Howe broke the law. But so did Babe Ruth and Grover Alexander. Steve Howe is coming to the aid of the victim in this crime. Himself. The addict could have said to hell with the man, the game, the team, the family, the world. Most of them do. Some of the storied heroes of the grand old game, in a sense, did. Steve Howe didn't."

After wrestling with the situation, Ueberroth permits Howe to play the '86 season for Class A San Jose. After pitching five effective innings for them he declares, "If I don't have a (Major League) job real quick now, you know something is rotten in Denmark."

Instead of a promotion he is suspended by the club for again testing positive. When this suspension is up, San Jose releases him.

April 2006

Howe, who has been signed and released by several minor and major league teams, and who has been arrested for cocaine possession and then with criminal possession of a weapon at Kennedy Airport in New York when a police officer spots a loaded .375 Magnum pistol in his carry-on baggage, and after being critically injured in a motorcycle accident a few years earlier while intoxicated, rolls his pickup truck on a remote California road and he is killed. The autopsy report indicates there were methamphetamines in his system. He left a wife and two children.

In Kansas City Lonnie Smith is having a good '86 season. He's hitting for a high average and stealing a lot of bases. That in itself is not surprising, though. He's been an All-Star, led the league in runs scored, stolen as many as 68 bases in a season, and twice hit over .320 in the World Series. He also has stories to tell.

He has admitted to being a heavy cocaine user while with the Cardinals in 1983.

"The majority of the time, I hid it on me," he says. "I had these Playboy socks with pockets in them and I'd stick it in there. I had ways of folding my clothes, 10, 12 pairs of pants in a suitcase. I learned it from a Latin friend in Venezuela. People who wanted to check wouldn't take the time."

He had a system all worked out with his supplier.

"We Federal Expressed it back and forth. I Federal Expressed the money, he Federal Expressed the stuff. He would use a phony address. I thought it was kind of creative in a way. He'd send me newspapers from Philadelphia and tape the stuff inside the papers."

He estimates that from some time in 1979 until June 1983, when he entered rehabilitation, he was spending between $50,000 and $60,000 a month on cocaine. He started buying an ounce at a time and then moved on to bigger and bigger quantities. Sometimes he would share it with teammates and friends but most of the time he did it by himself because "it's so expensive and it goes so fast, you like to hoard it."

"I think it slowed me down, not just running but my mental thinking," he says. "I wasn't as alert. My body was running down."

He admits that the more he used the less he cared about the outcome of the games. All he wanted to do was to get the game over with so he could use again.

His already shoddy defensive skills were getting worse, he was getting picked off base, and swinging at pitches way off the plate. His manager Whitey Herzog, could see there was something wrong.

"Whitey thought I was having problems but not drugs," Smith says. "He thought I was having emotional problems. No one wants to believe a guy is doing bad because of drug problems. But the more I did it, the worse I felt. My need kept getting greater and I couldn't fight that need."

Smith sympathizes with the Howe situation. "You're always tempted, he says. If you socialize with people, you run across the wrong people. You're tempted almost every day out of the year. It's not easy. There's no known cure for the disease."

Montreal outfielder Tim Raines was another user. "I had it in little gram bottles that I kept in my pocket," he says. "Actually, a lot of times I would put it in my batting glove and then in my pocket. I was trying to find ways of not getting caught." When he slid into a base, he knew how to protect his investment. "Usually," he says, "when I carried it in my pocket, I'd go in head first."

Expos president John McHale is convinced cocaine was the reason his team did not win the division in 1982 when most experts said they were the best team.

Whitey Herzog claims that when he took over as manager of the Cardinals 40 percent of the players were using cocaine.

Lonnie Smith, now apparently clean, still isn't a good fielder. Says one coach, "When he goes after a ball, it looks like he's running on a water bed." He isn't happy either, at least not with Ueberroth's demand that he and some of the others like Keith Hernandez, players the commissioner felt were the most egregious offenders, had to forfeit part of their '86 salary, perform community service, and agree to be tested randomly for the rest of their careers. He has to ante up $85,000 and put in 200 hours in the community.

"If I was to be disciplined, it should have been at the time I admitted my problem," he says. "To do it now, three years later, isn't right. The commissioner's ruling wasn't fair. He's not fining me for what I did in 1983, but what my role was in the trial."

Then he adds, "I'm not supposed to be talking about this, but I've been holding it in so long that I have to let it out. I'm so frustrated right now."

1987

Smith goes into a pawnshop and buys a Taurus 9-millimeter handgun. He intends to kill John Schuerholz, the Royals general manager, whom he blames for sabotaging his career. When he went begging for a job after leaving the Royals on bad terms, he was turned away by every club he approached. He blames Schuerholz who he says never believed he had given up drugs and told other general managers Smith was a troublemaker with a dangerous history.

"*If I couldn't get back to baseball,*" *Smith says,* "*I was going to take him with me. I was going to fly out there, wait for him in the parking lot of the stadium and pop him. If I got caught, I got caught. If not, I'd come on back home.*"

While taking a practice shot in his backyard, however, he held the gun incorrectly and the hammer snapped back badly slicing his hand. He decided instead to give the gun to his wife as part of their divorce settlement.

Has the commissioner been too lenient? Some baseball people think so. How is it going to be enforced? Why hasn't he addressed alcohol abuse, amphetamines, and anabolic steroids? Ueberroth counters that he would rather get players help than punish them.

31. Fight On

On-field fights seem to be "in" this season and the Mets lead the pugilistic parade. It's their arrogant, cocky, obnoxious attitude opponents say.

"There's a lot of jealousy around the league," Gary Carter says. "But we're going to play hard every day, and if the people we're playing don't like it, that's their problem."

Their latest fight begins with a bumping match between the Reds' Eric Davis and the Mets' Ray Knight. When Davis says something, Knight, a former Golden Gloves boxer, unloads a right cross to the face of Davis. Benches empty and the melee is on.

"Knight is one tough cookie," Carter says. "He's the nicest guy, but when you see that fire in his eyes, look out, boys."

Four Mets—Darling, Teufel, Aguilera, and Ojeda—are later involved in a barroom brawl with two off-duty policemen. Afterwards, someone comes up with a T-shirt reading "HOUSTON POLICE 4, NEW YORK METS 0."

Tough guys, those Mets.

"They're just so offensive, literally and figuratively," the Reds' Ted Power says. "They have an air about them like the Dodger teams in the '70s. They're real cocky. When they get beat, it's like, how did that happen?"

"All this gung-ho New York Mania," says the Reds' Dave Parker. "I've seen better. I've been on better. I'd love to meet them in the playoffs. We'd beat them."

Harbor no doubt about it. The Mets aren't well liked and Carter is their poster boy for provocation. His *#*# curtain calls after home runs are just too much. The last time he pulled that, the Atlanta pitcher plunked Strawberry with the next pitch.

Then there's George Foster with his I-could-care-less bat-flip when he is walked.

"Everybody hates the Mets," says Parker. "Everybody."

Carter says it all comes down to jealousy because ... well, simply because they're better than everyone else.

"We've got some fire," Johnson acknowledges. "You can't have all Boog

Powells and Brooks Robinsons. You have to have a few Frank Robinsons, too. Being cocky is not a bad attitude as far as I'm concerned."

Fight on, Mets. Your manager has your backs.

Although the Mets look as if they're going to cruise to the pennant, it doesn't stop them from continuing their aggressive ways. In a game against Cincinnati, Strawberry is ejected for arguing a called third strike, Howard Johnson is accused of intentionally kicking a dropped third strike away from the catcher leading to the an ejection, and a fight breaks out when Reds outfielder Eric Davis steals third and elbows Ray Knight, who then belts Davis with a right cross leading to four more ejections.

This leaves the Mets so thin that they have to play Carter at third and pitcher Roger McDowell in right field. In the tenth inning Johnson has McDowell move back to pitcher to get the last out, with pitcher Mario Soto moving to right. Then in the 11th Johnson puts Orosco back on the mound, moves McDowell to left field and Mookie Wilson to right. With this the Reds' Rose puts forth his own protest, claiming that since Orosco was already in the game, he shouldn't be entitled to the eight warmup pitches he takes. In the 13th, McDowell goes back to pitching and gets Tony Perez to line out to Orosco now back in the outfield. The Mets eventually win the contentious game.

One player who is not happy, however, is George Foster. Despite his lack of production, Foster is irked that Johnson is batting him in the sixth and seventh spots in the lineup. He should be batting cleanup. Fifth, maybe, but no lower than that.

When he pouts, Johnson sits him down. For the time being, rookie Kevin Mitchell will play in Foster's spot. To no one's surprise, Foster does not take the demotion well.

Yes, his numbers are down he argues, but he would be much more productive in the four or five spot. Why can't Johnson see that?

What Johnson sees is the highest paid player in franchise history not hitting.

A five-time All-Star outfielder, he had been an important member of the Big Red Machine, hitting as many as 52 home runs one season. It looked as if he was on track to become one of the game's all-time greats. The Mets shelled out $10 million for a five-year contract expecting him to be the centerpiece for their rebuilding efforts. In his first year with them he hit only 13 home runs while batting .274.

Now he is a moody loner and the team is no longer sure how much he can, or wants to, contribute.

Foster, never the most talkative player, goes to the press with his pique.

"When a ballclub can, they replace a George Foster or a Mookie Wilson with a more popular white player. I think the Mets would rather promote a

Gary Carter or a Keith Hernandez to the fans so parents who want to can point to them as role models for their children rather than a Darryl Strawberry, a Dwight Gooden, or a George Foster."

Or so said the report in the press. Foster says, "I don't remember saying 'a more popular white player.' I said something that was taken out of context."

A few days later Foster is released.

He was let go because he dared suggest the issue was racism, say some people.

Not at all, say the Mets. He was released because he was reduced to pinch-hitting status, a role in which he was unproductive. It happens all the time.

Besides, the player who replaced him, Kevin Mitchell, is black.

Yes, but the player who took his place on the roster, Lee Mazzilli, is white.

Everybody on the team understands Foster is a bit of a loner who is sensitive and easily hurt. It was said that one reason he was willing to leave the Reds after the 1981 season is that he felt that Pete Rose and Johnny Bench were receiving too much credit for the team's successes at his expense.

Perhaps the player he was closest to on the Mets was Ray Knight. They had played together for a while in the minors. Knight calls him a "solid man" who is "close to the Lord," and whom he described as being very emotional and upset at having been let go.

"A lot of guys thought for a long time he should be gone," Knight says. "I feel badly he's gone. But I understand it completely. I know a lot of guys here thought he was not really part of this team. They thought he quit. He never quit. A lot of people look at the surface. I knew in his heart he didn't quit."

Some players hope Mookie Wilson, the only black still on the team who predated Foster, will step up and take a bigger leadership role, but that is not really in his makeup.

Despite their undeniable successes on the field, there is an increasing awareness that the atmosphere in the Mets clubhouse is slowly disintegrating.

Now, on top of everything else, they've got to deal with the racism charge.

32. Renaissance Scholar in a Baseball Cap

One man paying particular attention to the accusations of racism and social justice in baseball is Dr. Bart Giamatti. "On matters of race, on matters of decency, baseball should lead the way," says the new National League president.

As Joe Garagiola noted, "One thing you can be sure of, you'll never hear anyone say I knew someone exactly like Bart Giamatti."

A bookish man with street smarts, a lifelong literary man, he is, of course, a lifelong Red Sox fan, for according to the writer John Cheever, "all literary men are Red Sox fans. To be a Yankee fan in literary society is to endanger your life."

J.D. Salinger, the famous writer/recluse/Red Sox fanatic, would probably have agreed. Apparently he has been to many games at Fenway.

On the elocution spectrum, Giamatti is far removed from most of baseball's spokesmen. Where Yogi Berra says of baseball, "It ain't like football. You can't make up no trick plays," Giamatti says, "It breaks your heart. It is designed to break your heart. The game begins in spring, when everything else begins again, and it blossoms in the summer, filling the afternoons and evenings, and then as soon as the chill rains come, it stops and leaves you to face the fall alone."

Giamatti was born in Boston and went to Yale University from which he graduated magna cum laude. He then stayed on to earn his Ph.D. and settled into the life of an academic at Yale and Princeton where he was a professor of comparative literature, an extremely popular teacher, his specialty was the comparison of English and Italian Renaissance poets. It is probably safe to say he knew more about Dante Alighieri, Petrarch, and Giotto than Joe Garagiola did.

As a joke, when he stepped down as master of Stiles College at Yale, his students presented him with a moose head that they had rescued from a yard sale. When the new master took over, Giamatti, in his most professorial academic voice, told him, "I have only one solemn duty to convey to you. Take care of my moose."

On more than one occasion he has spoken about how his two great loves, baseball and literature, are as spiritually connected as Tinker and Chance. The game of baseball is, he says, "an oft-told tale that recommences with every pitch, with every game, with every season. Tales of striving to leave home and then return go back at least to Homer. All literary romance derives from the Odyssey and is about rejoining."

Baseball has never seen anybody like him. That Major League Baseball should choose the author of *Play of Double Senses: Spenser's Faerie Queen* as one of its top executives is nothing short of remarkable. The bearded, beer-bellied, cigarette-smoking intellectual doesn't even look like a baseball man. He is a chubby, shortish man, often seen wandering around the Yale campus wearing rumpled slacks and a sports jacket topped by a Boston Red Sox cap, and, on many summer days, with a little radio pressed to his ear listening to a Red Sox game.

And he certainly doesn't talk like a baseball man. When discussing the journeymen players who make a contribution to the game greater than their rewards, he uses the word "maldistribution." When discussing rising salaries, he uses the word "déclassé." Adding football-like wild card teams to the playoffs isn't "bad," it's "abhorrent." He knows that the name of Seaver's home town, Fresno, means "ash tree," and he has referred to a record string of strikeouts as "an auto-da-fé that has never been bettered."

As befitting a scholar of a long-gone time, Giamatti brings to his new office as strong a sense of the past as he does a concern for the future. Call him a traditionalist and a staunch defender of values. With respect to drugs, he says baseball has a "moral obligation," not a "public relations issue." About instant replay, he says, "Never. It rests on the naive assumption that you can transfer the responsibility for judgment to technology." About the designated-hitter rule, he says it "takes away from the manager one of his most important acts of judgment — when to hit for the pitcher."

He also writes about the game with considerable skill. He knows, for example, that prepositions are not words you end sentences with. He can also define "gerund" and he has a real penchant for the poetic in his prose:

> Of course, there are those who learn after the first few times. They grow out of sports. And there are others who were born with the wisdom to know that nothing lasts. These are the truly tough among us, the ones who can live without illusion, or without even the hope of illusion. I am not that grown-up or up-to-date. I am a simpler creature, tied to more primitive patterns and cycles. I need to think something lasts forever, and it might as well be that state of being that is a game; it might as well be that, in a green field, in the sun.

When told that *Esquire* magazine called him one of the smartest men in America, he averred that it must have been a humor issue. He doesn't want his erudition to come across as arrogance and he certainly doesn't want to appear to be "too brainy" for the business he is now in. He's certainly smart enough to "dumb down" when necessary.

Still, there are those who question his qualifications for the job.

He's probably never laid down a drag bunt in his life.

To which he responds that people who bring this up "seem to think that all a university president does is sit under a green tree conferring with shepherds." He says he believes the challenges offered by baseball will be similar to those offered by academia but instead of dealing with faculty and administrators, he'll now be dealing with players and owners.

He says that in high school his athletic accomplishments were limited to carrying water and keeping score, but that he has always harbored a great affection for "the fundamental grid, the geometric beauty of baseball." He says that his first baseball glove was left behind by an American soldier in Italy and picked up by his father, a professor of languages at Mount Holyoke College.

His lack of athletic skills may have been at least partially a result of Charcot-Marie-Tooth disease, an inherited neurological disorder from which it has been said he is afflicted.

His administrative background suggests he knows how to handle the challenges to which he refers. When at 39 and after one of the most extensive and lengthy searches in American academic history, he was chosen as Yale's president, he was also challenged by huge problems. Facing a $16 million deficit, he was asked by William Bundy, presidential search committee head, to redesign the university so as to become "the Cadillac Seville of education." Presumably he meant maintaining the quality while keeping the costs down. He was also facing significant faculty vs. administration tensions exacerbated by a strike.

He threw himself into the task with great vigor, passion, and eloquence, leavened always by a self-deprecating sense of humor. "Call me Bart the Refurbisher," he says. "I've spent $20 million on deferred maintenance and will only be remembered by people who like to go through steam tunnels. If my name goes on anything, it will be the Giamatti Memorial Wiring System."

That he was so successful at Yale augers well for baseball.

"There are a lot of people who know me who can't understand for the life of them why I would go to work on something as unserious as baseball," he says. "If they only knew."

Because baseball is an integral part of our society, he understands the biggest problems facing the game are those of trying to adapt to the rapidity of changes in that society.

And about drugs?

"That's part of our environment that has to be confronted on many levels. It isn't just sending helicopters to Bolivia or busting street-corner peddlers.

There is an entire spectrum of approaches—law enforcement, education, public awareness—that must be taken. Everyone should be aware of the ruinous effects drugs have had on our society."

During the baseball strike of 1981 he had written an open letter spelling out his views on the situation.

"The people of America care about baseball, not about your squalid little squabbles. Reassume your dignity and remember that you are the temporary custodians of an enduring public trust.... You are evidently so enthralled by your mucky pelf and your self-serving stratagems that you have forgotten what your trusteeship means. I will tell you."

Although the baseball owners may not know exactly what "pelf" is they have given him control of theirs. He is baseball's first professor since Casey Stengel retired.

When he accepted the job as National League president he said, "Dante would have been delighted." There are nods all around, even from those who wonder who this Dante guy is and whether he could ever hit a curve ball.

He is a man incapable of acting capriciously in the face of difficulty or of letting troubles roll off his back. He carries them with him always, not because he chooses to, but because he is incapable of acting otherwise.

"The largest thing I've learned," he says, "is the enormous grip that this game has on people, the extent to which it really is very important. It goes way down deep. It really does bind together. It's a cliché and sounds sentimental, but I have now seen it from the inside."

He knows he will face the pressures, the problems with which the game is confronted, but he also knows that his passion for the Red Sox will not abate. National League owners have even instituted a mock kangaroo court for him. "I'll be fined $500 every time I mention the Red Sox," says Giamatti. "If Boston finally makes it to the World Series, it's going to be difficult going to Fenway Park and rooting for the National League team."

Mike Barnicle, *Boston Globe* columnist, once wrote, "Baseball is not a life and death matter, but the Red Sox are."

Giamatti is so passionate, so concerned, so committed, some wonder if he will be able to bear up under the pressure.

Some of the pressure is coming from Ueberroth who is urging the club owners to control their spending on this year's amateur draft. The word has gone out that around $100,000 is the limit for the top players. There is also an agreement that if a team fails to sign its No.1 pick, it will get two selections in the 1987 first round, and if it flagrantly violates the limit, it will lose the 1987 pick. The top two picks this year, Jeff King and Greg Swindell, have both signed for close to the $100,000 figure, but baseball executive are carefully watching Patrick Lennon who is asking for $250,000 from the Mariners, and maybe more for the Red Sox pick, the 6' 3" outfielder Greg McMurtry, who is considered the best athlete in the draft.

While Ueberroth is struggling with finding reasonable solutions to baseball's financial problems, rumors continue to circulate that he is actively campaigning for the 1988 vice presidential nomination. For this, if for no other reason, a lot of attention is being directed to Giamatti, who could well be an ideal replacement.

You just can't have too many Renaissance scholars in high places. Giamatti, though, shows no inclination for any other office than the one he now holds.

September 1989

Giamatti, a heavy smoker, dies suddenly of a massive heart attack. He was 51.

Both his sons, Marcus and Paul, will attend the prestigious Yale School of Drama and go on to have successful professional careers as actors. In the highly successful film Sideways, *Paul's character, Miles, looks at a picture of himself as a younger man standing with a man in sunglasses, his father, Bartlett. Like his father, he is a devoted Red Sox fan.*

33. Gambling on the Game

Pete Rose's salary for the 1986 season is a tidy $1 million. He has a lot of pocket change to throw around if he cares to and he often does.

Even casual fans of the game know who "Charlie Hustle" is. He is revered for his gristle and determination, admired for his "never-give-up" attitude. Fathers point him out with glee to their sons as he streaks down to first base on a routine walk.

See that? That's the way the game should be played.

Henry Aaron says, "Does Pete Rose hustle? Before the All-Star Game he came into the clubhouse and took off his shoes—and they ran another mile without him."

He plays hard. Everybody knows that. He's the antithesis of the lazy player but says, "I don't mind lazy players, as long as they're on the other side."

He holds so many records it's hard to count them all. Most importantly, though, he holds the record for the most career hits, a record he wrestled away from that bastard Ty Cobb. It came a year before when he lined a slider from the Padres' Eric Show (who would die a few years later of a drug overdose) into short left field. As Rose rounded first amidst popping flashbulbs, flying confetti, and streaming toilet paper, he saw the ball bound high and he thought about going for two, but uncharacteristically, he skidded to a stop and retreated to first.

"I wish I had took two," he said later about the historic hit. "I should have went into second base when the ball bounced high. That would have been a great way of getting the record, with a head first slide into second."

Told of the historic event, Mickey Mantle, emphasizing his slugging prowess over Rose's small-ball hitting, declared: "If I'd-a hit that many singles, I'd-a wore a dress."

Later Rose would insist that if he had used steroids, "I would have got 5,000 hits." Instead he did it like Cobb did, always working on his game, studying pitchers, taking batting practice until the shaggers keeled over, and always hustling.

Rose won about everything there is to win in the game—three World

Series, three batting crowns, one Most Valuable Player Award, two Gold Gloves, the Rookie of the Year Award, and he made 17 All-Star appearances playing five different positions.

Now he is a player-manager of the Cincinnati Reds, but it looks as if the "player" part of the job description may be close to being dropped even if he does say, "I'd walk through hell in a gasoline suit to keep playing baseball." When the season started he was 45. He has already outlasted Cobb by a year. Some players go gracefully into that good night, not Rose. He'll keep fighting as long as he can.

Pete, the fighter, don't quit.

Despite his popularity, however, the Reds owner, Marge Schott, has not seen fit to include a picture of Rose in the team's media guide. In fact, there are no pictures of players in the guide. There are, however, 12 shots of her Saint Bernard, Schottzie.

Rose is intense but outgoing at the same time. He loves the spotlight. A real media hound. He loves the company of the guys in the clubhouse. He loves doing what guys do—drinking a little beer, playing a little poker, and shooting a little bull—just so long as the guys remember who he is. Off the field there is something of a child-like quality about him, a description he'd probably reject.

"Doctors tell me I have the body of a thirty-year-old. I know I have the brain of a fifteen-year-old. If you've got both, you can play baseball."

He spends so much time with the boys that his ex-wife quips that it was too bad she wasn't a second baseman. She might have seen more of her husband.

When he wasn't around, it was common to hear Pete-ain't-the-brightest-bulb-in-the-pack lines or other similar observations.

Pete's a few cans short of a six pack — six cans. A few snowballs short of an avalanche. A few puppies short of a pet shop.

Cincinnati broadcaster Joe Nuxhall once said of Rose, "I'll tell you how smart Pete is. When they had the blackout in New York, he was stranded 13 hours on an escalator."

Rose himself used to say the only books he ever read were the several variations of the "Pete Rose Story."

You don't have to be a great intellect to be a good baseball manager. Baseball smarts work just as well, maybe better, and Rose had plenty of those. He wasn't born with great natural ability. He didn't have the athletic skills of a Willie Mays or a Mickey Mantle, but he worked like the devil to develop those he had. He liked to tell that story. It made him seem like the hustling, street smart, self-made player he promoted. He liked it when people said he may not have been the most talented guy around, or the smartest either, but he was one helluva ball player. Can't take that away from him.

No one jokes about his playing, but that's about the only part of his life that escapes.

Wade Boggs, Steve Garvey, and Pete Rose are in a bar. A pretty woman walks by and Boggs says, "I'm going to ask her out." Garvey replies, "You can't do that, she's carrying my baby." To which Rose added, "You wanna bet?"

Rose has a friend with whom he is frequently seen hanging out — Tommy Gioiosa. They have known each other since 1978 when Rose saw him playing catch with Pete Rose, Jr., in the parking lot of their spring training hotel. This stumpy little one-time junior college second baseman, now a car detailer, wore his hair just like Rose's. Little by little the two men with the Prince Valiant haircuts got to know each other.

"He's a very handy kid," Rose was to say. "Tommy can fix anything."

Tommy eventually moved in with Rose and his family and could be found in the Reds' locker room with the frequency of a clubhouse attendant. Tommy, the sycophant, became Rose's gopher. He'd go for coffee, beer, or about anything else his famous buddy asked for. He'd go for more new friends to introduce to Rose. People like Ron Peters.

Peters owned Jonathans Cafe in Franklin, Ohio, a town of 12,000 named after Benjamin Franklin. From there it is about a 40-minute drive down Route 75 to Riverfront Stadium where the Reds play their games. Peters is doing very well for a small-town café owner. He owns a Jaguar and a Corvette bought with cash, and he owns a $200,000 home. He must sell a lot of burgers at his café. Oh, but his 1985 federal tax return showed an income of less than $26,000. He probably invested wisely.

A few years later, Peters remembers it differently. "I had everything. I had the world by the tail. In a small town, I had a restaurant/bar that was grossing $1 million a year. My clientele was anybody and everybody in Franklin — everyone from hod carriers to lawyers. Everyone knew what I was doing — even the police chief."

Peters visits Rose frequently. Rose likes him. He's gregarious and he's smart.

Not everyone agrees. Rose is urged to steer clear of Peters and Gioiosa.

That ass-licking sycophant Gioiosa is going to lead you down a dead-end road, and you ain't gonna like it much.

Both those bums are nothing but trouble.

It's not the biggest secret in baseball — Rose is betting on games. Can't say he wasn't warned. Again and again he heard the admonitions. Again and again he ignored them.

It's a disease many highly successful people catch. They think that because they were so successful in one thing, they can be successful in anything. Gambling, for instance.

Now Rose has played in more than 3,600 games and has been in who knows how many clubhouses. Maybe he doesn't read many books and maybe he isn't the brightest guy in the clubhouse, but surely he saw the sign hanging in every one of them saying that betting on baseball can lead to expulsion from the game.

It's there in big letters, Pete.

August 1989

A five-page document is faxed to each Major League club. A. Bartlett Giamatti, now commissioner of baseball, and Peter Edward Rose, retired baseball player and manager, are the signatories. The document begins:

> On March 6, 1989, the Commissioner of Baseball instituted an investigation of Peter Edward Rose, the field manager of the Cincinnati Reds Baseball Club, concerning allegations that Peter Edward Rose engaged in conduct not in the best interests of baseball in violation of Major League Rule 21, including but not limited to betting on Major League Baseball games in connection with which he had a duty to perform.

The document also includes the following language:

> THEREFORE, the Commissioner, recognizing the benefits to Baseball from a resolution of this matter, orders and directs that Peter Edward Rose be subject to the following disciplinary sanctions, and Peter Edward Rose, recognizing the sole and exclusive authority of the Commissioner and that it is in his interest to resolve this matter without further proceedings, agrees to accept the following disciplinary sanctions imposed by the Commissioner.
>
> Peter Edward Rose is hereby declared permanently ineligible in accordance with Major League Rule 21 and placed on the Ineligible List.

If anyone knows what Rose is going through these days it is Denny McClain, who sits in the Federal Correctional Institution in Talladega, Alabama. Eighteen years earlier he had finished the season 31–6 for the Tigers. He was the first pitcher since Dizzy Dean in 1934 to win 30 games in a season. That year, after the Tigers had the 1968 pennant sewn up, McLain, the most dominant player in the game, purposely served up a fat pitch to Mantle, the creaky-kneed slugger who was nearing the end of his career. With that home run, Mantle passed Jimmie Foxx on the all-time home run list.

Denny McLain is all heart.

On March 16, 1985, a jury of nine women and three men in the U.S. District Court in Tampa found him guilty of racketeering, conspiracy to commit racketeering (including loan-sharking), extortion and possession of cocaine with intent to distribute it. The story told in court was a messy affair complete with mobsters, loan sharks, drug traffickers and heinous deeds such as threats to cut off ears. For his part, McLain received three consecutive eight-year sentences for the racketeering, conspiracy and extortion charges, and the remainder of the 23-year sentence on the drug charge.

McLain admits to the bookmaking charges, but denies the others.

Are you listening, Mr. Rose?

Betting on baseball isn't anything new. Punters were putting down bets when bases were still posts. Gamblers appeared at games just about when shortstops did. In the early 1870s the professional clubs had to put in a rule to prohibit a player from betting on his own team and to withhold his pay if he bet on another team. What an idea!

One of the earliest pioneers of the game, James Whyte Davis, wrote in 1872:

> If you wanted to place a bet on a horse race or a prize fight all you had to do was to go to any one of hundreds of saloons, billiard parlors, or coffee houses that were widely known to arrange such things. Or if you preferred, you could just as easily lose your money playing chuck-a-luck, draw poker, roulette, faro, or keno. It was never hard to find someone to take your money. The city was home to any number of gambling halls, lavishly decorated dives with thick carpets, soft chairs, and marble tables where for a pittance one could buy a brandy and a segar so as to lose one's money in faux style. I read someplace that in our city alone as many as 30,000 people earned their living off the gambling industry.
>
> Was it any surprise then that gamblers took such an interest in base ball? It's a chancy game played by men prone to mistakes whether inadvertent or resolute. I can't say how much money was changing hands regularly as a result of games. No one can, but neither can anyone deny that it was insidious and pervasive. Because gambling had become so much a part of base ball, spectators were wont to think that any game which their team lost when highly favored, was because the "fix was on." In most cases it wasn't, but so long as the suspicions surfaced, the game remained tainted. And because they so often played three-game championship series, the temptation, or even thought of temptation to purposely split the first two games so as to force a third game with a big gate was always in the air. Suspicion, justified or not, was everywhere. It is but a short step from gambling to fix. A sure thing is a whole lot better than a chance.

As if that wasn't enough, in 1882 the board of directors of the National League met in a secret session to try Richard Higham, one of the League's umpires, on the charge of crookedness preferred against him by the president of the Detroit Club. Higham himself was present at the formal trial. Apparently the charges were based on letters written by Higham to gamblers advising them to bet on certain games in which he umpired. As a result of the trial, by a unanimous vote, the League directors expelled him.

In the early years of the twentieth century, Hal Chase, aka "Prince Hal," was considered one of the best fielding first basemen ever to have played the game. He was also considered one of the dirtiest — the "Black Prince of Baseball." It was well known that he bet on games and widely believed that he threw them when appropriate. He fielded more allegations of corruption than he did ground balls. For a long time, the league scolded him, and then looked the other way.

He paid pitcher Jimmy Ring $50 to throw a game against the Giants. Formal charges were brought against him by the squeaky-clean Dale Murphy of his day — Christy Mathewson. The league president, however, acquitted him for lack of concrete evidence.

Then in 1919 the infamous Black Sox Scandal was headline news all over the country. It seems the White Sox players were furious with team owner Charles Comiskey for his "tightwad ways," including charging players to launder their uniforms. So, as the story goes, a group of players led by first baseman Chick Gandil met with gamblers and agreed to throw the World Series.

Take that Comiskey, you player-cheating, cheapskate, bastard.

In the trial that followed, the eight accused players, including Shoeless Joe Jackson, were acquitted, but the game's first commissioner, tough guy Kenesaw Mountain Landis, wanted to send a message to the public that the game was cleaning up its stained image. He needed scapegoats, and these eight men would do perfectly. The judge handed down his ruling:

> Regardless of the verdict of juries, no player who throws a ball game, no player who undertakes or promises to throw a ball game, no player who sits in confidence with a bunch of crooked ballplayers and gamblers, where the ways and means of throwing a game are discussed and does not promptly tell his club about it, will ever play professional baseball.

When it became known that Prince Hal won $40,000 by betting on the Reds in the World Series, Landis banned him from the game as well.

"I wasn't satisfied with what the club owners paid me," Chase said some years later. "Like others, I had to have a bet on the side and we used to bet with the other team and the gamblers who sat in the boxes. It was easy to get a bet. Sometimes collections were hard to make. Players would pass out IOUs and often be in debt for their entire salaries. That wasn't a healthy condition. Once the evil started there was no stopping it, and club owners were not strong enough to cope with the evil."

Nelson Algren wrote of the Black Sox Scandal, "Benedict Arnolds! Betrayers of American Boyhood, not to mention American Girlhood and American Womanhood and American Hoodhood."

Baseball's need to promote its image as a clean, fair, family-friendly game never stops. As soon as one problem is explained/legislated/buried/denied away, it seems new ones surface.

The McLain problem is just that. Detroit catcher Bill Freehan wrote of the 1969 season, "The rules for Denny just don't seem to be the same as for the rest of us."

In a *Sports Illustrated* article, McLain is quoted as saying,

> All of a sudden you wake up one day, you look around and say, "How in the hell did I get here?" Then you have to admit to yourself: I put myself here. No one else. Now what am I going to do to get out? There comes a point when you finally admit to yourself, hey, I've made some mistakes and I'm sorry. I'm genuinely sorry for what I did. Now please let me get on with the rest of my life.

How much Rose knows about Prince Hal, Denny McLain, Chick Gandil, and the others isn't clear. A reasonable guess is that he knows little but wouldn't give a damn if he did.

But those are of little matter now. He's got more important things to attend to.

1998

Rose serves as a "guest ring announcer" at several WWE wrestling matches. During a match between Kane and the Undertaker, he is subjected to a Tombstone Piledriver from Kane. To get revenge, he later appears as the San Diego Chicken and attacks Kane.

2004

Rose releases his autobiography, reversing fifteen years of denials and admitting he bet on baseball games while playing for and managing the Reds. It is seen by many as an attempt to persuade Major League Baseball that he should be eligible for induction into the Hall of Fame.

Rose hasn't brought a championship to the Reds yet as manager, but this could well be the year. He honestly believes that if you work hard enough at something you can master it. After all, isn't he a perfect example of this? Surely his work ethic will rub off on the team. Surely they can parlay a blue-collar approach into the division title. Charlie Hustle will mold the team in his image, simply because his ego can't have it any other way.

He has seen so many great players fail as managers because the naturally talented don't have to study and learn the techniques to play the game on a high level. It's pure instinct. No one ever had to tell Willie Mays how to determine the best angle to run down a fly ball. He just saw the ball in flight and with his great speed, ran to where he knew it would come down. Rose had neither that level of instinct nor the foot speed. He learned to compensate — study batters' tendencies so he could "cheat" in the direction the batter was more likely to hit the ball given the pitcher's approach to that batter. So as to minimize the lack of running speed, he learned the little tricks of getting a quick jump as soon as the ball was hit. Willie most likely saw a pitch that looked like it was going to be a strike and then swung at it. Good things often followed. Rose learned to study pitchers' little tell-tale giveaway signs when they were about to deliver a certain pitch so as to give him an edge. He wasn't guessing as much as predicting based on careful observation.

Rose sees himself as a teacher who has so many things to teach that he has no doubt he can be as great a manager as he has been a player — if only the damn players will listen.

34. The Way They Used to Play

Cal Ripken, Jr., doesn't gamble on baseball. He doesn't do drugs. He cares about how he is perceived by the public. He wants to be seen as a player who demonstrates what he considers the old-fashioned American values of Pete-Rose-like hard work, but to that he wants to add an image of integrity. He wants to be seen as pure *Saturday Evening Post*, a jut-jawed John Wayne of the diamond. When he finally retires he wants to be thought of as an ambassador for the game.

Six weeks into the season and Ripken is hitting below .250.

So, Cal, what is a 6' 4", 225-pound power-hitter doing playing shortstop anyway? Why don't you move to third?

Ripken says playing third base would make him "feel like a spectator."

But you don't have the athleticism of an Ozzie Smith. You don't even dive for balls.

"I don't dive and do fancy things," he responds, "but if you play where you're supposed to play, every play is routine." He says he learned that from one of the best fielding shortstops ever, Mark Belanger, who claimed that diving for balls was a waste of half a step.

His manager, Earl Weaver, comes to his defense citing the fact that Ripken set the AL record for assists in 1984. "What's so bad about that?" asks Weaver. "He's smart. He goes back on pop-ups better than anyone I've ever seen. Sure, he'll eventually move to save his bat, but he's 25. He's the All-Star shortstop, and not just because of his bat."

Okay, but wouldn't a day off here or there help his average? Look, he's played in 638 straight games and more than 5,750 consecutive innings. Surely that's taken a toll.

"What good does three hours off do me?" he asks before going back to shagging balls in the outfield.

"The boy loves to play baseball. Baseball keeps him fresh," says his coach-father.

The Orioles argue that he's one of the most intelligent players in the game and it can't hurt to have an intelligent shortstop. Down the line maybe third base. For now he's the All-Star shortstop and that's where he'll remain.

Cal Ripken says that growing up he played more soccer than baseball. He also says he was a pretty good basketball player in high school but gave it up because he didn't have any hair on his chest or underarms. He was embarrassed to wear the uniform. At least the baseball shirt covered up his perceived teenage deficiencies.

In high school he was mostly a pitcher. In his senior year he posted a 0.79 ERA, but when he wasn't pitching they let him play shortstop. Most of the scouts were interested in him as a pitcher, but he liked playing every day so his father, a long-time professional baseball coach, advised him to try the shortstop route and if he didn't make the grade there he could always come back in a couple of years as a pitcher.

He was drafted by the Orioles, his father's team, with the understanding that he would be given a chance to show what he could do at short, or at least in the infield. His first stop was with the Bluefield Orioles in West Virginia. He was 17 and he struggled on their weedy field, making 32 errors in 63 games with a low batting average and no homers. Some of his teammates figured the kid was only there anyway because his father was a coach for the Orioles. In time the hitting came around and so did the fielding and he moved his way up the minor league ladder. One day while with the Oriole's Triple-A team in Rochester, he took an early swing in the batting cages and felt something pull in his right shoulder. The team sat him down, talked of putting him on the disabled list, but finally opted against it.

Maybe the kid ain't gonna make it. If he gets hurt just swinging a bat who knows? Some guys get injured a lot, some don't. Some guys play hurt, some don't.

Some guys play in really long games. It was one of those cold, windy New England nights in Rhode Island in 1981 when everybody—fans, players, umpires, and coaches—wanted to get the game over with as soon as possible. It was cold enough that they had a fire going in an oil drum sitting in the dugout. As these things are wont to go, the game was tied at the end of nine innings—the last thing anyone wanted. Hampered by stiff and cold muscles, the players trudged on. Neither team scored in the tenth. Neither team scored in the eleventh through the twentieth either. Then finally, Rochester pushed over a run in the twenty-first.

There weren't many fans left, but the few who persisted let out a sigh of relief. Finally!

But soon "finally" turned to "oh, no!"

Pawtucket eked out a run to tie the game in the bottom of the inning. On they went. No one scored in the twenty-second, twenty-third, or thirtieth. In the thirty-second, Rochester manager Doc Edwards sent a runner home in a desperate effort to end the marathon affair. The ball and the runner looked as if they were about to arrive at the same instant.

"Out" called the umpire as if even he was disappointed to have to call it that way, but he had no choice. By this time, everyone was so exhausted and cold, the umpires huddled and decided the only humane thing to do was to suspend the game.

To be continued...

Some weeks later, when the game was resumed, the press and TV cameras assembled to record the historic event. They didn't have to wait long.

In the bottom of the thirty-third inning, a Pawtucket single sent the winning run home.

Like everyone else's average, Ripken's took a dive in that game. Going 2-for-13 will do that.

In August, Edwards told Ripken he was going up to the Orioles. With Lenn Sakata playing shortstop and his father coaching, he found himself in the lineup at third base.

Going into the '86 season, Ripken holds the Major League record for consecutive innings played at 5,457.

August 1997

The game between the Orioles and Mariners at Baltimore's Camden Yards is scheduled for a 7:35 start. However, when the big banks of lights are turned on, only a few bulbs along the first-base line are illuminated. After a delay of nearly 2½ hours, umpire Al Clark calls the game.

Davey Johnson says it was the right decision, if for no other reason than Randy Johnson, whose fastball has been clocked over 100 mph, was to be on the mound for the Mariners.

A story begins making the rounds of clubhouses a few days later.

The story goes like this: Cal Ripken's friend, the actor Kevin Costner, who has probably acted in more baseball-themed movies than anyone else, has been labeled by Esquire *magazine as one of the 100 sexiest stars in film history, and by* People *magazine as one of the 50 most beautiful people in the world. Cal Ripken's friend thinks Cal Ripken's wife is also one of the 50 most beautiful people in the world.*

On the day of this game, Ripken says goodbye to his wife, gets in his car, and begins driving to Camden Yards. On the way he realizes he has left his wallet at home so he turns around and heads back to retrieve it. When he walks in the house he finds Costner with his wife. The two men get into a scuffle in the midst of which Ripken is cut and bruised. There goes the consecutive game streak.

When Peter Angelos learns of the injuries he arranges for the stadium lights to malfunction. The game is cancelled and the streak remains alive.

That's the story.

The story gains traction when Costner is accused of performing a sex act while having a massage at a prestigious hotel in Scotland.

September 20, 1998
Cal Ripken, Jr., announces he's taking himself out of the lineup. He just says it, very typically Cal, "This is what I'm going to do." Ryan Minor takes his place.

Cal's father, Big Rip, is a master sergeant drill instructor of a baseball man. He's tough, he's gruff, he'll drill the fundamentals into any player, whether superstar or hanger on. Once, one of the Orioles front office men showed up at their spring training site at 7:30 in the morning to find Big Rip sitting at his office in his full uniform, including cap. The phrase "tough old coot" doesn't seem to be enough.

He's so old school he makes his manager, Earl Weaver, seem New Age.

Manager of the Aberdeen Pheasants in South Dakota was one of the many positions he held in a 13-year minor league managerial career. Once on a 12-hour bus trip from Duluth to Grand Forks, the bus driver became so tired that the manager took over in the middle of the night while the team slept and was still driving when the light came up the next morning. Just before noon the bus broke down and someone had to go for help. Not wanting to waste a perfectly good morning, Ripken sent his players out into a nearby field and hit golf balls to them which they shagged in their gloves.

With his perpetual cigarette and tobacco-yellowed fingers he barks instructions to everyone including his two kids, Cal Jr. and Billy. This stern man of craggy face and stoic disposition is a teacher by instinct and what he teaches most are fundamentals and respect for the game.

"I was always one to stress fundamentals, sports or anything," he says. "There's a basic way to do things, a fundamental way to do things. You have to know the proper way to go about it before you can do it properly."

His blue-collar work ethic has been passed down to Cal, Jr., and to Billy. Cal is in his fifth year with the Orioles and on his way to a Hall of Fame career. Billy is in the minors and won't come up until next season and is on his way to a career that is remembered as much for his infamous baseball card as for anything else. The Fleer card showed Billy holding a bat on his shoulder. In clear view on the knob was the expletive "fuck face."

Big Rip was not amused.

It's not always the ideal situation having your tough-guy father as a coach. Sometimes the players are careful not to say anything about Big Rip when Junior is around. Still, Junior doesn't have to worry any longer about people thinking he's there because of his father. That he's there on his own merits is beyond questioning. He's already been Rookie of the Year and league MVP. And he plays every day.

No one on the team asks him about his work ethic. They see where that comes from. He readily credits his father for instilling in him the conviction of his ways. "When you feel that you are right, you must stand up for what you believe in" is a message he's heard often from his father. Although according to Junior, his father could be "stupid stubborn," he has learned much from him and the mutual respect runs deep. "Stubbornness" must be a Ripken trait

Joe Torre says that Junior is a bridge, maybe the last bridge, back to the way the game used to be played. "Hitting home runs and all that other good stuff is not enough. It's how you handle yourself in all the good times and bad times that matters. That's what Cal showed us. Being a star is not enough. He showed us how to be more."

As baseball poet Donald Hall wrote, "Baseball is fathers and sons playing catch, the long arc of the years between."

There was a time, though, when it was anything but for the Ripkens. For many years Big Rip was away, first as a minor league catcher who never made it to the majors, and then as minor league manager, while Cal stayed home with his two brothers, sister, and mother. They saw little of each other.

"I feel cheated in a manner of speaking," says Cal, Jr., now 25. "I guess I'm making up for lost time. I see him every single day. It's nice."

To please his father, he began playing when he was eight. Cal, Sr., says he didn't force the game on his boys, but in a way he did, because that was how they could earn praise from the stoical father. Cal, Jr., says the look on his father's face says it all. He sees that look a lot these days.

When Cal, Jr., was a Little Leaguer, his father sometimes gave him and his teammates pamphlets to read, little booklets about the dangers of drug abuse. Play the game the right way, his father would insist and you don't need drugs. The game is its own high. Some of the boys thought he was a corny tough guy, but there was admiration too because he was a professional baseball man. Cal, Jr., when asked what his father did, liked to be able to say that. None of the other boys could and that made him feel important.

35. The Image of the Game

The Orioles hold a meeting to discuss the impact drugs are having on the game. They've all read about the cocaine scandals in Pittsburgh and Kansas City. They all know where and how they can get drugs if they choose to. The drug-pushing hangers-on are around subtly advertising their game-enhancing wares. And who is there to keep the wolves at bay?

Need a little giddy-up in your game?

Wanna get back from that injury a little faster?

Look at the drinkers and the coke guys, they slump faster than the setting sun. But if you're smart enough to try these uppers, well, you'll gain an edge ... and fast.

Remember, performance equals money.

The Oriole players, acting totally on their own, without approval from the Players Association, come up with their own plan—voluntary drug testing.

To no one's surprise, Cal Jr. strongly supports the plan. Looking back on it he says, "We were local players standing up for ourselves, really. We didn't need the union to do that."

When veteran Eddie Murray also backs the plan, most doubts vanish. "Steady Eddie" was already in his ninth year with the club and was one of the top players in the game. There really was a "Tale of Two Eddies"—a bristly enigma, and a carefree gentleman. To the media he was often diffident, even rude. To his teammates he was usually playful and open. After a 1979 article enraged him, he shut out the media and he kept up the silent treatment for years.

In the clubhouse, though, when he speaks, players tend to listen.

Of the drug testing plan, Cal Jr. says, "When you look around and see guys like Eddie Murray backing this, you know it's the right thing to do." Pitcher Mike Boddicker adds, "We made a gesture to show the fans of Baltimore that we had nothing to hide."

In the past, players on some teams had voluntarily agreed to drug testing in exchange for guaranteed contracts, and some had opted for testing to improve their image with the public. This is the first time, however, that players decided to participate in a plan as a team.

The first active player to sign a contract with a drug-testing clause was Steve Yeager, at the time a catcher with the Dodgers who was later traded to the Mariners.

According to the Baltimore plan, all the players who signed on were to be tested independently through the Johns Hopkins Hospital and Medical School. The tests would be conducted on a confidential basis from three to six times a year. Should a player's test prove positive, treatment would be strictly between patient and doctor.

General manager Hank Peters believes the program will remove the cloud of mistrust that is currently hanging over baseball. "We've long been concerned with the individual welfare of our players," says Peters, "and the magnitude of the drug problem in baseball has certainly damaged the image of our game."

Attorney Ron Shapiro, who represents a number of the Orioles players, is the driving force behind the plan. "The program is not being implemented as the result of a known problem on the ball club," Shapiro says, "but it is rather an effort to stay ahead of any problem." Nevertheless, it's public knowledge that outfielder Lee Lacy and second baseman Alan Wiggins have had problems with drug abuse in the past.

Since the testing isn't required in any contract and because the Oriole management won't see the results, the players hope that any opposition from the union will be blunted.

Donald Fehr, executive director of the Players Association, however, downplays the plan. He is playing his evil owners vs. misunderstood players card and the whose-fault-is-it game.

The Association files a grievance arguing that any drug-testing clauses in the contracts are unenforceable. The federal arbitrator hearing the case agrees, ruling that clubs may not get the results from any drug test by bypassing the union.

"Every sport is coming out with a drug program now, and we need to get something for ours," says Dave Anderson, the Los Angeles Dodgers' player representative. "It's a hot issue right now and we need to get going. We're going to get some bad publicity saying that baseball players don't like drug testing, and that's not the issue."

Maybe, but that's not the way much of the public sees it and that is a concern to Ueberroth and the owners, most of whom were disappointed with the arbitrator's ruling.

"I am very, very disappointed. It's a bad day for baseball. It's a bad day for the players, it's a bad day for America," says Bill Giles, owner of the Phillies.

"I see it as a union boss looking to justify his existence," says Mike Stone, president of the Rangers. "This ruling could have an adverse effect on granting long-term contracts to players. I'll be damned if we're going to risk several million dollars and have no guarantees."

"I think it's surprising in light of what happened to Len Bias and Don Rogers," says Reds' general manager Bill Bergesch. "I think it's a crime."

"I think it sounds pretty American to me," says the Royals' Dan Quisenberry.

Trying to address the problem is not a mistake, but going around the Players Association and enforcing it in each player's contract apparently is. This is not an issue that is going to go away quickly or easily.

The media's hand-wringing at every new revelation of any player using any drug of choice brings scores of column inches and sound bites.

Pete Rose used methamphetamines. How do you think he got the name "Charlie Hustle"?

And the Mick! Partied his ass off.

Willie Stargell, "King of the Greenies."

The self-righteous pronouncements of Ueberroth and some owners that players should be required to sign contracts with mandatory drug-testing clauses because they owe it to the fans, does not sit well with everyone. They see it as pure hypocrisy arguing that what the owners really mean is that the owners owe it to the owners. When players' performances deteriorate because of drug use, they lose money. End of argument.

Ueberroth, who sells himself as the commissioner of the fans, serves at the pleasure of the owners, and the owners aren't above driving a wedge between the owners and the players. From both a contractual and a public relations standpoint, they've come out on the short end of recent labor negotiations with the union. As long as they're on the "right" side of the drug issue, they believe they can curry favor with the fans when it comes to the real issue — salaries. It is escalating salaries that drives their "holy war" against the evils of drugs.

Drink plenty of beer in the grandstands by all means, but never ever smoke pot.

36. It Pumps Up Your Confidence

Jose Canseco writes in his book *Juiced*:

Is it cheating to do what everybody wants you to do? Are players the only ones to blame for steroids when Donald Fehr and the other bosses of the Major League Players Association fought for years to make sure players wouldn't be tested for steroids? Is it all that secret when the owners of the game put out the word that they want home runs and excitement, making sure that everyone from trainers to managers to clubhouse attendants understands that whatever it is the players are doing to become superhuman, they sure ought to keep it up?

Canseco could always hit long home runs. When he was playing for the minor league Modesto A's, young fans would chant "Loot, foot," every time he hit one of his 500-foot fence-clearing blasts. Teammates dubbed his bat "The Savoy Special," after Roy Hobbs' bat in Bernard Malamud's *The Natural*.

Along with his twin brother, Osvaldo, he grew up playing high school ball in a Miami suburb, having moved there when both were infants.

"He got by on natural talent back then," says coach Sal Pimotta of his lanky third baseman, "but he didn't have his priorities quite straight. He was more interested in socializing than in baseball."

He came out of Coral Park Senior High School a 165-pound weakling, Canseco says, and didn't begin to hit home runs until he found the weight room where he worked out regularly and added 35 pounds of muscle to his frame.

In the 1982 draft that included Dwight Gooden, Shawon Dunston, and Bo Jackson, he was chosen in the 15th round by Oakland. He began using liquid testosterone mixed with Deca Derbol before the start of the 1985 season. When he arrived in spring training, people were amazed at how much his work in the weight room had paid off. He thought he should have made the Athletics right then, but they sent him to Huntsville, Alabama, for a little more seasoning. When he put up huge numbers there, they moved him up to Triple-

A Tacoma, where among his other feats, he became the first player ever to hit a ball completely out of their stadium.

Now he was a legitimate prospect and stories about his incredible power were everywhere. By early September he had hit 40 home runs with 140 RBIs and an average over .300. The A's called him up.

Now, in his first full season, he is showing the power the Athletics expected and more speed from a big man than they might have thought. The tall, muscular player with the engaging smile and smooth powerful swing has made himself extremely popular with the Oakland fans. When he comes to bat, stadium concession lines shrink and fans edge forward in their seats. Either he or the Angeles' Wally Joyner is likely to win the Rookie of the Year Award, but as good as Joyner is, he doesn't have Canseco's power or dramatic appeal.

On the cover of their media guide, the team refers to him as "The Natural." Comparisons to Mickey Mantle and Reggie Jackson are everywhere. So are the young girls who turn out in droves to see this striking 6-foot, 4-inch, 220 pound Cuban-American muscle man. He is, ironically enough, considered to be unassuming, modest, even shy.

"I don't see myself as a hero," he says. "I'm still just a rookie who's trying to do the best he can."

Others see it differently. "The word around," says Brewers coach Frank Howard, "is that he has a great chance to be baseball's next superstar This young man's for real."

The Athletics know what they have in their young slugger, but they also know they have to be careful about putting too much pressure on him.

"I am concerned that some people are expecting too much out of him," says ex-manager Jackie Moore. "Don't expect 400-foot home runs from him every time. He's human, too."

"Sure, some people say I'm one of the greatest," Canseco says, "but some others say I'm not really so great, that I'm overrated. All I really wanted to do was come up to the Major Leagues, be consistent and let my talent take over."

His father, an oil company worker, has a big satellite dish installed at his Miami home so that he can record all of Jose's at-bats no matter where he is playing. Neighbors can hear him screaming exhortations at the screen each time his son comes up. Jose calls him almost every day and he continues his ritual of paying Jose $5 for every home run he hits—a leftover from his younger days. Hitting home runs pays.

Shortly before his mother died in 1984, she went to a psychic who told her both her boys were destined to be famous sportsmen.

Jose doesn't disagree. "Whatever is going to happen in the future will happen, regardless of what they say about me. Whatever is going to happen is predetermined; it's going to happen anyway."

Looking back on how he got to where he is, he says the Athletics were never that high on him, that there was prejudice against him as a 15th round pick and a Latino player. They saw Rob Nelson, a first-round pick, as their big power-hitting hope, but all Canseco saw was a flabby, out-of-shape first baseman who would go on to amass all of four home runs in a five-year Major League career.

When his mother was dying, he says he made her a promise that no matter what it took, he would become the best player in the world.

This, he says, it what drove him to bulk up.

This, he says, is why he turned to steroids.

This is his explanation.

He says at first he was chary about putting something like steroids into his body, but the more he did it, the easier it became. He didn't talk about it with people outside his close circle of friends that included his brother and his girlfriend, both of whom injected him at various times. He was more interested in developing strength and stamina than in adding bulk, but of course, the bulk came too. As writes about it in *Juiced:*

> And I tell you now: Steroids were the key to it all. I was such an improved player, and I think it was because steroids not only give you a lot of physical strength and stamina, they also give you a mental edge. Think of it this way: whenever you drink one of those energy drinks or eat one of those health bars, even before you finish the thing you're feeling better. It could just be sugar water and a candy bar, but mentally, you're feeling like you could run up a wall. It pumps up your confidence like you wouldn't believe, and for any athlete, that's a very potent combination. When your physical ability is there, your strength and stamina are there, and when your confidence level is up as well, the combination can carry you a long way. Wow, I realized those chemicals work.

He claims he eventually learned to inject himself ambidextrously, working both legs alternately. He experimented with different steroids and then combined them with human growth hormones.

If anyone on the team suspected he was using these drugs, they never said anything to him.

Then too, he says, seeing a beautiful lady can also boost your testosterone level and Jose does a lot of beautiful lady-looking.

November 2011
Major League Baseball and the MLB Players Association announce the signing of a memorandum of understanding that includes mandatory testing of blood for human growth hormone for the first time at the Major League level.

The Athletics are trying to climb out of the cellar in their division, and so they are trying lots of new players. Like a game of musical chairs, players are coming and going all season. The shy Canseco feels like he has no real friends on the team, yet he has been so hyped that hopes for the team's revival rest firmly on his broad shoulders. He is hitting a lot of long balls, but striking out a lot, too. He says he really doesn't have much of a sense of what he is doing at the plate other than see ball, swing hard, and sometimes hit ball.

In a game against the Angels, he comes up to bat against Mike Witt. He sees a pitch to his liking, swings hard, and hits the ball — a low line drive that shortstop Dick Schofield leaps to snare. The ball goes over his head. As the radio announcer calls it, "There's a line drive over short. It's in the gap. It's gone."

That's one strong kid, that Canseco.

"He has a body like an Adonis, can hit the ball as far as anybody who's ever come into the game and he's just a kid," Frank Howard says.

"Notice the massive chest and biceps, the results of intensive weight lifting that added 50 pounds of muscle to this 15th-round 1982 draft choice. See pop-ups become home runs to dead center," writes Joel Bierig in the *Chicago Sun Times*.

January 2008

A story appears in The New York Times *claiming Canseco offered to keep the Tigers' Magglio Ordenez "clear" in his new book if Ordonez invested in Canseco's movie project based on* Juiced, *his book implicating Mark McGwire and Jason Giambi, among others, of using performance-enhancing drugs.*

According to the paper, "a person in baseball with knowledge of the situation" claims that the matter has been referred to the FBI.

Canseco denies the blackmail story.

When the team announces they have just signed Jose's twin brother, Ozzie, owner Wally Hass figures they can write Ozzie's name in the lineup and then send Jose up in both spots and no one will be the wiser.

After all, if Jose's going to cheat anyway, they might as well go all the way.

37. Lawyer on the Bench

Although smiling, white-haired Tigers manager Sparky Anderson casts a kindly avuncular figure, he calls White Sox manager Tony LaRussa a "baby" for offering his opinion about a recent incident when Detroit outfielder Dave Collins charged the mound after Floyd Bannister hit him with a pitch.

"Any manager who speaks out is only a child," says Anderson. "He's a baby. Maybe I'll have to talk with him. Maybe I can help."

LaRussa has heard these types of comments from Anderson before. "Let's just say, if he has something to say, I'll be interested to talk with him." He says the record will show that the Sox and the Tigers have had numerous fights before. "Check on who started each one of these," he says.

A week later Collins follows his attack on Bannister with one on Boston's Al Nipper, who says, "Why doesn't the guy wear a dress?" So Tiger teammate Dave LaPoint buys a white dress with blue trim, pins on a note saying, "Love and kisses, Al," and places it in Collins' locker. Collins puts it on, saying, "I don't date ball players."

After going 26–38 to start the season, the White Sox fire LaRussa six weeks after giving him a vote of confidence and replace him on an interim basis with hitting coach Doug Rader. Pitching coach Dave Duncan is also replaced.

Apparently LaRussa's support of Duncan contributed to his release.

Ever since he was hired in 1985, White Sox general manager Ken "Hawk" Harrelson has been at odds with LaRussa.

March 2007

Police grow suspicious when the SUV is stopped at a light that went through two cycles of green and a driver behind it had to go around, police said. Police find LaRussa slumped over in the driver's seat of the running SUV, which is in drive. LaRussa has his foot on the brake and does not respond to knocks on the window. He finally wakes up and parks the car. Police say they notice the smell of alcohol on his breath, and a field sobriety test is conducted. He fails.

After he is arrested on a DUI charge, LaRussa says, "I accept full responsi-

bility for my conduct, and assure everyone that I have learned a very valuable lesson and that this will never occur again."

The word "genius" sticks to Tony LaRussa like "hot dog" does to Rickey Henderson and "boring" does to Steve Garvey.

Hands down, the best strategist in the game.

Manages a game like nobody else.

He understands and relies on statistical analysis like no one else ever.

What do you expect? He's a lawyer, isn't he?

He does have a juris doctor degree from Florida State University and he did pass the bar exam but he never practiced law. "I decided I'd rather ride the buses in the minor leagues than practice law for a living," he admits. And ride the buses he did because most of his playing career was spent in the minor leagues. In limited Major League action with the A's, Braves, and Cubs, he failed to reach a .200 career batting average.

He knew the game, though, even if he couldn't play it well and it was no surprise when the White Sox tapped him to be their manager in the middle of the 1979 season. He was 34.

"The toughest thing for me as a young manager was that a lot of my players saw me play," he says. "They know how bad I was."

When asked what the relationship would have been had LaRussa the manager had to deal with LaRussa the player, he responded, "Tony the manager would have really liked and respected Tony the player except he would have never played him because he was trying to win."

With less than two years managing experience in the minors, he was eager to tap the brains of some of the best he had played for. "When I first became a manager, I asked Chuck Tanner for advice. He told me, 'Always rent,' and 'You can have money piled to the ceiling but the size of your funeral is still going to depend on the weather.'"

In 1983 he was named Manager of the Year and, in some people's thinking, soon became manager of the decade. He is, however, apparently not good enough for the Chisox.

Is he bitter? He says he's not.

"Hawk called me the most stubborn person he ever has been around," LaRussa says at a crowded press conference. "I knew I was resisting him. It wasn't a healthy situation."

Tony, given the obviously widening rift between you and Harrelson, did you see the firing coming?

"You can't have a situation where you don't have a lot of teamwork, togetherness, trust and confidence in each other's opinions. Hawk deserves a chance to have his ideas work and win this year. There is plenty of season left."

What about Dave Duncan? Do you think he was treated fairly?

"Duncan has suffered since he's been in Chicago because he's not a back-slapper."

Neither are you, Tony.

"I believe my reputation is all right in this game," he said. "If there are any openings I believe I'll be considered."

With that, LaRussa goes to his Sarasota, Florida, home to wait for the phone to ring, but with every day his ire rises ... slightly. Reports begin circulating that he baited Harrelson by purposely waiting hours before returning the chief's phone calls and that he played "Beat the Hawk" by not treating fairly players whom Harrelson had added to the roster.

"I just didn't really feel I was part of the club right off the bat," pitcher Joe Cowley says. "For some reason, and I don't know how to put a finger on it, now I feel like a part of the ball club. Hawk was the one responsible for getting me over here. I don't know if Tony took offense to that and made it a little tougher on me because I was 'Hawk's boy' or whatever you want to say. I've always learned to keep my nose out of front-office business because it's a crazy world. I've been with the Yankees, so I should know."

"If there's a player on the club who said all that stuff, it's an excuse for coming up short," LaRussa says, "and if it's someone in the front office, they're covering their ass for problems that occurred. There isn't anything I did with the White Sox I won't stand up and be accountable for. I'd like to stand up and challenge the jerk who would say anything different."

While the feud is still festering, LaRussa gets a call from Roy Eisenhardt of the A's. Would he like to come out west and take over the team 20 games below .500 with the worst record in professional baseball? They could use someone with his hard-nosed personality and would welcome a strong manager at the helm. They have some good young talent on the team in Jose Canseco, they have Mark McGwire waiting in the wings, and they have some sock in old Dave Kingman, who, despite his frequent grumpiness, has hit 65 homers in the past two seasons. They also have a number of Spanish speakers, and LaRussa, who grew up in Tampa, Florida, speaks Spanish.

Three weeks of unemployment seems about enough.

Okay, he says, if you'll also agree to hire Dave Duncan.

Done.

38. Bunyanesque Feats

One question immediately facing LaRussa as he takes over the A's is how will he deal with the perpetually crabby Kingman? Maybe a better question would be how will Kingman respond to the no-nonsense LaRussa? The new manager is well known to put great emphasis on baseball fundamentals, and his designated hitter is well known to practice few of them. The hulking long-haired slugger hits home runs—long ones, and lots of them. That, however, is about all he does on a baseball diamond. In the field he is bad enough that he might have been a star on Stengel's early Mets. Phillies broadcaster Richie Ashburn once remarked during a break in play devoted to the repair of Kingman's glove, "They should have called a welder."

2004
 In order to honor Kingman, BaseballEvolution.com announces an annual Dave Kingman Award, "to the player who displayed the best power stroke without demonstrating an ability to do anything." In short, the Dave Kingman Award will be given to the player "doing the least with the most."
 The Hardball Times *claims Kingman's name today is something of a bitter joke: "a synonym for sluggishness, unpopularity, and dysfunctionality. Every discussion of bad fundamentals, bad fielding, and bad behavior inevitably leads to a Kingman mention."*

After leading the University of Southern California to the College World Series championship and being named an All-American, Kingman was drafted by the Giants in the first round. When the Giants called him up, they tried him in the outfield, at first base, third base, and occasionally even as a pitcher. He was an atrocious fielder wherever they put him. After the 1974 season, when he committed 12 errors in 59 chances, the Giants couldn't find a place to hide him in the field so they sold him to the Mets who couldn't either.

His inability to regularly catch the ball combined with his sour clubhouse demeanor caused him to be traded about as frequently as Billy Martin was fired. In 1977 alone he played for four different teams. The A's are his seventh.

Basically a shy man, he is frequently sullen and abrasive and certainly doesn't endear himself to his teammates. "He has the personality of a tree trunk," says former Mets catcher John Stearns. "Dave Kingman was like a cavity that made your whole mouth sore," says former Cub Bill Caudill.

The press isn't enamored of him, either. Apparently unhappy that female reporters were breaching the sanctity of the locker room, he once sent a gift-wrapped box to one of the interlopers, Susan Fornoff, a *Sacramento Bee* writer. The reporter opened the box to find a live rat with a note tied to its tail that read, "My name is Sue."

"From day one, he asked me to stay away from him, and I've tried to do that," said Fornoff.

"This is a man's clubhouse," Kingman says. "If someone can't take a simple joke, they shouldn't be in the game." Looking at Fornoff he shouts, "Kleenex," and then throws a box of tissues in her direction. "Anyone want to cry? Kleenex! Man's clubhouse! Tears! Anyone want to cry?"

The club fines Kingman and tells him to apologize to Fornoff, but in a negotiated deal, he agrees to a bigger fine without an apology. The rat, now named "Kong," is given to a five-year-old whose dad is a friend of a stadium guard. Later Kingman tried to buy the rat back for $75 to give to his wife, saying "she likes pets."

Another time he poured a bucket of water on a reporter.

Apparently anyone who can hit a round ball a long way with a round bat doesn't have to be a nice guy. "Why is it there are so many nice guys interested in baseball?" asked Hall of Famer "Old Stubblebeard" Burleigh Grimes. "Not me, I was a real bastard when I played." To prove it, he once threw at a batter in the on-deck circle.

While playing for the Cubs, Kingman, who did have a strong arm, once let loose a mighty throw from deep in left field. The ball sailed wide of the plate, through the dugout, and into the bathroom where it landed in the toilet bowl. Chicago columnist Mike Royko quipped, "The immortal Dave 'Ding Dong' Kingman. If he's ever voted into the Hall of Fame, they should put the toilet bowl there, too."

Royko needn't concern himself with Hall possibilities. Despite an impressive number of home runs, he has little else to recommend him. Going into the '86 season he has hit 407 home runs at a home runs per at bat pace exceeded only by players named Williams, Killebrew, Kiner, and Ruth. He has, however, also struck out at a pace exceeded by no one else who has ever played Major League Baseball.

"Everybody's always talking about my strikeouts," he says. "If I played every day, I could strike out maybe 400 times. I have no idea how many home runs I could hit if I played every day. I've never played every day."

There's a reason, Dave.

Two college professors, one from the Yale School of Management and one from the UC San Diego Rady School of Management — who either had tenure and so didn't need to do research on anything important, or didn't have tenure and thought their new research project would get it for them — came up with the idea for a scholarly study of "moniker maladies," based on the premise that names define destinies, and people like their names enough to "unconsciously approach consciously-avoided name-resembling outcomes." Among the conclusions in the paper "When Names Sabotage Success" are (1) C- and D-initialed students get lower grades than A- and B-initialed students and as a result get into lower ranked graduate schools, (2) Baseball hitters whose names begin with K strikeout 18.8 percent as compared to 17.2 percent for all other hitters, a large enough difference to be considered statistically significant.

Conclusion: Should Dave Kingman change his name to Dave Bingman he would not only strikeout less often but he could also get into a better graduate school when he retires. Alternatively, should he change it to Dave Wingman, perhaps he would walk more often, something he almost never does now.

As a character in the movie *Bull Durham* says, "Strikeouts are boring — besides that, they're fascist."

Kingman also holds the records for the lowest batting average ever recorded for a first baseman with enough plate appearances to qualify for a batting title and the lowest average ever for a player during a season in which the player led the league in home runs. He also led the league in home runs one season while compiling a batting average lower than the Cy Young Award-winner, Steve Carlton.

During his 16 seasons in the Major Leagues, Kingman has come to bat 6,677 times and either struck out or walked 2,424 times. Figuring he averaged about 400 at-bats a season, that means he has played six years without ever hitting the ball.

Despite his shortcomings on the field and his abrasive nature off it, he continues to find employment — albeit briefly — with clubs who fall in love with his Bunyanesque feats.

Fans love home runs and club owners love fans. As Babe Ruth said, "I never heard a crowd boo a homer." When Mickey Mantle was asked if he ever went up to the plate trying to hit a home run, he replied, "Sure, every time."

The Mighty Caseys in the game are always among the most popular players of their day. When in 1911 Frank "Home Run" Baker led the league with 11 round-trippers, he was not only hugely popular but he was frequently referred to as the greatest hitter alive.

Despite the fact that a ball that clears the outfield fence by one inch counts the same as one that clears it by 1,000 inches, fans love the "tape measure jobs" — the long blasts that evoke the ohs and ahs. Major League Baseball once created a promotion: "Chicks Dig the Long Ball." And the longer the better.

It is perhaps the most Olympian moment in all of sports. According to writer James Lincoln Ray, "It's the only time in any competitive game when the ball is considered live and the defense is wholly powerless to stop the other team's offense from scoring."

Even on the radio, the home run call can captivate.
That ball is going and it ain't coming back!
They usually show movies on a flight like that!
Bye, bye, baby!
Forget it!
Holy Cow!
Whattaya think about that?
Goodbye, Dolly Grey!
It's outta here!
Adios, Pelota!

Now the long-ball hitters such as Jackson, Gibson, Strawberry, Canseco, and Kingman are, or soon will be, among the highest paid players in the game

No one will ever know who hit the longest ball ever in a Major League game. Hyperbole rules the day. Shots as long as 620 feet have been claimed, although upon close inspection, these claims appear to be greatly exaggerated. Mickey Mantle, who undoubtedly hit some of the longest ever, was said to have hit a ball in 1963 that would have gone 620 feet had it not collided first with the right field facade. Almost everyone in the stadium that day said the ball was still rising when it hit the structure, but people who claim to know about these things say that was an optical illusion and the ball was really on its way down. It was nevertheless, a herculean blast of indeterminate distance.

According to the *Guinness Book of Records,* "The longest measured home run in a Major League game is 193 m (634 ft) by Mickey Mantle (USA) for the New York Yankees against the Detroit Tigers at Briggs Stadium, Detroit, Michigan, USA, on September 10, 1960." As with much in that book, this is almost certainly a gross overstatement worthy of P.T. Barnum.

Several physicists have been attracted to the burning scientific question: How far can a mortal really propel a baseball with a piece of wood? Conclusions arrived at independently state that at sea level, under normal temperatures, with no wind, the human limit is between 450 and 470 feet.

Even the normally conservative *New York Times* went hype-happy after Kingman launched a mighty blast they labeled "a huge parabolic fly." According to their "authoritative" estimate (the *Times* after all, will print nothing but) the ball flew 630 feet. They concluded: "Home owners outside left field here may find their insurance rates going up when Kingman and the Mets come back. In the last two days his three homers have banged off the fragile-looking frame houses with ominous thuds."

While with the Cubs, Kingman once hit three home runs in a game against the Dodgers. After the game, the irrepressible Tommy LaSorda was asked his opinion of Kingman's performance, to which he replied:

> What's my opinion of Kingman's performance!? What the fuck do you think is my opinion of it? I think it was fucking horseshit! Put that in, I don't fucking care. Opinion of his performance!? Jesus Christ, he beat us with three fucking home runs! What the fuck do you mean, "What is my opinion of his performance?" How could you ask me a question like that, "What is my opinion of his performance?" Jesus Christ, he hit three home runs! Jesus Christ! I'm fucking pissed off to lose the fucking game. And you ask me my opinion of his performance! Jesus Christ. That's a tough question to ask me, isn't it? "What is my opinion of his performance?"

39. Here Comes the Judge

According to several eyewitness accounts, the half-eaten ham sandwich found in the locker of Dwight Evans shortly before game time was planted there by Red Sox coach Rene Lachemann. The coach, however, is loudly proclaiming his innocence. He is, he insists, the son of a hotel chef and as such has cultivated culinary tastes far superior to lowly ham sandwiches, especially those without moutarde en grains mustard or, at the very least, dijon.

This sandwich has mayonnaise. Mayonaise! Does that sound more like Lachemann or Evans?

Witnesses are called, evidence weighed, and opinions considered. One point is clear, though: the offending partially-consumed repast violates long-standing team policy about eating so close to game time. Legal precedent applies here. The fine for the guilty party has been set at $5.

Players assemble for Judge Don's ruling. He is known to be a fair arbiter in the mold of Oliver Wendell Holmes, Jr., only bigger and a much better hitter. His decision as Grand Pooh Bah arbiter is not likely to win appellate action. Finality rules the day. Lost appeals simply double the fines and virtually all appeals are lost.

After carefully weighing all that has been presented, Don Baylor hands down his judgment. Lachmann is hereby fined $5 for perjury, sabotage, and presumably having eaten the missing half sandwich. In his court, Baylor declares, digestion is nine-tenths of the law.

Every Sunday before home games, Judge Don brandishes his spiral notebook in which he has recorded all possible violations, including, but not limited to, missing cutoff men, hitting into double plays, and failing to get a man home from third with fewer than two outs. These are all $5 fines. In the event of a shutout, every player in the starting lineup gets hit with a $1 fine. Failing to stand on the first step of the dugout during the National anthem will also cost the player $1. When he was with the Yankees, Phil Niekro was superstitious about needing to be in the dugout tunnel during the Anthem, and so handed the Judge his weekly fine in advance.

It's hard to imagine how much someone like Dave Kingman would have had to dish out had he been on this Boston club. Just the thought of a Kingman-Baylor showdown brings up ugly pictures.

There are numerous other sins and fines, some of which are known only to the designated-hitter-cum-chief-justice. When, earlier in the season, Roger Clemens struck out 20 Mariners, he was fined $5 for giving up a hit to Spike Owen on an 0–2 pitch. When Steve "Psycho" Lyons was thrown out trying to steal third on his own with Wade Boggs at the plate, he was hit with a fine so large that according to the Judge, "He'll need to take out a personal loan to pay the fine."

According to the highest, although seldom applied, standards of jurisprudence, when the Judge himself is guilty, the fine is quadrupled. When he hit into a double play earlier this year, he coughed up $25. He says the money held by collector Jim Rice will go to a championship party. There are no qualifications to this pronouncement, no "ifs." So far they have almost $1,600 — and it's only June.

The biggest contributor to the party fund is probably pitcher Bob Stanley, who has already parted with $75 in fines for fraternizing 15 times. To Baylor, fraternizing with the enemy makes you an instant bête noire. What do you mean laughing it up with the first baseman? You're supposed to be beating his brains out. Pull up going into second base? Tell me it's not so. Wishing another player good luck? Why would you want another player to have the luck? You need the damn luck.

In April, Bruce Hurst felt the wrath of the Judge when he did just this. Hurst made an egregious mistake when he wished Wally Joyner good luck before a game. He was fined $5 for sending greetings, one Mormon to another.

For repeat offenders, the fine is doubled, "especially if their name is Steve Lyons," says Baylor with a laugh. In April, Baylor had fined him $5 for applying black anti-glare greasepaint under his eyes even though he wasn't in the starting lineup.

Baylor's kangaroo court is more than a frivolous fun way to raise money. It is a team-bonding event that has been used by teams before.

"The court is all in fun, but it's more than that," says second baseman Marty Barrett. "It has brought us together, made us aware of all the little things we do on the field. Little things that win games."

The origins of the term "kangaroo court" are obscure. Oddly, it does not seem to have originated in Australia, but rather in the American West of the 1850s. None of the theories of its origin, however, are particularly plausible. The most likely possibility is that "kangaroo courts" initially tried "claim jumpers," and the name arose from associative wordplay. In any event, they apparently have their places in baseball clubhouses.

The gavel-wielding Baylor brought the court with him to the Sox when he came over from the Yankees in March. His addition to the team can neither be overlooked nor dismissed. Either by taking aim at Boston's Green Monster left field wall or simply by his presence in the locker room, he makes a huge contribution to this team. He is exactly what people mean when they talk about leadership — on and off the field. Before he arrived, the team had a well-deserved reputation for being a collection of individuals — 25 men going in 25 directions. Baylor would have none of it and the results are showing. By mid-June they have the best record in the American League, helped along by his 13 home runs, nine of which either tied or put the Red Sox ahead.

Clemens says, "From the moment he walked into the clubhouse last spring, there wasn't any doubt who our leader was." Jim Rice may be the titular captain, but he serves primarily as the court enforcer — and a very dedicated one at that.

The role of Baylor as savior sits uneasily with him, and some outside the club think Rice is upset with Baylor's dominance. "I know there are people trying to say that I have replaced him as the so-called leader," said Baylor, "and that we really don't get along. That's not true. We have no problems. We get along very well. He is the captain. He's earned the right and deserves it. It's not like in New York where you have a guy like Willie Randolph, who has been around 10 years and has to be a co-captain. Jimmy has put the numbers on the board and deserves to be captain."

Rice agrees. "I think we complement each other very well. We both are veterans and know what it takes to win. We've both been to the well. He can handle pressure. I can handle pressure. It's just a matter of who is at their best at a given time. I'm not going to hold back just because Baylor is behind me."

Most ballplayers consider themselves "tough," dedicated to their team and teammates, and "hating to lose." With Baylor, it's true. He's a straight-shooting, square-jawed tough guy on and off the field, much of which he learned from fellow tough guy, Frank Robinson, when he came up with the Orioles. Robinson was the chief justice of the Orioles kangaroo court and he wasted no time in introducing the intense young outfielder to the law of the ballplayer as he interpreted it, and that meant no nonsense and little leniency.

There is a proper way to play the game, period. You will play the game the proper way, period. If you don't play the game the proper way, you will face the consequences, period. And you will act like a professional ballplayer at all times. So sayeth Judge Frank. For losing his composure and not acting like a professional ballplayer one day early in his Major League career, Judge Frank presented Baylor with a red toilet seat. Point made.

"Don was so competitive on the field he would get very upset if he didn't get a hit," recalls former Oriole shortstop Mark Belanger. "In court we would egg him on and get him so mad he'd swear at someone, and then get fined for that."

Born in Austin, Texas, Baylor who describes himself as a "brown neck," grew up in a black ghetto. He says he experienced racism in the 1960s while playing in minor-league towns like Marion, Virginia, and Wytheville, Tennessee, where "a beer-bellied hillbilly ... called me everything but a nigger."

He had been offered a scholarship to play football under legendary Universtiy of Texas coach Darrell Royal, which would have made him the first African American to play football at Texas. However, he chose baseball and in 1967 was drafted in the second round by Baltimore. He played with the Orioles, Athletics, Angels, and Yankees before coming over to the Red Sox.

There probably isn't a player who wouldn't want him as a teammate. Anybody who has played for both Charles O. Finley and George Steinbrenner, who has seemingly played through more injuries than there are body parts to injure, who leads the world in getting hit by pitches because he is always willing "to take one for the club," and who is leader nonpareil, is a great addition to any club.

It's not a matter of chance that he has been selected as the Boston players representative to their union.

Despite being hit by pitches more than 200 times to set an American League record, the only time he acknowledged pain was when he was hit by a Nolan Ryan fastball that left his wrist numb for a year.

Baylor knows that to be a leader means putting into practice what you preach, and so he plays hard every play of every game. Probably no one since Frank Robinson goes harder into second to break up a double play. He also knows the only real training for leadership is leadership. No one doubts he will be a manager one day.

March 2003
Baylor who has been diagnosed with multiple myeloma will undergo stem-cell replacement surgery and spend most of the winter lying in one hospital bed or another, watching Oprah *and* Dr. Phil, *commuting from the Memorial Sloan-Kettering Cancer Center in New York to the City of Hope National Medical Center near Los Angeles.*

"There's a fairly high upfront success rate, somewhere in the vicinity of 60–70 percent," says his doctor about the possibility of complete remission. "The problem is that there are 'recurrences.'"

"My bones are as hard as a rock," says Baylor.

He assures everyone that he expects to be back on the Mets bench as a coach when the season begins.

March 2004
Baylor is back with the Mets almost a year to the day since his cancer was diagnosed.

40. Baseball Exorcist

As a hard-throwing high schooler, Nolan Ryan could propel a baseball faster than anyone in or around little Alvin, Texas. All the "throwing through a brick wall," "lamb chops past wolves," and similar metaphors were being tossed around by observers like Texas steers in a tornado.

Didn't see the ball but it sure sounded fast.

Looked about the size of a watermelon seed as it hissed by.

He's so fast, better start swinging while he's on his way to the mound.

Brings up memories of the old Ring Lardner line, "He's got a gun concealed about his person. They can't tell me he throws them balls with his arse."

Reggie Jackson says that Nolan Ryan is the only pitcher he faces that makes him go to bed before midnight. "He's the only guy who puts fear in me," he adds. "Not because he can get me out but because he could kill me."

Cy Young insisted that pitchers, like poets, are born, not made. You can't teach a kid like Ryan to throw that hard.

No one around had ever seen anyone like him and the scouts came flocking. They could see (or hear) the speed but there was a problem. The problem was he could throw hard but where it would go, well, that was quite another story. In one high-school playoff game he threw a ball that fractured the hitter's arm. Then with a new batter in the box, his next pitch hit the batter in the head, shattering his helmet. Thankful he could still stand, the shaken player trotted to first base. At least he was still alive. The next batter with fear in his eyes, appealed to his coach for mercy. Hitting against Ryan didn't seem like a good idea if he was to continue to live a healthy and productive life.

His coach probably understood, but somebody had to stand in the box and at least look like a hitter, even if it were only for show. The batter timidly took his place and swung at the first three pitches he saw, missing them all. It was better to strike out on three pitches than risk the possibility of fouling one off and having to face another. Getting a hit was out of the question.

Things weren't a whole lot different in the years to come. Says Reggie Jackson, "Every hitter likes fastballs, just like everybody likes ice cream. But you don't like it when someone's stuffing it into you by the gallon. That's what it feels like when Nolan Ryan's throwing balls by you."

"He's a baseball exorcist — scares the devil out of you," says former Tiger outfielder Dick Sharon.

He once hit Boston's Doug Griffin behind the left ear. "He wasn't moving," Ryan said. "His eyes were rolled back up in his head. I thought I'd killed him." Griffin missed 51 games after being hit and was never as good again. Within three years he was out of baseball, done at the age of 30.

The Mets gambled on the wild flamethrower by selecting him in the twelfth round of the 1965 free-agent draft, and after a brief call-up in 1966 when he was the second-youngest player in the league, he was returned to the minors to work on his control. He made the team for good in 1968, but the Mets, not quite sure what they had in Ryan, used him primarily in relief. Despite his ability to throw hard, he couldn't break into the starting rotation headed by Tom Seaver.

When blisters on his throwing hand began to appear, he took to soaking it in pickle brine, and despite the trainer's cautions, he continued the practice. For the next few years he pitched well for the Mets but grew tired of the big city life and asked the Mets to trade him. After the 1971 season, the Mets granted him his wish and sent him along with three other players to the Angels for the well-past-his-prime, and injured, shortstop Jim Fregosi.

Upon hearing of the trade, Fregosi said, "It's very tough to judge if California got enough for me."

Get enough? It ranks as one of the worst trades in history as Ryan goes on to become one of the game's greats and Fregosi ends up playing in only 146 games for the Mets.

Two years later, Ryan broke Sandy Koufax's record for strikeouts in a season, to which Koufax responded, "Yeah, and he also surpassed my total for bases on balls in a single season by 91. I suspect half of those guys he struck out swung rather than get hit."

How can he throw so hard? Chalk part of the answer up to genetics, part to his work ethic, and part to his conditioning. According to former Astro trainer Doc Ewell, Ryan's power, like Popeye's, comes from vegetables:

> Of all the athletes I worked with, Nolan is right up there with Joe DiMaggio and Gordie Howe. He's a perfect physical specimen because he takes such good care of himself. I've often eaten with him, and you can tell by what he orders — so many yellow, so many green vegetables — that he knows himself so well. People talk about his arm, but I think the real key is the way he lives.

Still, he has his critics, foremost among them Angels general manager Buzzie Bavasi. For all of his brilliance, and his four no-hitters, Ryan has been only slightly better than a .500 pitcher. When Ryan demanded to be paid $1 million a year, Bavasi said he could just as easily replace him with two 8–7 pitchers and save a lot of money, adding, "I think my plumber could do that." Contract negotiations were bitter and unproductive.

"What I'm looking for in a contract will be three to five years because I feel this will be the last contract I sign," said Ryan at the time.

That was seven years ago. He's still pitching and still drawing criticism.

After Bavasi balked, and wanting to play in Texas, he signed with Houston as a free agent.

He strikes out batters unlike anyone else who has ever played the game and yet he never wins the Cy Young Award or a World Series game.

For the past few seasons he has continually battled injuries and has made several trips to the disabled list. Last season for the first time, with the Angels, he posted a losing record. Still he struck out almost a batter for every inning he pitched, and still the fans pour into the stadium when he pitches. The Ryan Express is always worth the price of admission.

"I always wanted the fans to feel, when they walked out of the ballpark on the night I pitched, that they were glad they came and they felt like it was worth their effort and expense to come to the ballgame," he says.

But both the praise and the criticism continue.

Yes, he strikes out a lot of batters but he doesn't win enough games.

Yes, he is putting up Hall numbers but how can you compare him to the greats with his winning percentage?

Yes, he'll probably strike out a zillion batters in his career, but he adds almost five runners per game because of walks.

Yes, he's good, but is he really worth the incredible amount of money they're paying him?

Yes, he's got a lot of flashy no-hitters, but he's not in the same league with Seaver, Carlton, or Clemens, let alone Koufax or Mathewson.

The phrases "one of the greatest pitchers ever" and "one of the most overrated pitchers ever" are constantly being trotted out by both fans and press.

When former catcher Gene Tenace was asked how he fared against Ryan, he said, "I got this one hit off him — it was an accident. I told him that: Mister Ryan, it was an accident!"

Perhaps it is because he is one of the best pitchers in the game but maybe not the best, that he comes in for so much criticism. As author Elbert Hubbard wrote, "To avoid criticism do nothing, say nothing, be nothing."

There may be disapproval of Nolan Ryan the pitcher, but scant little of Nolan Ryan the man. He has always been an old-style gentleman in the tradition of Christy Mathewson. He has maintained his dignity in the face of criticism and never made excuses, or blasted management, or lambasted the media, or complained about the fans' demands.

Although there are no records to prove it, he has likely signed more autographs than any player in history — and he has never charged for one. He often carries three pens—one blue felt tip, one black felt tip, and a red ballpoint. This way when requests come his way — as they usually do anyplace he goes— he is prepared to sign just about anything put before him, almost any time, any place.

"We drove to a concert one day early in spring training, just after we got down there," says his former manager, Kevin Kennedy.

"It was Nolan, myself and my coaches, and we all went to see Wynonna Judd. We were pulling out of Charlotte County Stadium after a workout, and Nolan was driving. We had guys chasing him down. We were getting some gas, we were all in Nolan's car, and there was a guy running up at him. He'd run after us all the way from the stadium. I mean, you don't know if it's somebody trying to hurt him, or what. But Nolan stopped. He actually stopped and was going to sign the guy's card, except the guy didn't have it with him. It was his buddy's card, who was still back at the stadium, and the guy gets mad when Nolan won't go back. I mean, I don't think people understand what he goes through. Here he's making a concession, and he gets chased down in the parking lot of a Circle K when we stop to get gas. And that has to happen to him every day of his life."

The autograph sickness has reached epidemic proportion with Ryan, but still he signs. He signs pictures, and cards, and balls, and hats, and jerseys by the thousands every year. He signs for kids who line up after every game he pitches, he signs for adults who run into him in the streets, he signs for the clerical staff in the front office, and he signs for clubhouse attendants and batboys before games. In every town in which he plays he will station himself by the team bus before it leaves for whatever stadium they will be playing in that day, pens at the ready.

"People get in line by the bus and I sign for them, and that's the only time I sign when I'm on the road," he says. "It has to be organized. If it's not, you have people getting three or four autographs, and some won't get any. And then you get people all crowded up around you, and you end up ruining shirts and coats with ink marks that won't come out. So if you don't organize it and get it in a line and make it orderly where people can police themselves, you just won't get it done."

A Honus Wagner baseball card once sold for $2.35 million — and it wasn't even signed. Signed Nolan Ryan cards are among the least expensive star cards.

Such is the nature of supply and demand.

Nolan Ryan, the competitive, hard-working, clean-living gentleman from Texas, is, whether he likes the phrase or not, an American hero and a role model to many.

But not everyone. As with the issue of his ranking in the baseball hierarchy, there are some who question his ranking in the "heroes roll call." Jeff Millar, co-creator of the *Tank McNamara* comic strip, has made fun of Ryan because of the huge number of national commercials Ryan does, implying that Ryan sells himself to any and all bidders.

"This guy Millar is not a Nolan Ryan fan," Ryan says, adding:

> He's taken shots at me for 15 years. He's out of Houston, and he's been on my case ever since I signed there. I think a lot of it is that he has problems with athletes making the money that they do. He's real outspoken about saying that athletes shouldn't be role models. He even brings me into his speeches, in public. He did that one time in front of a tennis association when my wife was at the meeting, and it was quite embarrassing for her and the people who were there with her.
>
> I've never met him, so I was surprised by it. But there are certain areas of our society that resent athletes and the money they make and the recognition they get. And I can understand that. Our society puts more emphasis on sports and entertainment than it does some of the important things. I just am disappointed he's singled me out because he thinks I represent something, when the reverse of that is true. I do try to be a positive influence on kids. I do try to do as many things as I can to be a good role model for kids.

Charles Barkley insists he's not a role model: "Just because I can dunk basketballs doesn't mean I should raise your kids." The much overused phrase, however, is pinned on Ryan again and again. Fathers dream of sons pitching like Ryan; mothers dream of sons behaving like Ryan.

Ryan also comes in for censure when he is involved in a fight with Robin Ventura.

> Now, if Robin would've come out there and stopped before he got to the mound, that's something different. I wouldn't have attacked him. But when he came out and grabbed me, I had to react to the situation. That's what I try to tell people, but it looks like I used him for a punching dummy when people play the clip. A lot of criticism came out of that tape.

Even gentlemen have their limits.

2008

Statues of Ryan adorn City Hall in his hometown of Alvin, Texas, and Rangers Ballpark in Arlington. Nolan Ryan Field at Alvin High is located near the Nolan Ryan Expressway, not to be confused with the Dallas Nolan Ryan Expressway.

Hal Lanier pulls Nolan Ryan from a game in late July, citing a sore elbow, and Ryan is miffed. "I think it was premature. I don't agree with it," he says when informed he's on the DL. "For some unknown reason they've decided to put me on the DL. They didn't give me any say. I think I can pitch, but that hasn't changed their thinking." Lanier is the manager and he thinks it would be better to have a healthy and rested Ryan available for the stretch run.

Well, if nothing else, now he'll have more time to sign autographs.

41. All About Money

Jeremy Miller is nine. His father has promised him this trip to the sports memorabilia show at the downtown Convention Center. Jeremy's baseball card and autograph collection is the envy of his friends. His father got him into the hobby when, at six years old, he began taking him to Red Sox games. They would always arrange to arrive during batting practice so they could move down along the rail by one of the baselines and there wave a card or program in the direction of a player in hopes of getting a much-sought-after signature. More times than not they came away with at least one, and, on a good day, Jeremy might head back to his seat with two or three. Once they even went out to the bleachers with a collapsible fishing pole and hung a program and a ballpoint pen on the end of the line which they lowered almost to the ground. That's how they got Baylor's autograph, but the ushers came and made them stop, so they went back to the foul line idea and sometimes waited outside the stadium after a game in hope of catching an interesting player on his way to his car, which is how they got a Boggs.

Collecting cards and autographs is special for Jeremy because it is something he shares with his father and there aren't a lot of things a nine-year-old can do so happily with a father. Collecting is also like connecting in a small way with the athlete, like taking a little part of him home.

The memorabilia show is an opportunity to get some autographs that are missing from his collection — specifically that of Carl Yastrzemski. To have a legitimate Yastrzemski, well, that would elevate his collection almost to the level of his father's, which includes a Mantle.

They arrive at the Convention Center in a state of considerable anticipation. Standing across a table only a few feet from Yaz will certainly be a highlight of his young life and his father will beam with pride at having so pleased his only son. There are many card dealers here offering all sorts of things from the impossibly expensive, like a Tris Speaker card, to the ridiculously mundane, like a Steve Lyons card. The show might also present an opportunity to trade some duplicate cards or autographs with others. But it is the opportunity to get a Yastrzemski that roils the blood in both father and son.

As they near the designated table, there he is in a polo shirt and jeans—the great Yaz. It's always strange to see athletes out of uniform, but he looks good—still trim and healthy—like he should still be playing. Jeremy's father hates to see the old athletes looking paunchy and balding and so he avoids old-timers games. He likes to remember them as they were in the prime of their playing days, graceful athletes playing a boys' game like few could.

As they approach the table a man standing in front tells them, "An autograph is $6. We take cash or credit cards. Sorry, no checks."

Jeremy's father's face sags. He's never heard of an athlete charging for an autograph before. What's wrong with Yaz? Is he really a greedy SOB? Didn't he get paid a small fortune to play the game? Why is he trying to rip off a kid who idolizes him? Is he so hard up that he needs a few $6 donations?

He puts these and similar questions to the man who delivered the disappointing news. It turns out the man is a lawyer named Paynter. "Over the years we've had a lot of ballplayers come to our shows," Paynter says, and then adds:

> We've generally paid them something—in the early years it was basically just mileage money, to pay for their gas. But it has escalated. The asking price for personal appearances has gone up and up, especially for the superstars. And in this case, instead of paying Carl Yastrzesmki a flat fee, we agreed to charge $6 an autograph, which would go to him. On top of that we flew him in first class and put him up in a hotel for two nights. Plus we flew in the businessman who was representing Yastrzemski, and the businessman's son.

He insists that Yaz is really a great guy, but that these days none of the top athletes make public appearances for free anymore. Because he doesn't want to disappoint his son, Jeremy's father forks over the $6.

It's too bad it has come to this, he thinks to himself. Everybody in the game is out to make a quick buck. Baseball has become all about money. It shouldn't be that way.

To Jeremy, it's just the way things are.

A few days later Jeremy's father reads that Yastrzemski took in $7,500 for signing his name at that show. He'll never think of Yaz the same way again.

42. The Big Silence

Casey Stengel once said, "Left-handers have more enthusiasm for life. They sleep on the wrong side of the bed and their head gets more stagnant on that side."

As to the unasked question, several players in baseball history have been nicknamed Lefty, but has any player ever been called Righty? No, but right-handed reliever Donnie Moore is called "Lefty" because of his flaky nature. The first pitcher to have earned that sobriquet is said to have been pitcher/outfielder John McMullen in the 1870s, who eventually gave up baseball to become the world's first opera singer named Lefty.

To make his point clear, St. Louis pitcher Greg Mathews wears a t-shirt proclaiming "EVERYBODY IS BORN RIGHT-HANDED. ONLY THE GREATEST CAN OVERCOME IT."

The pitcher whom fans these days call "Lefty" may be enthusiastic about life but he isn't talking about it. Steve Carlton is an intimidating and dominating pitcher, one of the best of his generation, but he isn't talking about that either.

He became an immediate success when he made his debut with the Cardinals as an imposing 6' 4", 20-year-old in 1965. Then after learning to throw his signature pitch, a hard slider that broke down and in to right-handed hitters, he became the game's leading strikeout pitcher. He realized how effective the pitch could be when, on an exhibition tour of Japan, it completely fooled the great Japanese slugger, Sadaharu Oh.

Going into this season he has already won 314 games, a record that puts him in the top 15 on the all-time list, and has struck out the side 124 times in his career.

In 1970, though, after a protracted contract dispute that saw him miss all of spring training, he had an uncharacteristically poor season, losing 19 games. Two years later he was traded to Philadelphia and won 27 games in his first season with them.

"We hadn't been able to sign Carlton," says former Cardinals general manager Bing Devine. "There was no free agency, so he didn't have the freedom to say, 'sign me or else.' He was being very difficult to sign for the ridiculous amount of $10,000 between what he wanted and what we'd give him. Many times Mr. Busch gave me a little leeway in the budget, but in the case of Carlton, Mr. Busch developed the feeling that Carlton was a 'smart-aleck' young guy, and I'm not used to having young smart-alecks tell me what do."

The press, looking for an excuse for his poor season, settled on his unorthodox training methods.

Lefty always worked hard to keep himself in top condition. There was no question about that. His strenuous workouts included strengthening his arm by twisting it in a bucket of rice and his legs by maneuvering them through a trench filled with rice. He was also quite proficient in martial arts.

He may be in the best shape of any pitcher, but you don't get to pass judgment on yourself; others do, and they were particularly critical of him. What happened to turn the man who had gone 27–10 the year before and won the Cy Young Award for a last-place team?

Some writers painted him as a sulking weirdo.

What can you expect of a guy who's into transcendental meditation and est?

He mumbles karma-esque things to himself.

He talks about a search for serenity and concentration when what he ought to be searching for is his slider.

The guy's a whacked-out nut case.

A story has it he's a closet lush.

He sure as hell can't get along with managers.

Carlton has a way of tuning out distractions—on and off the mound. He is reclusive, refuses to sign autographs. He has studied martial arts and Far East religions. He is "a wine connoisseur." And he pisses people off.

"I believe he said some things about stuff other than baseball that he regretted," McCarver said in a 1980 *Inside Sports* article.

Lefty became particularly upset when a reporter covering spring training dropped in uninvited to a party he was hosting and wouldn't leave. Lefty had enough. He stopped talking to the press and reading the papers. He felt he was letting the criticism creep into his life and it was affecting his performance on the mound. The "Big Silence" was on.

The press upped the criticism, but he had several great seasons, winning the Cy Young Award two more times. After he went Marcel Marceau, there was no going back to a chatty Lefty. He has not spoken to the press since.

What a jerk, some think. He owes it to the fans.

Somebody getting his kind of money damn well should have more respect for the game.

April 1994

An article in Philadelphia Magazine, *written by former player turned novelist/journalist Pat Jordan, quotes Carlton as saying such things as "The Elders* of Zion rule the world" and "twelve Jewish bankers meeting in Switzerland rule the world."

Carlton denies making the statements.

Jordan insists, "Everything I wrote, he said."

Jewish groups demand his induction into the Hall of Fame be delayed until he apologizes. His induction is scheduled for July.

Carlton says the article has almost no truth in it. "I specifically deny saying anything that could be interpreted as offensive to Jewish people."

"I go to the interview," says Jordan. "I write down what people say. If he decided he doesn't want to say it now, that's his problem. I couldn't have made that stuff up."

"I've known Steve for 29 years, and I can say categorically that he's not an anti–Semite," says McCarver. He calls the comments "contradictory, not anti–Semitic."

Carlton has been known to espouse numerous conspiracy theories.

A representative of the Jewish Community Relations Council suspects that Carlton has always felt this way, since these views are not suddenly picked up late in life. "Remember, he didn't talk to the press," he says.

Last season, the always marvelously conditioned Lefty suffered the first serious injury of his career when he damaged his rotator cuff. Going into the season, the Phillies were concerned that he might not be up to anchoring what was already a shaky staff. If he couldn't, there was little chance that this season they would be anything but a bunch of base-stealing fools.

By the 21st of June, the team is 15 games behind the Mets when they send Carlton to the mound against the Cardinals. He lasts five innings, giving up six hits, six walks, and six bases on balls. After 14½ seasons with the Phillies, he is released by the team.

He's lost something off both his fastball and his slider, say his frequent critics, many of whom are still irked by his silent treatment. You can't fool Mother Nature. However, at 41, Lefty still thinks he can be a productive pitcher and that his rising ERA can be explained by a slow return from the surgery. The Giants, who are a game and a half up on Houston in the National League West, agree and sign Carlton.

Then came the big surprise: "Lefty Talks."

"It's been 10 years since I've done this," he says at a press conference. "Pardon me if I make mistakes."

Apparently, Giants president and general manager Al Rosen talked him into this.

Sometimes players nearing the ends of their careers will go to great lengths to stay in the game.

"You can't make a move like this and not talk to the media," Lefty adds.

He says he was happy with his last start in Philadelphia and that he thought he had worked out 90 percent of his problems. Despite having won a total of only five games in the last two seasons, he insists his arm is sound.

The Giants manager, Roger Craig, is a wily handler of pitchers and will see what Carlton can add to a staff headed by Mike Krukow and Vida Blue.

"It's fair to say Al and Roger impressed upon him the 'hum baby attitude' that exists here," says Giants publicist Duffy Jennings.

The suddenly chatty Lefty says he chose San Francisco over other teams that also wanted him because "I love this city. I've always loved San Francisco. It's a hell of a city."

He makes it clear that he may be talking now, but don't expect him to do it every day, and certainly not after losses. The press will just have to be satisfied with whatever scraps of oral arcana he is willing to throw their way.

He starts his first game for the Giants on Willie McCovey Hall of Fame Day at Candlestick Park. The results are not good. He last only 3⅓ innings, giving up 8 hits, 2 walks, and 3 runs to the Cards.

By the end of the first week of August, when they send Lefty out against the Reds, the Giants have slipped 5 games behind Houston. He is hit hard again, giving up 7 runs in 3⅔ innings. The Giants give him his release. He had won one game for them thanks to his own 3-run homer and had hit the 4,000 mark in strikeouts.

Lefty announces his retirement — and talks about it.

"Upon reflection, I realize I've reached a career milestone never accomplished before by a pitcher ending his whole career in one league," he says. "Further, I realize that the San Francisco Giants are committed to the young players in their organization, especially the young talented men on their pitching staff."

On the same day, George Foster announces his retirement from the Mets. He wants to play, but the Mets no longer want him. Only Jim Rice earns more per season than he does and now that he has lost his starting position in left field to Kevin Mitchell and has been ineffective in coming off the bench, the Mets feel it is time to cut him loose.

No, it's not because of his racial comments, the Mets brass insists. "He took the news very poorly," Cashen said. "He was quite broken up. It's very difficult for me and for him, but mostly for him. He indicated that he still wants to play but first he would go home and think about it. He's a proud athlete... But we don't want unhappy people around. He hadn't adapted to his part-time role. We've had a rocky road together. Now his rocky part is over, and that's sad."

That quickly, baseball lost two of its best players ... but not for long.

43. Mid-Season Form

Although they own 18 World Series rings among them, Sparky Anderson, Dick Williams, Pete Rose, and Whitey Herzog are all last-place managers in the middle of June.

To make matters worse, the Cardinals are not only in last place, but they have been asked to return their National League Championship rings to the manufacturer because some of the stones have fallen out. Jeff Lahti, for one, isn't interested. "The way we're playing," he says, "they might not let us have them back."

In mid–June, the Red Sox sweep the Yankees in a three-game series putting them 6½ games in front. Despite owning the best record in the American League, they are anything but complacent. Five times in the past 14 years they were in first place after the All-Star break only to miss out on the pennant.

"Everywhere we go, we have to hear about how we always collapse," says Dwight Evans. "In Toronto, a guy wrote a column calling us 'the Boston Chokers,' and we won two out of three. In New York, they'll call us a lot worse. But it's different this year. We used to win with slugging and hope to get by with pitching. We're not the slugging team we used to be, but this year we have the pitching. Sure, we have a bunch of guys hurt, but we have Roger and Oil Can."

The Sox are scaring everyone with their new-found pitching brilliance. "Pitching's the whole game of baseball," says Sparky Anderson. "Hitting means nothing. It's almost a useless art."

They're going to have to do without Boggs for a while, though, after he is shelved with a sore rib injured while straining to wrench off his tight cowboy boots. He can only laugh when, for the All-Star Game, the American League players are presented with a pair of Justin cowboy boots.

Then before a game a few days later while in the clubhouse treating the ribs, he gets a call telling him that his mother had just been killed in Florida when her car was struck by a truck that ran a red light. Boggs flies into a rage, thrashing anything he can get his hands on. The team trainer has to administer a sedative.

Clemens is pitching particularly well. After showing Henderson two mid-90s fastballs, he strikes him out with a wicked sharp-breaking curveball. Rickey turns to Clemens and yells, "If you're going to do that, I'm not bringing a bat."

In July Tom Terrific says he has been "pitching like an idiot the last couple of weeks," and once again presses the White Sox to trade him closer to his home in Connecticut, saying he will quit if not traded. Since Boston is a lot closer to his home, and since the Yankees are still within striking distance at the beginning of July, and since Seaver claims a "deep affection" for McNamara, and since he has put a gun to the head of the White Sox, he is traded straight up to Boston for Steve Lyons.

"I'm happy to be here," Seaver says upon arriving on the first flight he could catch. "Up to this point, this has been a very difficult year for me. This is a breath of fresh air."

At the very least, the 41-year-old hurler can help mentor Boston's exceptionally young pitching staff.

When Seaver makes his first appearance for the Red Sox, he receives three standing ovations before he has even thrown a pitch — when he starts warming up, when he walks in from the bullpen, and when he takes the mound against the Jays. Each time he tips his hat in acknowledgement which, as many people noted, was three more times than Ted Williams did in his entire career. During the game the fans shouted, "Sea-vah, Sea-vah."

"I'd like to earn this kind of feeling with performance," says Seaver. "The Red Sox got into first place without me. I have to prove to them I can still pitch effectively. When I feel I've contributed, then I'll be really happy."

A few days later he picks up his 308th career win and anticipation builds that he may get the chance to pitch against the Mets in the World Series, a team he led there 17 years earlier.

In mid–August, the White Sox, beginning to lose contact with the Angels, make two desperation moves: they pick up the briefly retired Steve Carlton and the briefly unemployed George Foster.

With Lefty, the thought is the National League hitters learned to lay off his slider, but since the American League hitters haven't seen it, they'll swing at it for a while. Never mind that a Cubs official claims his "fast ball" was clocked at 80 mph in his last game with the Giants.

Justifying the acquisition of Foster, Hawk Harrelson says, "We think the man can still hit. We're taking a shot. We're just trying to cover ourselves. We haven't thrown in the towel on the division title."

And, no, they aren't concerned with his problems while with the Mets. Nevertheless, Foster insists he would still be with the Mets if the story with his racial comments hadn't come out. He reiterates that his comments were taken out of context and misinterpreted.

The Mets, happy to have Foster off their payroll, are running away with the division, maintaining a lead over the second-place Phillies of between 16 and 20 games.

44. Like Attila the Hun

Dick Gossage, aka "Goose," with his thick mustache and long sideburns is an imposing figure on the Padres' mound. He scowls, he grimaces, he propels his big body forward as he unleashes his "high hard one." His Attila the Hun act and his fastball have made him one of the game's most dominant relievers.

He relies on his natural aggression and the instincts that tell him he can throw a ball past anyone, anytime.

Growing up in Colorado Springs he lacked the confidence to picture himself as a professional baseball player. His father thought otherwise and pushed him in that direction. "I'd usually just get all embarrassed, when he'd say he thought I'd pitch in the big leagues," the Goose says. "I still thought players like Mickey Mantle had to be fictitious people."

Somewhere along the way he came to believe in himself. Basically a one-pitch hurler he is the "fireman" who comes into the game when the situation demands—and that means anytime from the sixth inning on. He's a durable workhorse.

Two men on in the seventh and the starter running out of gas in a close game? Call for the Goose. There is no pampering, no waiting for the ninth.

January 2006
Gossage insists the state of the game is deteriorating. "It pisses me off to say Barry Bonds is the greatest hitter. He's playing in a wussy era. The game is soft. You never get thrown at today. Last thing a hitter has to worry about today is getting hit. The first thing Hank Aaron had to worry about is: Am I going to survive this at-bat because I'm black."

The Padres know what they have in Gossage and they don't hesitate to call on him with great regularity. Since he came over to San Diego in 1984 as a free agent, he's been racking up innings like he's being paid by the out. No sense of being a "closer." No one else has ever pitched as many long saves of 4 to 9 outs. During two seasons he pitched more than 130 innings in relief.

After the 1973 season, the Padres were on the verge of being sold and moved to Washington, D.C. The move seemed to be such a fait accompli that new uniforms were designed and the baseball card company, Topps, printed Padres' player cards with Washington Padres on them. At the last minute, McDonald's co-founder Ray Kroc stepped in, bought the team with hamburger money and kept the team in San Diego.

When Kroc died in 1984, he left his widow, Joan, with stewardship of Ronald McDonald, his considerable fortune, and ownership of his baseball team. Joan Kroc, daughter of a railroad worker, met her future second husband while playing piano at a bar in St. Paul, Minnesota. He told her that two years earlier he had opened a hamburger stand in Des Plaines, Illinois. "I was stunned by her blond beauty," he wrote later in his autobiography.

Mrs. Kroc, unlike Mr. Kroc, mostly kept herself out of the baseball side of things in favor of the money side of things. She commissioned a sprawling house in Fairbanks Ranch and purchased a 300-foot yacht, the Impromptu; a helicopter, the Luvduv; a private Gulfstream jet; and a fleet of gold Cadillac Sevilles. She also gave away a lot of money—billions to causes ranging from nuclear disarmament to the San Diego Zoo and to flood victims in North Dakota. She tried to donate the Padres, too, to the City of San Diego, but Major League Baseball would have none of it. Public ownership of teams was something up with which they would not put.

An enlightened owner, she started Major League Baseball's first employee-assistance program for players and staff with drug problems.

She remains a popular San Diegoan for support of many local causes including a sizeable donation to assist families of the 21 victims slain at a McDonald's in San Ysidro. Her popularity, however, does not extend to Goose Gossage.

With the team floundering in mid-summer, they ban beer in the clubhouse, and Gossage goes into a fit of rage, berating Kroc for "poisoning the world with her hamburgers." This does not sit well with the Padres' owner, nor does it sit well with the Padres' president, Ballard Smith, when Gossage adds, that Kroc and Smith are "gutless, spineless people." "All of a sudden, we're being treated like 14-year-old kids," he says. "It stinks. I guess Ballard Smith and Joan Kroc don't have anything better to do. Their life is so boring."

The Goose, never known for his subtlety on or off the mound, is just warming up. Although he feuded with George Steinbrenner while with the Yankees, he says he prefers Steinbrenner to Smith. "I'd rather have a guy like George who wants to win every game than have the guy we have here who doesn't know anything and doesn't care. He [Smith] cares more about our citizenship than winning. He wants choir boys and not winning players. What are we in this game for, to show what good people we are or to win games? I never sang in a choir. I didn't know you had to go to church before you could play baseball."

Mrs. Kroc, who pays the Goose $1.2 million to throw baseballs past hitters, and the executive who had brought the best damn power pitcher in the game to his club, decide that Gossage can spend the next month eating in vegetarian restaurants for all they care, but he certainly won't be playing for their team. They'd rather rely on their choir boys than the smokeballer they think would be better served by primal-scream therapy. They're in last place anyway, so how much worse can it get?

The job of informing their reliever that he is being suspended is passed down to Steve Boros, the manager.

"Steve called me and said, 'Can I come up to your room?' And I said, 'Sure, come on up.' And he hands me a piece of paper that says I was suspended. I couldn't believe it. I mean I just couldn't believe it," Gossage says.

While the Players Association prepares an appeal, the Padres get on with their woeful season.

That their chief choirboy, Steve Garvey, isn't hitting with anything like his normal consistency isn't helping.

45. Looking for Heroes

Earlier in his career, it looked as if Garvey was a shoe-in for the Hall of Fame. Coming up with the Dodgers in 1969, he showed he could hit for a good average, he could hit for power, he could field his position well, and most importantly, he could do it every day. From September 3, 1975, to July 29, 1983, he played in 1,207 consecutive games, anchoring the Cey-Russell-Lopes-Garvey longest-ever infield. He played on five pennant winners, set an NLCS record with 8 homers and 24 RBIs, was MVP of both the 1978 and 1984 NLCS, led the league in fielding percentage five times, and won four Gold Gloves. Lawrence Ritter and Donald Honig included him in their book *The 100 Greatest Baseball Players of All Time*.

In 1983, after fourteen years with Los Angeles, he exchanged his Dodger blue for Padres brown. "Instead of looking like the American flag, I look like a taco," he said at the time.

He was still a good baseball player, a boringly good player. Lacking the charisma of a Reggie Jackson or a Rickey Henderson, he was seen instead as a solid, if dull, player. As Rick Reilly wrote in *Sports Illustrated*:

> Steve Garvey lines up his colognes by the amount unused. He arranges his Polo shirts by pastel. He'll keep vacuuming a clean carpet just to admire the parallel patterns he makes. His shirts are monogrammed. When he was a batboy, the bats rested trademarks out, knobs up, in the order of the day's starting lineup. He would save his allowance to buy Ban-Lon shirts. (He had 16 in varying colors.) He would sometimes re-iron his mother's ironing, just to get it exactly right. As a player, he would sweep the dugout steps. When he joined the San Diego Padres, he suggested a reorganization of the bat and helmet racks. Much tidier. In his closet in his pink-and-pink house in Del Mar, Calif., all the shirts are on hangers, facing left. There are no blue jeans. On the floor, the shoes are treed and the toes all point outward. Muss his hair, go to jail. You can bounce a quarter off his bed.

He is the quintessential Boy Scout in spikes. He is trustworthy, loyal, helpful, friendly, courteous, kind, obedient, cheerful, thrifty, brave, clean, and reverent. If he doesn't help old ladies across the street it's only because he's on the field and not on the street. Quipped Don Rickles, "Steve Garvey is not sure whether he wants to be the first baseman or the pope. He's so goody he goes out behind the barn to chew gum."

His uniform never looks dirty; neither his countenance nor his hair ever looks ruffled. He is the "Ken" of Ken and Barbie leading a Norman Rockwell life.

He was the star athlete in his Tampa high school and the two-sport star athlete at Michigan State University who married the prettiest catch around and fathered two beautiful girls.

His wife, Cyndy, is the quintessential California beach girl — summer-eyed, blonde, and statuesque. Never mind that she was born in Detroit. She has the looks and charm worthy of the television personality she has become. She hosted the television show *Games People Play*, with Bryant Gumbel, and co-hosted *The Morning Show*, with Regis Philbin. If Steve Garvey is a star, so is his wife.

Rick Riley called Garvey a role model's role model, a "dinosaur somebody uncrated from the 1950's and couldn't get back in the box." "I try to walk around as if a little boy or little girl was following me," Garvey once said.

Need someone to represent the club at a charity event? Garvey will do it. He has collected more distinguished service awards from charities than he has room on his walls to hang them.

Need someone to appear at an autograph-signing session on behalf of the club? Garvey will be there and he'll hand out home-baked cookies while he's doing it, too, if you need that.

A junior high school in California decided to trade in its Abraham Lincoln name for that of Steve Garvey Junior High School, "Home of the Panthers."

In 1975, shortly before the fall of Saigon and a year before an American president was forced to leave office for criminal acts, a handsome, jut-jawed, Frank Merriwell-like Steve Garvey, reaching for a throw at first base, is on the front cover of *Sports Illustrated*. "STEVE GARVEY, PROUD TO BE A HERO," it says. At a time when an angst-ridden America was looking for heroes, it appears that Steve Garvey was arriving on a white horse just in the nick of time.

Thousands of Americans were dying in Vietnam, but Major league players weren't among them. Major League players weren't going to Vietnam. At worst, their clubs arranged for them to be put in local National Guard units.

One of Garvey's teammates in spring training a few years earlier was a very promising young outfielder, with a great arm and more speed than any Dodger this side of Willie Davis. His name was Roy Gleason. Ted Williams had been so impressed with him that he personally recruited him for the Red Sox. However, he wanted to play with the Dodgers and so signed with them as a free agent.

"I thought I was going to be a superstar," he says.

So did the Dodgers. Late in the 1963 season they called him up. On September 28, with the Dodgers behind, 12–2, in the bottom of the 8th, they sent Gleason up to pinch hit. He found a low fastball to his liking and drove it down the left-field line for a clean double. He scored when Moose Skowron reached safely on an error.

Led by Sandy Koufax and Don Drysdale, the Dodgers went on to face Mickey Mantle and the Yankees in the World Series so Gleason had a World Series ring.

Before he got a call from the Dodgers again, he got one from Uncle Sam. "I went from the highest of highs, to the absolute low," he said. At his military induction ceremony he refused to take the pledge. "I told the officers that they had made a mistake."

Mistake or not, he was sent to Vietnam for eight months—the only Major League player who ever served in that war.

"It was so hard, sitting in the jungle and thinking what could have been," he said.

So while Steve Garvey and the other young Dodgers-to-be were getting ready for their starring years, he was keeping his arm in shape by lobbing grenades. He kept track of his Dodgers the best he could. Then on a July day during which Don Sutton relieved Don Drysdale in a losing effort against the Astros, a shell exploded in a tree above Gleason, tearing holes in his left calf and wrist. A chopper lifted him from the battlefield leaving all his belongings, including his World Series ring, behind. Baseball career over.

If he listened carefully he could probably hear the Dodger Stadium announcer: "Ladies and gentlemen, introducing the Dodgers' all-time leading hitter, batting 1.000 forever, the great Roy Gleason."

Several years later during a game at Dodger Stadium, Cubs outfielder Rick Monday rescued a flag that was about to be set on fire by two war protesters, saying, "If you're going to burn the flag, don't do it around me. I've been to too many veterans' hospitals and seen too many broken bodies of guys who tried to protect it." He was later traded to the Dodgers for Bill Buckner.

So while Gleason is forgotten by the fans, Steve Garvey is being portrayed as a hero. A baseball card even comes out with Garvey standing in front of the word "Heroes" in bold gray script.

The concept of a sports figure as hero goes back at least to ancient Greece and the Olympic Games where heroes were considered semi-divine, that is, born of the union of a mortal and a divine parent. As such, the great athletes were said to be "born of the gods."

Traditionally, the word has been applied most often to those figures who perform exceptional acts, usually self-sacrifice or risking themselves while saving others during time of war. Sergeant York is a true hero in this sense. Often heroes are those who are seen to have done something outstanding for society — Nelson Mandela for example. The word is certainly used more freely now, though, if for no other reason than it sells newspapers.

In addition to physical prowess, perhaps only when a baseball player is seen to have made an outstanding contribution to society should the player be considered a true hero.

Roberto Clemente is an obvious example. Throughout the '60s the Puerto Rican-born Pirates outfielder was one of the game's greatest players, all the while engaged in charity work. When in 1972, Managua, Nicaragua, was hit by a massive earthquake, Clemente immediately began arranging emergency relief flights. He quickly learned, however, that the flights never reached the quake victims as they had been diverted by the corrupt Somoza government.

Clemente then accompanied the next shipment hoping that his presence would allow the shipments to get through. On New Year's Eve, shortly after takeoff, the flight with Clemente aboard crashed into the sea. It appears that the plane was overloaded, had a history of mechanical failures, and was being operated by a poorly trained crew. Although the pilot and parts of the plane were recovered, the only trace of Clemente that ever surfaced was a case belonging to him. Teammate and close friend Manny Sanguillen was the only Pirate not to attend the funeral. He even went diving in an effort to find Clemente's body.

Jackie Robinson overcoming the racial hatred that was hurled at him is another obvious example of a true sports hero.

Psychologists tell us that we grow up needing heroes and so the media feeds the need by constantly promoting candidates for our choosing. Who we then select from the slate of candidates probably has more to do with our needs than the accomplishments of the nominee.

"There is no universal hero," says sports psychologist Richard Lustberg. "Subjectively, the hero is created within you. Heroes are created as a great way to escape from whatever you need to escape from, and they can supply for you whatever you need."

It's been argued that sports heroes play a bigger part today than ever before because of the increasing number of homes without fathers. In the absence of father figures, sports figures can make effective stand-ins.

There seems to be a longing (maybe a need) to lionize boys and men who play games so much better than we do, because when we identify with their successes our self-esteem is bolstered. So, too, is our connection with our community — the others who share our allegiances to the players and the teams they play for. We feel better about ourselves when our heroes lead our team to victory and we share that feeling with others of the same conviction.

Ah yes, but when they fail, as they so often do...

Garvey, as *Sports Illustrated* reminds us, has been a hero all his life. He is a smiling, good-natured character from a storybook.

He lectures frequently about ... his life as a hero:

In 1971 I went to Orthopedic Hospital in Los Angeles to visit a boy named Ricky Williams, who was suffering from cancer. The boy had just had an operation to remove the lower part of a leg, and he was in a bad way. It was a hollow feeling, seeing him there on the bed. His mother said, "Thank you for coming." The doctors said he had an 18 percent chance of living. He was heavily sedated. I took his small hand in mine. His mother said, "Ricky, Steve Garvey's here." And I started to feel a little squeeze from that 10-year-old's hand. He started opening his eyes. Although he couldn't talk, when he opened his eyes it also opened mine. I could feel the strength in that little boy's hand. I knew then that Steve Garvey had a place.

Last year on an annual night for crippled children at Dodger Stadium, Ricky Williams walked from the dugout to first base with Steve Garvey. "I don't really believe that I have any special powers. But Ricky that night gave me a medal, with an inscription that said, 'To Steve Garvey. Thank you for giving me the will to live.'"

Garvey has aspirations of running for political office when his playing days are over. Governor Garvey has a nice alliterative ring to it. And after Governor, who knows? If Reagan the baseball announcer can be president, why not Garvey the baseball player? He did sign up as an Athlete for Nixon during the 1968 campaign.

Along the way, maybe a little television exposure. "People in TV have told me," he says, "'If you want to quit playing ball today, we'll get a series for you. You know, playing somebody with short hair—whether it's a police story, a Gentle Ben, or whatever. Middle America.'"

Mr. Middle America was born to nice middle-class parents in a nice middle-class section of Tampa. He lived in a nice house with a dozen grapefruit trees in the backyard. He developed his nice swing and Popeye-like forearms by hitting the grapefruits with a broomstick.

When the Dodgers finally drafted him he was ecstatic because he had been a Dodger fan ever since his father, a Greyhound bus driver, transported the team when they came to Tampa to play spring training games. He idolized Gil Hodges, the big, affable gentleman. "I sincerely believe that there is such a thing as a Dodger," he says. "I don't think there's such a thing as a Padre or a Brave or a Met. I sincerely think that I was born to be a Dodger."

He came up originally as a third baseman, but his throwing was too erratic so they moved him to first base. In 1974 he had a dream season—MVP of the All-Star Game, MVP of the National League, Gold Glove Award, .389 average in the National League playoffs, and a .381 average in the World Series.

Never being shy about self-promoting, he says, "It could have been the best year a professional ballplayer ever had."

Now as his batting average is dropping into the .250s, there are alarms not missed by the Padres' brass. It is the fourth year in a row that his batting has diminished.

Yet he is still smiling, still keeping every hair in place, still signing autographs and meeting the public with the zeal of a politician, still being introduced as "a perfect gentleman," and a "testament to the game of baseball and the American way of life." He is introduced at banquets as "a great ambassador for Tampa. A great ambassador for baseball. A great ambassador of the almost-lost-art of being a perfect gentleman."

Not everyone agrees, however. Many of his teammates simply don't like him — Don Sutton, for instance. When he gave an interview to Tom Boswell of *The Washington Post* in 1978, he was quoted as saying, "This nation gets infatuated with a few names. All you hear about on our team is Steve Garvey, the All-American boy. Well, the best player on this team for the last two years—and we all know it — is Reggie Smith. Reggie doesn't go out and publicize himself. He doesn't smile at the right people or say the right thing. He tells the truth even if it sometimes alienates people. Reggie is not a facade or a Madison Avenue image. He's a real person."

To no one's surprise, Garvey and Sutton squared off in a you-can't-say-that-about-me-in-the-papers, fist-swinging brawl in the Dodgers clubhouse and had to be forcibly restrained by teammates. Heroes have to stand up for themselves.

Both players came away from the altercation with numerous scratches on their faces. Garvey appeared groggy when he said, "I don't think these things should come out like this in the public. If someone has something to say, they should say it to my face." Said Garvey, "I'm only human. I have always tried to set an example for the Dodgers both on and off the field."

Teammate Ron Cey says that all the players know Garvey is nothing more than a public relations man. Jay Johnstone quips, "Anybody who has plastic hair is bound to have problems." "Mr. Perfect," as he is sometimes referred to, probably thinks the term is a compliment.

Some teammates, too, have grown tired of his quest to find every microphone and television camera in sight, and, to many, he is seen as a selfish, egotistical player.

Maybe, but you can't argue with his offensive numbers, can you?

Except he hits an empty .300 with few walks and a lousy on-base percentage.

Well, there's no argument about his brilliant 193-game errorless fielding streak.

Except he has poor range and an even worse arm. The streak was due more to his failure to range for balls to his right than it was flawless fielding. And most of the time he refused to throw the damn ball. He rarely even attempted a first-to-second-to-first double play, a refusal that drew the wrath of the seldom wrathful Lasorda and a few of his teammates.

But don't forget his streak of 1,207 consecutive games played. That shows, at the very least, durability and grit.

Except when the streak got long enough to draw the attention of press and fans, he played so tentatively in the field and on the base paths, gingerly protecting his chase of Gehrig's streak of 2,130, that he looked more like a ballerina than a ballplayer. The broken hand that ended the streak was a fluke injury and didn't occur on a particularly aggressive slide. Unlike Ripken, Garvey was not great enough to make people think of other things besides the streak later in his career.

All right, so maybe he's a flawed hero. Aren't they all? He is, however, a solid citizen espousing the highest values, a role model for all young men.

Cyndy Garvey, however, has other thoughts. The daughter of an abusive father, she met and married Steve at 20 while both were at Michigan State. He was already a handsome star athlete and her ticket out of her oppressive family situation. But within a year or so, "I knew something was wrong," she says. "There was a lack of consciousness, remorse. There was an emotional lacking."

She had planned to go to medical school, but Steve insisted she should be available for him, so those plans were shelved. She would be there for him, despite the fact that he was seldom there for her. He rarely came home, rarely called, and paid little attention to their two young daughters. She was, in her own words, "an emotional hostage" to the All-Star player.

"My husband was so controlling," she says. "He'd say things like, if you don't get everything straight here in the house, I just might not come home after this road trip… It might not have been a beating, but the isolation, a look in the eye. It's not always a bruise."

Unable to take it any longer, they were divorced in 1981 and Cyndy moved out of their house. The next day Steve's girlfriend moved in.

To some fans, Cyndy was seen as an ungrateful gold digger and she was faced with a barrage of how-dare-you-abandon-the-hero stares and comments. She was getting little child support, couldn't eat, couldn't sleep, and accidentally overdosed on sleeping pills.

"For a long time, people would tell me, 'I can't understand how you could leave him. You're nothing without Steve Garvey,'" she says.

One day in the middle of the '86 season while Steve is struggling to keep his fast-fading career alive with the Padres, a man stops her while she is in the cleaners with her oldest daughter. "So you're the bitch who left Steve Garvey," he says.

1989

Cyndy Garvey publishes a tell-all book, The Secret Life of Cyndy Garvey, *in which she reveals the details of her marriage.*

Cyndy tells a story about the time she was Christmas shopping and ran into Nicole Simpson. Nicole grabbed Cyndy's sleeve and whispered, "He's so charming and people think he's so wonderful. No one would believe me. If they didn't believe you, they won't believe me."

Her book was later found by Nicole's bed after she was killed.

Several paternity suits are filed against Steve and he admits to fathering children to two mothers.

Where he once was considered a candidate for state or national office, Garvey is resigned to hosting game shows and infomercials.

Do stories about the sexual conquests of heroes tarnish the image of the hero or elevate him to the level of envious stud? Probably both. Wilt Chamberlain once amazingly claimed he had sex with twenty thousand women. What is even more amazing is that he still had time to play basketball.

Major League baseball players spend some six weeks in spring training every year and play at least 81 games on the road. That's a lot of time in hotels, a lot of time away from wives, friends, and family, a lot of time to engage in "sexcapades" if they are so inclined, and many are. Their celebrity status is a "chick magnet" that some players aren't at all shy about deploying.

It's not unusual to find players whose sense of self is tied to their ability to "score" in the non-baseball sense. Sociologist Seven Ortiz calls it the "adultery culture." Players may pick up young ladies in bars, making sure that other players see them.

Sexual dalliances maketh the man.

What a guy!

As Joseph Campbell says, a hero has a thousand faces.

The writer Daniel Boorstin makes a distinction between the hero and the celebrity. The hero is distinguished by his achievement, the celebrity by his image. The hero creates himself, the celebrity is created by the media. The hero is a big person, the celebrity is a big name. No doubt there are more celebrities in baseball than heroes.

46. Wally's World

In the popular film *National Lampoon's Vacation*, Chevy Chase and Beverly D'Angelo, aka the Griswolds, take their kids on a cross-country trip to Los Angeles to visit "America's Favorite Family Fun Park," aka "Wally World." Says Clark Griswold, "I must be crazy... I'm on a pilgrimage to see a moose!"

But, says the Moose, "Sorry folks! We're closed for two weeks to clean and repair America's favorite family fun park!" Clark responds as Billy Martin would have suggested, by punching the moose in the nose.

The film was hugely successful, earning more than $60 million at U.S. box offices.

One night at Anaheim Stadium, a big sign appears proclaiming the place "Wally World."

You are now an official celebrity, Wally Joyner.

Gene Mauch was certainly right when he replaced the aging Carew and his 3,000 hits with Wally Joyner and his 0 hits. He knew the kid could hit for average but he's also showing some power, something Mauch didn't expect based on Joyner's minor league numbers.

"I knew he was going to be good. I didn't know he was going to be this good this quick," says Mauch.

It hasn't taken long for the baby-faced player to become a fan favorite, particularly with kids, and he seems to be enjoying the Wally World connection.

Wally has a smooth swing and after every pitch he steps out of the box and taps each shoe with his bat to clear dirt. Little kids all over Southern California are copying Big Wally's mannerisms and now Wally World banners are popping up all over the stadium.

"I don't consider myself a phenom," Joyner says. "I'm just enjoying this."

"Wally's a very stable young man. I've met his parents and I can understand why. They're classy people," says Mauch.

Wally is another personification of the hard-working, clean-living, All-American kid. He smiles a lot, is generous with the media, and good with the fans—all hot dogs and apple pie stuff. With his easy-going manner and boyish charm he is the Angels media department's prized gem, so they promote him whenever and however they can.

The fact that he is white and Opie Taylor-like doesn't go unnoticed.

He's such a bonanza for the media that everywhere he goes he's in so much demand that some other players are feeling slighted. Reggie Jackson has been a media favorite for so long that now he says of the demand for Wally quotes, "It's boring, it really is." The media is beating this like a drum, Jackson says, but Wally is just too damn nice to turn down all the requests.

"It's been an overkill," says third baseman Doug DeCinces. "You guys [reporters] are breathing on him every time he turns around."

"It doesn't bother me that much," Joyner says. "Our public relations department has done a great job of keeping it under control. It's part of my job."

"Hello, Wally, this is the beat writer for the *Walla Walla Gazette*. I realize it's 7:30 in the morning. I'm sorry to bother you, but I thought we could do a story connecting you with our name. You know, Wally and Walla Walla. That sort of thing. So if I could have 15 minutes of your time."

"Sure, no problem."

As the season moves on, there is considerable concern around Wally World that Joyner might be wearing down. He has played two full winters and started every spring training exhibition game and now that his batting average is plummeting, the team has banned off-field interviews. This comes after two Los Angeles papers do an at-home-with-the-Joyners piece. Wonderful Wally's popularity is a publicist's dream, but a manager's nightmare.

47. Family Values

As the Angels are leaving the field after a 2–0 night-game win at Yankee Stadium, Wally Joyner feels something hit his arm. Thinking it is a comb thrown by a fan, he looks down. "It was this big Bowie knife. The thing had a five-inch blade on it," he says. "Next thing I remember was being in the dugout."

Gary Pettis, the center fielder, picks it up as they trot off and gives the weapon to Mauch.

Johnny Carson gets laughs when he says that before Game 1 of the World Series an honorary fan will throw out the first brick. The players are not among the laughers.

"I've had whiskey bottles and darts and other things thrown at me there," says Orioles center fielder Fred Lynn. "But a knife?"

Who threw it? Of the some 28,000 spectators at the stadium, surely someone watched the strong-armed idiot let go with the weapon.

What guy? I didn't see no guy!

Like with a subway stabbing, no one comes forward.

Earl Weaver says when he's at Yankee Stadium, he never looks up as he walks from the mound back to the dugout, but rather he pulls his cap down over his eyes to avoid the paper clips often thrown at him there. Ray Miller, the pitching coach, says he once had a coke thrown in his face.

A Blue Jays game this season begins with a U.S. Marine and Royal Canadian Mounted Police color guard and the traditional playing of the national anthems. Both contingents might have come in handy later in the game as rowdy fans cause the game to be stopped at least a half dozen times with reckless forays onto the field. One woman runs around hugging policemen, a man parades around the field flourishing a Union Jack flag, and several men play dodge-the-security-guards with varying degrees of success.

The situation degenerates to the extent that Baltimore manager Earl Weaver declares he is playing the game under protest. "When you've got a delay for five minutes on a 3–2 pitch in 2–1 game, well, that's important to me."

Toronto's Lloyd Moseby feels the breeze of a bottle whizzing by. "Yes, a

Remy Martin bottle came flying near me," says Moseby of the wayward missile. "That's just not Toronto. It's not Toronto."

Apparently some Toronto fans have a better taste in liquor than they have sense.

Toronto security eject 126 fans. "We've got great fans in Toronto, but I don't know who those fans were," manager Jimy Williams says.

In recent years, Mickey Rivers was hit in the head with a bolt in Boston and Dave Parker felt a flashlight battery zing by his ear in Pittsburgh. Reggie Jackson was so used to coins flying by that he sometimes took to wearing a batting helmet in the field during practices. One day he collected $34 worth of the little round missiles.

In Atlanta earlier in the season, three fans ran onto the field and joined the lively brawl between teams.

The problem of rowdy fans goes back to the earliest days of the game when the Plug Uglies and Dead Rabbits gangs made their feelings known in unsavory ways during matches between the Brooklyn Eckfords and the New York Mutuals, as ruffians, gangs, and pickpockets roamed the stands.

Ueberroth is concerned. His says fan safety is a primary concern — that and drugs ... and player salaries. "You can't have somebody watching everybody in the park. And you can't stop a kook from doing something crazy," says Bob Aylward, director of business affairs for the Baltimore Orioles. But there's a lot you can do."

Like limiting baseball's sacred cow, beer sales, for example. Suds have always been a part of the ball-going experience. Breweries own the Cards, Expos, and Jays. Cut out the brewski and you lose fans, turn the taps up full and you get unruly behavior. Some parks even sell hard liquor, and, in most, fans can buy as much beer as they can carry back to their seat. In many parks, a fan doesn't have to stagger back to the concession stand, since vendors will deliver beer to the fan. The call of "beer here" is as familiar to most fans as "play ball."

"Essentially, White Sox Park used to be the world's largest outdoor bar," says Aylward. Now most teams cut off beer sales after the seventh inning. For a time, the Tigers close the bleachers altogether as a message to their naughty fans. Now they sell only low-alcohol beer with the hope that fans will get full and/or sick on the stuff before they get drunk. The Red Sox have hired local football players as bouncers, and at Ueberroth's urging seven teams have set aside beerless family sections.

Owners still remember that night back in 1974, when the struggling Indians hosted a 10-cent beer night at their "Mistake by the Lake" stadium. In the first inning it looked like a good idea drawing more fans than they had seen in some time. In the third inning it looked like a lousy idea as the tipsy fans spilled over onto the field and proceeded to tear up the sod. The "sod and suds" night forced the club to forfeit the game.

The instant celebrity status offered up by TV cameras is another problem teams are tackling. When that little red light comes on, some fans begin acting like half-wits drawing attention to themselves. The solution? Ueberroth says turn off the red lights. That way no one knows whether they're on TV or not — not even the East Boston teenager wearing an Ozzie Osborne "Too Drunk to Fuck" t-shirt.

Joyner was fortunate he was not injured by the invisible knife thrower, but it was a close call. Strides are being made to curb rowdyism, but there is more to be done. Baseball has to be seen as a safe, family-friendly affair. This is not the NFL or English soccer. After all, it is fathers playing catch with their sons ... and daughters. When the game was first getting going as a spectator sport in the mid–19th century, the clubs thought that having women present would help cool passions when things got a little too boisterous. So they put up special canopies or tents just for the ladies. Of course, they were usually far removed from the action in case a gentleman player in the heat of the moment inadvertently let loose a foul word. Starting with the Knickerbockers, players were fined for using profanity. The fine was six cents.

In the mid–1850s, the *Clipper* newspaper wrote of the desirability of having ladies at the games:

> Let our American ladies visit the ballfield and the most rough or rude among the spectators would acknowledge their magic sway, thus conferring a double favor upon the sports they countenance, because the members of our sporting organizations are usually gentlemen and always lovers of order, but they can no more control the bystanders than they can any other passengers along a public highway. When ladies are present, we are proud to be able to say that no class of our population can be found so debased as not to change their external behavior immediately, and that change is always for the better.

Last year a student concerned about marijuana smoking in Fenway Park said, "On July 20, a friend and I went to a Red Sox game; our seats were in the right-field bleachers. As the game started many people around us lighted marijuana cigarettes. We don't mind if people smoke marijuana — that's their business, but not in a public place where fathers bring their children. During the third inning, the smoke had overcome us, so we left."

"Beer here."

"Pot here."

Ueberroth's absolute, most primary concern is the bottom-line financial stability of the game, which masquerades as a heartfelt expression of the owners' commitment to morality and family values.

In the patois of Wall Street, family values sells. Baseball wants the fans' respect because baseball wants the fans' dollars. And it's working. Ticket sales are up, and watered-down beer sales are up. Now, keep pushing the image.

48. As Mellow as Mr. Rogers

The Cubs, already 17½ games behind the Mets, decide it's time for a new manager to replace Jim Frey, who Bill James says "has the emotional intensity of a comatose eggplant."

Frey goes quietly, with his parting words about his team being, "If they quit on me, shame on them."

G.M. Dallas Green taps Yankee third base coach Gene Michael. The two men then dredged up the usual hiring clichés and prepare to get on with the Cubs' depressing season.

Says Green, "I think he'll do a great job with our club."

Says Michael, "My philosophy is winning."

Michael then admits that he isn't sure he wants to manage, doesn't know anything about the Cubs or how to manage without a designated hitter, and then is thrown out of his first game, later admitting he didn't know the rules.

"I can learn," says Michael. "I was a slow learner as a hitter but not slow at the game."

A career .229 hitter, he labored in the minor leagues until he was 28, played for nine years, mostly for the Yankees, and then had two short stints as Yankee manager, being fired both times by Steinbrenner.

Before his first game with the Cubs, he said he had been looking forward to a relaxed summer as a Yankee coach and was not eager to get back into the pressure cooker again. When asked to further explain his managing philosophy, he says, "All we have to do is win 50 of our next 56 games and everything will work out."

As the season progresses everything does not work out well for either the Cubs or their new manager. They are quickly falling far behind the runaway Mets, Green is unhappy with Michael, and on-field problems are mounting.

When outfielder Keith Moreland is thrown out at first base on a one-hop drive to right field, Michael says nothing to him. Green is angry at Michael's lack of toughness with the players.

When their young shortstop Shawon Dunston takes his time getting to first base after a third strike gets away from the catcher, Michael decides to get tough and has stern words for him. Dunston responds with an obscene gesture.

After a run-in with umpire Dave Pallone, Michael is suspended for three games, turning the club over to coach John Vukovich. When Michael returns, he expresses concerns about Vukovich who he thinks may be after his job.

Green says if it bothers Michael to have Vukovich in the dugout as a coach, he'll just have to deal with it. "If Gene really feels that way, they should talk about it," says Green. "He should go eyeball-to-eyeball with Vuke and say, 'You worry me.' But I can't do that for Gene. He has to do it himself. It's only an unhealthy situation if they can't work it out, and then it goes back to 'I' vs 'we.' Hey, if they can't work it out, then I'll work it out for them."

As Green himself claims, "I'm a screamer, a yeller and a cusser. I never hold back." He and Lasorda would probably place 1–2 in a Major League profanity-laced tirade contest, although in which order isn't clear.

Given Green's coarseness and Michael's Mr. Rogers mellowness, the ongoing tensions between them doesn't really surprise anyone.

The two questions on the minds of all Cubs watchers is how long will Michael last, and did Green hire Michael in the first place because he saw him as a yes man who would play the cards dealt him?

"He's my manager, dadgummit," says Green who's never been one to admit mistakes.

After speculation appears in the papers that Green is going to reassign Michael to a front-office job, the manager asks for a meeting with the president during which he tells him, "I should be the manager until I'm fired," and says he should not have to read Green's published comments about his job status.

Marla Collins, a curvaceous, lovely young woman is a Cubs' ball person. Wearing skin-tight short shorts and a number 86 Cubs jersey, she chases down rolling foul balls to the delight of the beer-bellied crowd and has been doing so for the past five years.

She is wildly popular to the Wrigley Field hootin' 'n' hollerin' crowd.

"Hey," says a Cubs' season ticket holder, "when you're a Cubs fan you gotta have something to look forward to, and it sure ain't winning."

Marla is a winsome lass with a big smile, an endearing giggle, and a beguiling personality. Naturally she is photogenic and therein lies her problem.

One day in July, someone in the Cubs' front office opens a copy of *Playboy* to read the editorial, only to find his otherwise prim eye scanning an eight-page photographic spread of an attractive and, of course, nude, young lady in various provocative poses. Several photos include fully-clad Cubs' players Shawon Dunston and Leon Durham, and the venerable Cubs' announcer Harry Caray. Upon closer inspection, the object of the men's attention turns out to be none other than Marla, the popular ball person.

Goodbye, Marla.

Surely she understands that the Cubs are homespun American family entertainment. For the sake of everything that is decent in this country, it is time to stop chasing balls, Marla. Family entertainment will always trump degeneracy in the Cubs' world.

"But doesn't everybody in the family take their clothes off at some time or another?" Caray asks.

When Dallas Green is asked for his reaction he says he doesn't have a reaction.

But, Dallas, you're known for answering all the tough questions.

"I don't have a reaction," he insists. "Isn't that an answer?"

"Why the hell would they want to fire her?" Caray adds. "She didn't do anything wrong."

The note telling her that her Cubbies services will no longer be needed is sent to her unsigned.

This is not going to sit well with some fans who are struggling to find something enjoyable in this disastrous season.

"I think that might have been part of the problem — that I was a little more popular (than the team)," she says. "Obviously, their job is to promote the team and not me. All of a sudden, I'm becoming a little too popular."

The Cubs have a long tradition going back to 1876 when they were called the Chicago Orphans and they have always tried to present wholesome entertainment for their fans. Since they don't win much, they have to sell something else.

"They believe more, I think, in conservative ways," says Ms. Collins, the ex-ball person. "When it comes down to it, I think they're pretty much a group of ultraconservative people."

In August, she appears as a "guest ball boy" at a minor league Madison Muskies game.

She is driven onto the field in an open blue Cadillac and handed a dozen roses by the club president. Then a male belly dancer gyrates.

"She can do it better," one beer-guzzling fan shouts.

The Muskies faithful cheer wildly with every foul ball she chases down and boo the unwitting catcher for picking up a loose ball.

Harry Caray misses her.

Gene Michael, though, has other things on his mind. His team is playing poorly. Speculation is rife that like Collins, Michael will not see the next Opening Day.

49. Misunderstood

Like the Cubs, the Red Sox are in a very long non-championship drought, but unlike the Cubs, they are having a good season largely because their pitching staff is leading the league in earned run average, not something the Sox have been known for. Says John McNamara, "I don't know what it was like in the past, but from the time I arrived here last spring I tried to tell people, 'Pitching determines pennants.'"

"I don't care how good your pitchers are, if you have that great number one stopper, the entire staff is affected," says pitching coach Bill Fischer. "Clemens is that great number one stopper."

The last time the Red Sox staff led the league in earned run average, Babe Ruth was a rookie pitcher.

By mid–June the Sox already had fifteen complete games from their starters. The Yankees had one. Yet, when called on, their bullpen has been particularly effective, so much so that the irrepressible Sammy Stewart has dubbed the group "The Savings and Loan Association." He explains that they specialize in saving but are sometimes loaned out as starters.

Boston is eight games ahead in its division when Oil Can Boyd wins his 11th game on July 8th. Then piece by piece their dream season begins to unravel. Jim Rice, hitting .331, hurts his knee, and outfielder Tony Armas goes on the disabled list. So, at various times, do pitchers Wes Gardner, Steve Crawford, Bruce Hurst, and Al Nipper. Sammy Stewart's arm is hurting, too, and he sees a doctor.

When their lead shrinks to three games, Boyd is in the University of Massachusetts Medical Center under an agreement the club claims has been "mutually agreed upon."

His examination, say the Sox, will include drug testing and a mental examination. They are awaiting word on whether or not he will be available again this season. They are not optimistic. Only one pitcher in the league has won more games this season, but the ugly thought that his career may be prematurely over hovers like the clichéd black cloud. Maybe he's gone too far, burned too many bridges, yelled too many obscenities to ever again be a productive member of the team. Some club officials think so. Some think for the sake of club chemistry and sanity, they'd be better off without him.

A week earlier when he learned he wasn't selected for the All-Star Game, he went on a clubhouse rampage, throwing anything he could get his hands on. He screamed obscenities at one of his few close friends on the team, Al Nipper, and then turned his wrath to McNamara ending with, "Go ahead and fine me."

"I've been in this game for 34 years, and it was the worst thing I've ever seen," says McNamara. "He's lost even his last friends."

The next night when Boyd didn't bother to show up for the game with the A's, the club slapped a $6,450 fine and a three-day suspension on him. The club, though, is not only worried about his behavior, they're also worried about his decelerating fastball. By the sixth inning in his last start, it had dropped into the 70s.

The night of his explosion, Boyd was stopped in his car by police looking for drugs. They didn't find any. Four days later, the police showed up at his house saying they were tipped that Boyd was involved in drug transactions.

"We tried to hold him still," Chelsea detective sergeant Jack Phillips says. "He said he had a gun and was going to blow our brains out."

A complaint was filed against Boyd charging him with assault and battery and disorderly conduct.

Just a year earlier he looked as if he was going to be a superstar and the anchor for the Red Sox team for years to come. Reporters asked him what he thought about a possible matchup with Gooden in that year's All-Star Game. "Who?" he asked with all the seriousness of an innocent.

Doc Gooden, probably the best pitcher in the game.

"Tell him to come to the All-Star Game and learn pitching from The Can," Boyd said.

Doc-vs.-The Can becomes a hot topic for writers and an obsession for Boyd. Then when he was left off the team, he shouted, "This is the last All-Star Game they won't invite Oil Can Boyd to."

As the season moves on, his productivity declines and he is prone to sudden mood swings. He is late so many times, the club can barely keep track of the fines and he appears to be on the verge of fighting just about anybody and everybody in the clubhouse.

Now stories are circulating that despite his $375,000 salary, Boyd has serious financial problems. The implications are that drugs are at the root of the difficulties.

No one knows what to expect from him, so the Sox general manager, Lou Gorman, drags out the standard, "We'd like to see him pitch again, but I think what everyone's feeling now is concern over his well-being."

While hospitalized, he is given a pass to leave the hospital for a few hours and then while driving in his car with his wife, Karen, they are stopped for speeding and Boyd is arrested for an old motor vehicle registration violation. He eventually waives his right to a jury trial and pays a fine.

After a few weeks in the hospital, Boyd issues a statement through his attorney. "I have been given medical clearance to return to baseball and I am eager to rejoin my teammates as soon as possible. I feel good and hope that I can get back on the mound very soon. My medical tests and evaluations have been completed and the summary of the results have been given to the Red Sox. I know what my difficulties are and I have taken positive steps to deal with them."

The Red Sox say they haven't received the results of any tests and that he is still suspended from the team and that if there is to be any resolution of the suspension, it will include "not only medical advice and assistance, but also financial counseling in an endeavor to ease outside burdens that have been a source of stress for Boyd."

A few days later, after a complete medical examination which includes negative tests for drugs, Boyd is reinstated. The team says a counseling and support program has been put together for him by the club, Major League Baseball, and the Players Association.

"Any problems he's got, he can come to certain people for help," says Gorman. "We hope they will get him through the rest of the year."

Back in Meridian, Mississippi, Boyd's family and friends are upset with what they've been reading and hearing about him. He's really a good kid they say, while acknowledging that he can be overly emotional and hard on himself.

But Ledarrack Wilson, a friend of Boyd's since childhood and best man at his wedding, says, "That's The Can. Can's my best friend, but he always got his own way, and when he didn't, he flew the coop. We'd lose a game as teenagers and he'd cry, take off in a rage and we wouldn't see him for two days."

Boyd's mother says people don't understand just how much of a perfectionist her youngest son is. She says he wouldn't go to school if she hadn't perfectly pressed the pleats on his pants.

Boyd admits that because of his tantrums, he started seeing a psychiatrist when he was 12. "Those tantrums almost cost me my career, too," he says.

> In the summer of 1977, before going to Jackson State, I struck out 17 in seven innings in a semi-pro game at Meridian. I had a no-hitter going, the umpire missed a pitch for a walk, and the next guy hit a double that scored him all the way from first. I told the umpire that it was his fucking fault. He threw me out of the game because you can't swear on the ball field. I went wild. I took my uniform off and left the park in my underwear. I sat in my daddy's car, crying, kicking, cussing, fussing. The next day my daddy said there were a lot of scouts in the ballpark, and they all left. I got so mad at him telling me that, that I walked 20 miles from that pasture all the way back to Meridian. I misunderstood him; I

thought my daddy had told me I would never make the big leagues because I was too hotheaded.

My sophomore year at Jackson State I put on my worst display ever, playing the University of New Orleans down there. It was an all-black team against an all-white team, and they're yelling, "Nigger, nigger, nigger..." and I'm going crazy. This New Orleans player runs across the mound and calls me a "nigger" and a "hot dog," so I chased him to the first base line and fought him. They didn't throw either one of us out, and the next inning he hit a blast off me. He was running round the bases, shaking his fist and it made me so mad that I let him beat me that I just lost it. I went so crazy — I took my hat off, I started undressing on the mound, I got so mad that I felt as if my clothes were burning up. I was that mad, madder than they saw me in Boston ... and they wonder about temper. I went off the mound, threw my spikes into their dugout and I came off the field again in my underwear. My teammates looked at me like I was crazy. Stay away from him. Coach Braddy kept yelling at me, "This was the biggest game of the season and you act like that? Like a spoiled baby?" Then I fought my brother Neal, right there. I just want to win too bad, sometimes.

Boyd's father, Willie, was a good semi-pro pitcher for the Meridian Braves in his day and he, too, had something of a temper. When he couldn't get organized baseball to give him a chance, he gave up the game and became a singer known in the area for his rendition of "He Pulled the Trigger, But You Took His Life."

At one point, all five of The Can's older brothers played together on the Braves and all had aspirations of playing in the Major Leagues. One of them, Don, did sign with the Cardinals but he only lasted one year in their system.

"The Boyds carried a mark of baseball," The Can says, adding:

When I went off to play pro ball in 1980, I told my mother, "This is it. The last of the Boyds. I gotta make the big leagues." When I made it, it took a burden off the family because they were so into baseball. When I was called up to Boston in September 1982, I called them when I arrived at the Sheraton and said, "We made it. We all made it," and they all cried. Brother Don told me, "Since you got there, my life has just stopped, because to be a Boyd is to be a baseball player."

Everyone in our neighborhood, in Meridian, knew that these six boys were such good players that one of them had to make it. The other ones didn't make it for racial problems, or because scouts didn't pass through here.

Even now, The Can is wont to break down when talking about his family and how his brothers were denied chances for baseball careers. He is a proud, emotional man. His family insists he is badly misunderstood.

Where has all his money gone? Well, for one thing he is sending a lot of it down to his family. He is making payments on several condominiums and cars for his brothers, he has loans to pay off, and he isn't making nearly as much as some people think. Jim Rice gets $2 million to patrol the outfield; Boyd gets $375,000. In April he called down to Meridian to arrange for his mother to quit her job at a Kentucky Fried Chicken drive-through and move into his condominium. "He is so careful with his own money," says his brother Don, "that last spring he wasn't eating properly and that's why his weight dropped to 133 pounds sending him to the hospital where they said he had noncontagious hepatitis."

He assumed all his bills were being paid by his agent, Dennis Coleman. "Then strange things started happening," Boyd says. "I got calls threatening me because I owed money. I told them my agent took care of that. Then my phone got shut off. I'd tell Dennis that I couldn't live on chump change, that something was wrong, but nothing happened." He adds that when he realized he had no money it hit him hard. So he got a new agent, his fourth in five years.

As to the All-Star Game meltdown incident, he explains that he was sure he'd make the team this year for sure. Why wouldn't he? He already had 10 wins didn't he? He called his family and made arrangements for them to make the 400-mile trip to Houston for the game.

"What better way than to have them see me in the All-Star Game?" he asks. "I wanted to pitch with some of those great players behind me, even guys I've had controversy with because they say I'm showing them up. I'd like to sit with them in the dugout and have them realize I'm not like that. It would mean a lot to have Lou Whitaker playing behind me. It would mean a lot to be able to say to Don Mattingly, 'Way to stroke the bat.' It took a lot away from me when Sparky Anderson didn't pick me last year. Then this year..."

Ken Schrom is chosen as an American League pitcher for the game. Oil Can Boyd is not.

Then, too, claim Boston tabloids, he's hanging out in Chelsea—coke heaven—and as everybody knows, coke costs money.

By The Can's own admission, "The city may be more than a country boy can handle."

The Sox certainly hope he learns to handle it, and fast, as both the Yankees and Orioles are breathing down their necks.

"Maybe getting away, cooling down and doing what I did was for the best," Boyd says after being reinstated by the club. "I'm getting my finances straightened out. I'm with family. I've got 13 or 14 starts left. I can help the Red Sox win the pennant. I'm no angel, but at least I'll admit it. Fire and desire got me to the big leagues, but I've got to control it. So all I need from here on in is the ball, because the one thing Oil Can Boyd wants most in the world is to pitch in the big leagues. They can take my money, they can take my car, but please don't mess with my family or take the ball out of my hand."

1995

Due to a contract dispute between the owners and the Players Association, the 1994 season had been canceled in August. After protracted negotiations broke down in January, President Clinton ordered both the players and the owners to resume bargaining and reach an agreement by February 6. When he was ignored, the owners decided to use replacement players for spring training and regular season games. Almost all Major League players abhorred the idea and expressed disdain for any Major Leaguer who crossed the line and joined the replacements.

Probably the most well-known player to do so was Oil Can Boyd. He was reportedly guaranteed $5,000 for reporting to spring training and another $5,000 when the season began.

Declared acting commissioner Bud Selig, "We are committed to playing the 1995 season and will do so with the best players willing to play."

When Oil Can is subjected to harsh criticism from other players, he says, "You've got to do what's good for The Can."

February 2012

Boyd gives a radio interview in which he claims he pitched while high on cocaine in every American League ball park, saying he always stayed up to 4:00 or 5:00 in the morning. "It ain't like you had time to go and do it while you were in the game, which I have (done) that ... and if I had went to bed, I would have won 150 ballgames in the time span that I played and ... I felt like my career was cut short for a lot of reasons."

The biggest reason he says is that he was an outspoken black man. "I can name 50 people that got third and fourth chances all because they weren't outspoken black individuals."

50. Who's In: Who's Not

If for no other reason than the starting pitching matchup, the All-Star Game has whetted the appetite for a Mets–Red Sox World Series. Gooden and Clemens are the two most exciting young pitchers in the game and both can get the radar guns to the brink of triple digits. "All last year we heard that a Dwight Gooden comes along once in a lifetime," says NBC's Tony Kubek. "Now we've got Gooden and Roger Clemens." For the first time in his early career, though, Gooden, baseball's Mozart, seems hittable. In his last dozen starts his ERA is up and his strikeouts down. "WHAT'S UP, DOC?" reads the headline in one paper.

At the All-Star break the Red Sox, Giants, Angels, and Mets are all in first place.

The Giants' success is something of a surprise, but it is leading to speculation that it will make it easier for the Giants to move to another city. The club desperately needs a new stadium. Their present one, Candlestick Park, sometimes known as "The Cave of the Winds," is windy, damp, cold, too far from the city, without access to suitable public transport, and disliked as much by the players as the fans.

"You know it's summertime at Candlestick when the fog rolls in, the wind kicks up, and you see the center fielder slicing open a caribou to survive the ninth inning," quipped performer Bob Sarlette.

The wind got so bad during the All-Star Game of 1961 that Giants pitcher Stu Miller was blown off the mound, resulting in the first wind-aided balk. Two years later the wind picked up the batting cage and dropped it in the middle of the infield.

Recently outfielder Chili Davis looked up at a minuscule crowd of less than 5,000 and called them "pathetic." "We have about 6,000 real fans," he says. "The rest are assholes who come out to see other teams beat us. They should pack up this team and get the hell out of here. If I were [team owner] Bob Lurie, I'd pack it up and take a hike. Adios. See you later."

The Giants, desperate to keep their relatively few loyal fans, installed a radiant heating system but it was largely ineffective. Celebrated attorney

50. Who's In: Who's Not

Melvin Belli filed a claim against the Giants arguing that his box seats, which cost him almost $1,600, were unbearably cold and that the heating system didn't work as advertised. Belli won his case.

Although he is courting other offers Bob Lurie would rather remain in or near San Francisco, but he needs help from the city fathers or, in this case, the city's mother, Mayor Diane Feinstein. She tells Lurie that the city is willing to kick in $40 million, but not a penny more. She says they're willing to pay for a Buick of a stadium, not a Cadillac. Lurie, who prefers a Seville, seems to be serious about moving the team and many baseball people are betting he will.

Denver seems the most likely candidate. Last year, Mark Knudson, now an Astros starter, was a sports writer for the *Rocky Mountain News*. His primary assignment was to cover the impending news of the Giants' move to Denver and to assemble a Denver Giants team guide.

Denver baseball fans were excited.

Does "I Left my Heart in Denver" work well as a song?

If ever a city needs an All-Star Game, it's Houston. The sun has set on this Sun Belt boomtown. As the Saudi Arabians keep pumping out more and more crude, a huge surplus of oil is building up here. Stories of unemployment and the continued skid in oil prices dominate the newspapers. Clearly an anticipated $40 million All-Star infusion will be a big lift.

The game can't hurt the Astros either, because even though they are only one game out of first place in the National League West, their attendance at the Astrodome is down 27,165 from last season.

The day before the game, the National League beats the American, 8–7, in a home run hitting contest with Strawberry and Joyner hitting four each and Dave Parker getting three. Jose Canseco, gets one and then says, "The Dome is a hard place to hit home runs. I heard that before I came and now I believe it. Maybe it would be an easier place to hit homers if they hung a fence from the roof."

Huh?

The relay-throwing contest ends in a 3–3 tie. The Cubs' Ryne Sandberg teams with Parker and Gary Carter to beat Jesse Barfield, Frank White, and Lance Parrish. Later, the White Sox' Harold Baines teams with Cal Ripken and Parrish to beat Strawberry, Hubie Brooks, and Tony Peña.

As usual, Oil Can Boyd gets a lot of attention. "I am dismayed to read about what happened with Boyd in Boston," American League manager Dick Howser says. "I feel sorry for what happened. There are always some good players left off but I can't make excuses for the team we selected."

As usual, there's some griping about who was and who wasn't selected for the teams. Hernandez gets the nod over 10-time All Star Garvey and 17-

timer Pete Rose. Three-hundred-game winners Carlton, Seaver, and Sutton aren't in the game. Neither is Reggie Jackson. Wally Joyner is, though. He's the first rookie selected by the fans to start a midseason classic.

It is while driving home to watch the game on television that Boyd has his run-in with the police.

"He kept insisting he had a gun and he was going to shoot somebody," Detective Sergeant Jack Phillips says of what he thought was going to be a routine car stop. "At this point, we did just an immediate search of the area. We didn't locate any gun. That was kind of our concern, especially when he turned his back and reached into his pockets. Weapons is the first thing you look for. Dope is secondary. We came up with nothing. He just became crazy. He kept screaming that he didn't have any dope."

"I just want to pitch, man," Boyd says after he is suspended. "I can't pitch."

The American League wins the game, 3–2. Clemens is chosen as the game's Most Valuable Player.

51. Signs of Confusion

During the All-Star Game, American League Manager Dick Howser seems confused at times, so much so that the broadcasters comment on it.

Howser is an experienced and successful manager, who during a seven-year managerial career never finished lower than second place. He's considered a knowledgeable and tough baseball man who took over as Yankee skipper in 1980, leading them to an AL Eastern Division championship. He is perhaps better known, however, for being one of the few managers who consistently stood up to Steinbrenner. When Steinbrenner would call the manager's office, Howser was wont to pick up the phone and tell the boss, "I'm busy," and then hang up.

In the second game of the 1980 American League Championship Series, third base coach Mike Ferraro waved Willie Randolph home with two outs in the top of the eighth inning, only to have him thrown out at the plate. Steinbrenner jumped from his chair letting loose a string of profanities, all caught on national television, and immediately announced he wanted Ferraro fired on the spot. After the game, Howser said he wouldn't do that, and so Howser was fired.

The Royals hired him to finish out the next season. In 1982 and 1983, he guided them to second-place finishes. The team, ravaged by drug problems, was then pretty much torn apart in what was reasonably expected to be a rebuilding year. Howser, though, took his young team to the division title in 1984, and then in 1985 to their first and only World Series title when they defeated the Cards in seven games.

No question about it, Richard Dalton Howser is considered one of the brightest and most able managers around, so why is he now exhibiting signs of confusion? He's not old (50), he's certainly not a fool, and he's not known to play Casey Stenglesque games.

Ferrraro, now Howser's third base coach, says, "About four or five days ago, he started calling guys by the wrong names," Ferraro said. "We knew he wasn't feeling good, but we just thought it was stress."

A few days before the All-Star Game, Howser gets Royals catcher Jim

Sundberg confused with pitcher Bret Saberhagen. Ferraro says, "And then on Saturday he told [batting coach] Lee May we weren't going to [have batting practice] on Sunday. After the game he came in and told the fellas, 'If you want to hit tomorrow, it will be at 11:30.' Lee said, 'Dick, you said we're not hitting tomorrow.' Dick said, 'Did I say that?' He was forgetting what he was saying."

Barely 48 hours after guiding the American League to victory in the All-Star Game, Howser is admitted to Kansas City's St. Luke's Hospital complaining of a sore neck.

The next day, team physician Dr. Paul Meyer, pointing at the Royals' general manager, John Schuerholz, says, "We would ask him who is this man? He didn't know. We asked him who won the game last night and he said the Royals, but he didn't know the score."

Dick Howser has a brain tumor. "This is a large tumor," Meyer says. "If it is benign, as we hope it is, then the plan will be to remove it. If it is malignant, then you have to resort to radiation-type therapy, or chemotherapy. It's in the frontal area where emotions and personality are centered."

"Every now and then something happens to slap you in the face and remind you that all these little things you're worried about don't amount to anything," says designated hitter Hal McRae. "We knew the skip wasn't feeling good, but we just thought it was stress and worry."

The frontal lobe tumor is determined to be malignant and a three-hour operation is performed, during which only a part of the tumor can be removed. He is sent home and told that he will undergo a series of radiation treatments — five a week for five weeks.

After a second brain operation Howser says, "What happens if Dick Howser couldn't manage? I think you all know — they'd bring somebody else in. But I feel like I can do it. What I can't stand is staying away from baseball."

When the tumor continues to grow, he goes to California for experimental treatment in which cancer-killing cells are injected into the tumor. Wearing a golf cap over his shaved head and looking noticeably thinner, he says because of his strong religious faith, he remains optimistic. "That's the only way you can look at this game. I look at baseball the way I look at life and that's day-to-day. As important as managing is to me — and I think about things like left fielders and designated hitters almost every day, my health comes first."

"Every day is a fight," he adds. "It's not fun. It's all day-to-day with me. Some of the reports I don't know about. I don't want to know about. Some of the reports were good. I'm sure some were real bad."

Ferraro will finish the season as Royals manager. Howser says he is planning to be with the Royals next year when they open spring training. Family, friends, and teammates say they are sure he will.

June 1987

Howser died at 2:45 P.M. at St. Luke's Hospital, a spokeswoman says. His wife, Nancy, was at his bedside.

In spring training he had attempted to return as manager, but was so weak he had to give it up after two days.

"This is a sad day for baseball," Ueberroth says in a statement released by his New York office. "Dick Howser was one of the great men of our game."

A Dick Howser Award is established to be presented annually to college baseball's top player.

52. The Tony Gwyn of Pitching

On a muggy Tuesday afternoon in September, the first-place Astros send Nolan Ryan to the mound against the struggling Cubs and their young left-hander, Jamie Moyer. Both are gone by the time the game heads into extra innings. With the score tied at 4, the Astros finally manage to add three runs in the top of the 17th inning. When in the bottom of the inning, Cubs catcher Jodi Davis singles, Gene Michael sends in a young pitcher the club had recently brought up. It is Greg Maddux's first Major League appearance — and he's a pinch-runner. At 20, he is the youngest player in the league. After the Cubs re-tie the game, Maddux is sent out to pitch.

His catcher is Tom Martin, a long-time minor leaguer who himself had just been called up a month earlier. Martin and Maddux had been roommates in the minor leagues and now were rooming together again with the Cubs. After getting the first batter to ground out, Maddux gives up a home run to Billy Hatcher and takes the loss.

Martin's big-league career consists of 13 at-bats and one hit.

"I did not know then how good he would be," Martin says. "He didn't either. Nobody did. He is never satisfied, and he's an incredible competitor. Not many people are blessed with that kind of ability. He's always studying, doesn't take anything for granted. Tony Gwynn was the batter who made studying video popular. Greg Maddux is the Tony Gwynn of pitching."

Maddux grew up in Spain where his father served in the Air Force. It was father, Dave, who introduced Greg and his older brother, Mike, to the game. Later, when they moved to Las Vegas, it was Mike who caught the attention of scouts. Dave, though, told them, "You will be back later for the little one."

Since Greg was a skinny kid without much of a fastball, scouts had doubts about his potential. Little guys like that break down easily.

"Sure, I remember 'Doggie' when he first came up," says Billy Williams, then a Cubs coach. "He was a scrawny little kid who couldn't have weighed 160 pounds soaking wet."

One afternoon a teammate, pointing to Maddux sitting in the dugout, told a security guard that the batboy shouldn't be allowed to sit in the dugout that many hours before the game.

In this, his first taste of big-league life, he makes five September starts for the team playing out the string in a lost season.

His first start is an 11-hit win over the Reds, ending the Cubs' 7-game losing skid. Maddux is ahead 10–0 when Dave Parker drives in the Reds' first run in the fifth inning with his 2,000th career hit. "He hit some pitches nobody's ever hit off me," says Maddux of Parker's three-hit game. "They were all out of the strike zone. Amazing."

In his last start, he goes up against his brother. It is the first time brothers faced each other since the Niekro boys in the early '80s.

"You can't put a price on bragging rights, especially for him," Mike says. "God forbid, he gets a hit off me. I'll be hearing about it Monday dinner, Tuesday dinner. Some things you never hear the end of."

Greg beats his older brother, striking out seven while walking none along the way, and sets a trend he will continue for a long time.

"The last time I faced him, I think, was in the back yard playing Wiffle Ball," Mike says after the game. "I think we both hit about .700 in the back yard."

January 2008
Greg Maddux is making his annual appearance at the baseball camp of his old roommate, Martin. He is working with a kid, telling him to hold his glove at a certain point, and then throws the ball right to it from 120 feet away.

"I played with Mike and Greg," says Martin. "Both of them are guys you want your son to grow up and be like."

Maddux's arrival may have garnered scant attention from fans and the press, but the same cannot be said of another newcomer.

53. Challenges to America's Game

In early September, the Royals call up Bo Jackson from the Memphis Chicks. The college football player who won Most Valuable Player awards in both the Liberty and Sugar Bowls and then picked up the Heisman Trophy surprised a lot of people, telling the Tampa Bay Buccaneers "no thanks" after they made him a first-round draft choice in June and choosing instead to play baseball for the Kansas City Royals. The Buccaneers were prepared to sign him to a contract making him the highest paid rookie in NFL history at more than $7 million. He settled for a $100,000 salary and a ticket to Memphis. He also passed up a possible shot to make the U.S. Olympic team as a sprinter.

"We shocked the world," said Royals general manager John Schuerholz modestly.

"Everybody sat up and asked, 'Why would this guy play baseball and spend six months or a year in the minors when he could go to football and be an instant millionaire?'" Jackson said, "I had to do what makes me happy, and right now that's baseball."

The Royals were never sure they could convince Jackson to play baseball but they felt he was worth the gamble. Their scout said he was the best prospect he'd seen in 50 years and doubted he'd ever see another one as good again. When the Royals brought him in to tour their stadium, pitchers Bret Saberhagen and Bud Black showed up wearing Auburn t-shirts and big smiles. Then when other teams passed on him, figuring he would opt for football, the Royals gambled and selected him in the fourth round.

"We felt there was some glimmer of hope that existed for us to sign Bo Jackson," Schuerholz said. "We also had some legitimate concerns that he would say, 'I'm going to play football.'"

Schuerholz was nervous as they began the negotiations. Football is gaining a stronger hold on many young athletes—particularly African Americans. There are a number of reasons: television's glamorization of the sport, the possibility to play as a professional without spending years in the minor leagues, and potential lucrative commercial tie-ins. On the downside, there is a greater chance for serious injury.

Baseball is in a battle with football for the loyalty and dollars of the fans. While baseball attendance figures are going up, this may be due more to the increase in population, because football attendance is going up at an even higher rate.

No doubt Jackson could play either sport, or even both sports, but his decision comes as a surprise to many.

Bo knows baseball and baseball knows it has a strong drawing card with the Heisman winner.

Way to go, say baseball fans.

What a fool, say football fans.

Of course, many fans follow both sports, but most have a "favorite" sport and professional football is moving to the front of the pack ... but not with everyone.

"Anybody who watches three games of football in a row should be declared brain dead," declares Erma Bombeck.

Any way you look at it, says former pitcher Jim Bouton, baseball players are smarter than football players. "How often do you see a baseball team penalized for too many men on the field?" he asks.

"I don't like American football," says Jim Jarmusch. "I think it's boring and ridiculous and predictable. But baseball is very beautiful. It's played on a diamond."

Baseball has been, ever since the 1870s, generally referred to as the "National Pastime" or "National Game." "It is," opines Saul Steinberg, "an allegorical play about America, a poetic, complex, and subtle play of courage, fear, good luck, mistakes, patience about fate, and sober self-esteem."

In the mid–19th century there were a lot of ideas floating around about which sport should be considered America's national game. One paper even opined that of all the games played in this country the two that would become the most popular were baseball and coits. Apparently the St. Andrews Coit Club and the New York Coit Club were going at it full tilt. Other papers lobbied for cricket or lacrosse. The thought was that the Greeks had their Olympic Games; the Spaniards, the bull fight; the French, fencing; and the English, their much-loved cricket.

The Americans wanted a game to call their own, not one borrowed from another culture. Baseball fit the bill. It was fun, it provided good exercise and, at a time when there was still considerable animosity over things British, it was seen as American and was intrinsically linked in the minds of many with patriotism.

"Baseball? It's just a game — as simple as a ball and a bat. Yet, as complex as the American spirit it symbolizes. It's a sport, business — and sometimes even religion," wrote broadcaster Ernie Harwell.

From the 1870s until the early 1950s, at least, baseball was king. It was our game, America's game, pure and simple, no question about it. Then came a new toy that changed the way Americans came to see sports. Television was taking hold of households with the speed and ferocity of a plague and it quickly discovered that by broadcasting football it could sell lots of time for deodorants and razor blades. Heretofore football had been primarily consigned to colleges and universities and only marginally to professional teams. Television changed all of that.

In 1950 the Los Angeles Rams became the first team to televise its entire schedule. Television and professional football entered into a partnership that would prove to be a boon to both. Then in 1958, the so-called "Greatest Game That Was Ever Played" took place between the New York Giants and the Baltimore Colts. This dramatic sudden-death overtime game was carried live on NBC and became the watershed moment in professional football history. Writer Tex Maule said of the contest, "This, for the first time, was a truly epic game which inflamed the imagination of a national audience."

Now, in 1986, Ueberroth and the baseball owners know that they are in for a long battle in trying to wrest back from professional football the loyalty (and dollars) of the fans.

December 2005
  A Harris survey shows that professional football continues to surge in popularity with 33 percent of adults who say they follow sports stating it is their favorite sport. Baseball follows at 14 percent, college football at 13 percent, and auto racing at 11 percent.

  Since 1985 professional football has risen nine points in popularity and auto racing six. Baseball has dropped by nine points.

  Professional football is most popular among African Americans and Generation X (those aged 28 to 39). African Americans are least likely to say baseball is their favorite sport, and those with a post-graduate education are least likely to name professional football their favorite.

  Baseball does best among Hispanics and Echo Boomers (those aged 18 to 27).

  College football is particularly popular among Republicans. Auto racing is most popular with those with a high school education or less and fares the worst among those with a post-graduate degree.

Ueberroth is thrilled with Jackson's signing. Giamatti is thrilled. Kansas City is thrilled. Baseball fans are ... hopeful.

"What made it more doable was his attitude that he really loved baseball," Schuerholz said. "And more so his attitude that dollars alone wasn't going to make his decision for him. He demonstrated that there are some principles and there are some people that dollar bills can't buy."

The general manager began to breathe easier.

When the deal was done, the Royals had one of the greatest athletes in the world.

"I'm so happy now, they could send me to Pee-Wee ball," Jackson said.

Even the great athletes, though, can find baseball a difficult game to learn well enough to play on the Major League level. In his first 31 at-bats for the Chicks he struck out 14 times, had two hits, one RBI and a .065 batting average.

"This is going to take some time," he said.

But not a lot of time. By the middle of September he's raised his average to .333.

Still some baseball people are skeptical and compare him to John Elway. Their arm strengths are comparable, but Elway was neither as quick nor as powerful as Jackson, and he remained a fringe minor leaguer in the Yankee system before moving on to a Hall of Fame career as a football quarterback.

"When people tell me I could be the best athlete there is, I just let it go in one ear and out the other," Jackson says. "There is always somebody out there who is better than you are."

Jackson, though, looks like a baseball player, a very good baseball player and the Royals have slated him in to be their regular left fielder in 1987. Now, for the remainder of this season they will give him a chance to show their fans what the future of their franchise will look like and it looks like Bo Jackson running down balls in the alley and hitting monster home runs.

Lots of talented young players come up as "the next" Mantle, Mays, Koufax, or someone else who looks like, hits like, throws like, or runs like a great player of the past. For any number of reasons—pressure, misjudged skills, injury, character—disappointment often follows. Bo Jackson, though, does look like the real deal. He looks like the next great star in baseball.

March 1992
Bo Jackson, in an exhibition game, hits a ground ball to the Tigers' shortstop. Unless the ball is booted or thrown away, it's a sure double play. Jackson heads for first, virtually dragging his leg with him. It's not a pretty sight. Then seemingly out of sympathy, the Tigers' first baseman, Cecil Fielder, steps off the bag and holds up both his big arms, waving off the relay throw from the second baseman.

Jackson is trying to prove that the left hip he injured in a NFL playoff game while a running back with the Los Angeles Raiders would allow him to play baseball again.

"It hurts just watching him," says Gene Lamont, Chicago's manager.

And it's not just the running and fielding, it's the hitting, too. He swings with all upper body. There are no legs left in his swing at all.

Al Davis, the ornery owner of the Raiders, got Jackson to sign a contract by offering a contract comparable to the best running backs, but allowing him to play with the Raiders only after the baseball season was done. Davis knew a good football player and a good publicity angle when he saw one.

Jackson proved he was still a superb running back. In one Monday Night Football game, he ran over the Seahawks' loudmouthed star linebacker Brian Bosworth in a 221-yard rushing performance after Bosworth boasted he would shut down Jackson.

Now the hip injury looks like the end in both sports may be near for two-sport Bo Jackson.

"Back before I injured my hip, I thought going to the gym was for wimps," he says. Everyone nods. He says he's not ready to give it up yet.

He will hang on for a while then retire far short of what might have been.

"He might be the best player who ever lived," says teammate Buddy Biancalana about Jackson.

That's a pretty bold statement.

Except there's much to support it.

Such as?

Well for one, he's the fastest player in the game today.

But he's no Mantle.

Close.

They say the Mick did a legendary 3.5 seconds from the right side of the plate to first.

Jackson did 3.62. And he's got a cannon for an arm.

As good as Jesse Barfield's?

Maybe.

Power?

In his first week in the league he hit a 475-foot homer, said to be the longest ball ever hit at Royals Stadium. Oh, yes, and he also had a four-hit game that first week.

The first time he faced Oil Can, Boyd tells him, "I am The Can, and I am going to come right at you with my best shit, and if you can hit it, I want to see how far Bo Jackson can hit The Oil Can."

Okay Jackson, see what you can do.

The first pitch he sees he launches over the 71-foot-high scoreboard at Fenway Park. The ball lands more than 500 feet from home plate.

54. Making Waves Is Dangerous

The Angels picked up Donnie Moore late in the 1985 season and he immediately proved to be the missing piece in their bullpen.

Moore was anything but an instant hit in professional baseball, bouncing around like a pachinko ball between nine major and minor league clubs before finding success with the Braves in 1982.

What happened? Why all of a sudden was he almost unhittable? How did he go from being a stiff to being a stud? Where did his 1.92 ERA for the Angels come from?

Simple, he says. He learned the split-fingered fast ball.

It was four years ago and he was struggling to get outs for the Braves' AAA team in Richmond, Virginia. He was still throwing hard but the batters knew he didn't have an off-speed pitch so they were ready for him. His first inclination was to master a changeup. "I tried about every way you could throw one," he says.

Oh, he could throw it all right, just not over the plate. Then one night after getting shelled in Richmond, pitching coach Johnny Sain suggested he try the split-finger pitch. Thrown properly it looks like a fastball but it runs out of steam just before it gets to the plate. Because they tend to swing early, batters hate it.

Moore had toyed with the pitch before but never in a game. When Sain asked him about it, "I said no," explained Moore. "I said I didn't have that much confidence in it. He said I should use it. He thought it was a hell of a pitch. He said, 'That's why you're in Richmond, in Triple A. You should work on it, throw it, work on it.' I did that, and it was the difference in me. That's what got me back in the big leagues."

He was always known as a hard worker so it wasn't a big surprise that it finally all came together for him. Says Moore, a strapping, good-natured man, "Maybe I'm just a survivor."

The split-finger is being hailed as the pitch of the '80s. Thank you, Roger

Donnie Moore unleashing his split-fingered fastball against the Red Sox in the '86 ALCS. He gave up four runs in the Series, including the home run to Henderson he could not forget.

Craig. The San Francisco manager serves as the pitch's chief cheerleader, and split-finger mania is spreading about as fast as pitchers can learn it. Because he has gotten so many requests from players, managers, and coaches about how to best throw the pitch, Craig has written out a complete split-finger owner's manual and sends it out free of charge.

"I think it will change things in the '80s, but I think too many people are jumping on the bandwagon," says San Francisco pitcher Greg Minton. "I don't think that many guys will be able to throw it that well. It will be outstanding for the guys who do master it."

Moore begs to differ. "I think it is the pitch of the future," he says. "I think it's going to be a pitch like the slider was. Now almost everybody throws a little slider. I think in years to come, it's going to be the pitch."

When he was in high school Moore developed an itch to win a Texas state title but that didn't seem possible at his school. The only thing to do was to transfer to a school that had a reasonable shot. He checked out the possibilities and decided on Lubbock's Monterey High. Bobby Moegle, the baseball coach there, could easily envision Moore on his mound and the victories that would surely follow, but he was also a realist. His school of over 2,000 students was white — all white. The fans in the stands were white, and this was Texas.

Does this big, well-meaning kid have any idea what he would be up against, some wondered. It's difficult enough facing the challenges of top high school batters without having to cope with the abuse he would inevitably face. The kid can pitch, but it would certainly be easier for everyone if he stayed put — "everyone" meaning both player and coach.

Moegle was already a legend in the area. He had spent some time as a Cardinals farmhand and an Army infantryman, and so ran his team like a boot camp. Even by Texas standards he was as tough and hard-nosed as they come. He was also meticulous in his game preparations. Before each season he administered a 263-question test to all his players. The test was about the fundamentals of baseball.

Want to play for Coach Moegle? Study, pass the test, or go back to Home Ec classes.

His stringent disciplinary measures were so draconian that war stories about him have become Texas myths.

When a player was a few seconds late for practice, he made the poor kid run laps around the field. Three hours later when practice was over and darkness was descending, the coach set up a lawn chair and knocked off a few chapters of *Gone with the Wind* without saying a word to the exhausted, but still jogging player.

After a bitter loss, he had the players run back to their motel lugging all of their gear while he lectured them on fundamentals from the window of the bus.

When a player running laps and on the verge of throwing up complained he was about to die if he didn't stop, Coach Moegle told him to keep running because he would pass out before he'd die.

When an outfielder misjudged a fly ball that hit him on the head, the coach had him wear a red helmet at every game and practice for the rest of the season.

Among team members there was always more respect than love for the ornery coach. They may not all have liked him, but they knew he knew how to win. Yes, there would be difficult days under this Patton-like disciplinarian and, yes, there would be difficult days for a black kid in an all-white school, but as Moegle put it, "Donnie was on a mission, and nothing could stop him."

Nothing did stop him. In his three years with the Monterey Plainsmen the team went 91–6. As a sophomore, Moore mostly played right field, but in his second year he went 15–1 on the mound, played right field when he wasn't, and hit .414. In his senior year he was 18–4 and they were in the state championships. Moore won the semi-final game, and then came back to close the clincher. The Plainsmen were ahead, 2–1, in the last inning with two outs a runner on third, and a 3–2 count on the batter when Moore beckoned the coach to the mound. "Coach, I'm nervous," Moore whispered. "Hell, I'm nervous too," said Moegle. "You just get back on that rubber and cut it loose, and I like our chances." Moore struck out the batter on the next pitch and the Texas state championship was theirs.

"Donnie was the savior we'd been looking for," Moegle says, "his hand always out for the ball no matter how hurt he was."

As the school's only black student, Moore was something of a loner, albeit a popular one, attested to by the fact he was voted among the school's five most popular students. This was a school with a strong athletic tradition and everyone could see Moore's contribution. Once when the Texas skies opened up during a pivotal game against arch-rival El Paso, Moore disappeared for a few minutes and then reappeared with a big wheelbarrow full of dirt to spread around so that the game wouldn't be suspended. Maybe the groundskeepers had been cut from the budget, but he wasn't about to let a 3–1 lead go to waste.

A quiet kid. Moore kept a lot to himself because he had to. In his situation, making waves was dangerous and so he learned to put a lid on his emotions. He pitched well, smiled when appropriate, and stayed out of trouble.

Moegle would go on to become the winningest baseball coach in high school history.

The 31-year old Moore came to the Angels in 1985 and quickly became their bullpen go-to guy. His 31 saves were a vital part in getting to within one game of winning the division title.

Now expectations for the Angels are high and manager Gene Mauch is counting on him to be a dominant closer. Moore is not disappointing, and the Angels are playing consistent ball, posting a winning record every month other than May and remaining in front of the Rangers, albeit not by much.

The Angels' eclectic collection of gray-hairs and greenhorns are being led

54. Making Waves Is Dangerous

by their slam-the-door reliever Moore, their Rookie of the Year candidate Wally Joyner, and a resilient, if less powerful, Reggie Jackson.

Jackson whines some about DH-ing, but last year playing 81 games in right field showed that catching fly balls before they bounced at least once has become a challenge for him.

Still, Moore is regularly closing out enough games that prospects for a championship look promising.

55. The Fine Art of Cheating

Mike Scott is unquestionably the Astros' ace but he's finding winning difficult. Despite not allowing more than two earned runs in ten consecutive starts, he is only 3–3 during that span and he is irked — annoyed not so much by his record, but because the team has decided to promote his strikeout prowess by handing out placards with a big red "K" so that fans can hold them up all over the stadium each time he gets two strikes on a batter. Scott thinks this is lame-brained promotional idiocy. Now every time he gets two strikes, he looks up into a sea of red "K" cards which makes him overthrow. Despite this, he leads the league in strikeouts. Maybe the placards have a subliminal effect.

The Cubs' manager, Jim Frey, thinks there's another reason — Scott's cheating.

"I think he scuffs the ball," Frey says. "I don't know how much he does it, but I think he does it to get out of tough spots."

Last year Frey sent a piece of sandpaper to the National League office he claims was found on the mound during a Scott-pitched game. "The hitters think he scuffs it," Frey says. "On his strikeouts, the ball is doing something."

The Astros say he's become a strikeout pitcher since he's relied more on his fastball.

Scott says it's because he's learned the art of the split-fingered pitch.

The team publicist hopes it's the placards.

Frey claims it's the sandpaper.

In a game against the Giants last season, Scott was accused of scuffing the ball. He received a warning from the umpires, but no other action was taken other than ejecting Giants manager Roger Craig for arguing the play.

To make matters worse, he's been trying to teach Nolan Ryan his trick. National League hitters are thankful that, so far at least, he has been unable to master it. Maybe when you're throwing 100 mph you don't need it.

"There's no doubt in my mind that Mike Scott is doing something to that ball," says Giants general manager Al Rosen. "And that surprises me because he's a fine young man and good enough pitcher that he doesn't need to cheat."

And how can you stop cheating like that?

Sentence the offender to life without baseball, says Rosen. "That will stop it. If a player is caught with irrefutable evidence, he shouldn't be allowed to play again. No player would take a chance then."

He thinks the prevalence of cheating is endemic in baseball and becoming worse than ever. Scuffed balls and corked bats are the most obvious examples. "And they're getting better at it," he says. "The problem is so severe, and it's a terrible message we're sending to the public."

And what about your players, Mr. Rosen? Are you suggesting they're all clean?

"I never said that. All I can tell you is the Giant players have been informed that if they are ever caught cheating, don't expect any support from the club. They know I abhor cheating."

Baseball players make a lot of money when they play well, less when they don't play well. "If you don't succeed, you won't be in your profession for long," says outfielder Chili Davis. "In our society, it's not about good or bad. It's about who's on top. If you're caught roughing up the ball or corking your bat, that's cheating. But short of that, I would do anything I could to hit the ball 20 feet farther and help my team win. I owe it to my teammates."

Is there a difference between gamesmanship and cheating? Some (most) players think not. An outfielder dives, traps the ball, comes up holding the ball high to convince the umpire he caught it before it hit the ground. Gamesmanship or cheating? The shortstop knows he misses a tag on a sliding runner, but flips the ball back to the pitcher suggesting he made the tag. Gamesmanship or cheating?

Donna Lopiano, director of the Womens' Sports Foundation, former world class softball pitcher and teacher of a Sports Ethics course at the University of Texas, says, "Gamesmanship is just another word for cheating. It's one thing for a pitcher to say to a batter, 'Would you like a changeup?' and then throw you a fastball. It's another thing to see what you can get away with."

In baseball, as in other sports, there is cheating and then there is cheating, a distinction that may be harmless enough when a pitcher smears a little gooey stuff on his fingers trying to get a better grip on a cold night, but it can be argued that it represents the kind of moral relativism that can justify just about anything

Gene Tenace, one of Gaylord Perry's many catchers in his long career once said, "I can remember a couple of occasions when I couldn't throw the ball back to him because it was so greasy that it slipped out of my hands. I just walked out to the mound and flipped the ball back to him."

"When you walk by, he smells like a drugstore," says Billy Martin.

Perry, who didn't work very hard at denying he doctored balls, even wrote a book, *Me and the Spitter*, about how he cheated, and he still made it to the

Hall of Fame. When he retired he said, "The league will be a little drier now folks."

He claims (brags) that he perfected the fine art of sniffing red peppers to make his nose run so that he could throw a snot ball, and learned to rub Vaseline along his zipper under the (correct) assumption that umpires wouldn't dare check there.

He reportedly approached Vaseline about endorsing their product but received a postcard reply saying, "We soothe babies' backsides, not baseballs."

Perry made getting away with cheating seem like fun and the fans joined in.

Yeah, of course he's cheating but look at how cleverly he gets away with it.

He's brilliant at breaking the rules and laughing at the suits who rule the game — a perfect anti-hero, a rebel with a cause and a tube of KY jelly.

Cubs pitcher George Frazier has an ERA this season of over 5.00. Nevertheless he will later claim that without the spitter he wouldn't even be in the Major Leagues:

> I got started with the spitter in 1983 with the Yankees. Billy Martin was my manager, and he took me aside and told me to throw it. I told him I didn't have to, and he said throw it here or don't throw it in Triple-A. Later, I learned from the best in the business, Gaylord Perry. He said, "You look kind of bad doing it. Let me show you a few things." I don't feel a bit guilty. It was just a nice equalizer. ... I threw a spitter for five years and never got caught.

Spitters have been a part of the game at least since Bobby Mathews threw them in the first Major League game, pitching for the Fort Wayne Kekiongas.

Don Sutton occasionally throws a wet one. Everyone knows it, including the umpires. Once, when an umpire came out to check for a little dab of Vaseline that Sutton might use to load up a ball, or for a little piece of sandpaper for roughing it up, he reached into Sutton's pocket and found a note saying "Not here." Then under Sutton's belt, he found another note — "You're getting warmer."

This season, in a battle of 41-year-olds, Don Sutton earns his 299th win against Tom Seaver. It is the greatest combination of total victories since 1926 when Walter Johnson and Red Faber pitched against each other. Ken Harrelson, though, is dismissive of Sutton's performance. "He scuffed so many baseballs that had to be thrown out, we outfitted all the Catholic Youth Leagues of Chicago," he says.

After Norm Cash won the batting title in 1961, he later admitted to using a corked bat the entire season.

Yes, the fine art of cheating in baseball has long been winked at.

Young players naturally emulate those Major Leaguers they see on television and in the ballparks. Why not? They're so very good at what they do, they're worthy of emulation. What they see is that some forms of cheating are okay, tolerated, and even celebrated; others are not. Tricking an umpire into thinking you've caught a trapped ball is commendable. Stealing signs is not.

55. The Fine Art of Cheating

Of course, baseball is not alone when it comes to issues concerning cheating. In the second round of this year's NBA draft, the Detroit Pistons take Dennis Rodman, who will go on to a successful career of pulling and tugging on opponent's jerseys when the referees aren't looking, with the tacit understanding that "it ain't cheating if you ain't caught." What illegal activities go on at the bottom of football piles staggers the imagination.

The line between colorful eccentricity and outright cheating is blurry. Is a little pine tar on your fingers okay but a little spit not? Once upon a time spitters were legal and quite a few pitchers made their living throwing them. Then, partially as a result of Ray Chapman being beaned and killed by a pitch said to be a spitter, it was partially outlawed in 1919 when, in a stroke of dubious logic, each team was allowed to designate two pitchers who were legally allowed to throw it. A year later, extending their string of questionable decisions, they outlawed the pitch for anyone not then throwing it, but grandfathered in an escape clause allowing any pitcher who was throwing it then to continue to do so until the day he retired. Burleigh Grimes took full advantage of the exception and continued throwing the pitch effectively until the day he quit the game in 1934.

Cheating in baseball goes back to who knows when. The first organized clubs in the mid–19th century were made up exclusively of men who considered themselves "gentlemen"— doctors, lawyers, stockbrokers, and bankers. Of course, gentlemen don't cheat, they insisted. According to the rules by which they played, the pitcher was to deliver the ball underhanded where the batsman requested. There were no called balls and strikes. Since there was no intent for the pitcher to gain an advantage on the batter, gentlemen didn't need such things. The pitcher simply delivered the ball so the batter could put it in play and thus begin the action of the game. Then some dastardly cheaters (we could hardly call them gentlemen) actually intentionally tried to deceive the batters. Some even started delivering "curvers" so as to try to get the batter to miss the ball. So the inevitable battle between pitcher and batter was begun by cheaters.

In those earliest days the game was played to 21 "aces" or runs, no matter how many innings it took. Some players, employing their own form of gamesmanship, would stall the game by not swinging at good deliveries until it became too dark to continue and thus save their team from defeat.

The top-hatted umpire generally only made calls when requested by a player. If he was in doubt about a play such as whether a ball was fairly caught (it was an out if caught on the fly or on one bounce), he might ask any spectator present for his opinion. Since the intent of the game was to offer exercise and healthy enjoyment to the participants, with winning and losing being only an incidental complement, there was less inclination to press for an unethical advantage. Of course as the inevitable competitive urge took over so did the inclination to find "competitive edges."

Charlie DeBost, one of the game's pioneers in the 1850s, complained: "I saw a game once where Eddie Brown of the Mutuals stole the third base. Although the play was very close, he jumped up and offered to take on any of the Eureka players who cared to fight him. As those taking him up on his offer rushed to the base, he ran home with the winning run. Is this fair trickery or cheating? Either way, it stunk to heaven."

As the game became more competitive, so did the efforts to win at any cost. Stories are told about the old 19th century Baltimore Orioles with John McGraw, who apparently weren't above hiding extra balls in the outfield grass so that there would always be a handy spare to outfox a surprised base runner.

Dave Bresnahan, though, may win the prize as the most outrageous cheater in professional baseball history. A second-string catcher with the Williamsport Bills of the Class-AA Eastern League, Bresnahan peeled and sculpted a potato in the shape of a baseball and then drew laces on it with a red pen. Catching in the fifth inning with the potato concealed in his glove and a runner on third base, he threw the potato ball over the third basemans's head and into the outfield hoping the runner would think it was an errant pickoff throw. The runner took the bait and headed home. "So then the runner tried to come home," Bresnahan says. "And I tagged him with the ball. He was out."

So was Bresnahan, who was fined and then released by the Bills' parent club, the Indians, for what they considered to be an egregious affront to the dignity of the game.

2001

The U.S. Postal Service announces it is issuing a stamp commemorating what is often considered the most stunning moment in baseball history — Bobby Thomson's "shot heard 'round the world" — that prompted Russ Hodges' oft-repeated sound bite scream that memorializes the play and forever torments every Dodger fan: "THE GIANTS WIN THE PENNANT!! THE GIANTS WIN THE PENNANT! THE GIANTS WIN THE PENNANT! THE GIANTS WIN THE PENNANT! Bobby Thomson hits into the lower deck of the left-field stands! The Giants win the pennant and they're goin' crazy, they're goin' crazy! HEEEY-OH!!! I don't believe it! I don't believe it! I do not believe it! Bobby Thomson ... hit a line drive ... into the lower deck ... of the left-field stands ... and this blame place is goin' crazy!"

The Postal Service will go ahead with the issue despite the acknowledgement that by dint of cheating, Bobby Thomson knew what pitch he would be seeing. Giants manager Leo Durocher had smuggled a coach with a telescope into the clubhouse overlooking center field. The coach picked up the catcher's sign and then pressed a button that activated a buzzer in the dugout indicating what pitch was coming. Durocher then had another coach signal Thomson.

Columnist Frank Deford, senior contributing writer at *Sports Illustrated*, argues that, of all the sports played in this country, baseball leads in premeditated cheating:

> Ironically, while now the idea is to lighten a bat in order to swing it faster, by inserting cork or sawdust or even, in one memorable instance, little rubber balls, the idea years ago was to make a bat a sturdier cudgel by hammering nails into it. Interesting about baseball, isn't it? You never hear about this sort of stuff in sports like golf and tennis, where the players also use the equivalent of bats. Only in our national pastime has such nefarious behavior always been part and parcel of the game.

Cubs president Andy MacPhail puts it this way: "There is a culture of deception in this game. It's been in this game for a 100 years. I do not look at this in terms of ethics. It's the culture of the game. I wish we'd get away from it, but it is what it is."

Not everyone, though, is interested in cheating. When the student theater club at Allan Hancock College ordered tickets for its fall play from a printing company in Arkansas, they received more than 50,000 World Series tickets instead. However, rather than using or selling them, they sent them back. Had it been a business club that received the ducats, their members would undoubtedly have known how to turn them into a sizeable profit, but since they were only actors, no one could expect them to know any better.

56. Best and Worst

By fall the pennant races have all the suspense of a game of solitaire played by a sneak. A nine-game spread between the leaders and the chasers has been about as tight as any race has gotten. The Mets have been so dominant that the other teams might well have been playing in another league. For the season, they outscore their opponents by a whopping 181 runs.

The fans in Boston, Anaheim, Houston, and in one borough of New York are happy, but Ueberroth and the powers that be in baseball know that tight races and narrow margins sell tickets. Winning just barely at the last minute beats runaways every time. Snatching victory from the jaws of defeat probably goes back at least to the caveman facing the saber-toothed tiger — kill or be killed. Competition between relative equals is always more dramatic than watching a bully beat up a weak sister.

Gary Carter says he doesn't miss the drama of a tight race. "I'd rather it be this way. It takes the pressure off. I've been in enough exciting races, enough close ones to last a lifetime."

Shortstop Rafael Santana disagrees. He misses the pressure of last year when they were tussling with the Cards all season, even if they did come in second. "Last year we would come to the park early every day. Three o'clock or even one o'clock for a 7:35 game. It felt good to be here. You wanted to come here and think about how we were going to win. You wanted to do everything you could to win. It's different this year. We come to the park at five on the bus, and wait for the game. It's nice to have a big lead. But I miss that. I liked the pressure. Last year, I'd wake up, and the first thing I'd think about was, how are we going to win tonight? This year, the first thing I think of is breakfast."

With the pennant chases over, the only drama left in the regular season seems to be the American League batting race between Mattingly and Boggs, both hitting around .350. The season will wrap up with a four-game Yankee-Red Sox head-to-head. "I hope it comes down to those last four games," says Mattingly, who is closing in on the Yankees' all-time record for hits. "That would be neat."

56. Best and Worst

Rafael Santana gets low fives as the Mets are introduced before the first game of the '86 World Series.

In the early '80s the Yankees expected "Bye Bye" Balboni to be their regular first baseman for years to come. The kid from Brockton, Massachusetts, could hit those long tape-measure home runs, so that, like Gibson and every other white kid who hits long home runs, he was compared to Mickey Mantle. In the minors he hit long balls with such frequency that he had "superstar" written all over him. He could hit the ball far when he hit it at all. The problem was that he swung and missed so often that the Yankees soon were looking for someone else to play first. That's when they turned to "Donnie Baseball," Don Mattingly.

The nickname, hung on him by Kirby Puckett, came because by his own admission that's about all he did. "I don't have a lot of hobbies," he says. "I pretty much play the game and go home."

Gooden once said of Mattingly, "I'm glad I don't have to face that guy every day. He has that look that few hitters have. I don't know if it's his stance, his eyes or what, but you can tell he means business."

He began his career in Oneonta, New York, where for a quarter they'd send a bus to his rooming house to pick him up for the ride to the playing field. He was a 180-pound, 19th-round draft pick Punch-and-Judy hitter, but he made contact often enough that the Yankees called him up in 1984. He quickly found himself locked into a season-long close battle with Dave Winfield for the batting title. On his last at-bat of the season, trailing Winfield by a couple of points, he got a bad-hop single off the glove of the second baseman, giving him the title.

According to a poll in *The New York Times*, Major League players consider Mattingly the best player in the game. The praise comes rolling in.

EARL WEAVER: "I've never seen anyone like him."
SPARKY ANDERSON: "Mattingly's from another planet."
BOBBY COX: "He's simply the best."

Red Sox hitting coach Walt Hriniak says, "The guy's hitting .350, making a million-something dollars a year, his team is 10 games out, they got to their hotel at four in the morning, and he's underneath the stands in the cage at 3:30 in the afternoon. Look at the way he plays the game — hitting, base running... He's the best first baseman in this league, by far. He's the best. He's the greatest I've ever seen, and he's everything this game should be."

Boggs says he is looking forward to the head-to-head confrontation with Mattingly but he sits out the final games with what he says is a slight hamstring pull. Mattingly goes on a tear, collecting hits like they were paychecks, but ends the season five points behind the sitting Boggs.

A New York tabloid runs a big headline across the back page — "CHICKENED OUT." Boggs is quick to let Mattingly know that's not the way he sees it. "If you read one quote that even hints at my questioning you, then it's been twisted or it's a fabrication," he says. "You know me. We're friends. If I were you, if I were hurting and had the playoffs to think about, then I'd do the same thing. The team comes first."

February 2008

Mattingly, who despite a .307 lifetime average, is often called the best Yankee player to never have played in a World Series or been elected to the Hall of Fame. When he is passed over as manager of the Yankees, he agrees to become batting coach for the Dodgers. However, after filing for divorce, his wife is arrested and charged with public intoxication and disorderly conduct. Mattingly, not wanting to leave his youngest son on his own, postponed his taking up the position.

He appears in several TV "True Dads" public service announcements in a campaign to encourage men to take an active role in their children's lives.

If the Mets are clearly the best team in the league this year, then the Pirates are just as clearly the worst. After ESPN sportscaster Tom Mees refers to the Pirates as "pitiful," their public relations man, Joe Gallagher, demands equal time. "You can call us lousy, but not pitiful," he insists. He then informs players that they will have to pay $25 apiece for individual copies of the 1986 team photo.

56. Best and Worst

So how about this for the team slogan: "We're not pitiful, just lousy and cheap."

When the team originally known as the Pittsburgh Alleghenys went on an early-season five-game winning streak, outfielder Steve Kemp had said, "It proves if we work together we'll be all right." Despite the presence of their young slugger Barry Bonds and his 16 home runs, the Pirates finish 44 games out of first place, the worst record any team will put up in the decade.

Writers drag up a number of early-season prognostications.

Cubs' manager Jim Frey had predicted, "I think the Chicago Cubs will be the big baseball story of the 1986 season. I really do — if we're healthy, that is." The exceptionally healthy Cubs finish fifth, 37 games out. Frey is fired.

LaRussa had predicted, "We have an explosive lineup. Once we get the key, we'll blow people off the map." The White Sox, last in the American League in hitting and in home runs, hadn't even waited for the end of the season to fire the genius.

Cardinals third baseman Terry Pendleton had predicted, "We want to prove 1985 was no fluke. We have something to prove. And remember, we haven't changed that much from last year." Without many changes, the Cardinals go from world champions to 28½ games out in the National League East.

Coming off a grim 1985 season in which the Braves were dead last in the NL in pitching, tenth in hitting, ninth in fielding, and finished 19 games behind the Dodgers, they brought in Chuck Tanner to manage. He said he was going to alternately hug and kick his players to turn the team's fortunes around. Neither the hugging nor kicking worked as they come in last in the NL West, 23½ games behind Houston.

In September, the Mets and Red Sox play an exhibition charity game in Boston that is billed in the press as a possible preview of the World Series. When the Mets' bus breaks down outside the tunnel leading from the airport to downtown, some of the players hitchhike to their hotel. "When you're 20 games up," Mookie Wilson says, "nothing bothers you."

In some circles at least, anticipation is building up that a Red Sox–Mets World Series might actually happen. Major League Baseball would love to see it, Peter Ueberroth would love to see it, Bart Giamatti would love to see it, so would NBC, many in the press, and naturally the fans of the two teams. It could be sold as the first matchup in 75 years of teams from New York and Boston. It could be sold as a matchup of last year's once-in-a-lifetime sensation, Dwight Gooden, against this year's once-in-a-lifetime sensation, Roger Clemens. It could be sold as the potential end of the Babe Ruth Curse for the Red Sox.

Of course, there is always the danger of a Houston-Anaheim Series played in their shopping mall-like stadiums. NBC and MLB shudder at the thought.

The Mets' 17-game lead late in August is the biggest in the National League since the end of the 1975 season when the Reds were 20 games out front. They had been on a magic number watch since Labor Day. When they do clinch, some fans run amuck and seem to think that, given their season-long superiority, destroying things is their right. Like a swarm of destructive locusts, fans run onto the field with the mob mentality of a jailbreak, tearing up the infield, the outfield and about anything else that can be torn up. Maybe they got the idea for celebratory vandalism from the Detroit fans who torched downtown Detroit as a tribute to their Tigers' winning everything two years earlier. Mayhem took the place of cheers.

"Ballclubs ought to administer IQ tests before selling seats to the characters who feel they have a right, or perhaps an obligation, to go galloping onto the field and capture souvenirs of a championship," writes Hal Bock of the AP. "Maybe a moat would help. Or chicken wire to keep the crazies fenced in, preventing them from doing any significant damage, except to each other. What do you do with a captured clump of grass? Watch it turn brown? What a wonderful souvenir. If you want a Mets cap, you buy one at the souvenir stand. You don't swipe it from a player who is running for his life."

So now if a player turns an ankle on the newly patched sod or a game is lost because of a needless bad hop, the fans can take the credit or the blame.

"We've got a first-place team and last-place fans," says Shea groundskeeper Pete Flynn. "These people don't deserve a winner."

Anticipating a possible Rambo-esque on-field invasion when they clinched, the Mets had 200 security guards at the ready, cut off beer sales early, and made numerous requests that fans stay off the field at the end of the game.

"I never saw 56,000 people come out on the field before," Wally Backman says. "I'll just have to figure out my escape routes."

Following the Joyner knife-throwing incident and a knife thrown earlier in the season at the Dodgers' Franklin Stubbs, these riots at least seem to pose more of a threat to the grass than to the players.

Last year a pregnant woman was shot in the hand at Yankee Stadium while watching a game with her husband and two sons. Now, after the mayhem at Shea, she says, "I'd never walk into another stadium again. I'd be too nervous. All the drinking and marijuana. You never know when someone is going to go berserk. I don't want to go to any kind of stadium ever again. It's just not worth it, especially if you have children."

Fans can be unruly in other ways, too. Last year, fans at Yankee Stadium booed the Canadian national anthem, "O Canada," before a game against Toronto. This season, Jim Rice had his hat stolen by a fan while he was sprawled on the ground following a base-running collision. Rice confronted the thief only to have racial invectives shouted at him. Rice took off after the fan, chasing him into the stands, followed quickly by Boggs, Clemens, Boyd, and McNamara. If nothing else, it said something about the team unity.

March 2011

A 42-year-old Giants fan, Bryan Stow, is critically injured when he is attacked by two Dodgers fans in the Dodger Stadium parking lot after the Dodgers and Giants open the season. Stow, a paramedic and father of two, sustains severe injuries to his skull and brain and is placed into a medically induced coma. Lawyers for Stow say his medical care is expected to cost more than $50 million.

There is considerable speculation that Steinbrenner wants to move the Yankees to New Jersey so events such as this only give him more excuses to do so.

The New Jersey Yankees? Is nothing sacred?

Of course, despite the thinking of some in the I-love-to-hate-New-York crowd, it isn't the only home for the unruly. At Arlington Stadium in Texas, a free baseball night backfires when, armed with their new round missiles, fans take out their frustration on the Rangers after they blow a lead to the Brewers.

But before the Series come the divisional playoffs, with plenty of opportunities to screw up and miss out on the big show. Huge favorites have fallen in these baseball minefields before. Still, the opening matchups look enticing — Scott against Gooden and Clemens against Witt. There are some nice generational battles shaping up, too, between the "old boys' who can trace their debuts back to the '60s — Seaver, Jackson, Sutton, and Ryan with a combined 78 years of Major League experience — and the "kids" who might be playing into the next century — Gooden, Clemens, Strawberry, and Joyner with a combined 10 years.

The New York media, never short on hyperbole, have lionized their Mets as if they were the Yankees of the '50s. They won their division, they were expected to win their division, and they are expected to do so for years to come. After all, they represent the most important city in the most important country in the world.

Houston, despite its population of around 6.5 million, is considered small-town America to many New Yorkers. If the Mets were about to play a team from Chicago or Los Angeles that would be one thing, but Houston? Who knows anything about the Astros? Okay, they have Nolan Ryan, but other than that? They weren't even supposed to win their admittedly weak division. As an important baseball team, they're about as recognizable as the Colt 45s, their original name when they were created as an expansion franchise in 1962. They later changed their name either to reflect their new indoor stadium, the Astrodome, or the ersatz plastic grass on which they played.

"This is one heck of a place just to be in and watch whatever is going on," said Bob Hope on the opening of the Astrodome in 1965. "If they had a maternity ward and a cemetery you'd never have to leave!"

For their first seven years they never finished higher than eighth place in the league.

The Mets versus the Astros? New Yorkers are already booking the train to Boston.

It isn't until September 25 that the Astros clinch the division, but when they do, they do so in grand fashion with Mike Scott throwing a no-hitter.

Scott, who came up through the Mets' system, debuted with them in 1979 but was not particularly effective. Through the 1982 season he had a 14–27 record and was unhappy with what he considered a sloppily run team. When the Mets traded him to the Astros, he felt he had a new opportunity. His results there, though, weren't much better for his first two seasons. Then in 1985, Roger Craig taught him the split-finger fastball and he picked up the scuffed baseball pitch. Presto, he was an 18-game winner!

"That may have been the most dominating performance I've ever seen," said Craig of a Scott no-hitter. "I told one of my coaches in the fourth or fifth inning, 'We're not going to get a hit off of him.' It was unbelievable."

"I'm numb, I'm tired, but this is fantastic," Scott says after the game. "Right now, I hope I don't fall down and pass out."

Roger Craig wants to make sure everyone understands he is the master teacher of the split-finger pitch. "Why did it have to be me who taught him the damn thing?" he adds. "Now he throws it as well as anybody ever has. The really amazing thing is how hard he throws it. I was on the other side when Don Larsen pitched his perfect game, but this was the most overpowering no-hitter I've ever seen."

Scott has been brilliant all season. Only four times in his 36 starts did he allow more than three earned runs and is used to pitching on three days' rest. It isn't out of the question that he could pitch Games 1, 4, and 7.

The Astros catch something of a break when, because television executives make baseball bow to the NFL schedule, the Astros will have the home field advantage that should rightly have gone to the Mets. Not only are they a much better team at home, but there is a feeling that the rubes from Texas can be overwhelmed by the boisterous New York crowds.

Then, too, they have geared their style of play to the indoor Astrodome with its tailor-made pitching mound and plastic surface. When the stadium opened it had real grass with a glass roof. When fielders complained of the glare, they painted the glass white. Surprise, surprise, the grass died. So they went to the Monsanto chemical company for what they then called Chemgrass. The company didn't have enough to cover the entire field but they came up with enough for the infield which was installed in April 1966. Then in July, when the team was on an extended road trip, they covered the outfield. Later, Joe Namath was to make the rug famous when he was asked if he preferred Astroturf to grass, he said, "I don't know. I never smoked Astroturf."

Hal Lanier, their manager, has his players running on the turf at every realistic opportunity and some that aren't. He'll send runners regardless of the score or who's on base. Throw out one runner, and he'll send the next. He knows, too, that Gary Carter only threw out 20 percent of opposing base stealers. Expect a track meet.

Everyone hates a bully except the bully's friends. With the always hateable Yankees unavailable as the team-of-the-month to scorn, the Mets will serve as a reasonable stand-in. "There are 24 other teams who will be Astros fans beginning October 7," says one Philly. "The Mets are the only team in baseball that high fives in batting practice."

The Mets are good, the Mets know they are good, and the Mets let you know they know they are good. They irritate just about everybody but their own fans but there is no denying that their starting pitching is the best in the league and they can come up with more ways to score than just about anybody. In Carter they have a player who seems to thrive under pressure, and even though Strawberry drew boos from the Mets' faithful during a prolonged slump, he has the potential to become the Big Apple's next Mr. October. Or at least so promotes the Mets' brass.

The reigning Mr. October, however, isn't ready to cede the crown. Reggie Jackson and the Angels have played well all season against the Red Sox. In Mike Witt they have a pitcher who in any other year might have been the odds-on favorite for the Cy Young Award. They also have a general manager, Mike Port, who has set this team up well for the postseason. "The Angels in the past have died in the clutch," says one rival manager. "The players never had any motivation. Well, Port has about eight of them worried about being free agents once the season is over, so for the first time, he's got at least one third of the ballclub playing for their careers."

Everyone knows Clemens is the man in Boston. The schedule is set up for him to pitch the first game and then have five days off before he pitches again. During the regular season, when he had this much rest he was 8–0 including the 20-strikeout game. Seaver might be a question mark because of a tender knee, but they've still got Boyd ... assuming he shows up. In Boggs they have one of the great hitters in the game and, assuming there's enough chicken and beer on hand, he should lead a solid offense.

When Clemens carries off both the Cy Young and American League MVP awards for his great season, not everybody is happy about it.

The Cy Young, sure. But the MVP to a pitcher?

Hank Aaron calls it "a joke." "Everyday players cannot win the Cy Young Award and pitchers should not be able to win the MVP award," he says. "The pitchers have their own MVP award and it is the Cy Young. I feel very strongly about that."

National League MVP Mike Schmidt agrees. "The MVP should be reserved for an everyday player, a guy who puts his neck out seven days a week," he says.

Responding to the Aaron comment, Clemens says, "I wish he were still playing. I'd probably crack his head open to show him how valuable I was."

No one is arguing about the Cy Young Award, though. Clemens wins that unanimously, joining Denny McLain and Ron Guidry as the only two to have done so in the AL since the writers began giving the award to the best pitcher in each league. McNamara says, "It would have been the robbery of the century if he hadn't won."

And so Clemens puts his trophies in a case that will need to be greatly expanded over the years.

The last time the Red Sox played in the World Series against a team from New York was in 1916 when they beat the Brooklyn Robins in five games. The Robins, led by their young outfielders, Casey Stengel and the Wheat brothers, Zack and Mack, had been known as the Dodgers earlier, and would revert to that name later despite requests to call the team the Brooklyn Canaries. Four years earlier the Red Sox had been in the Series against John McGraw's Giants led by the great Christy Mathewson. It took the Sox eight games to win the Series because Game 2 was called a tie due to darkness. In that eighth game the Sox's Smokey Joe Wood surrendered a run in the top of the tenth, but Boston rallied for two runs off Mathewson in the bottom of the inning to take the Series.

That was 75 years ago. An omen?

57. The Cowboy and the Goat

The American League playoffs bring together two teams with long histories of searching for a World Series Championship — 25 years for the Angels, 68 for the Red Sox. The Red Sox are looking to "reverse the curse," the Angels to win it all for Mr. Autry.

Mr. Autry is as revered a baseball owner as anyone in the game — maybe more so — and is seldom called Gene. He is, and will remain, Mr. Autry. Everybody loves Mr. Autry, a true American cowboy, a hero.

Now 79 years old, his first job was as a telegrapher for the St. Louis–San Francisco Railway, but he spent a lot of his spare time singing and playing his guitar at local dances. He was known as "Oklahoma's Yodeling Cowboy." His popularity led to a recording contract and a job with a radio station in Chicago where he hosted his own show, the *National Barn Dance*. His first big hit recording was "That Silver-Haired Daddy of Mine." Later came his Christmas hits, "Here Comes Santa Claus," "Frosty the Snowman," and "Rudolph the Red-Nosed Reindeer."

His popularity was immense. Who in America didn't know who "The Singing Cowboy" was? He is the only celebrity to have stars on the Hollywood Walk of Fame in all five of the recognized categories — recording, motion pictures, radio, television, and live theater.

Among his many fans was that great cowboy singer himself, Ringo Starr. "Gene Autry was the most," Starr says. "It may sound like a joke but go and have a look in my bedroom. It's covered with Gene Autry posters. He was my first musical influence."

In 1934 Autry began what became a long career in films making B westerns, always playing under his own name, always riding his horse Champion, always with his sidekick Smiley Burnette, and always singing.

He only played true-blue parts where good always triumphed over evil, and the American way of life was celebrated. His characters were always men of high moral character who stood for everything that was good, decent, and fair. He was a good guy who urged youngsters to be just like Gene and to live their lives according to his Cowboy Code.

1. The Cowboy must never shoot first, hit a smaller man, or take unfair advantage.
2. He must never go back on his word or a trust confided in him.
3. He must always tell the truth.
4. He must be gentle with children, the elderly, and animals.
5. He must not advocate or possess racially or religiously intolerant ideas.
6. He must help people in distress.
7. He must be a good worker.
8. He must keep himself clean in thought, speech, action, and personal habits.
9. He must respect women, parents, and his nation's laws.
10. The Cowboy is a patriot.

It was un–American not to like the singing cowboy, World War II pilot, and ardent baseball fan. (Forget about his progressively more destructive drinking and numerous extramarital liaisons. He kept a tight lid on these things.)

He was widely respected for living a life on-screen and off that adhered to his Cowboy Code, and his love of America's National Game only endeared him to the public that much more.

In 1937, the town of Kenton, Ohio, was on the verge of disaster due to the Great Depression. Its one major industry, the Kenton Hardware Company, was laying off most of its employees. They were desperate; the town was desperate. It was Gene Autry who came riding to the rescue by allowing the struggling company to make a toy cap gun based on his own pistols and bearing his name. The town's fortunes turned around almost overnight. The Gene Autry cap gun became known as the toy that saved a town, and millions of bad guys were shown their just rewards at the barrel end of an "Autry." Today, if you can find one, they can fetch hundreds of dollars.

Douglas B. "Ranger Doug" Green, lead singer of the western music quartet Riders in the Sky, says, "In this era of difficult moral choices, we must ask ourselves ... what would Gene Autry do?"

While millions of kids were devoted Gene Autry fans, Gene Autry was a devoted baseball fan. Why not? It is America's game, pure apple pie and mother. Doesn't it stand for all that is right about this country? It's a meritocracy where you succeed when you deserve to. It promotes hard work and discipline — all the values of the cowboy.

For years there had been talk of moving an existing team to the West Coast. In the '40s it looked as though the St. Louis Browns would be the team to make the move to Los Angeles. Permission was granted and a schedule was drawn up for the team to head west. Then came the bombing of Pearl Harbor and any thought of moving a team to the precarious West Coast was shelved. If the Japanese attack, the West Coast would be the first place hit. In the early '50s the idea of moving the Brown's re-surfaced, but in the end the team moved to Baltimore and became the Orioles. The Washington Senators toyed with moving to Los Angeles and the Philadelphia Athletics' move to Kansas City was seen as a temporary stop on their eventual way west.

The Dodgers and Giants eventually made the first moves, but in 1960 when the National League decided to expand by adding the New York Mets, the American League announced it would place an expansion team of its own in Los Angeles to begin play in 1961.

First the master promoter Bill Veeck had the inside track to operate the franchise, and then the game's other master promoter, Charles O. Finley, came into the picture. The Dodgers, however, shuddered at the thought of competing with either and moved to block the expansion. Gene Autry to the rescue. He paid the Dodgers $300,000 for the exclusive rights to the name "Angels" and purchased the new franchise.

In the early years they shared Dodger Stadium with the Dodgers, but they insisted in calling it Chavez Ravine when they played there. In 1966 they moved a few miles down the freeway to their new stadium, "The Big A" in Anaheim. The name came from the 230-foot-high A-shaped scoreboard. A few years later, the scoreboard came crashing down in an earthquake.

Welcome to the shaky world of Southern California.

Led by big Steve Bilko and little Albie Pearson, at 5' 5", the team completed its first season with the highest winning percentage of any first-year expansion team ever. During the '70s they put decent teams on the field headlined by Nolan Ryan and Rod Carew and finally reached the playoffs in 1979, which they lost to the Orioles. They clinched their second AL West championship in 1982, the season in which Reggie Jackson joined Baylor and Carew to power the team, but lost that battle with the Brewers.

Now they're hoping the third time is the charm and that the team led by Gene Mauch, "The Greatest Manager Who Never Won" in his first 25 seasons of managing, can take them all the way.

"You have to bear in mind that Mr. Autry's favorite horse was named Champion. He ain't ever had one called Runner Up," says Mauch.

Game 1 sees Roger Clemens, the American League's best pitcher, up against Mike Witt, the American League's almost-best pitcher. Six days earlier, Clemens had been hit on the elbow with a line drive and there was concern over the elbow and his inactivity since. Witt, the 6' 7" curveballer, dominates and the Angels win the game, 8–1.

The what's-with-McNamara crowd is at it again.

What idiot would leave Clemens in for 148 pitches when they were getting trounced?

Although he shut down Reggie Jackson, Clemens doesn't look like Clemens.

"I felt reasonably strong, and the cold definitely didn't bother me. Neither did the elbow," says Clemens. "I felt no weakness at all until after the sixth inning. I just got hit pretty well and that's the way it goes. We'll know tomorrow just how the elbow really is."

In Game 2, Bruce Hurst throws what he calls a "nifty 11-hitter." It is a poorly played game won by the Red Sox, 9–2. "The last time I saw a game like this," says Don Sutton, "our coach wouldn't take us to Tastee-Freeze for a milkshake afterward."

Oil Can Boyd, or as Mauch calls him, "dipstick," gesticulates wildly from the mound and stares down the Angels' hitters in Game 3. Boyd, who had to be restrained by teammates from going after the home plate umpire after a call at the plate, also serves up a couple of hanging sliders for home runs as the Angels win, 5–3. "Mr. October," Reggie Jackson, is the hero with his run-scoring single.

Now add Al Nipper to the cadre of the complainers. When told that Clemens would come back and pitch the fourth game on short rest, he storms out of the clubhouse refusing to talk to reporters.

Never one to pass when the little red camera light comes on, Reggie steps into the dead-air void. "We're just up 2-1, it's 'advantage Angels,'" he says. "But in the next game they have their best pitcher going, the best pitcher in baseball this year, and I think they're really going to have their backs to the wall if they don't win."

Game 4 looks like it's going to be Clemens' game. He's got a three-run lead with but three more outs to get. Coming off the high-pitch count in his first game, McNamara asks him how he's feeling before going out to wrap it up. "I'm fine," says Clemens.

He's not. He gives up a homer and two singles before McNamara takes him out in favor of their top reliever, Calvin Schiraldi.

Mac's done it again, scream his critics. Doesn't have a clue about when to pull a pitcher.

Schiraldi promptly surrenders one run, and then after the bases are loaded, he blows two fastballs past Brian Downing, before trying a backdoor slider that plunks Downing, sending the tying run in.

"It was," Schiraldi would say, "the stupidest pitch of my life. I tried to throw the perfect pitch and choked it."

Two innings later in the 11th he gives up the winning run.

After the game the distraught reliever sits in the dugout for a long time, his face buried in a towel. Judge Don deploys teammates to shield him from the press.

57. The Cowboy and the Goat

Oil Can sits sobbing uncontrollably in front of his locker. The team doctor comes over to console him and then, a few moments later, leads him safely away from the media.

Naturally the choke issue comes up.

Why not? They haven't won a World Series since 1918. Or maybe it's the old Curse of the Bambino raising its ugly head again.

"I toss that away as trash," says Joe Sambito. "Anybody who drags that out didn't put much thought into the question. When someone says something about choking and the past haunting us, I take it personally."

Say what you want, Joe. Some of the fans know better.

It's the goddamned Curse again. Anybody don't see that is just plain nuts.

In the Sox locker room, Don Baylor is sulking because he didn't get a chance to hit. "I'm a fucking cheerleader," he says.

The Red Sox have their backs to the wall, down three games to one with another game to play in Anaheim. The team that specializes in breaking hearts seems to be about to do it again. McNamara says he avoided the Knute Rockne speeches before Game 5. "I just said a few words that I thought were appropriate to a few individuals."

The Angels are concerned that their hot-hitting first baseman Wally Joyner is hospitalized for a bacterial infection in his right leg and will miss the game.

Going into the sixth inning, it's the Red Sox up, 2–1. Dave Henderson is in center for the Red Sox, having replaced Tony Armas for defensive purposes. With two outs, he messes up a routine fly ball when he lets it drop for a double. Then the Angels' Bobby Grich lifts a towering fly ball to deep left center. Henderson goes back to the track, leaps, and appears to make the catch, but the ball deflects off his glove and over the wall for a two-run homer, giving the Angels a 3–2 lead. Henderson throws his arms up in despair and Bruce Hurst kneels on the mound with his head down as Grich jubilantly circles the bases. "I thought I had it all the way," says Henderson.

He's the defensive replacement? Way to go, McNamara.

The Red Sox get out of the inning without any more damage when Reggie Jackson strikes out swinging.

The Angels, though, are able to add two more runs in the seventh and stretch their lead to 5–2. Baylor tells his teammates, "We may have only nine outs left in this season, so let's make them quality at-bats and, if we go out, go out with our heads high."

Some of the Red Sox batters are having trouble concentrating because of a fluttering banner in the center field bleachers and ask for it to be removed. The banner reads "ANOTHER BOSTON CHOKE."

Then with one out in the ninth, Baylor brings the Red Sox to within one by belting a two-run homer. After a pop out and a hit batsman, Mauch hands the ball to his stopper — Donnie Moore.

Moore has finished 99 games in his two years with the Angels and has racked up 52 saves. He's been an All-Star and a legitimate Cy Young Award candidate. He walks very few batters and his sharp breaking split-finger pitch keeps balls in the park. No question he is the right choice — unfortunately.

Moore will face Dave Henderson, who looks as if he might be the goat of the game for his fielding miscues.

With the count 2–2, Henderson asks for time and steps out of the box.

"We're ballplayers. We fail most of the time," Henderson will later say. "I had to step out of the batter's box and gather my thoughts."

Moore is used to the pressure. Stoppers have to be, and he's a good one.

"We were down to the last pitch, the last out," Baylor said after the game. "The emotion was unbelievable."

Moore stares down at Bob Boone, his catcher, looking for the sign. Is there any doubt? His best pitch is the split-fingered fastball. He's not going to go with anything else, is he? No. Moore knows it, Boone knows it, many of the fans in Anaheim Stadium know it, and Henderson knows it.

Henderson wiggles his bat a few times and waits. Moore winds up and delivers the expected pitch. Henderson is ready for it and sends it on a line over the left-center-field wall.

The once-raucous Big A goes eerily quiet as if all the air has been sucked out of it. Baseball is like that. A team's fortunes can change in a matter of a few scant seconds. Victory or defeat can hang in the air and drop almost without warning.

To most of the Angels fans, this seems as if it is the most unlikely of occurrences. The ever-reliable Donnie Moore has let them down at the most important moment. In baseball parlance, he has gone from hero-in-the-making to goat on one pitch.

As Neil Steinberg wrote in *Forbes Magazine*, "More than any other sport, baseball lends itself to the phenomenon of The Goat, a fallen star who lives in a parallel purgatory, watching his lifetime of achievement outweighed by the stigma of a single moment of bad performance and bad luck, a unique aspect of a game with a long memory, a game whose defining poem is about the lack of joy in Mudville after the mighty Casey has struck out."

"If you kill someone, they sentence you to life," says Ralph Branca, who gave up the shot "heard 'round the world" by Thomson. "You serve 20 years, and you get paroled. I've never been paroled."

Moore is despondent, but despite the emotion-draining drama of Henderson's home run, it doesn't win the game for Boston. The Angels battle back, tie the game in the bottom of the ninth, and don't finally lose until the 11th.

Baylor and Grich have been friends since they were both drafted in the 1967 amateur draft by the Orioles. "What do you think?" Grich asks Baylor at the top of the 11th. "Greatest game I've ever played in," Baylor replies. Grich slaps Baylor's hand. "Me, too, partner."

"I'm tired," says McNamara. "The season was long and tough and we were on the brink of elimination today. Believe me, I'll sleep on the plane tonight."

After exchanging 11-inning victories in less than 24 hours, the Angels move on to Boston and feebly drop their last two chances, 10–4 and 8–1. The Angels' World Series dream is over.

July 1989

Ever since "the Pitch," Donnie Moore was booed every time he came out of the Angels' dugout. Two years later he was out of baseball, his money had run out, his house was for sale, and his marriage apparently on the rocks. Now he is dead by his own hand.

According to police, he first shot and seriously wounded his wife and then shot himself.

Moore's 17-year-old daughter Demetria and her two brothers, aged 7 and 10, were unhurt. She says:

> We came back and we found them arguing. The next thing I know, he had a gun and he shot. I heard several shots and I saw my mom shot. Then, we all ran to the car. We were just trying to hurry up and go to the hospital. And, I guess, while we left ... while we were gone, my two brothers were still at the house with my father. And only one brother witnessed my Dad actually committing suicide. But I just wish we (had been) there for him. If he would've talked to us none of this would have ever happened.

Friends and former teammates react with equal measures of surprise, grief, and anger.

Dave Pinter, his agent: "He blamed himself for the Angels not going to the World Series. He constantly talked about the Henderson home run. It was that important to him that the Angels make it to the World Series. He couldn't get over it. I tried to get him to go to a psychiatrist, but he said, 'Don't need it. I'll get over it.' Even when he was told that one pitch doesn't make a season, he couldn't get over it. That home run killed him."

Former teammate Brian Downing: "He wasn't treated fairly. He was treated like [expletive]. Nobody remembered the great things he did. All they remembered was that one pitch. And it ruined his life. Despite the way he acted, that he didn't care ... he was a very sensitive guy. No one cared about him after 1986. He was buried. And that's bull. No one wants to give him credit that he got us to the playoffs. Well, that one home run is not the reason we lost. He always said to me, '[The boos] don't bother me,' but he put up a big facade. He was a tough guy, but I can't believe it didn't bother him."

Boston pitcher Bob Stanley: "Life is more important than that stuff. You think about it, the wild pitch that helped lose Game 6 of the '86 World Series to *the Mets, but not enough to kill myself. I didn't kill myself and I hear about that pitch all the time. It seems that people remember the last thing that happens. That's just the way it is in this game. You have to accept that."*

Boston outfielder Dave Henderson: "No, I'm not upset. I don't know. I guess there's a connection. I heard he had a lot of family problems and everything. I'll tell you what — baseball can't be that serious that you'd take your life. There's got to be a lot of other stuff. I saw that the next year. He got booed before he hit the mound. That is nothing new in baseball. I learned a long time ago, when I saw Yaz booed in Boston, we're all going to get booed in baseball. I was booed my first five years in baseball. That's why the connection can't be that strong. Maybe a minute part. But there had to be other things."

Tonya Martin, Moore's wife, says he would often come home after pitching at Anaheim Stadium and burst into tears.

At least 80 active or retired Major League ballplayers have been known to have committed suicide. The first on record was Frank Ringo, who in 1889 killed himself by ingesting morphine. Whether or not his .192 lifetime batting average had anything to do with it is unclear.

On a lighter note, Dan Quisenberry, acknowledging the stress the game can put on players, says, "Once I tried to drown myself with a shower nozzle after I gave up a homer in the ninth. I found out you can't."

Moore will come to be regarded as the quintessential example of the one-blunder theory. This, however, misses the point that Moore suffered from bouts of severe depression and was battling substance abuse. He also had a very complicated and occasionally abusive relationship with his wife.

Without a doubt giving up the home run to Henderson stung him deeply, but it did not cause him to take his life.

58. Just What Everyone Wanted

"You've got a team here that's so invisible," writes columnist Robert Strauss about the Astros, "Casper the Friendly Ghost is asking for a try out; so disrespected, Rodney Dangerfield pushes them out of the way; so anonymous, their mothers don't even send birthday cards. Let's face it, with the exception of Nolan Ryan, these guys would be better noticed if they were playing in Reykjavik."

So it's the inconspicuous Astros against the anything-but Mets.

They head into the playoffs boasting the two top pitching staffs in the National League. The opening game will feature a matchup between the 1985 Cy Young Award winner Dwight Gooden and Mike Scott, who threw a no-hitter to clinch the division title for the Astros. There doesn't figure to be much of a drop off in the second game either, which will feature Nolan Ryan and Bob Ojeda. In the hitting department, the Mets would seem to have the edge with Dykstra, Backman, and Hernandez at the top of the order and Strawberry and Carter supplying the power.

The Mets have been the best team in the league all season, but in addition to their pitching, the Astros have one thing going for them — they play their games indoors on a plastic rug under a plastic roof. The very thought of an indoors World Series makes some people shudder.

That ain't baseball. It's ... it's ... something else.

"It's a very tough park to play in," says Astros utilityman Davey Lopes:

> Anybody who comes here is thankful it's only for two or three days. There are seams, boards, platforms, you name it. It's almost like there are potholes out there. A New York cab driver would feel at home. People used to say, "How can you go wrong on an artificial surface? There are no bad hops. How can you mess up?" Those people ought to take a look at this surface. There are actually high and low spots.

It's a dreary, gray, plastic place even with the television klieg lights turned on full bore.

"People say down here, 'But if we didn't have the Dome, it would be too hot to play here in the middle of the summer. We couldn't have a team.'"

Yeah, and what's wrong with that?

If God meant for baseball to be played indoors, he would have put roofs over every empty lot in New York City.

In the first game, the Astros, who have learned to adjust to the vagaries of rug baseball, make a number of superb defensive plays behind the overpowering Scott, who strikes out 14 to the deafening, almost frighteningly loud, roar of the Astro fans. They have learned well the wall-of-sound routine that bounces off the hard roof.

The Mets, true to their reputation, grouse, bark at the umpire, argue, and whine. They also lose a brilliantly played game, 1–0. It is a dramatic, emotion-packed, close game that some will call one of the best postseason games in memory.

Gary Carter, true to his reputation, says there's no doubt Scott is throwing a scuffed ball — the pitch that floats away from the batter as if it had wings.

"That ball did something that I've never seen a baseball do," says Carter. "There's movement on that ball that I've never seen. There wasn't any rotation on it at all."

Several times he asks the home plate umpire, Doug Harvey, to examine the ball.

Harvey obliges but opines that the evidence is inconclusive. It could be the Astroturf that's marking up the ball.

"I wasn't afraid or worried," Scott says in yet another of his non-denial denials. "Sometimes the ball comes out of the bag with marks on it. Sometimes it gets scuffed when it's hit or when it goes in the dirt."

He doesn't mind when batters think that he might be throwing a dirty pitch. "Might" is a great ally to a pitcher.

At one point Keith Hernandez strikes out on a fastball right down the middle. Suspicion of a scuffed pitch can have that result.

In the second game, the Ryan Express holds the Mets hitless for the first 3 and ⅓ innings until Backman breaks through for the first hit and paves the way for a 5–1 victory. As so often happens when Dykstra and Backman get on base, the Mets win. Each had two hits, scoring three runs between them.

"You've got to get to Ryan early before he gets his rhythm going," Strawberry says. "His fastball was exploding at the start of the game. But later on, he didn't have quite as much on it."

When Ryan threw a knockdown pitch to Backman, it seemed to ignite not only Backman, but the whole team. After the pitch, he got up, brushed himself off, beamed a long hard stare at Ryan, and then proceeded to lash a single that triggered a three-run outburst.

"I think Nolan might have gotten a little upset," Carter says. "I think because Lenny is such a little guy. It was a real key to the win." Davey Johnson says the knockdown brought their aggression back. "I sensed some emotion in our dugout," he says. "That inspired us to go out and score more runs."

"We had the killer instinct tonight," Backman says. "We weren't going to wait around to see things happen. We were going to make things happen. There was no way we were coming out of here down 2–0. It doesn't matter who was out there."

The characteristics of the two teams is clear to all — the boisterous Mets, the low-key Astros. Few if any prognosticators think the meek will inherit the championship.

Bob Knepper will pitch for the Astros when the teams get to New York, but he hardly sounds confident. "Shea Stadium is one of the hardest places to play in because of the fans," Knepper says.

He gives up four runs in seven innings. Not a bad outing, but not good enough to win.

The cocky Dykstra is known for his barbed-wire toughness, not his power hitting prowess, but in one of the most dramatic climaxes in playoff history Dykstra, who connected for only eight homers all season, comes up with a two-run, one-out homer to give the Mets a 6–5 win.

"The last time I hit a home run in the bottom of the ninth to win a game was in Stratomatic baseball against my brother a couple of years ago. That's a game where you roll dice," says Dykstra. "I rolled some good numbers. Don't get used to this. You're not going to see too many like that from me."

"Lenny Dykstra? Who would have believed it?" Hernandez says.

The Mets lose the next game, 3–1, and they're peeved. In order to squeeze every dollar from their fans, the Mets have added extra seats down the left-field line. In a crucial point in the game, the Astros hit a little foul pop up down the line. It should be a routine play, but the new protruding boxes confuse the Mets' infielders and the ball bounces into the seats.

Third baseman Knight blames shortstop Santana for calling him off. "It was my ball," he says.

Santana says it was his ball all the way, but it was uncatchable.

"It was a much easier play for me," says Knight.

"I never heard him call for it," says Santana.

"When a guy calls for the ball, you should let him have it," says Knight. "I knew I could have made it."

The bickering Mets are at it again. Their fans think it's a good sign.

"The fact that they sold a lot of tickets ended up helping me out," says Alan Ashby, who takes advantage of his new life to drive the next pitch over the wall for a two-run homer.

Scott's line so far: He has not surrendered an extra-base hit in 18 innings. His 16 shutout innings is a record. So are his 19 strikeouts.

He doesn't hurt himself with his fielding either. With the Mets down 3–1, Dykstra comes to the plate in the ninth. The Mets' fans come to their collective feet and let loose with enough noise that it might have been heard over at Yankee Stadium. Dykstra singles sharply to center. If anything the noise increases as Backman comes up. He drops a drag bunt that Scott dives for. He scrambles to his feet, throws to first and nabs Backman by a step. He then gets Hernandez and Carter. Game over.

With rain giving the players an unexpected day off before the next game, the Mets, beaten now twice by Scott, up the ante on the whine tour.

How could the best hitting team in baseball be so thoroughly throttled by Scott? He's cheating, of course, and Backman's got a bucket of balls to prove it. "Every one of them was scuffed," he says. "Every single one of them. You know there are people in this game who cheat. I never knew until late in the game, but when you have 15 to 20 balls that have been scuffed you know it's not done by fouling them off."

But if he is cheating and everybody says they know it, how is he possibly getting away with it?

Davey Johnson says he thinks he knows how—sandpaper. "It is in his palm," he explains. "He doesn't rotate the ball, he just makes a grinding motion. It's blatant to me."

Johnson certainly isn't above deflecting attention away from the Mets' poor performances. "Look at these balls," he says fondling one in his hand for all the world to see. "They're all scuffed, and all scuffed in just about the same place, and they all came out of last night's game after foul balls and whatever. Isn't that unusual? That they've all got these marks here in just about the same place? I don't think Scott needs to do this. He could make a cueball dance. But something's going on out there and I don't like it."

The Astros' manager, Hal Lanier, says maybe the Mets are collecting all those balls because they want to get his autograph on them.

What do you mean scuffed? says Scott. "There was nothing wrong with them when I threw them."

"Yes, we can inspect the glove, but we're not going to go out there and take a man's shirt off," says umpire Doug Harvey.

Maybe, but let's get down to the nitty gritty. Do you think Scott is cheating?

"I had him at least five times during the season, so the first game of the LCS was the sixth time this year," says Harvey. "When Carter asked me to check the ball, I did. It was as clean as this desk. The man had just exploded two tremendous pitches. The man is one hell of a pitcher."

Maybe he's cheating. Maybe he's not. But the Mets think he is. Maybe the Mets don't really think he is but they need excuses and maybe a psychological ploy.

"Hey," Backman says. "God couldn't have gone out there and pitched better baseball the last month."

Is he suggesting that because God is governed by a higher moral code than baseball players, He couldn't have stooped to sandpapering a baseball?

"We're ticked and we're not going to take this lying down," Backman says. "I don't care if he scuffs 400 balls. I don't care if they're scuffed before the game. I don't think any pitcher can beat us three times in a row."

If the Mets are looking for excuses, they don't have to look much further than the Kid. Carter, who took a lot of heat when he played for Montreal because they seemed to live in a perpetual second place, isn't hitting. This was to be his chance to silence his many critics.

"He's pressing, there's no doubt about it," says Ray Knight. "Every time he makes an out in a pressure situation, it wears on him. He came so close for so long in Montreal and had to read all that negative press."

Strawberry has struck out 8 times in 14 at-bats but no one seems to be on his case. Carter, though, is not well liked and is an easier target.

"I think Kid is trying to make this his forum," says Darling. "Especially the way he always did to get here. The Kid likes to shine. Heck, we all like to shine."

January 2003
Carter hears that he has been elected to the Hall of Fame.

"I got overly excited and screamed," he says. "Now we can do a little celebrating. It is a grueling position (catching). My knees will tell you that. I've had nine knee surgeries. I've had a couple of broken thumbs, one on each hand. I can look back at it and say it's worth it to be enshrined in Cooperstown. I don't have any pain in my knees right now."

He announces he's lending his name and support to the American Life League, an anti-abortion organization opposed to legislation that contains exceptions for rape, incest, life of the mother, or fetal deformity.

Carter looks for and gets a chance for a measure of redemption in the next game. Going into the ninth inning, it's been all Gooden and Ryan. Ryan in particular has been nearly unhittable, giving up only two hits, striking out 12, and walking one. The only damage is a solo home run by Strawberry in the fifth. Like Ryan, Gooden has surrendered only one run, but unlike Ryan, he will pitch into the tenth.

"I let everything I had go in the ninth because I had never pitched 10 innings before," Gooden says after the game. "Then, when I came back to the dugout after the ninth, nobody said anything. It was like getting ready for the game all over again."

The Mets don't get their third hit until the 12th when Backman singles. Charlie Kerfeld, now pitching for the Astros, then throws wildly on a pickoff attempt and Backman scoots to second. When Hernandez is purposely walked, putting runners on first and second, Carter comes to the plate. The count goes to 3–2 and Carter fouls off two pitches before delivering a run-scoring single up the middle. The Kid has come through. The Mets are within one game of the World Series.

"I kept thinking positive," Carter says. "I wanted to have a positive frame of mind — no negative thoughts."

"If anybody deserves it, Gary did," Gooden says. "The other day when Gary hit one back to the mound, Kerfeld showed him the ball. That can come back to haunt you."

The Mets' complaining of showboating strikes some as ironic.

No one, least of all the Mets, expects the Astros to go quietly into that good night ... and they don't.

With the Mets now up three games to two, they send Ojeda out to face Knepper in what will turn out to be the longest game in postseason history.

Ojeda has been solid all year. He has neither the overpowering stuff of Gooden nor the savvy of Darling. All he did was lead the team in wins with 18 and post the lowest ERA among the starters. He has great control, good off-speed stuff, and what Carter calls "dead fish."

Explain, please, Gary.

"It's an off-speed pitch, like a palm ball," Carter says. "The bottom drops out of it. It's one of the deceptive pitches like Mike Scott's, but he doesn't throw it as hard. It looks so good when it's coming in, but it keeps going down and down and down."

The Mets are hoping Ojeda can softball the Astros to death.

September 1988

A year after a remarkable recovery from elbow surgery, Ojeda nearly severs the upper one-third of his left middle finger in an accident involving a pair of electric hedge clippers. All that keeps the finger attached is a small flap of skin

March 1993

During a spring training outing, Ojeda is sitting in a boat on little Lake Nellie. He is slouched just low enough that when, in the dim light of early evening and with a drunk Tim Crews driving, the boat slams into a dock. Ojeda comes away with only a badly cut scalp. His Indians teammates Steve Olin and Tim Crews are killed.

Deep depression, counseling at a hospital, and thoughts of suicide follow. "My whole world was crushed and everything changed," he later says. "One of the things I didn't want to do was to lose 'me' in all of this. I am unfortunately stronger — no one wants to get stronger that way. But the important thing is to go forward... I kept me around. Me has always been a competitor."

58. Just What Everyone Wanted

The Astros take a 3–0 first inning lead off Ojeda.

In the second, third, and fourth innings, both pitchers are in complete control and neither team threatens to score. Then in the Astros' half of the fifth, Billy Doran gets on via a force out and steals second. With Doran edging off second, Billy Hatcher singles. But Doran is thrown out at third and it looks as if the momentum may have changed.

But for the next three innings the Mets can only manage one single, and heading to the 9th, it looks as if the Astros have the game in hand. Knepper is completely dominating.

Then with their backs to the wall, Nails triples, Mookie singles, Mex doubles, and Straw and the Kid walk. With two out and three runs in, Backman walks to load the bases and it looks as if the Mets may yet pull this out. But Danny Heep strikes out swinging and the Astros escape without more damage. Game tied at three with the Astros coming to bat in the bottom of the 9th.

The Astros go out in order and the game heads to extra innings.

For the next four tense innings the Mets potent offense goes hitless and the Astros can manage only one single

Then in the 14th, Carter snaps the long drought with a single, Strawberry works a walk, Backman singles, and the Mets break through with a run. With two outs, Dykstra is intentionally walked to load the bases, and with Wilson at the plate the Mets could break the game open.

But Wilson strikes out swinging. Still with a one-run lead and the Astros' dormant offense, it looks as if the game will soon be over.

Not so, thanks to a Billy Hatcher home run, the Astros come back to tie the game in the bottom of the inning and maybe the Mets have run out of miracles.

In the 15th Carter singles but, with the always dangerous Strawberry at the plate, he is thrown out trying to steal second.

Strawberry opens the 16th inning with a pop fly double. Before the inning is over, Backman walks, Dykstra singles, and the Mets come up with 3 runs. Seems the Mets have found another miracle after all.

But, lo, in the bottom of the inning a walk and three singles gets the Astros two runs. With two outs they have a runner at second and their best hitter at the plate. Kevin Bass hit .311 during the season with 20 home runs and no one from either team has more hits in the playoffs. It looks as if the Astros may pull this out, but Jesse Orosco gets him on a swinging strikeout.

What a game. Mets 7, Astros, 6.

"If we don't win the World Series, this is all for nothing," Carter shouts. "To come this far and not get to the World Series would have been very sad."

Naturally the Mets' fans are ecstatic, but around most of the league there is mostly disappointment. Arrogance may be a kingdom without a crown, but the Mets are arrogant and they now have their sights set on the crown.

"If being confident in our team is arrogant, then call us arrogant, I don't care," Johnson says.

The Mets are the best team in the league. Anyone not sure of that only need ask them.

"Of course we've dominated the National League this year and there's no one who can say we didn't," Dykstra says.

It may have been the prayers. "I'm not ashamed to say this, but I said a little prayer when two were out," says Knight. "I was just praying everything would work out," adds Carter.

It was clearly a pins-and-needles game that had enough drama in it to engage even the most diffident.

The two league playoffs have produced tension-filled, nail-biting, emotion-draining games—exactly what Major League Baseball, the sponsors, the networks, and the fans wanted.

59. Disaster Wrapped in Catastrophe

Sport is never duller than when it is purely logical. This is a World Series in which to expect the unexpected and all the more fascinating for it.

Given the protracted drama of the playoffs, the first five games of World Series are relatively pedestrian. Darling pitches very well for the Mets but they end up splitting his two starts. Gooden pitches poorly and they lose both of his. Oil Can is even worse in his defeat.

"Sometimes in a seven-game series, the best team doesn't win," Ray Knight says. "Sometimes, drive and determination can overcome talent."

It ain't drive and determination, it's lousy playing. It's the errors and misplays like the one between Dykstra and Strawberry. And how about that wimpy throw from Dykstra? When you can't throw out Buckner who can you throw out?

In the third inning of the fifth game Buckner was on second, nursing a sore right Achilles tendon and limping on two bad ankles. The Red Sox had to figure the only way they could get him home would be in a wheelchair. But when Evans singles to center, third base coach Rene Lachmann sends the gimpy one home.

"I got to third base in good shape," says Buckner, "but the last 90 feet I couldn't turn."

When he finally made it to the plate he went in head first. "It was not a slide," he says. "I died at home."

Buckner as hero? He's paid his proverbial dues. It's about time.

By the time the fifth game ends, the bright No.1 lights up on the Prudential Center skyscraper towering over Fenway Park showing the number of victories the Red Sox need to wrap up the World Series.

But then comes Game 6 and it is anything but pedestrian. With Boston up three games to two, they send out Clemens to face Ojeda.

It's a sloppily played contest with more errors, wild pitches, and hit batsmen than earned runs. At the end of nine innings the game is tied, 3–3.

In the top of the tenth, the Red Sox get two runs, thanks primarily to another Henderson home run and a Boggs double.

In the bottom of the inning they quickly get two outs. One more and they're world champs.

The Shea Stadium faithful are stunned. After such a brilliant Mets season, it has come down to this.

How can the best team in baseball not win the Series?

Where did it go wrong?

It's a disaster wrapped in a catastrophe, an unmitigated calamity. A curtain of despair envelopes the stadium.

So now with the Red Sox on the brink and the Mets' chances seemingly nil, Kevin Mitchell abandons the dugout and goes to the locker room, where he is changing out of his uniform and about to make plane reservation for a flight back to San Diego, when out on the field, Gary Carter singles and the call goes out for Mitchell to pinch-hit. Hurriedly he re-buttons his uniform, not taking time to grab his cup, and scurries back through the dugout and onto the field.

Later he says he never wore a cup anyway, because "I couldn't find one big enough for my junk."

Mitchell lines a single to center field, sending Carter to second. When the next batter, Knight, follows with another line-drive single, Carter scores and Mitchell makes it to third.

Boston is still up by a run.

One out, one crummy out is all the Red Sox fans are asking for.

McNamara brings in Bob Stanley to replace Calvin Schiraldi and immediately third base coach Bud Harrelson motions Kevin Mitchell to come toward him. "Be alert! This guy's got a sinker," he tells the runner. Mitchell, never the most alert player in the best of situations, listens. Harrelson's advice was right on the mark. With Mookie Wilson batting, Stanley throws a sinker that should have been caught by the catcher and it gets away from him.

"I couldn't believe it when I saw that ball get away," Mitchell says later. "I just ran for my life."

Mitchell scores and Knight scoots to third.

In his autobiography, *Heat,* Gooden says Mitchell was "a very wild and sometimes very dangerous guy. I liked Mitch but I knew better than to ever fuck with him. I'd heard stories about his background in San Diego, some of which included rumors he'd hurt some people in gang-related violence."

Gooden goes on to relate a story about a time he and Meade Chassky, a card show promoter, dropped in unannounced to visit with Mitchell. When they arrived, they found a very drunk and angry Mitchell wielding a 12-inch knife and shouting at his girlfriend, "I told you not to fuck with me, but you don't want to fuckin' listen, do you?"

As Gooden relates the story, Mitchell for some reason thought the cops were following Gooden and Chassky and tells them to barricade the doors.

"You think I'm kidding? Do what I tell you," Mitchell shouts.

Not sure of the situation, and with Mitchell brandishing the knife, the three men barricade the doors with furniture, pull the blinds down, and then Mitchell rips the phone cord out of the wall.

When Gooden tries to get him to calm down, Mitchell shouts, "You calling me a liar, motherfucker?"

Then when his girlfriend tries to intervene, Mitchell grabs the girl's cat and quickly cuts its head off.

"I was horrified by the sight," Gooden writes. "Mitch was still holding the cat's head in one hand, while the body dropped to the floor, blood pouring out from where the head once was, limbs still twitching."

When confronted with the story, Mitchell denied it, saying, "Hell, I love animals."

Vowing to get even with Gooden, he says the pitcher was sucking up lines of cocaine, not him. "I'm a decent guy."

If the story is not true, why would Gooden concoct such a libelous story and then put it in his book? To deflect attention from his substance abuse problems?

Whether true or not, there is no question about Mitchell's wild ways. Questions always seem to swirl around him.

He has the talent, but does he have the will?

The guy's completely unpredictable — scary.

He always seems to be distracted by ... something.

At best his attitude is indifferent.

He could have been good, really good, but not with that attitude or his penchant for putting on weight.

Despite, or maybe because of, the attitude issue, he came in for more than his share of bizarre injuries, including, but not limited to, pulling a muscle while vomiting and breaking a tooth on a donut left so long in the microwave that it had hardened into a rock-like mass.

2000

Mitchell, who has already been arrested once for assaulting his father, is managing the Sonoma County Crushers, whose mascot is the Abominable Snowman, when he is suspended for punching the opposing team's owner.

Although he will never be ranked as one of the game's best defensive outfielders, Mitchell will make a remarkable bare-handed catch in St. Louis on a ball hit by Ozzie Smith that will go down as one of the greatest defensive plays ever.

Now as he trudges across the plate with the tying run, the Mets fans are in a frenzy.

We're back in the game. Is it possible?

Dare we think about a miracle?

Back in the locker room that Mitchell had unexpectedly left only minutes earlier, Hernandez, having made the second out of the inning, is sitting in Davey Johnson's director's chair sipping a beer and preparing to watch a Red Sox World Series clinching celebration.

"When we started to get hits, I sat up," he says. "When we scored the tying run, I jumped up and grabbed my glove. But then I thought, 'I'm not leaving. There are a lot of hits in this chair, so I sat back down."

Mookie Wilson is the batter, Billy Buckner is the first baseman, and what comes next is about to become part of the ever-expanding mythology of the game.

60. Symbol of Failure

When people say "the Buckner game," no further explanation is necessary. Although Billy Buck played in the Major Leagues for all or parts of 22 years, came to bat over 10,000 times accumulating 2,735 hits, and was credited with committing 146 errors, there is but one statistic most fans remember: 1, the number of balls that rolled through his legs and cost the Red Sox their first World Series win since the day that Corporal York almost single-handedly killed 25 German soldiers and captured 132 during the First World War, a Series that would have broken once and for all the Curse of the Bambino but instead proved its potency, a Series that would have brought honor and respect to the Crimson Hose, the Olde Towne Team, a Series that would have honored its greats— Cy Young, Tris Speaker, Lefty Grove, Joe Cronin, Jimmy Foxx, Babe Ruth, Ted Williams, and Yaz — a Series that would have ... would have...

But no, if not for Mookie's ground ball through the legs of Billy Buck, all this and more would have been theirs.

"Here I just experienced the best year of my life with a team, and I feel rotten," says Buckner. "This whole city hates me. Is this what I'm going to be remembered for? Is this what I've killed myself for all these years? Is a whole season ruined because of a bad hop?"

Line up the jokes.

"More than two and a half million people honored the world champions yesterday in New York," says the announcer on the radio, "and the parade finished with the Mets' team bus going through Bill Buckner's legs."

Boston's Zakim Bunker Hill Bridge is now called "The Bill Buckner Bridge" because cars pass easily through the bridge's Y-shaped legs.

After Matt Damon loses everything on one hand of poker in *Rounders*, the avid Sox fan sighs, "I feel like Buckner walking back into Shea."

Did you hear the sad news? Bill Buckner tried to kill himself the other day by jumping in front of a bus. Luckily it went right through his legs.

In the movie *The Comebacks*, the Boston manager is working on a crossword puzzle in the dugout while the game is in progress. He calls out to Buckner playing first, "Buckner, what's a six letter word for tropical fruit? I'm thinking it might be banana."

Buckner looks over at him. "This is the World Series, man. Are you crazy?" This is enough of a distraction to let the ball roll through his legs.

"It's papaya," says the manager.

To be "Bucknerized" is to be made the scapegoat for some heinous act such as ... missing a ground ball.

Sports scapegoating has long been a popular pastime for TVs' hottest reality show — sports, any sports, all sports. It's not just the fans. The media loves a scapegoat as much as, or maybe even more than, a hero. Want to see that ball roll through Billy Buck's legs again? No problem. It's been shown so many thousands of times that every frame is indelibly etched on the mind of every baseball fan; for those who watched it live on television, so is the description by Vince Scully:

> Can you believe this ballgame at Shea? So the winning run is at second base. With two out, three and two to Mookie Wilson. A little roller up along first. Behind the bag! It gets through Buckner. Here comes Knight and the Mets win it!

The Mets are not only alive, they are well and they will play the Red Sox in Game 7 tomorrow.

An attosecond after the ball rolled through Buckner's halting legs, a collective groan could be heard across New England. Not again! Then just as quickly came the silence. Local taverns filled with people watching the game went suddenly still. In one revolution of the ball, hope and anticipation were replaced by malice and spite. An instant ago the world championship was within their grasp; now all that was left was the grim certainty of the inevitable loss in Game 7.

They are right. The Mets win the next game, 8–5, behind home runs from Strawberry and Knight, and the world championship is theirs. It is the highest rated World Series game in the history of television.

Put away the champagne for ... what? Another 68 years or so?

If Buckner is destined to be American baseball's all-time scapegoat, then in Japan so is Colonel Sanders. Every fan there knows about the "Curse of the Colonel." According to popular sentiment, a curse was placed on the Hanshin Tigers baseball team by the KFC founder and mascot because of the Colonel's pique over the treatment of one of his store-front statues. It obviously works, too, as evidenced by the fact that the team hasn't won the championship series since.

The idea of scapegoating goes back at least as far as the bible. Leviticus tells us that a goat, with the sins of the people loaded on it, was sent over a cliff, thereby making the people feel much better about themselves. The ancient Greeks, in response to natural disasters such as plagues or foreign invasions, were known to practice a scapegoating rite by casting out a beggar or a criminal from their community.

Get out of here, you criminal, and never darken our town again. That'll teach you.

Psychologists say that it is normal for the scapegoat to feel wrongly persecuted and to be the target of misplaced vilification, blame and criticism. He is likely to suffer rejection from those whom the perpetrators seek to influence.

Now, at least, the woe-is-us Bosox fans have a living scapegoat on which to take out their ire and blame for their losses. After all, the old owner, Harry Frazee, is no longer around to castigate for selling the Babe and instigating the curse that followed. Ah, but Buckner is.

The fact that he was wearing a Chicago Cubs batting glove under his first baseman's glove only adds to the frustration. If any team other than the Red Sox knows what it is to miss out on World Series rings, it is certainly the Cubs.

What the hell were you thinking, Buckner!

How could you, Buckner!

He had no answers for such stupid question/accusations.

He will be pilloried for years with little thought about how this would affect him, and virtually no thought at all how it would impact his three kids who saw their father treated as a pariah.

The Mets celebrate their '86 World Series victory.

He will play a little more on increasingly fragile legs before being let go by the team, and then move 2,600 miles west to an Idaho ranch.

"I am a little bitter toward some of the things that have happened there," he will later say about his Boston experience. "It's unbelievable. You know what? This is the honest-to-God's truth. My first thought was, 'Oh fuck, we lost the game.' The second thought was, 'Oh man, we get to play the seventh game of the World Series.' I mean, I was having so much fun. You're trying to win, obviously, but I mean, if we won the game, it was over with. I'm thinking, 'We get to play another game, and we'll win.' There was no doubt in my mind we were going to win the last game."

Summer 2006
During a series with the Mets, the Red Sox host a reunion of their '86 team. Bill Buckner does not show up.

Over time, the vitriol is diluted by closer inspection of the facts of that fateful Game 6.

Game 7 is pushed back to Monday because of rain. "Then Monday I agreed to do an interview for *The NBC Nightly News*," says Buckner, "and all the guy kept asking me was, 'How can you look at yourself in the mirror? How can you face your teammates?' I went out for batting practice, and I thought one sign that said 'Nice legs' was funny, but when I got the standing ovation from the Mets' fans during the introductions, it wasn't so funny."

He isn't happy either about the Mets' replaying the error on the Shea Stadium message board in the middle of the fifth inning.

Very tacky, very insensitive, very New York.

Throughout the Series he looks more like Dennis Weaver playing Chester Goode in *Gunsmoke* than a professional athlete. He drags his bad leg like it is an unwilling passenger. He looks as if he were running in Army boots if he is running at all. He crawls to bases, limps to his position, and leans on his bat during the national anthem as if it were cane. He falls down chasing a popup.

During the season he has had nine cortisone shots trying to stay in the lineup.

But it wasn't always thus. Tommy Lasorda says when he signed him, Buckner could get down the line as fast as anyone in the game. Dick Vermeil recruited him to play football for Stanford and when asked which recruit he most regretted not coaching he said, "Wide receiver Bill Buckner. He could fly."

One April day in 1975 Buckner and the Dodgers were playing the Giants. In the third inning Buckner singled to right field and then with Garvey at the plate, he tried to steal second. "I remember it as if it were yesterday," Buckner says. "John Montefusco was pitching, Marc Hill catching. I'd just been trying to learn to slide from Davey Lopes, the way he barely hit the ground. I never did hit the ground, my foot caught under the bag and I flipped right over."

He wasn't right the rest of the season and his performance showed it. He had surgery in September to remove a tendon. He had surgery in October to remove bone chips. He had surgery the next winter that resulted in a staph infection. When the Dodgers traded him to the Cubs for Rick Monday, he showed up for spring training hobbling on a cane. The Cubs asked the league to annul the trade on the grounds that he was damaged goods.

"I was damaged goods," he says. "But I wanted to prove them wrong, so I played the first half of the season. It was a painful mistake. I never walked right again."

He tried everything he could to make the ankle good: acupuncture needles all over his body that made him feel like a pin cushion, DMSO on the ankle that made him feel like he had just eaten a bowl of garlic, and holy water that made him feel guilty. Nothing helped.

In order to stay in the lineup he took to soaking his ankle in ice for an hour before each game and then he soaked it again after the game. He worked out like a fiend and watched his diet carefully. He became a real health food nut and downed handfuls of daily vitamins. Nothing helped the ankle but he played.

Growing up he was the best athlete in his small California wine country town. He was also one of the smartest. He debated whether to attend Stanford or the University of Southern California, before deciding on USC. He would concentrate on his studies there and not even play sports, but the siren call of baseball rang in his ears when the Dodgers drafted him in the second round and he decided to put off his education for a while.

The Dodgers assigned him to their Rookie League club in Ogden, Utah, where his manager and mentor was a former Major League pitcher whose three-year career consisted of no wins and an ERA of 6.28. Tommy Lasorda liked his young 17-year-old outfielder and could see good things for him ... and for himself. Lasorda had a strong team that included several players who went on to play for him with the Dodgers, including Bobby Valentine, Tom Paciorek, Joe Ferguson, and Charlie Hough, but always looking to get a psychological edge, Tommy the master motivator had his players write letters to the then current Dodgers telling them they were on the way and looking for their jobs. Buckner wrote to the Dodgers' first baseman, Wes Parker, giving him the news.

"I visited the clubhouse after the season," Buckner says, "and you should have seen the look I got from Parker."

No one could ever think of Buckner as a Mr. Rogers. A mellow, laid back California kid he wasn't. He was a fighter and Lasorda kept telling him how much he loved fighters.

"Buck was always getting thrown out of games," says Lasorda. Throw helmets? He broke one a night. Finally I told him I'd fine him if he ever did it again. He made an out and I heard this banging. I look over and he was smashing his head against the wall so hard he was bleeding. One night in Triple A, he and Valentine collided going for a pop fly. Buck broke his jaw, and the front office told me to sit him out for five weeks. Buckner missed only one game and wound up hitting .335 and learned to spit and swear with his jaw wired shut.

He cusses at himself for missing pitches, swears at umpires for missing calls, and fights with opponents for breaking his bats and other assorted reasons. In a 1980 game in Montreal, he became so frustrated with himself for popping up that he smashed his bat down in anger, accidently breaking Carter's mask. The next week, Carter, himself no milquetoast, took Buckner's bat and broke it over home plate. Fight on. When Carter later rounded first base after a hit, Buckner was waiting for him and the brawl broke out. He was also involved in a violent fight with Cubs manager Lee Elia on the top step of their dugout.

Buckner's wife, Jody, is furious at a reporter who asked Buckner after Moore's suicide if he had ever considered suicide himself after his infamous error.

Popular mythology has it that ever since "the error," Buckner has been deeply depressed, is a mere shell of his former in-your-face-self, lives the life of a recluse, and is so anguished that he has contemplated suicide. Not so. He is irked, piqued by the way he has been treated. Maybe offended. He uses the word "bitter." Maybe a little defensive.

But the myth will always outstrip the reality.

"I didn't lose the World Series," he says. "Everyone knows one play doesn't decide a seven-game series. I can find 30 plays more important than that. That wasn't the only error or unearned run in that game. I give the Mets credit for winning, for not giving up."

He is not now, nor has he ever been, self-destructive. Though his miscue took on a life of its own, he is not tortured by his memories of it.

From his Idaho ranch he says, "I got a great life. I like the way things are going. I don't sit in the woods and think about it. Ever."

Does he expect the Red Sox fans to ever forgive him?

"I don't really care about forgiveness," he says.

Regrets?

After actor Charlie Sheen paid $93,000 for the ball he never stopped, he says, "I guess I should have turned around and gone after it."

Blame the media?

"You've got the Tim McCarvers of the world who, if I were sitting there talking to him, would say it's a team deal. 'You didn't lose the World Series.'

But the next night, he'd go on TV and say, 'Buckner lost the World Series.' It's the bandwagon that everybody jumped on. You'd have to say it was the media mostly because that's what everybody is influenced by."

Afterthoughts?

"Funny thing, the next year we went to Yankee Stadium and played the Yankees early in the year, and Mattingly hit a ball — of course, being in New York, you're hearing all this shit — Mattingly hit a ground ball, it was the exact same ball. And I did the exact same thing. That was one of the most embarrassing moments of my life. It was crazy. I mean, I was pretty good at ground balls."

Stephen Jay Gould, the eminent American paleontologist, evolutionary biologist, historian of science, and avid baseball fan, has written extensively of the Buckner error as an example of how "canonical stories distort our reading of actual patterns. The canonical story of Buckner's travail must follow a scenario that might be called 'But for this,'" Gould writes:

> In numerous versions of "But for this," a large and hugely desired result fails to materialize and the absolutely opposite resolution, both factually and morally, unfolds instead because one tiny and apparently inconsequential piece of the story fails to fall into place, usually as a consequence of human error or malfeasance.
>
> "But for this" can brook no nuances, no complexity, no departure from the central meaning and poignant tragedy that an entire baleful outcome flows absolutely and entirely from one tiny accident of history. "But for this" must therefore drive the tale of Bill Buckner's legs into the only version that can validate the canonical story. In short, poor Bill must become the one and only cause and focus of ultimate defeat or victory. That is, if Buckner fields the ball properly, the Sox win their first World Series since 1918 and eradicate the Curse of the Bambino. But if Buckner bobbles the ball, the Mets win the Series instead, and the curse continues in an even more intense and painful way. For Buckner's miscue marks the unkindest bounce of all, the most improbable, trivial little error sustained by a good and admired man. What hath God wrought?"

Now revisionist writers aided and abetted by revisionist fans and revisionist radio talk show hosts have decided that Buckner wasn't nearly as culpable as the myth would have it, that maybe he shouldn't take all the heat for the loss, and that maybe he's as much a scapegoat as anything else.

These freethinking souls point to several things.

Look, it wasn't even the seventh game of the Series for Pete's sake.

His error on the Mookie ball, at worst, cost them a game, not the Series.

The Sox weren't even winning the game at the time of the muff. The Mets had just tied the game on a wild pitch by Bob Stanley with Mookie at the plate. So even if Buckner had made the play the game wouldn't have been over. Why isn't Stanley who threw the wild pitch vilified like Buckner? Isn't he as much to blame?

Oh, yes, and how did the Sox even get into that situation? They screwed up two bunts in the eighth inning, allowing the Mets to tie the game in the first place.

Maybe Buckner shouldn't have been in the game at that point anyway. With his bum ankle he had reduced mobility, so often during the regular season McNamara replaced Buckner late in games with Dave Stapleton. So what was McNamara doing leaving in Buckner? You want to pin the horns on someone, put them on McNamara.

"McNamara kind of left that up to the players," says Buckner. "Marty Barrett was standing right there. Marty was a friend of mine, but he wanted to win and was a straight shooter. Mac said, 'Marty, should we switch?' And he said, 'Nah.' I mean, I had no problem either way. I think I was probably ok at that point. Early in the series, my Achilles' tendon was really sore, and I was having trouble. But by the end of the sixth game, I was moving all right. I felt like I was probably the best player to have at first."

Besides, Buckner insists, Stapleton was not above an occasional error. "I mean, he probably would have caught that ball, and I would've caught it 99 times out of 100, too."

So why is Buckner's goof what everybody remembers? Because it was so visually dramatic — a routine ground ball rolling unhindered through the legs. How visually dramatic is a wild pitch, or breaking ball without much bite that is lined into center, or a decision to leave one of your best players (albeit a gimpy one) in the game? Maybe if Buckner had mishandled a throw it would be different. Maybe it would even be different had the ball been off to the side. But through the legs in the sixth game of the World Series? That's the stuff of baseball legend.

"We jumped out to a lead early," Buckner says. "I got a couple of hits. Hurst just didn't have it. Oil Can was supposed to pitch then, but after the rainout, they moved Hurst up. He was our hot pitcher. He just ran out of gas."

Nevertheless, virtually every mention of Buckner reads with something like, "William Joseph 'Bill' Buckner (born December 14, 1949, in Vallejo, California) is a former Major League Baseball player who, despite an impressive 20-year career, is best known for a ground ball that rolled between his legs in Game 6 of the 1986 World Series."

Like Ruth's called shot, Bobby Thomson's "shot heard 'round the world," or Gibson's improbable World Series home run, the Buckner through-the-wickets error ranks high on the Most Memorable Moments of All-Time lists.

Bill Buckner will become a symbol for failure. In Japan where ski jumping is second in popularity only to baseball during the Olympics, Masahiko Harada is known as the "Japanese Bill Buckner." At the Lillehammer Olympics, Japan had the gold medal apparently locked up. It was Harada's chance to jump. "All he had to do," U.S. coach Alan Johnson says, "was fall forward." The ball was about to go through his legs. He got off the worst jump of his life and Japan lost the gold. Harada was crushed. He considered himself a national disgrace.

April 2008
The Red Sox are on the field receiving their 2007 World Series rings. As the fans stand and applaud, Buckner emerges from behind the Green Monster left-field wall, wiping the tears from his eyes. He goes to the pitcher's mound and throws out the ceremonial first pitch. The fans applaud wildly.

When he was asked to appear, he had to think it over. The memories were that painful. He hadn't been on that field in many years. Finally, after several days and repeated requests, he nervously agreed.

By their response, the fans tell him he is forgiven.

"I feel like the guy who got put away for a crime he didn't commit," he says, "and then the DNA evidence comes back 30 years later and the guy gets out of jail. What do you say for the 30 years he spent suffering? I don't feel like I've committed a crime."

It is a thunderous ovation, a hero's welcome.

"I would have to say in my heart," said Buckner, fighting back tears at the press conference that followed, "I had to forgive the media for what they put me and my family through. I've done that. I'm over that."

Some think him a traitor, but baseball allegiances can run deep. Bart Giamatti, President of the National League, was not so secretly pulling for the American League Red Sox. This Benedict Arnold/quisling/Judas/fifth columnist is actually hoping his employer loses the most important thing he has been hired to acquire. No, not "hoping," praying—and this from an agnostic with at least one atheist son. Here is a perfect example of how the deep-seated loyalty of a passionate baseball man can trump other fealties, how the fan can take precedence over the administrator.

When his Sox lose the sixth game he admits not to disappointment, or frustration, or annoyance, but its more violent cousin, rage.

Doubtless, the literature professor knows Shakespeare's line, "Oppose not rage while rage is in its force, but give it way a while and let it waste." It is not easy, though, to let it rest, for the loss gnaws at him, roils in his gut, and touches a lifetime of ingrained feelings.

The philosopher Josiah Royce said loyalty is the supreme moral good, and that one's devotion to something matters more than the merits of the thing itself. To Giamatti and the other Red Sox diehards, the game does matter. A Sox win and their spirits are demonstrably lifted; a loss and a degree of visceral depression settles in until anticipation of the next game and calculated victory replaces it.

As Donald Hall in *Baseball and the Meaning of Life* has so eloquently expressed, baseball loyalty is often generational:

> When you are small, you may not discuss politics or union dues or profit margins with your father's cigar-smoking friends when your father has gone out for a six-pack, but you may discuss baseball.... About the season's moment you know as much as he does; you may shake your heads over Lefty's wildness or the rookie who was called out last Saturday when he tried to steal home with two out in the ninth inning and his team down by one.

Peter Gammons, writing in *Sports Illustrated*, can't hide his lifelong loyalty to his New England heritage:

> Last Saturday night, after the clubhouses had cleared out and emotional exhaustion set in, the whole thing seemed to make sense. We in New England dwell on history because we are brought up with the English notion that we are what we are because of who and what came before us. The 10th inning of this sixth game was part of something bizarre and supernatural that is bigger than any of us. "Maybe they are going to win, maybe even Buckner will end up the hero," I told a friend. "But before we could find out what it feels like to win, we have to be made to suffer one last, excruciating time."

One thing about baseball: there is always tomorrow, always another game. Heaven bless Yogi Berra: it ain't over till it's over. "You can't sit on a lead and run a few plays in the line," says Earl Weaver, the retiring monarch of managers. "You've got to give the other man his chance."

The doubters, the second-guessers, and the anxious gather for Game 7 in the Series that will not die. The "whys" of Game 6 won't go away. Why didn't McNamara pinch-hit with Baylor instead of Mike Greenwall? All Greenwall could do was strike out. Why did Davey Johnson have Howard Johnson bunt instead of swinging away with a 3–3 score, two on and none out in the bottom of the ninth? All Johnson could do was strike out.

"You guys go ahead and second-guess," says McNamara. "But I don't understand. Baylor batting instead of Greenwall, or later Baylor batting instead of leaving Buckner in, is not such a big deal where I come from."

Yeah, well you're from California, maybe that explains your lousy decisions in this Series.

"I don't second-guess myself."

Maybe you don't, but we sure as hell do. While we're at it, why did you pull Clemens in the eighth? He was pitching great.

He wanted to come out because of a blister, says McNamara.

No, I didn't, says Clemens.

Either way, there is enough ire floating around to keep the I-told-you-so crowd happy.

The tantrum-prone Oil Can is irked that he was not pitching Game 7.

"I make decisions without emotion," McNamara says.

Boyd, who doesn't do anything without emotion, cries when McNamara gives him the word that Bruce Hurst will be starting. "It hurts so bad, what can I do?" Boyd says. "Bruce is on a roll and Mac thinks the Mets have a better left-handed lineup. It's just that it was my turn and after all I've been through… But I'm sorry, my sensitivities are going to show through every time. This one hurts more because I was so psyched to pitch the one game that means everything."

The erratic Strawberry is irked that Johnson pulled him in the ninth inning of Game 6 as part of a double switch. "I was kind of upset, kind of frustrated to be sitting in the locker room when the team needed me," Strawberry says. "It made me look bad. Obviously, he didn't have enough faith to keep me in the lineup. I played and contributed all year and I don't particularly like that happening in the World Series. Taking me out was a terrible mistake."

The calculating Davey Johnson is irked that Strawberry is irked. "When he said I was taking the bat out of his hands, he was thinking of his own personal situation," Johnson says. "I was thinking two or three innings down the road. When Darryl gets a few more years in, maybe he'll be managerial material."

The manager's favorite, Ray Knight, is irked that Johnson benched him in Game 2 against Clemens. "I'm shocked and embarrassed," Knight says. "My whole family was here. I've never been so unhappy."

The judicial Baylor is irked that he has been passed over several times when he thought his pinch-hitting prowess should have been called on.

Sid Fernandez, who ran up a 16–6 record this season as a starter for the Mets, is irked. He has appeared twice in relief, but hasn't started a game.

Sammy Stewart, the second-most-called-on reliever for the Red Sox this season, is irked that he hasn't been used at all in either the playoffs or the World Series. "I think he forgot about me," he complains. "I haven't forgotten about anyone," McNamara barks.

Sammy is a flake, a first-class practical joker, and one of the most truthful players around.

An example: Almost every player claims he works hard at the game, and in fact, is the first one to arrive at the park for every game, and the last one to leave. Not Stewart.

"I'm the kind of fella who comes to the ballpark the last minute," he says. "I'm also the first one to leave because I don't know how many minutes I'm gonna have left with those precious kids of mine. I love 'em to death."

His two children, both of whom suffer from cystic fibrosis, have a life expectancy of only 20 years.

"Cystic fibrosis is the No.1 killer in the world for children and that's always in front of me. But thank God, my boy hasn't been in a hospital now for seven months," he says, tapping the wooden frame on a clubhouse locker with his knuckles.

This big teddy bear of a man sometimes cries when he thinks about this. "My little boy has asthma on top of everything else," Stewart says. "Seeing him lying on the couch pulling his hair because he can't breathe is hard for me and my wife to take."

It's been a long season. On to the last game.

Since 1918, when Babe Ruth was their pitching ace, the Red Sox had been in three World Series before 1986. They've lost all three in the seventh game — 1946 when Joe Garagiola out-hit Ted Williams, 1967 when Bob Gibson beat them three times surrendering a total of three runs, and 1975 when Joe Morgan won the seventh game with a scoring single in the ninth inning.

Here we go again.

Of course it's the curse. How else could you explain it?

With the petulant Boyd sitting, the Sox send Hurst to the mound. Tom Seaver, who has helped the Red Sox since his acquisition, might have been the ideal choice in such a critical game, but he injured his knee in September and is not available.

April 1987

Seaver tries to make a comeback with the Mets after being released by the Red Sox when the two sides could not reach agreement on a contract. In a spring training game against the Mets' Triple-A affiliate he is shelled. "I've used up all the competitive pitches in my arm!" he says and retires to his vineyards in northern California.

In an ESPN poll among his peers, Bob Gibson, Nolan Ryan, Steve Carlton, and Don Sutton all agree Seaver was "the best" of their generation of pitchers.

Game 7 is at Shea Stadium. Hurst retires 15 of the first 16 Mets he faces and the Red Sox take a three-run lead against Darling. If the lead holds, Hurst could end up beating the Mets for the third time in the Series and become the Red Sox' greatest hero since Babe Ruth.

The Red Sox fans are hopeful but...

They're the Red Sox, for christsake.

The Mets tie the game in the sixth when Hernandez slaps a two-run single to left center on an 0–1 pitch. "I told my brother, who has been with me all week, that if there are men on base today, I'm going to be a key," Hernandez says. Carter follows with a looping fly that drops in shallow right field, scoring Backman from third.

Here we go again ... that curse.

In the seventh, paced by Ray Knight's home run, the Mets move to their own three-run lead.

Of course.

In the eighth, the Red Sox score two runs and have the potential tying run at second. The Shea Stadium crowd erupts with a cacophonic din.

Tom Boswell, the *Washington Post* columnist, can't help responding, "If noise, a wall of noise, a will of noise, can turn a Series, then it did this night," he wrote. "If a crowd can shake pitchers to their competitive soul, steal the marrow from their bones, then that is what happened to the Red Sox this soul-chilling evening as Schiraldi, Joe Sambito and, in the eighth, Al Nipper seemed to quake in the palpable volume."

The Red Sox can't get the run in from second. Then Strawberry's home run in the bottom of the inning begins a rally, getting the Mets back to a three-run lead.

The Mets fans, though, are anything but complacent.

Remember the message on the scoreboard in Game 6? The one that came on when the Red Sox were ahead by two runs with two outs and nobody on in the 10th?

Yeah, the one that said "Congratulations. Red Sox."

In the ninth the Red Sox go down in order. The season is over.

Boggs sits in the dugout, tears streaming down his face, for several minutes after the game, then showers and declines comment in the crowded clubhouse.

Most of the other Red Sox players are left with little more than the usual obvious clichés that are the right of the losers.

BILL BUCKNER: "There's nothing to be sorry about, it was a great Series."
JIM RICE: "We gave it a good shot."
DAVE STAPLETON: "We don't have anything to hang our heads over."
RICH GEDMAN: "It's real frustrating."
BRUCE HURST: "We showed our character. We had a chance to win it, but things didn't work out."

Ron Darling, who grew up following the Red Sox, had wondered before the Series began if a Red Sox victory "might not alter the way New Englanders view the world." After all, in the sixth game, they looked as if they would prevail, then suddenly it all went wrong and the New England Calvinistic tragedy played out again.

Of course the Red Sox figured out a way to lose it. It's fate, it's destiny, it's kismet.

The Mets lost the first two games at home and their ace, Dwight Gooden, lost two games and still they won. Until 2011, when the Rangers went one better, the Red Sox were the only team ever to be within one out of the World Series championship and not win it.

It just ain't meant to be.

"We were destined to win," says Darling.

The Mets are everything their many critics claim — arrogant, cocky, rude — perfect representatives of the arrogant, cocky, rude city they represent.

An estimated 2.2 million people show up in New York for what is being called the largest ticker-tape parade ever, larger even than that for Charles Lindbergh. A paper snowstorm envelopes lower Manhattan with confetti, computer printouts, and occasional software disks, some of it landing on the trees along City Hall Park, lending a surreal look to the wild event. Pandemonium reigns. Players ride in open cars, looking up at fans waving from open windows high above.

"I came to see Keith Hernandez because he's so cute," says 17-year-old Kathy Murphy.

"New York is very proud of this team and grateful not just for the winning, but the way they won it ... coming from behind," says Governor Mario Cuomo, sporting a Mets cap.

On sidewalks, fans burn Red Sox caps; in parking-lots-turned-discos they dance; in front of bars they drink.

They're obnoxious, those Mets fans.

They're New Yorkers, aren't they?

Hey, buddy, this is New York and there ain't no law against being annoying.

During the seventh game, 15 people were arrested at Shea for a variety of offenses, and the Red Sox traveling secretary had a 6-inch gash opened in his head courtesy of a filled can of soda thrown from the stands.

Okay, but it was better than the lawlessness that followed Detroit's Series win two years ago.

Maybe O. Henry said it best. "It couldn't have happened anywhere but in little old New York."

One of the most dramatic, problematic, and charismatic seasons in baseball history is over.

Bibliography

The Internet has been a boon to baseball researchers, providing an abundance of opportunities to locate information that once was much more cumbersome to track down. These opportunities are related to existing research methodologies but re-invent and re-imagine them in the light of new technologies and conditions associated with the Internet.

Many of the stories and quotes, and much of the statistical and biographical information in this book were collected from online sources.

Online Sources

Baseball Almanac
Baseball Library.com
Baseballevolution.com
Baseball-reference.com
The Boston Globe
Brainyquote.com
The Hardball Times
Houston Chronicle
Inside Sports
Los Angeles Times
Minneapolis Star Tribune
MLB.com
The New York Times
Newspaperarchive.com
SABR Biography Project
Searchquotes.com
The Sporting News
Sports Illustrated
Thinkexist.com
USA Today
The Washington Post
Wikipedia.org

Print Sources

Aaseng, Nathan. *Steve Carlton: Baseball's Silent Strongman*. Minneapolis: Lerner Publishing, 1984.

Adler, Bill. *Baseball Wit.* New York: Crown Publishers, 1986.
Anderson, Ken, and Melissa Roberts. *Nolan Ryan: Texas Fastball to Cooperstown.* Austin, Texas: Eakin Press, 1999.
Burman, Howard. *Gentlemen at the Bat: A Fictional Oral History of the New York Knickerbockers.* Jefferson, North Carolina: McFarland and Company, 2010.
Canseco, Jose. *Juiced: Wild Times, Rampant 'Roids, Smash Hits, and How Baseball Got Big.* New York: Harper Collins, 2005.
Carew, Rod, and Ira Berkow. *Carew.* Minneapolis: University of Minnesota Press, 2010.
Carter, Gary, and John Hough, Jr. *Dream Season.* New York: Harcourt Brace Jovanovich, 1987.
Dickson, Paul. *Baseball's Greatest Quotations.* New York: Edward Burlingame Books, 1991.
Dykstra, Lenny, with Marty Noble. *Nails: The Inside Story of An Amazin' Season.* New York: Doubleday, 1987.
Garvey, Cynthia, and Andy Meisler. *The Secret Life of Cyndy Garvey.* New York: St. Martins Press, 1990.
Garvey, Steve, with Skip Rozin. *Garvey.* New York: Times Books, 1986.
Gooden, Dwight, with Bob Klapisch. *Heat: My Life On and Off the Diamond.* New York: William Morrow and Company, 1999.
Gossage, Richard, and Russ Pate. *The Goose Is Loose.* New York: Ballantine Books, 2000.
Gould, Stephen Jay. *I Have Landed: The End of a Beginning in Natural History.* Leicester, UK: Harmony, 2002.
Henderson, Rickey, with John Shea. *Off Base: Confessions of a Thief.* New York: Harper Collins, 1993.
Hernandez, Keith, and Mike Bryan. *If at First ... A Season with the Mets.* New York: McGraw-Hill Book Company, 1986.
Johnson, Davey, and Peter Golenbock. *Bats: The Man Behind the Miracle.* New York: Bantam Books, 1986.
Markusen, Bruce. *Tales from the Mets Dugout.* Champaign, Illinois: Sports Publishing L.L.C., 2005.
Martin, Billy, with Phil Pepe. *Billyball.* New York: Doubleday, 1987.
Murphy, Dale, with Brad Rock and Lee Warnick. *Murph.* Salt Lake City: Bookcraft, 1986.
_____, with Curtis Patton . *Ask Dale Murphy.* Chapel Hill, North Carolina: Algonquin Books, 1987.
Pearlman, Jeff. *The Bad Guys Won!* New York: Perennial Currents, 2004.
_____. *Love Me, Hate Me: Barry Bonds and the Making of an Antihero.* New York: It Books, 2007.
Perry, Dayn. *Reggie Jackson: The Life and Thunderous Career of Baseball's Mr. October.* New York: William Morrow, 2010.
Perry, Gaylord. *Me and the Spitter.* New York: Saturday Review Press, 1974.
Pietrusza, David, Matthew Silverman, Michael Gershman, eds. *Baseball: The Biographical Encyclopedia.* New York: Total Sports Illustrated, 2000.
Puckett, Kirby. *I Love This Game: My Life and Baseball.* New York: Harper Collins, 1993.
Ripken, Cal, Jr., and Mike Bryan. *My Story.* New York: Dial Books, 1999.
Ritter, Lawrence, and Donald Honig. *The 100 Greatest Baseball Players of All Time.* New York: Random House, 1998.
Robinson, Kenneth, ed. *A Great and Glorious Game: Baseball Writings of A. Bartlett Giamatti.* New York: Algonquin Books, 1998.
Shaughnessy, Dan. *One Strike Away: The Story of the 1986 Red Sox.* New York: Beaufort Books, 1987.

Sokolove, Michael. *Hustle: The Myth, Life, and Lies of Pete Rose.* New York: Simon and Schuster, 2005.
_____. *The Ticket Out: Darryl Strawberry & the Boys of Crenshaw.* New York: Simon and Schuster, 2004.
Sowell, Mike. *One Pitch Away: The Players' Stories of the 1986 League Championships and World Series.* New York: Macmillan, 1995.
Thompson, Terry, Nathaniel Vinton, Michael O'Keefe, Christian Red. *American Icon: The Fall of Roger Clemens and the Rise of Steroids in America's Pastime.* New York: Knopf, 2009.
Thorn, John, ed. *The Complete Armchair Book of Baseball: An All-Star Lineup Celebrates America's National Pastime.* New York: Galahad Books, 2004.
_____, Pete Palmer, Michael Gershman, David Pietrusza, eds. *Total Baseball.* New York: Total Sports, 1999.

Video Source

The New York Mets 1986 World Series Collector's Edition DVD. A&E Home Video, 2000.

Index

Adams, Margo 41
alcohol abuse in baseball 5, 28, 38–40, 77–78, 80, 95; attitude vs. drug abuse 98–99, 155, 181; *see also* rowdyism
American League 30
Anderson, Sparky 14, 114–15, 209, 234, 262
Atlanta Braves 67, 149, 151, 263
autographs 115, 200–1, 203–4
Autry, Gene 118, 269–71

Backman, Wally 68, 80, 82, 84–86, 99, 107, 264, 277–83, 300
Baldwin, Doug 16–17
Baltimore Orioles 23, 112, 179, 271
baseball, as "America's game" 244–47, 270
baseball cards 177, 201, 203, 216
Baseball Chapel, Inc. 147–48
Baseball Hall of Fame 44
Baylor, Don 23, 194–97, 271, 273–74, 298
black players 34, 61
Boggs, Debbie 40, 41
Boggs, Wade 23, 36–43, 78, 103, 123, 155, 169, 195, 203, 209, 260, 262, 264, 267, 286, 301
Bonds, Barry 1–2, 58, 140, 142–44, 150, 152, 211
Boros, Steve 154, 213
Boston Red Sox 22–23, 31–32, 34–36, 108–9, 113–15, 118, 209, 230, 263, 267–68, 285–86; '86 ALCS, 271–75; '86 World Series Games, 285–86, 300–1
Boyd, Oil Can 23, 49–51, 109, 114–15, 123, 209, 230–35, 237–38, 248, 264, 267, 272–73, 285, 296, 299
Brock, Lou 44–47
Buckner, Bill 23, 52–53, 105, 109, 123, 216, 285, 289–98, 301

California Angels 115, 252, 267, 271
Canseco, Jose 23–24, 33, 37, 48, 102, 182–85, 188, 192, 237

Carew, Rod 54–55, 271
Carlton, Steve 16, 200, 205–8, 210
Carter, Gary 68, 92, 101, 145–48, 159–61, 237, 260, 267, 277–78, 280–82, 284, 286, 294, 300
Cashen, Frank 71–72, 88, 90–92, 97, 101, 145, 208
Chicago Cubs 227–29, 242, 263
Chicago White Sox 24, 108, 114, 172, 186, 210, 263
Cincinnati Reds 68, 264
Clemens, Roger 23, 36, 51, 115, 121–24, 196, 200, 208–9, 230, 236, 238, 264–65, 267–68, 271–72, 285, 298–99
Clemente, Roberto 100, 217
Coleman, Vince 120
Collins, Dave 186, 229
Collins, Marla 228–29
collusion, alleged owners' 3, 11,
Commissioner of Baseball 3, 6–7, 10, 16, 19, 21, 56, 112–13, 118, 129, 157–58, 170, 181
Continental League 128–29
contracts, player 12, 13, 16, 234
Craig, Roger 23, 67, 120, 208, 266
cricket 117, 245
"Curse of the Bambino" 31, 32, 35–37

Darling, Ron 74, 92, 106, 136–38, 145, 159, 281–82, 300–2
Detroit Tigers 17, 115, 186, 264
Doby, Larry 61
drugs in baseball 19, 21, 36, 99, 164–65; cocaine 20, 80, 95, 101, 153–54, 155–57, 235, 287; testing 113, 179–81; *see also* performance enhancing drugs
Dykstra, Lenny 68, 82–84, 107, 277–80, 283–85

Ehrhardt, Karl, the "Sign Man" 132–33

Index

Ferraro, Mike 239–40
Foster, George 4, 142, 147, 159–61, 208
free agency 11, 12, 14, 15, 16, 205, 267

gambling 3, 172
Garvey, Cyndi 220–21
Garvey, Steve 110, 146, 148, 150, 169, 187, 213–21, 292
Giamatti, A. Bartlett 162–63, 165–66, 246, 297
Gibson, Kirk 13–17, 23, 61, 113, 115, 140, 192, 261, 296
Gleason, Roy 215–16
"The Goat" *see* scapegoating
Gooden, Dwight 78, 87–97, 102–3, 106, 110, 124, 142, 145, 161, 182, 231, 236, 261, 263, 265, 277, 281–82, 286–87, 301
Gossage, Goose 2, 14, 211–13

Harrelson, Ken 108, 186–88, 286
Henderson, Rickey 23, 42, 44–48, 77, 187, 209, 214, 250, 273–74
Hernandez, Keith 2, 80, 98–103, 107, 136, 237, 277, 279–80, 282, 288, 300
Houston Astros 237, 242, 254, 265–66; '86 ALCS, 271–75
Howe, Steve 19, 153–56
Howser, Dick 23, 237, 239–41

Jackson, Bo 182, 244–45, 247–48
Jackson, Reggie 15, 27, 54, 56–61, 77, 114–15, 142, 183, 192, 198, 214, 219, 223, 225, 238, 253, 267, 271–73
Johnson, Davey 30, 68–76, 79, 83–84, 87, 89, 91, 94, 102–3, 107, 110, 133, 136–37, 146, 159–60, 176, 279–80, 284, 288, 298–99
Joyner, Wally 118, 183, 222–23, 226, 265

Kansas City Royals 239, 240, 244, 247
Kingman, Dave 189–93
Knickerbocker Base Ball Club 3, 116, 226
Knight, Ray 159, 161, 279, 284, 286, 290, 299
Koufax, Sandy 11–12, 199–200, 247
Kroc, Joan 212
Kuhn, Bowie 92

LaRussa, Tony 186–89, 263
Lasorda, Tommy 67, 125–26, 154, 228, 293–94
Lee, Bill 35–36
Leyland, Jim 140, 142
Los Angeles Dodgers 11–12, 119, 126, 127, 153–54, 216, 271

Maddux, Greg 141, 242–43
Mantle, Mickey 11, 14, 26, 47, 77, 88, 94, 102, 140, 155, 167–68, 170, 183, 191–92, 203, 211, 216, 247–48, 261
Martin, Billy 26–29, 46, 54, 57, 59–60, 155, 177, 189, 222, 255–56
Mauch, Gene 222, 224, 271–73
Mays, Willie 20, 33–34, 45, 65, 77, 134–35, 140, 142, 149, 168, 173
McLain, Denny 170–72
McNamara, John 50, 52, 109, 123–24, 210, 231, 264, 268, 272–73, 275, 286, 296, 298–99
Messersmith, Andy 12–13
Michael, Gene 227–29
Minnesota Twins 24, 60, 64
Mitchell, Kevin 286–88
Moegle, Bobby 251–52
Moore, Donnie 15–17, 249–50, 252–53, 273–76
Murphy, Dale 67, 148–52
MVP award 33, 54, 100, 146, 149, 168, 214, 218, 238, 244, 267–68

National Association of Base Ball Players 61
National League 30, 127, 128, 129, 271
Negro National League 61
New York Giants 30, 77, 132
New York Highlanders 30–31
New York Mets 69–70, 83–84, 104, 110, 118, 120, 130, 131–35, 161, 199, 208, 210, 248, 260, 261, 284; '86 NLCS 277–83; '86 World Series games, 285–86, 288, 290, 291, 292, 299, 300, 301, 302
New York Yankees 11, 16, 25, 26, 28, 31, 32, 36, 127, 260, 261, 265, 295

Oakland Athletics 24, 46, 56, 182, 183
Ojeda, Bobby 159, 282–83, 285
Olympic Games 7–8, 10, 140, 216, 245, 296
O'Malley, Peter 119, 154
O'Malley, Walter 127

Pawtucket Red Sox 122–23, 175–76
performance enhancing drugs: amphetamines 20; steroids 18–19, 84, 123, 143, 151–52, 182, 184–85
Peters, Ron 169, 180
Philadelphia Phillies 67, 119, 207
Pittsburgh Pirates 19–20, 67, 62–63, 120, 140, 141, 262–63
Players Association 6, 112–13, 180, 181, 213, 234
Prince Hal 171–73
Puckett, Kirby 23, 60, 62–66, 261

racism 56, 61, 161, 197
Reagan, Ronald 54, 112–13, 218
Rice, Jim 109, 123, 196, 264
Ripken, Billy 177
Ripken, Cal, Jr. 174–79, 220
Ripken, Cal, Sr. 177–78
Robinson, Jackie, 61, 217
Rose, Pete 4, 33, 35, 54, 56, 67–68, 77, 87–88, 126, 161, 167, 169, 181, 209
rowdyism, among fans 224–26, 264, 265, 302
Ruth, Babe 26, 31–32, 115–16, 190, 291, 296
Ryan, Nolan 67, 124, 133, 149, 197–202, 242, 265, 271, 277–78, 281, 300

St. Louis Cardinals 67, 99, 100, 120, 209, 263
salaries, player 4, 10, 11, 21, 26, 181
San Diego Padres 67, 109–10, 211–13
San Francisco Giants 67, 127, 189, 207–8, 236–37, 258
scapegoating 274, 290–91, 295
Schiraldi, Calvin 122, 272, 301
Schuerholz, John 158, 244, 246
Scott, Mike 254, 265–66, 278–80
Seattle Mariners 24
Seaver, Tom 23, 108, 114, 135, 200, 210, 238, 265, 267, 300
Shea, Bill 128–29, 135
Sheffield, Gary 93, 96
Smith, Ballard 212
Smith, Lonnie 37, 100, 157–58
sports heroes 139, 217, 99, 215, 216, 217, 218; as role models 20, 78, 105–6, 161, 201–2, 220; vs. celebrities 221
Steinbrenner, George 26–29, 47, 59–60, 212, 227, 239, 265
Stengel, Casey 116, 131–32, 189
steroids *see* performance enhancing drugs
Strawberry, Darryl 37, 68, 75–82, 84, 90–91, 93, 101–3, 106, 160–61, 192, 265, 267, 277–78, 281, 283, 285, 290, 299
Strong, Curtis 19–20
superstitions, in baseball 37–38, 194; *see also* "Curse of the Bambino"

Tanner, Chuck 19, 148–49, 187, 263
Turner, Ted 16, 150–51

Ueberroth, Peter 7–10, 112, 166, 225; drugs issue 19, 20, 21, 99, 113, 153, 157; player contracts 11, 16, 165
umpires 10–11, 21
union *see* Players Association

Valenzuela, Fernando 125–26

Williams, Dick 108, 110, 209
Williams, Ted 32–34, 61
Wilson, Mookie 83–84, 92, 104–7, 160–61, 263, 283, 286, 288, 290, 295
Winfield, Dave 27–28, 48
World Series 30; *see also* Boston Red Sox; New York Mets

Yastrzemski, Carl 203–4

www.ingramcontent.com/pod-product-compliance
Ingram Content Group UK Ltd.
Pitfield, Milton Keynes, MK11 3LW, UK
UKHW041925140426
5217IPUK00014B/317